Shojo Beat

ORESAMA TEACHER

Vol. 22

Story & Art by
Izumi Tsubaki

ORESAMA TEACHER

CHARACTERS AND THE STORY THUS FAR

PUBLIC MORALS CLUB

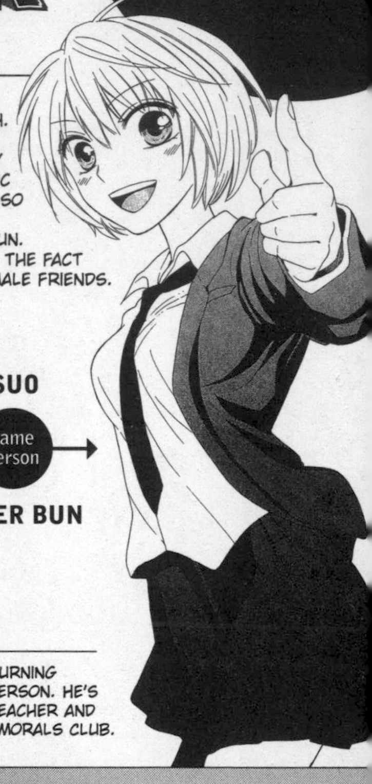

Mafuyu Kurosaki

THE FORMER BANCHO OF SAITAMA EAST HIGH. SHE TRANSFERRED TO MIDORIGAOKA ACADEMY AND JOINED THE PUBLIC MORALS CLUB. SHE ALSO PLAYS THE PARTS OF NATSUO AND SUPER BUN. SHE IS CONCERNED BY THE FACT THAT SHE HAS NO FEMALE FRIENDS.

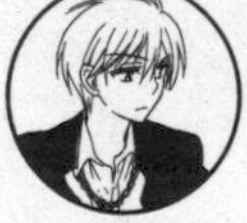

NATSUO

Same Person

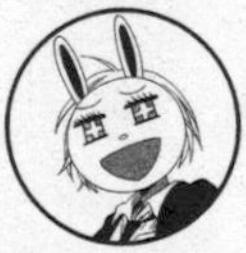

SUPER BUN

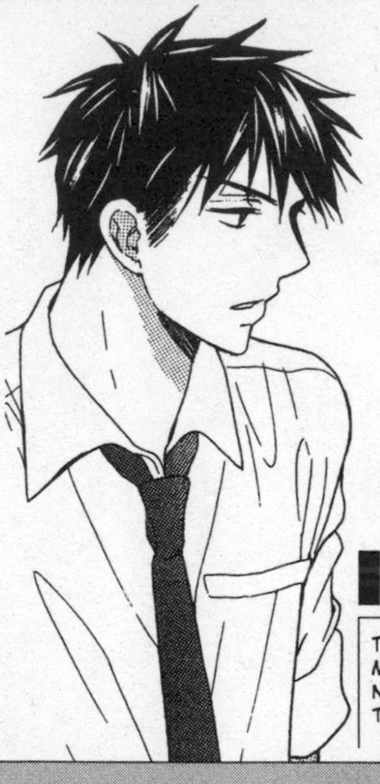

Takaomi Saeki

THE ONE RESPONSIBLE FOR TURNING MAFUYU INTO A TERRIFYING PERSON. HE'S NOW MAFUYU'S HOMEROOM TEACHER AND THE ADVISOR OF THE PUBLIC MORALS CLUB.

PUBLIC MORALS CLUB

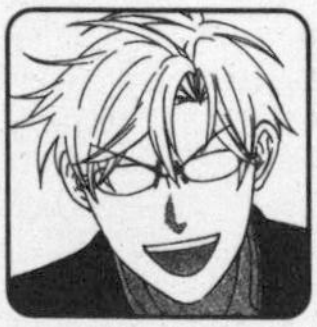

Shinobu Yui

A FORMER MEMBER OF THE STUDENT COUNCIL AND A SELF-PROCLAIMED NINJA.

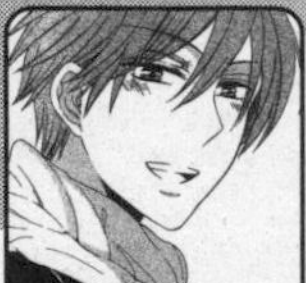

Hayasaka

MAFUYU'S CLASSMATE. HE ADMIRES SUPER BUN. HE IS A PLAIN AND SIMPLE DELINQUENT.

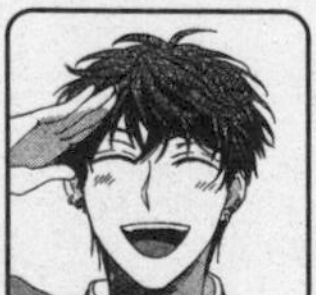

Aki Shibuya

A TALKATIVE AND WOMANIZING UNDERCLASSMAN. HIS NICKNAME IS AKKI. HE'S NOT GOOD AT FIGHTING.

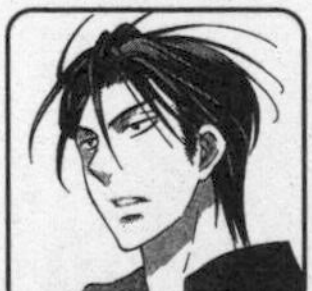

Kyotaro Okegawa

THE BANCHO OF MIDORIGAOKA. HE FLUNKED A YEAR, SO HE'S A SUPER SENIOR THIS YEAR. HE JOINED THE PUBLIC MORALS CLUB TO HELP MAFUYU AND HER FRIENDS.

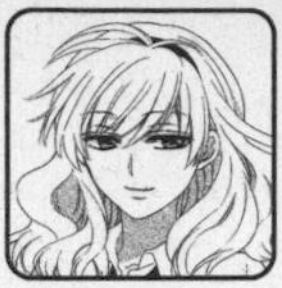

Runa Momochi

THIRD YEAR, CLASS THREE. HANABUSA'S CLASSMATE. RECENTLY QUIT THE STUDENT COUNCIL. MYSTERIOUS, AND HER MOTIVATIONS ARE VERY DIFFERENT FROM MIYABI'S.

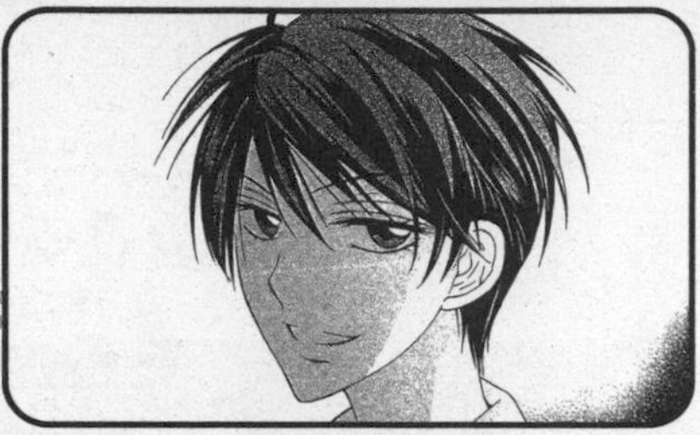

STUDENT COUNCIL

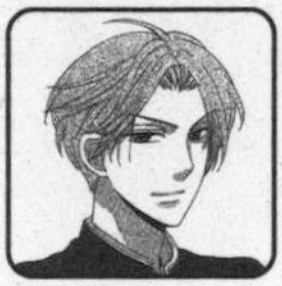

Shuntaro Kosaka

HE'S OBSESSED WITH MANUALS. HE DOES NOT HANDLE UNEXPECTED EVENTS WELL.

Miyabi Hanabusa

THE SCHOOL DIRECTOR'S SON AND THE PRESIDENT OF THE STUDENT COUNCIL. HE HAS THE POWER TO ENCHANT ANY WHO MEET HIS GAZE.

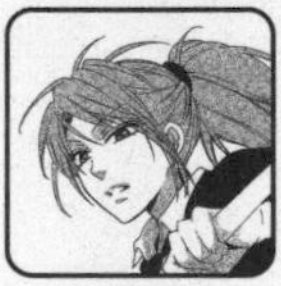

Wakana Hojo

SHE HAS A STOIC ATTITUDE AND WATCHES OVER HANABUSA. SHE HAS FEELINGS FOR YUI.

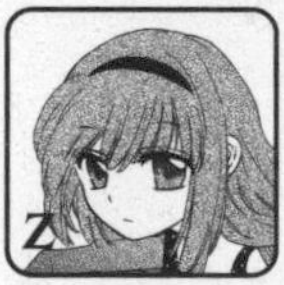

Komari Yukioka

USING HER CUTE LOOKS, SHE CONTROLS PEOPLE AROUND HER WITHOUT SAYING A WORD. INSIDE, SHE'S LIKE A DIRTY OLD MAN.

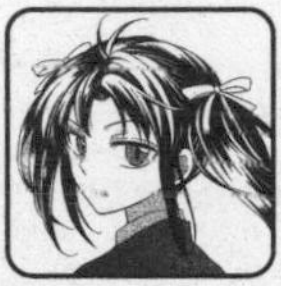

Kanon Nonoguchi

SHE HATES MEN. HER FAMILY RUNS A DOJO, SO SHE'S STRONG. SHE PLANS TO DESTROY THE PUBLIC MORALS CLUB OUT OF GRATITUDE TOWARD MIYABI.

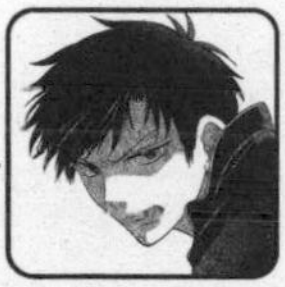

Reito Ayabe

HE LOVES CLEANING. HE GETS STRONGER IN DIRTY PLACES. HE IS A STUDENT COUNCIL OFFICER, BUT HE'S ALSO FRIENDS WITH MAFUYU.

Story

★ MAFUYU KUROSAKI WAS A BANCHO WHO CONTROLLED ALL OF SAITAMA, BUT ONCE SHE TRANSFERRED TO MIDORIGAOKA ACADEMY, SHE COMPLETELY CHANGED AND BECAME A SPIRITED HIGH SCHOOL GIRL...OR AT LEAST SHE WAS SUPPOSED TO. TAKAOMI SAEKI, HER CHILDHOOD FRIEND AND HOMEROOM TEACHER, FORCED HER TO JOIN THE PUBLIC MORALS CLUB AND SHE HAS TO CONTINUE TO LIVE A LIFE THAT IS FAR FROM AVERAGE.

★ THE PUBLIC MORALS CLUB AND THE STUDENT COUNCIL ARE FIGHTING FOR OWNERSHIP OF THE SCHOOL! YUI USES THE ART OF THE ECHO TO MAKE OKEGAWA AND SHIBUYA QUIT THE PUBLIC MORALS CLUB, BUT HE SOON REALIZES HOW MUCH HIS FRIENDSHIP WITH MAFUYU AND HAYASAKA MEANS TO HIM, AND THINGS RETURN TO "NORMAL."

★ THE SECOND SEMESTER BEGINS, AND RUNA MOMOCHI USES HYPNOSIS TO MAKE HAYASAKA LOSE HIS MEMORIES. HE ENDS UP SUSPENDED FOR FIGHTING AND MAFUYU AND THE OTHERS VISIT HIM AT HOME AND MANAGE TO RESTORE HIS MEMORIES. THEY ARE ABLE TO DEFEAT MOMOCHI AFTER LEARNING ABOUT HER PAST WITH HAYASAKA.

★ JUST WHEN THINGS FINALLY SEEM TO HAVE SETTLED DOWN, A SUPER BUN IMPOSTER SHOWS UP AMIDST A STRING OF PRANKS AGAINST THE STUDENT COUNCIL. THEN MIYABI, THE FORMER STUDENT COUNCIL PRESIDENT, IS INJURED FALLING DOWN A FLIGHT OF STAIRS AND HAS TO STAY HOME FROM SCHOOL. MEANWHILE, MAFUYU AND CREW CHASE DOWN THE FALSE SUPER BUN, BUT SHE MANAGES TO ESCAPE AT THE LAST MOMENT!

ORESAMA TEACHER

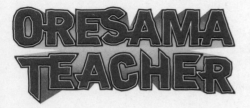

Volume 22
CONTENTS

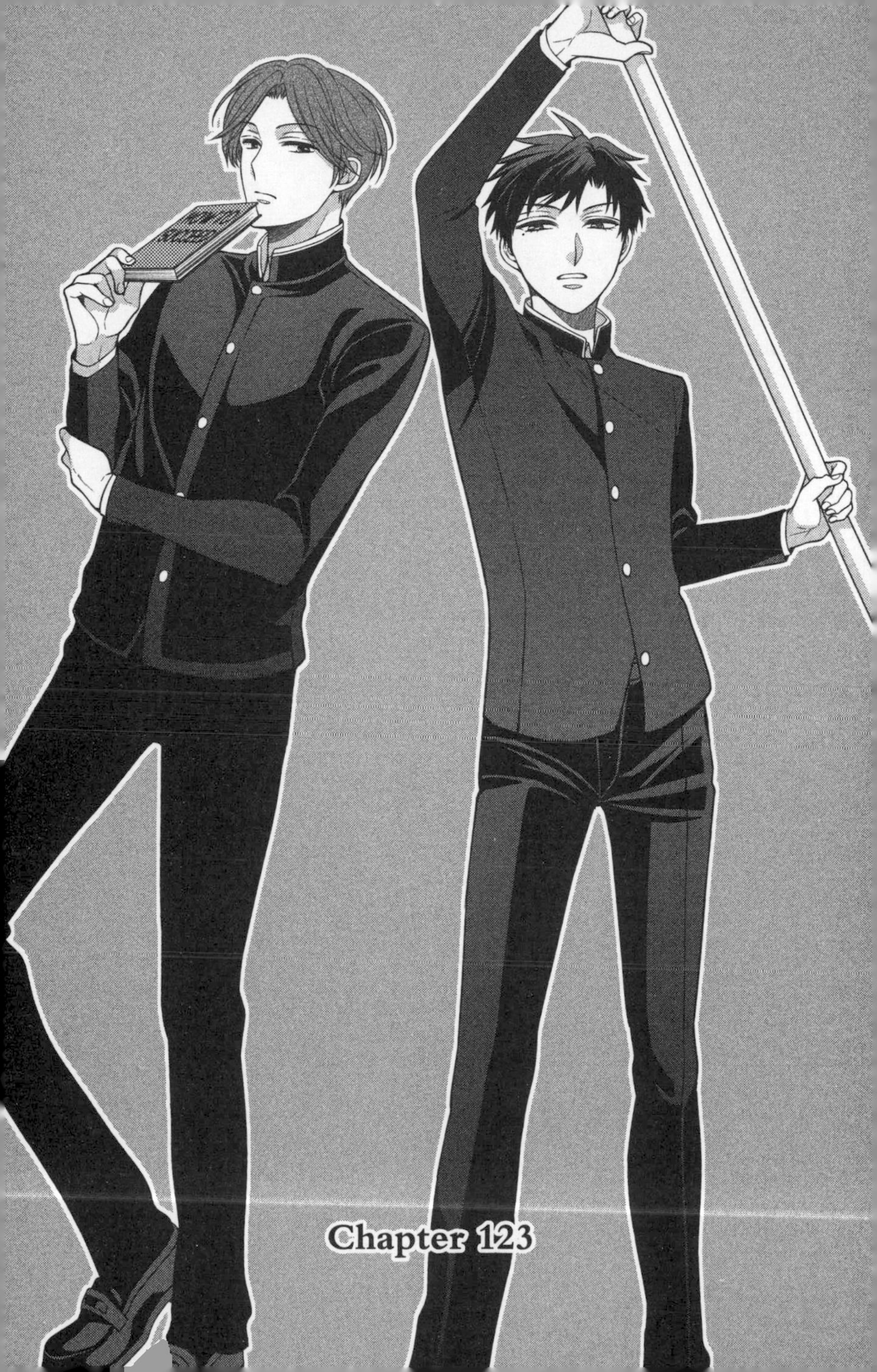
Chapter 123

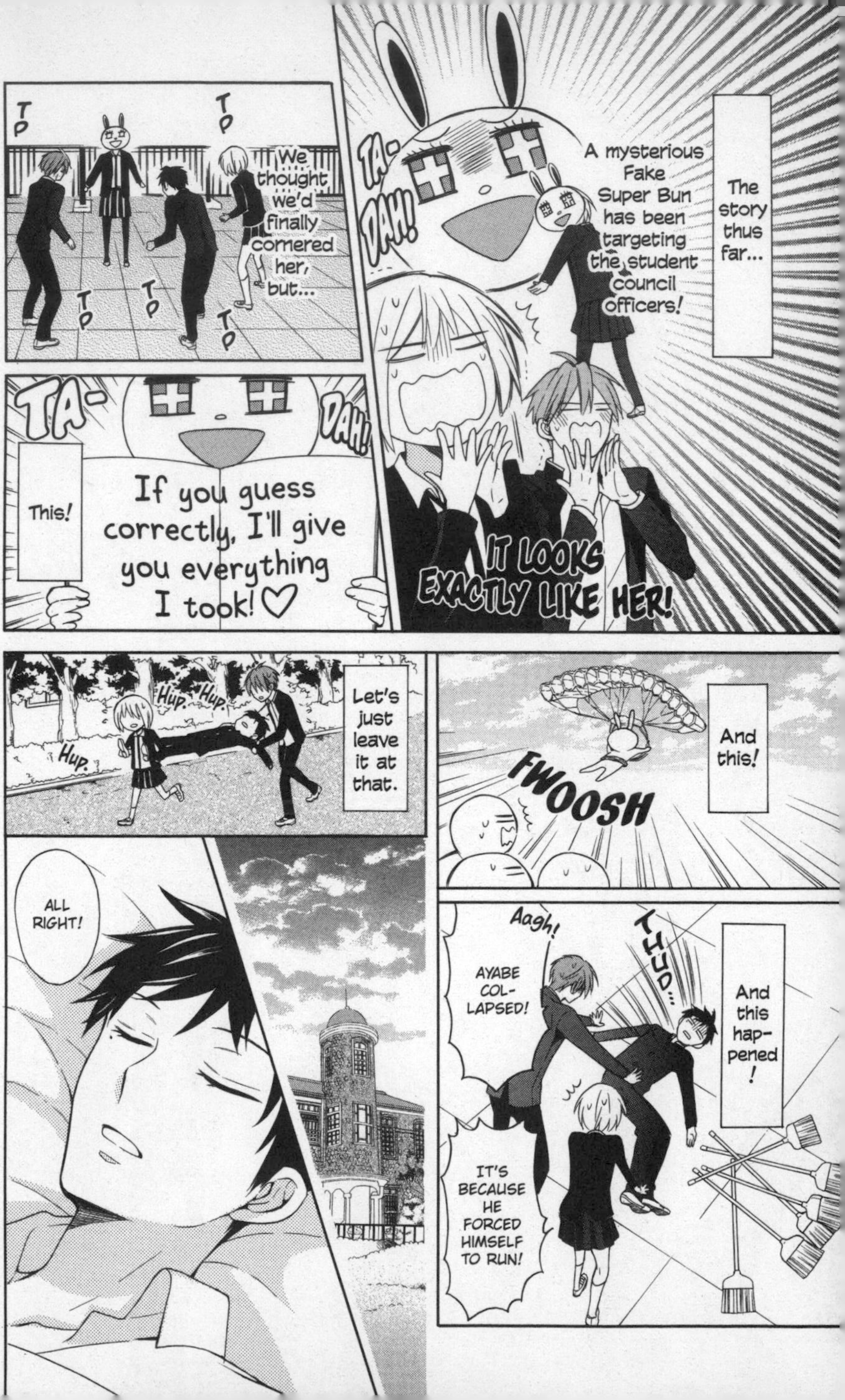
The story thus far...
A mysterious Fake Super Bun has been targeting the student council officers!
TA-DAH!
IT LOOKS EXACTLY LIKE HER!
TP
TP
We thought we'd finally cornered her, but...
TP
TP
TP
TA-
DAH!
This!
If you guess correctly, I'll give you everything I took! ♡
And this!
FWOOSH
And this happened!
THUD...
Aagh!
AYABE COL-LAPSED!
IT'S BECAUSE HE FORCED HIMSELF TO RUN!
Let's just leave it at that.
Hup.
Hup.
Hup.
ALL RIGHT!

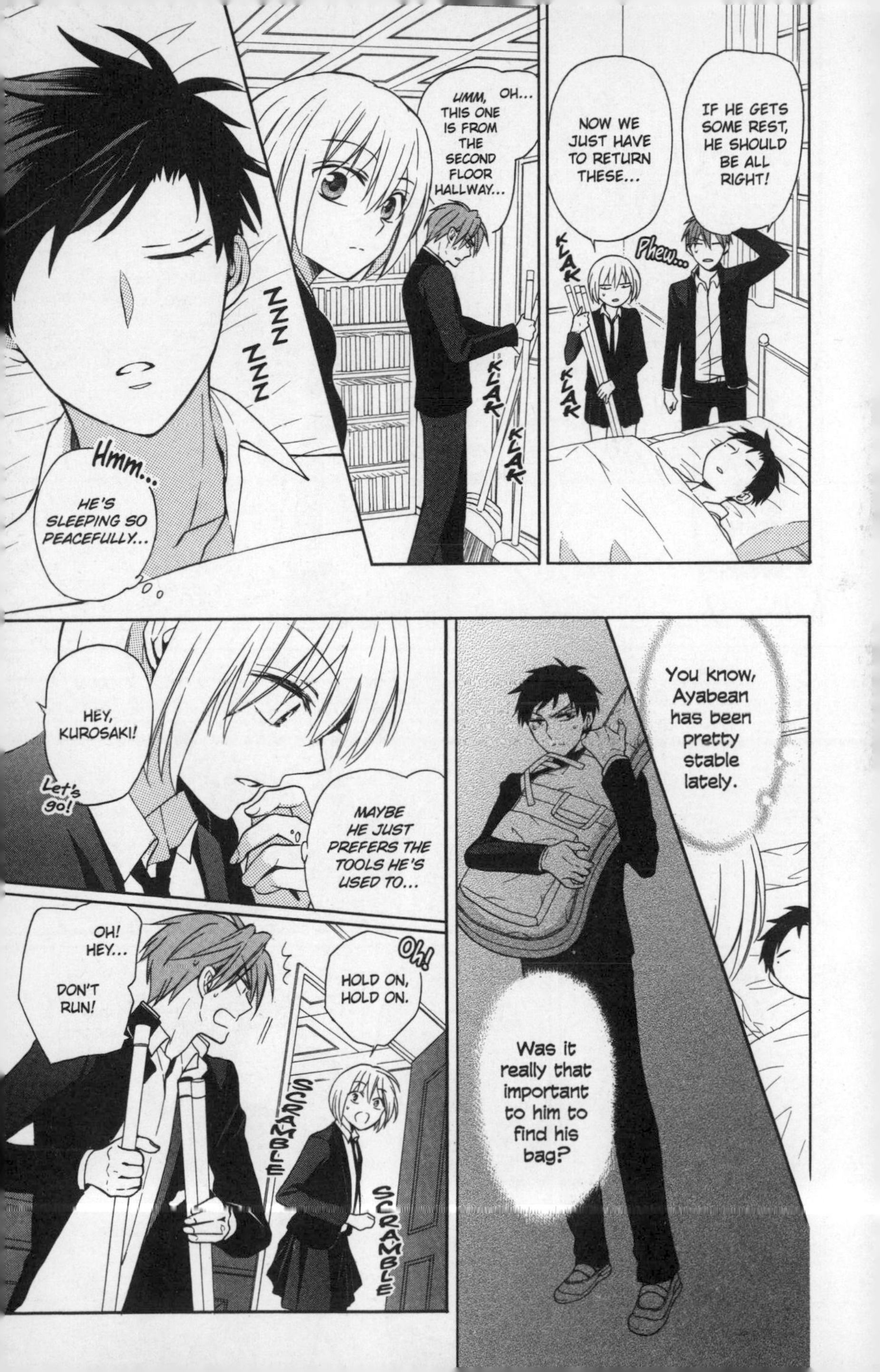
IF HE GETS SOME REST, HE SHOULD BE ALL RIGHT!
Phew...
NOW WE JUST HAVE TO RETURN THESE...
KLAK KLAK
OH...
UMM, THIS ONE IS FROM THE SECOND FLOOR HALLWAY...
KLAK KLAK
ZZZ ZZZ
Hmm...
HE'S SLEEPING SO PEACEFULLY...
You know, Ayabean has been pretty stable lately.
Was it really that important to him to find his bag?
MAYBE HE JUST PREFERS THE TOOLS HE'S USED TO...
HEY, KUROSAKI!
Let's go!
Oh!
HOLD ON, HOLD ON.
OH! HEY...
DON'T RUN!
SCRAMBLE
SCRAMBLE

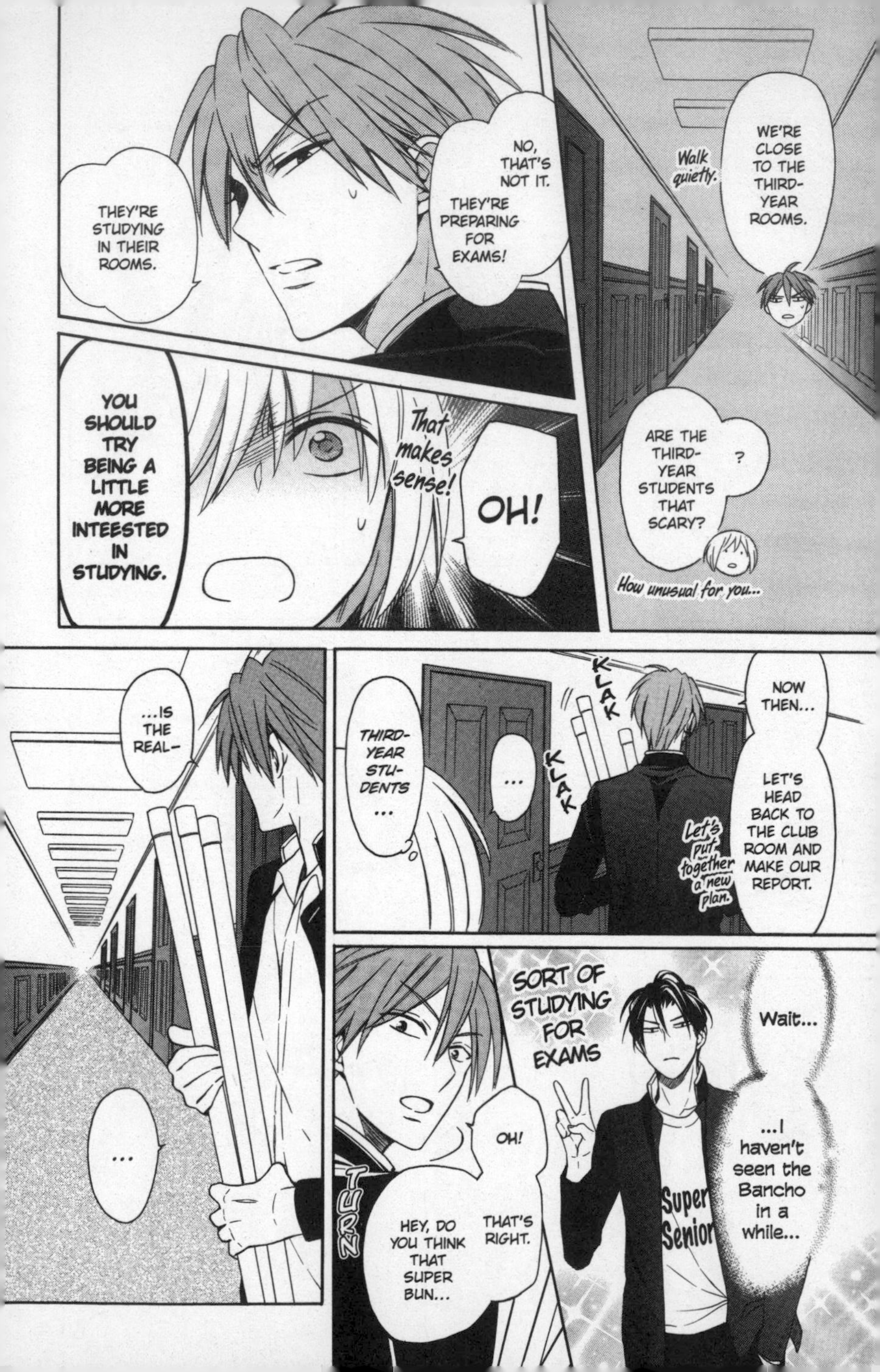
WE'RE CLOSE TO THE THIRD-YEAR ROOMS.
Walk quietly.
ARE THE THIRD-YEAR STUDENTS THAT SCARY?
?
How unusual for you...
NO, THAT'S NOT IT.
THEY'RE PREPARING FOR EXAMS!
THEY'RE STUDYING IN THEIR ROOMS.
That makes sense!
OH!
YOU SHOULD TRY BEING A LITTLE MORE INTEESTED IN STUDYING.
NOW THEN...
LET'S HEAD BACK TO THE CLUB ROOM AND MAKE OUR REPORT.
Let's put together a new plan.
KLAK
KLAK
...
THIRD-YEAR STUDENTS...
Wait...
...I haven't seen the Bancho in a while...
SORT OF STUDYING FOR EXAMS
Super Senior
OH!
THAT'S RIGHT.
HEY, DO YOU THINK THAT SUPER BUN...
TURN
...IS THE REAL-
...

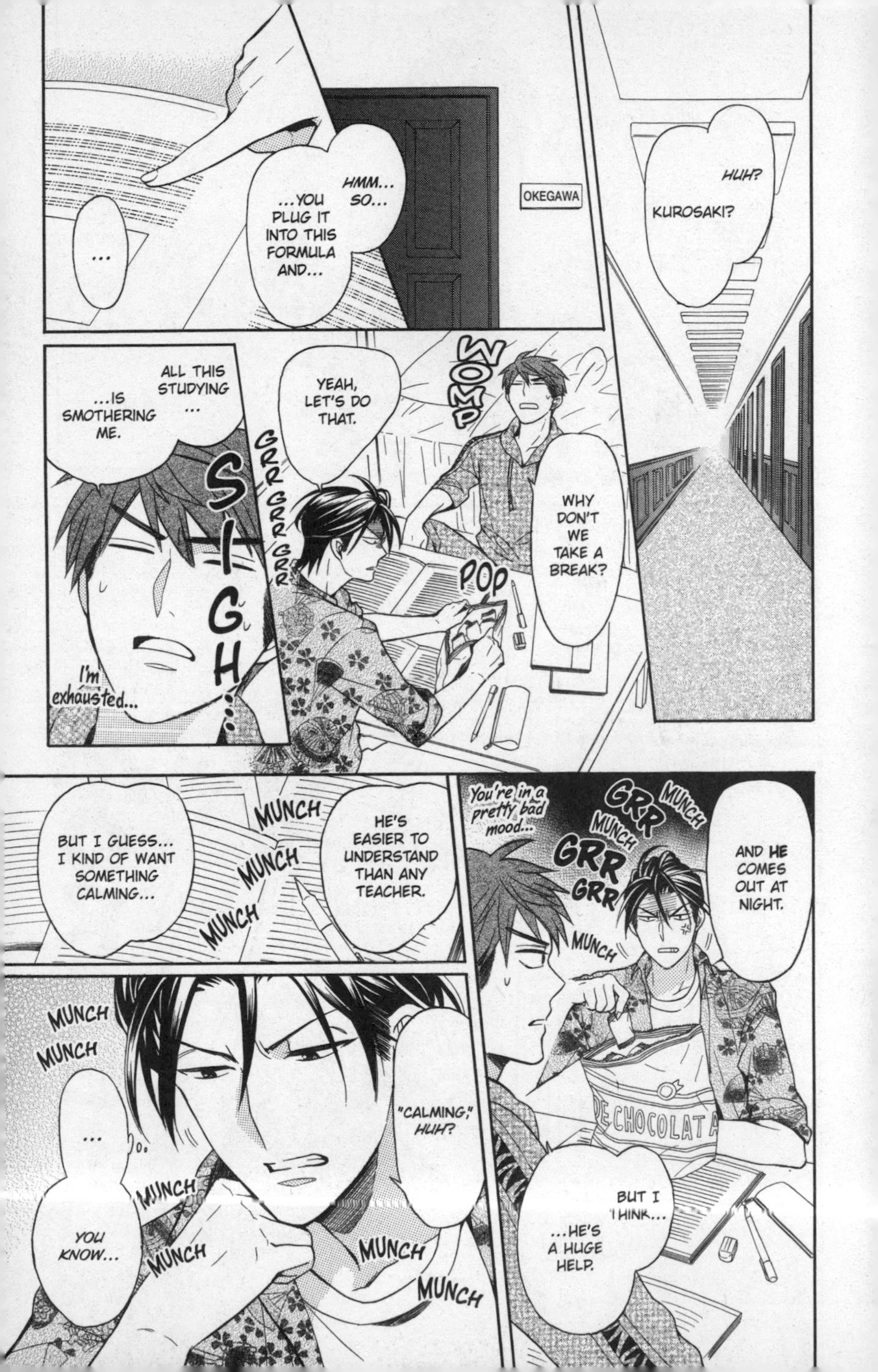
OKEGAWA
HUH?
KUROSAKI?
HMM... SO...
...YOU PLUG IT INTO THIS FORMULA AND...
...
WOMP
WHY DON'T WE TAKE A BREAK?
POP
YEAH, LET'S DO THAT.
GRR GRR GRR
ALL THIS STUDYING...
...IS SMOTHERING ME.
SIGH...
I'm exhausted...
AND HE COMES OUT AT NIGHT.
MUNCH
GRR
MUNCH
GRR GRR
You're in a pretty bad mood...
MUNCH
DE CHOCOLATA
BUT I THINK...
...HE'S A HUGE HELP.
HE'S EASIER TO UNDERSTAND THAN ANY TEACHER.
MUNCH
MUNCH
MUNCH
BUT I GUESS... I KIND OF WANT SOMETHING CALMING...
"CALMING," HUH?
MUNCH
MUNCH
...
MUNCH
YOU KNOW...
MUNCH
MUNCH
MUNCH

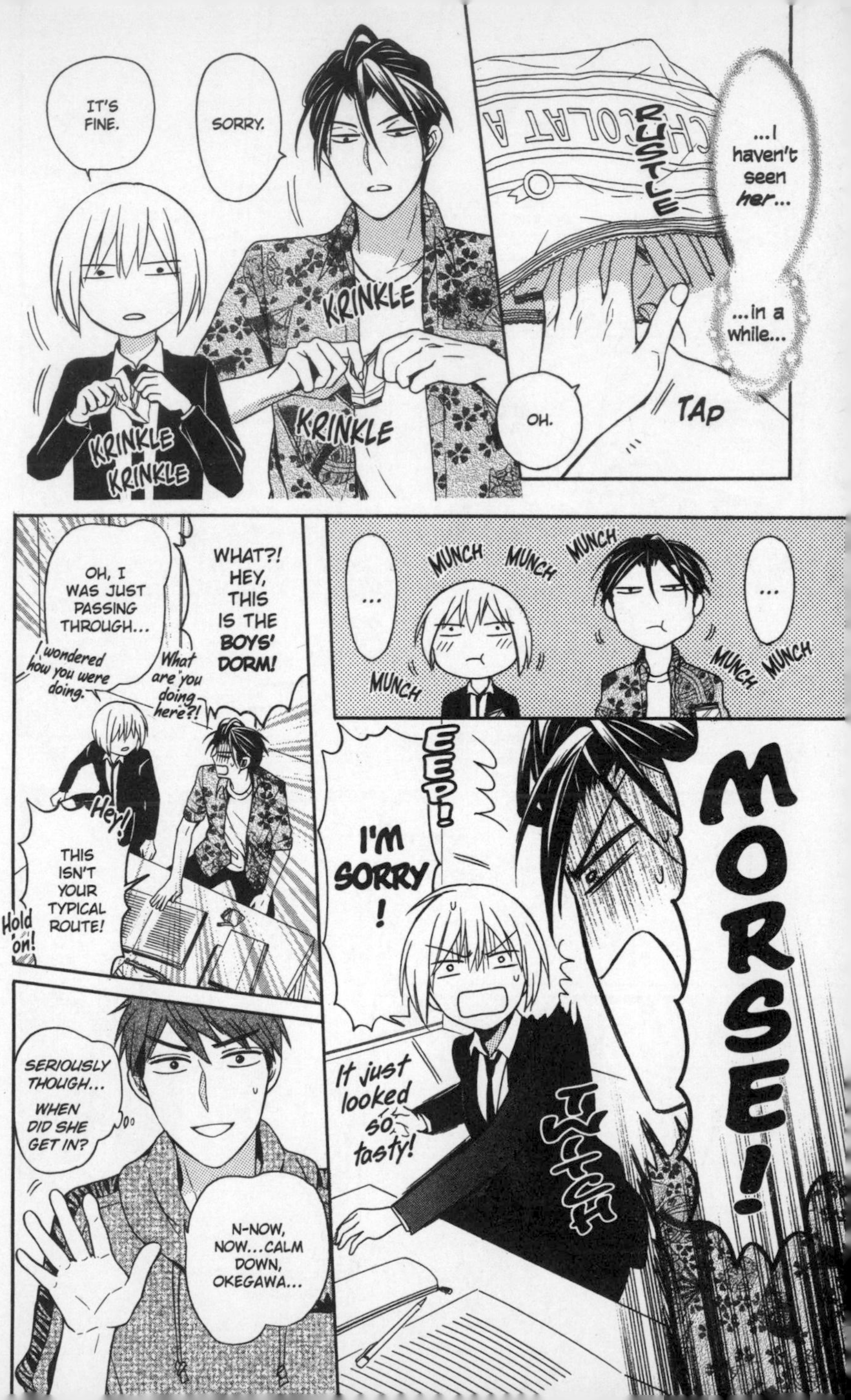

...I haven't seen *her*...
RUSTLE
...in a while...
TAP
OH.
SORRY.
IT'S FINE.
KRINKLE
KRINKLE
KRINKLE KRINKLE
...
MUNCH MUNCH MUNCH
...
MUNCH
MUNCH MUNCH
MORSE!
EEP!
I'M SORRY!
It just looked so tasty!
WHAT?! HEY, THIS IS THE BOYS' DORM!
What are you doing here?!
OH, I WAS JUST PASSING THROUGH...
I wondered how you were doing.
Hey!
THIS ISN'T YOUR TYPICAL ROUTE!
Hold on!
SERIOUSLY THOUGH... WHEN DID SHE GET IN?
N-NOW, NOW...CALM DOWN, OKEGAWA...

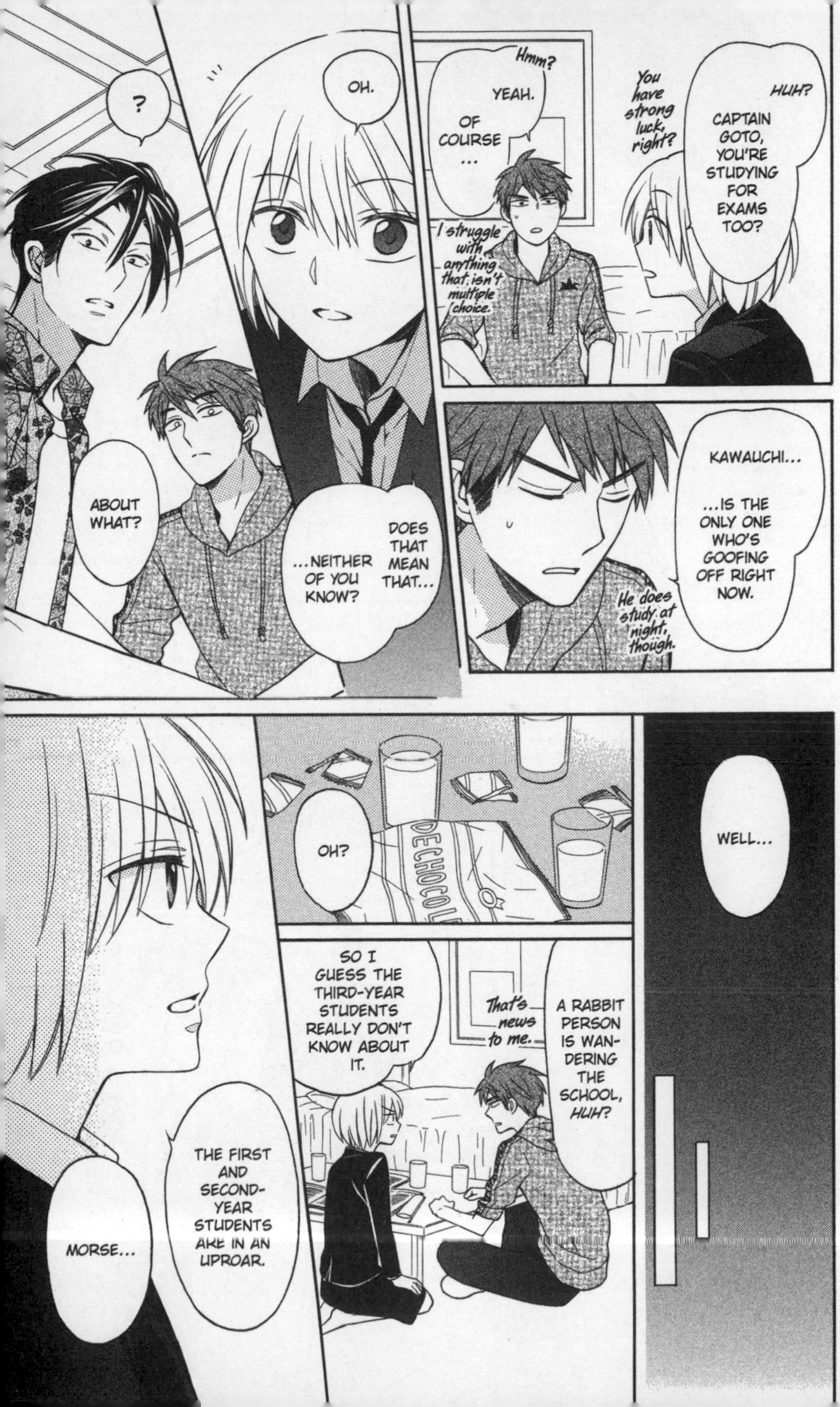
HUH?
CAPTAIN GOTO, YOU'RE STUDYING FOR EXAMS TOO?
You have strong luck, right?
Hmm?
YEAH.
OF COURSE...
I struggle with anything that isn't multiple choice.
KAWAUCHI...
...IS THE ONLY ONE WHO'S GOOFING OFF RIGHT NOW.
He does study at night, though.
OH.
DOES THAT MEAN THAT...
...NEITHER OF YOU KNOW?
?
ABOUT WHAT?
WELL...
OH?
A RABBIT PERSON IS WANDERING THE SCHOOL, HUH?
That's news to me.
SO I GUESS THE THIRD-YEAR STUDENTS REALLY DON'T KNOW ABOUT IT.
THE FIRST AND SECOND-YEAR STUDENTS ARE IN AN UPROAR.
MORSE...

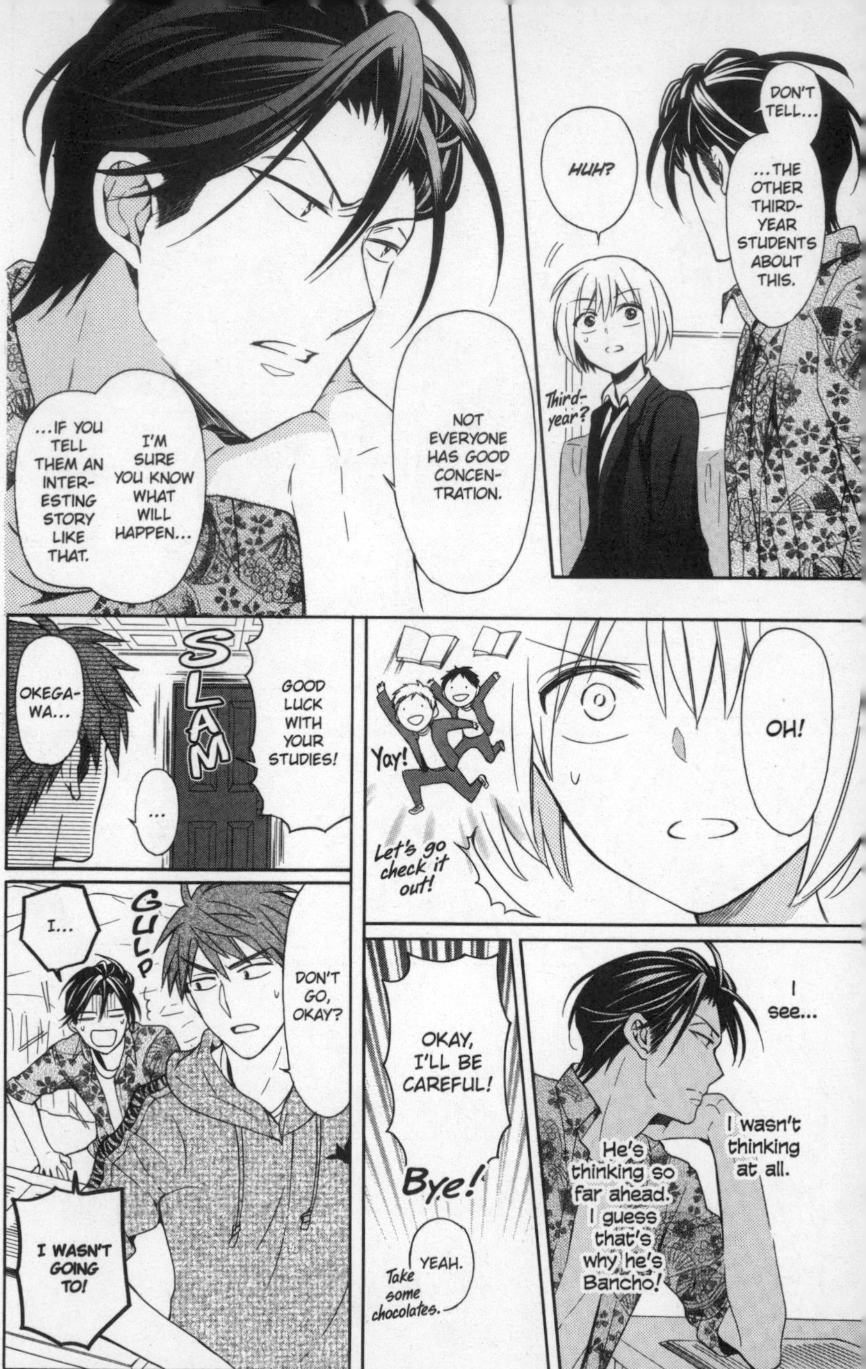
DON'T TELL...
...THE OTHER THIRD-YEAR STUDENTS ABOUT THIS.
HUH?
Third-year?
NOT EVERYONE HAS GOOD CONCENTRATION.
I'M SURE YOU KNOW WHAT WILL HAPPEN...
...IF YOU TELL THEM AN INTERESTING STORY LIKE THAT.
OH!
Yay!
Let's go check it out!
GOOD LUCK WITH YOUR STUDIES!
SLAM
...
OKEGAWA...
I see...
I wasn't thinking at all.
He's thinking so far ahead. I guess that's why he's Bancho!
OKAY, I'LL BE CAREFUL!
Bye!
YEAH.
Take some chocolates.
DON'T GO, OKAY?
GULP
I...
I WASN'T GOING TO!

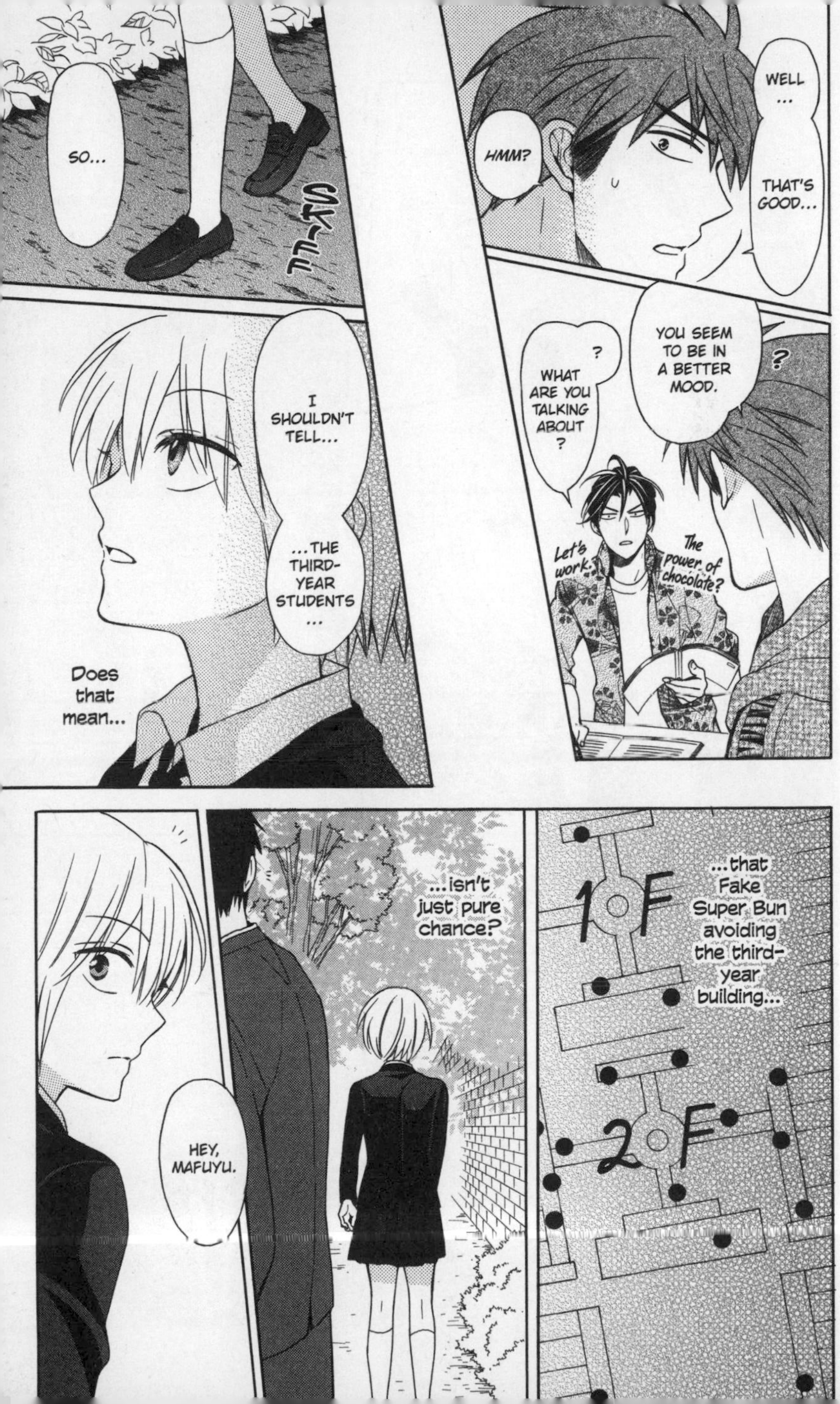
WELL ...
HMM?
THAT'S GOOD...
SO...
SKIFF
YOU SEEM TO BE IN A BETTER MOOD.
?
? WHAT ARE YOU TALKING ABOUT ?
The power of chocolate?
Let's work.
I SHOULDN'T TELL...
...THE THIRD-YEAR STUDENTS ...
Does that mean...
...that Fake Super Bun avoiding the third-year building...
1F
2F
...isn't just pure chance?
HEY, MAFUYU.

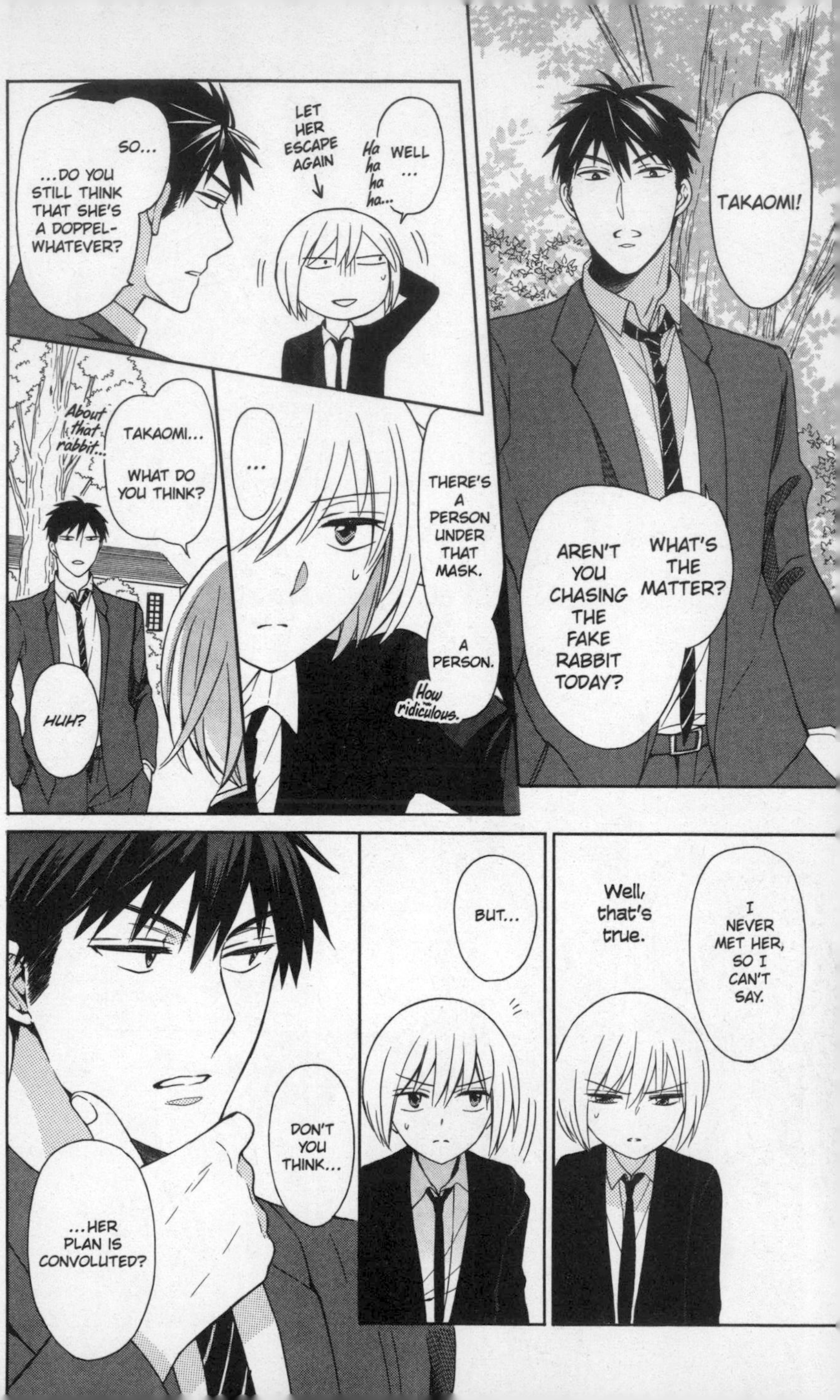
TAKAOMI!
WHAT'S THE MATTER?
AREN'T YOU CHASING THE FAKE RABBIT TODAY?
WELL...
Ha ha ha ha...
LET HER ESCAPE AGAIN
SO...
...DO YOU STILL THINK THAT SHE'S A DOPPEL-WHATEVER?
THERE'S A PERSON UNDER THAT MASK.
A PERSON.
How ridiculous.
...
About that rabbit...
TAKAOMI...
WHAT DO YOU THINK?
HUH?
I NEVER MET HER, SO I CAN'T SAY.
Well, that's true.
BUT...
DON'T YOU THINK...
...HER PLAN IS CONVOLUTED?

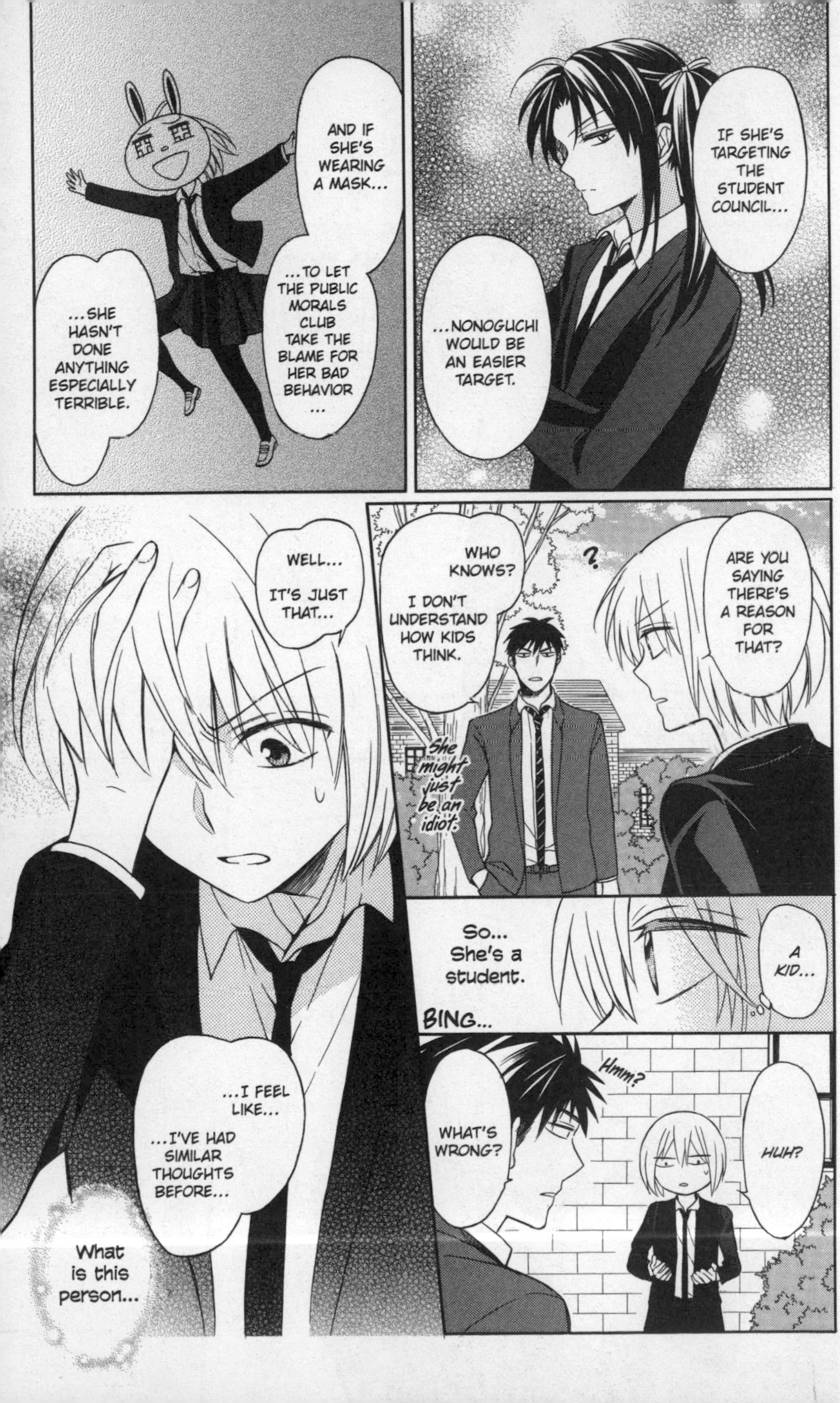
IF SHE'S TARGETING THE STUDENT COUNCIL...
...NONOGUCHI WOULD BE AN EASIER TARGET.
AND IF SHE'S WEARING A MASK...
...TO LET THE PUBLIC MORALS CLUB TAKE THE BLAME FOR HER BAD BEHAVIOR ...
...SHE HASN'T DONE ANYTHING ESPECIALLY TERRIBLE.
ARE YOU SAYING THERE'S A REASON FOR THAT?
?
WHO KNOWS?
I DON'T UNDERSTAND HOW KIDS THINK.
She might just be an idiot.
A KID...
So... She's a student.
BING...
HUH?
Hmm?
WHAT'S WRONG?
WELL...
IT'S JUST THAT...
...I FEEL LIKE...
...I'VE HAD SIMILAR THOUGHTS BEFORE...
What is this person...

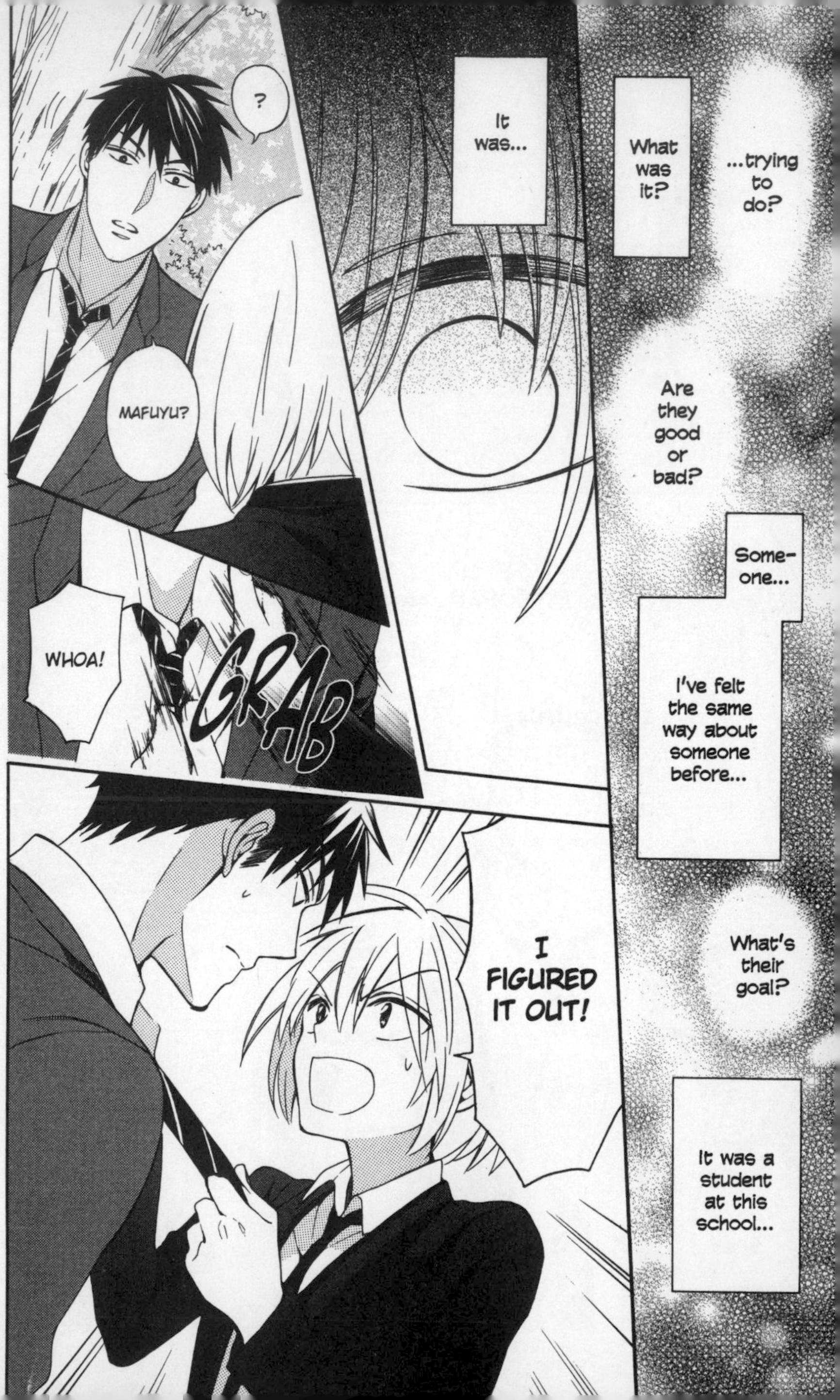
What was it?
...trying to do?
Are they good or bad?
Someone...
I've felt the same way about someone before...
What's their goal?
It was a student at this school...
It was...
?
MAFUYU?
WHOA!
GRAB
I FIGURED IT OUT!

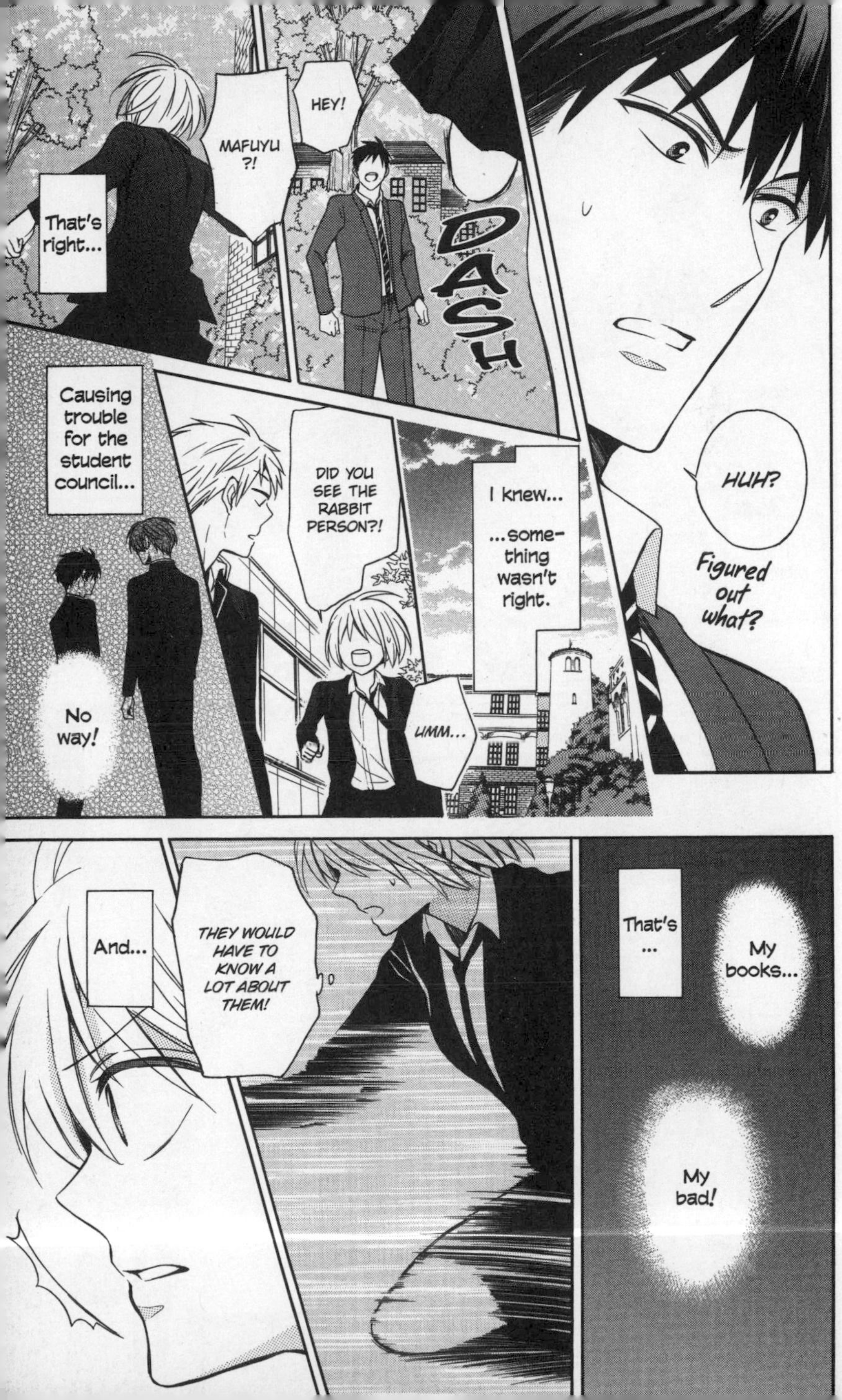
HUH?
Figured out what?
HEY!
MAFUYU ?!
DASH
That's right...
I knew... ...some-thing wasn't right.
DID YOU SEE THE RABBIT PERSON?!
UMM...
Causing trouble for the student council...
No way!
That's ...
My books...
My bad!
THEY WOULD HAVE TO KNOW A LOT ABOUT THEM!
And...

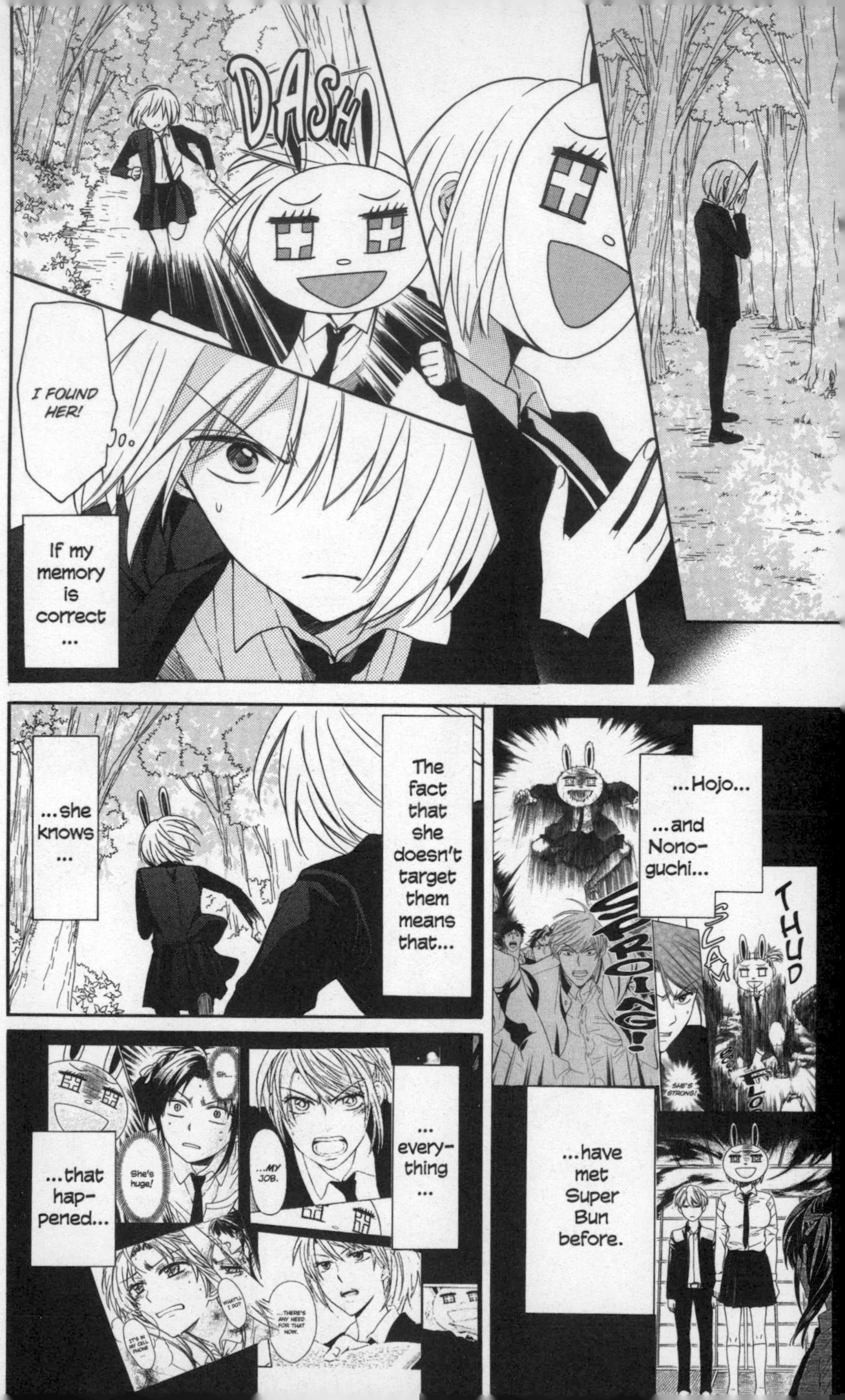
DASH
I FOUND HER!
If my memory is correct ...
...Hojo...
...and Nono-guchi...
SPROING!
SLAM
THUD
SHE'S STRONG!
...have met Super Bun before.
The fact that she doesn't target them means that...
...she knows ...
... every-thing ...
Sh...
...MY JOB.
She's huge!
...that hap-pened...
...THERE'S ANY NEED FOR THAT NOW.
WHAT'LL I DO?
IT'S IN MY CELL PHONE ...

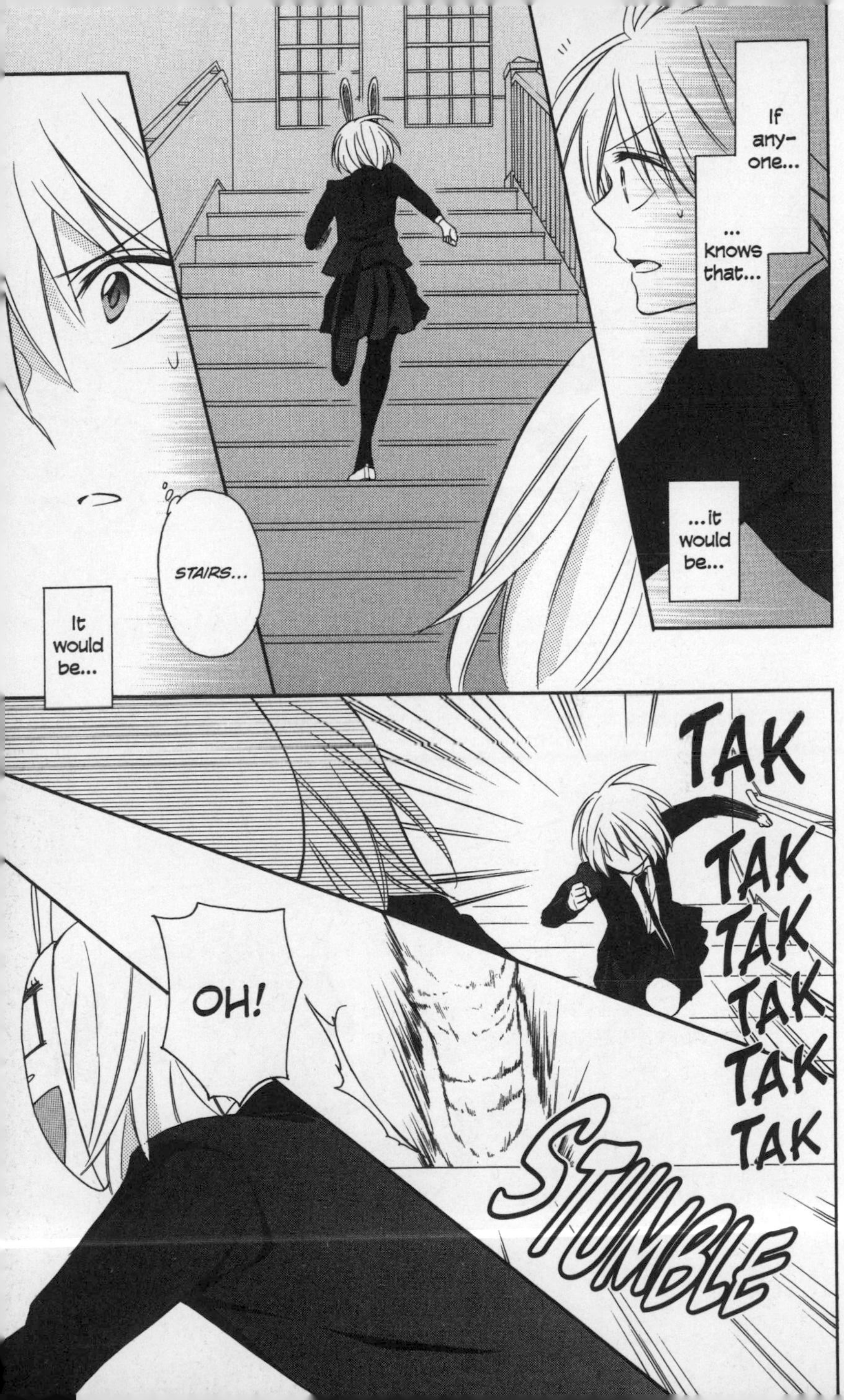

If any-one...
...knows that...
...it would be...
STAIRS...
It would be...
TAK
TAK TAK TAK TAK TAK
STUMBLE
OH!

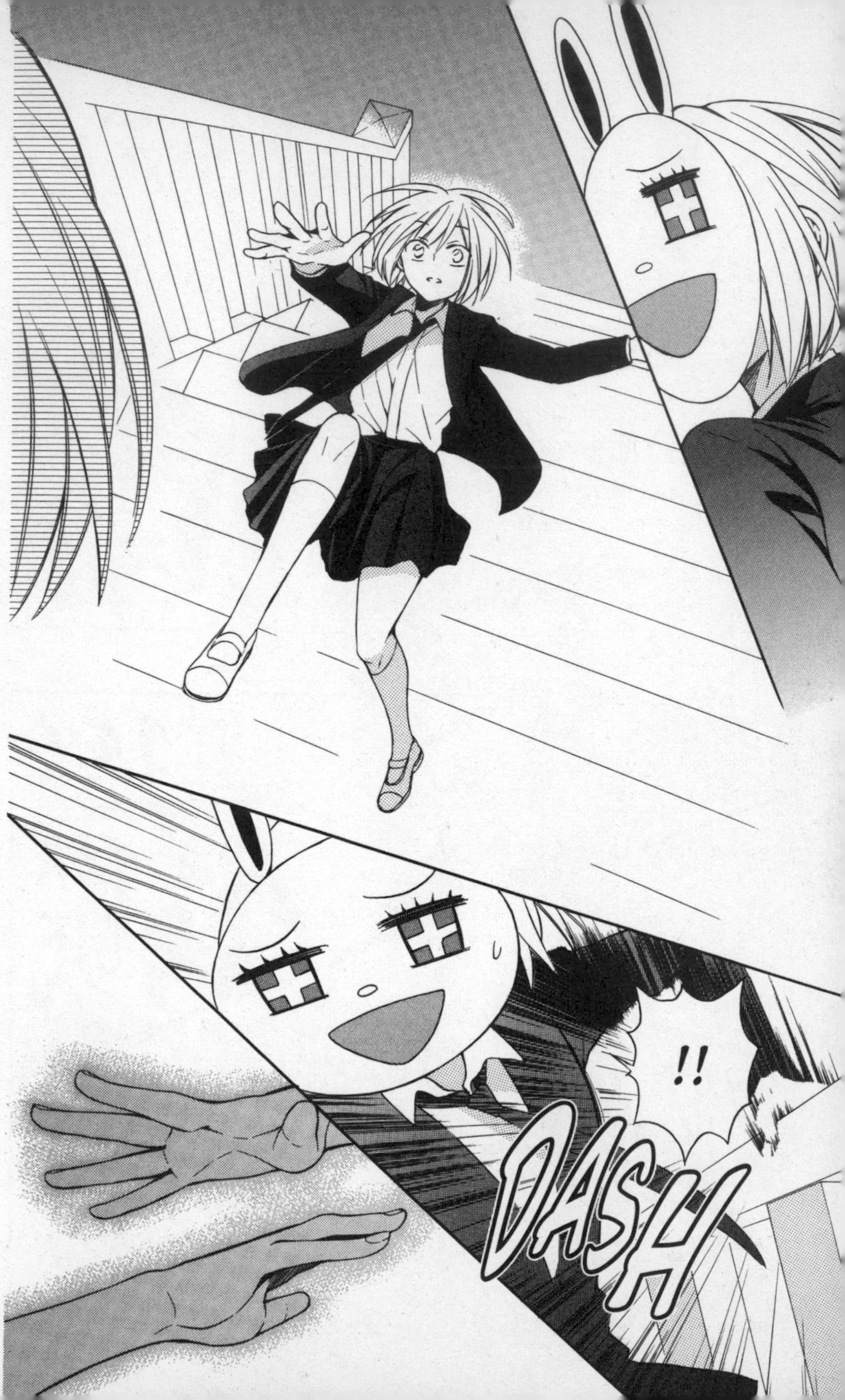
!!
DASH

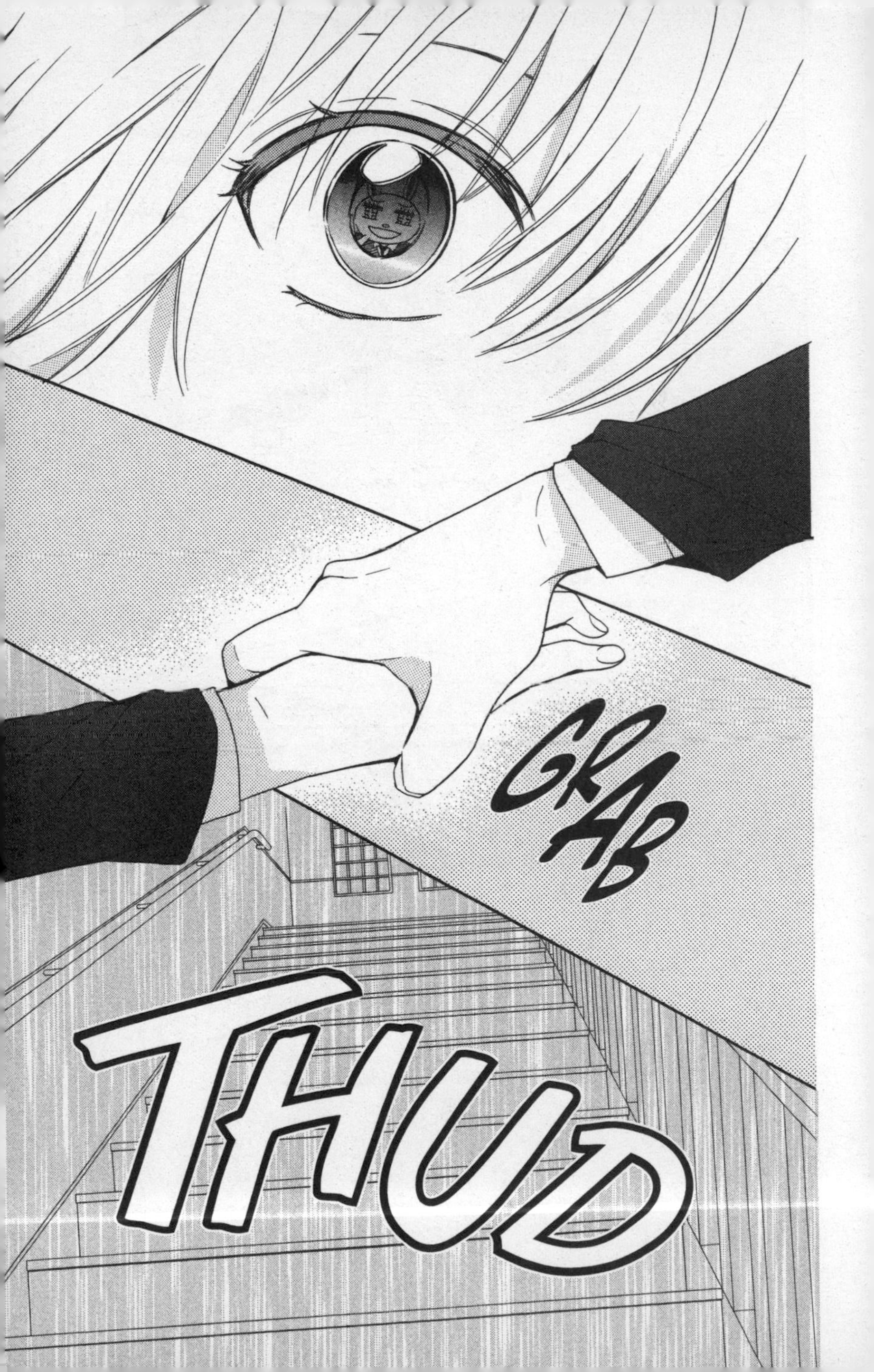
GRAB
THUD

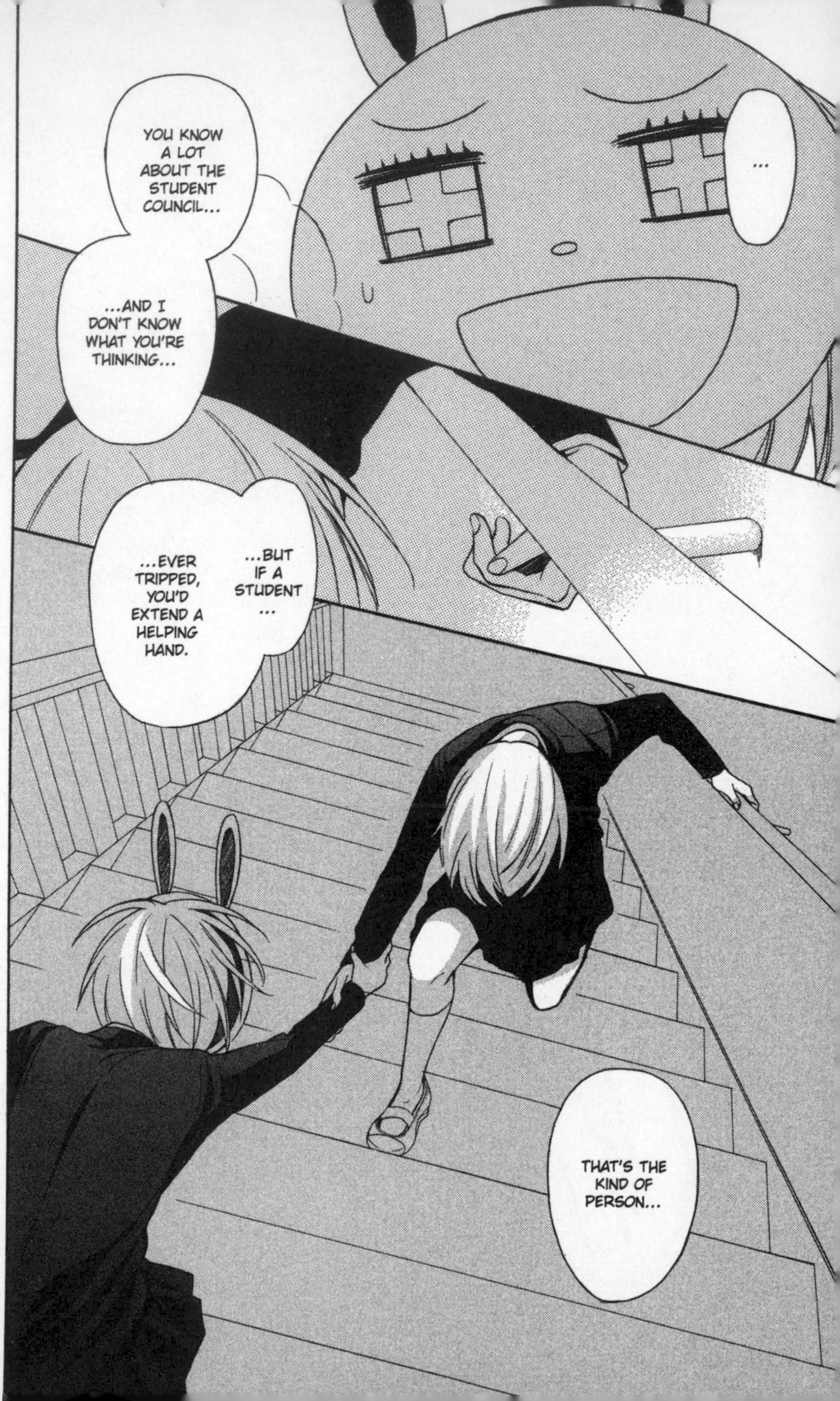
...
YOU KNOW A LOT ABOUT THE STUDENT COUNCIL...
...AND I DON'T KNOW WHAT YOU'RE THINKING...
...BUT IF A STUDENT ...
...EVER TRIPPED, YOU'D EXTEND A HELPING HAND.
THAT'S THE KIND OF PERSON...

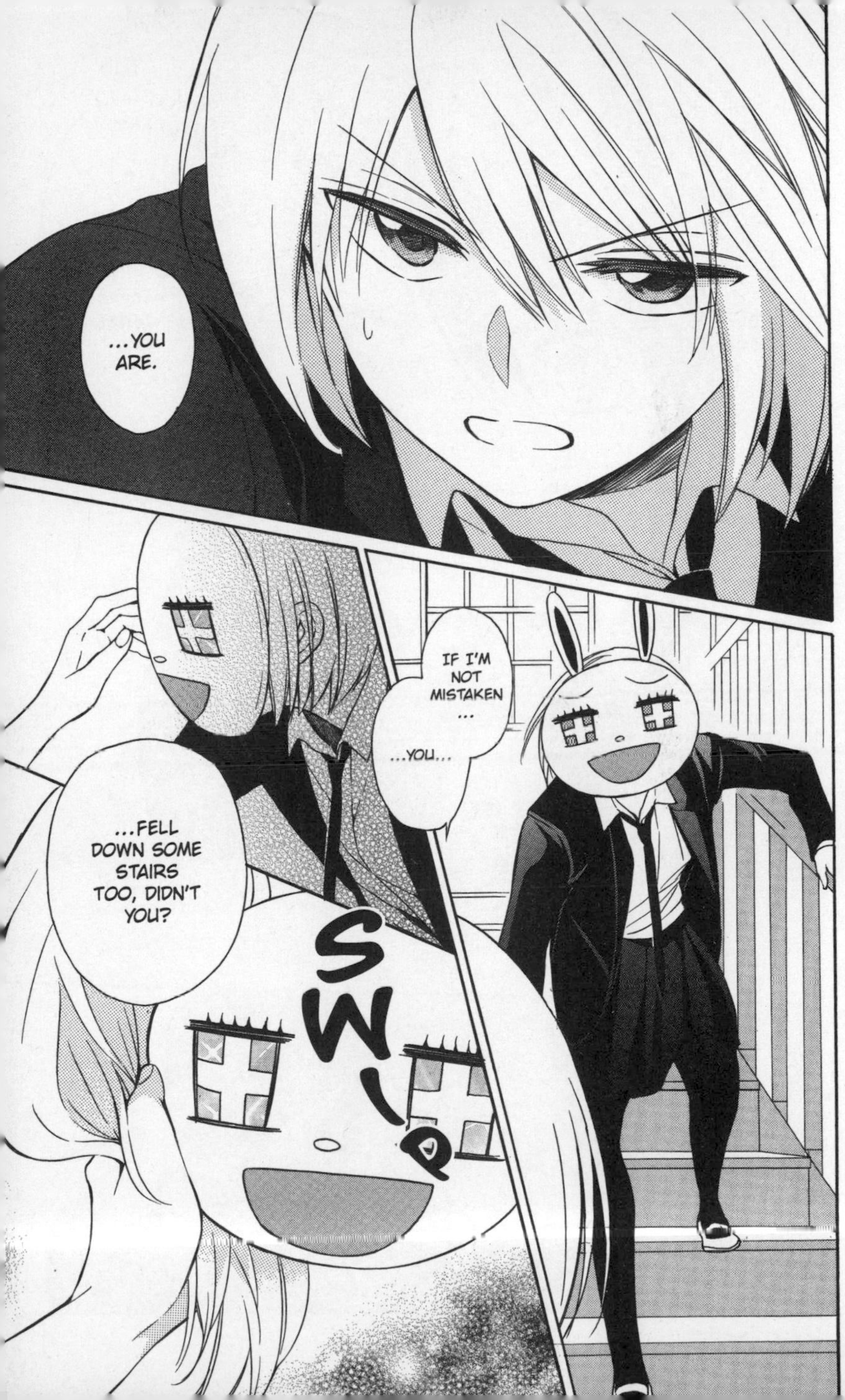
...YOU ARE.
IF I'M NOT MISTAKEN...
...YOU...
...FELL DOWN SOME STAIRS TOO, DIDN'T YOU?
SWIP

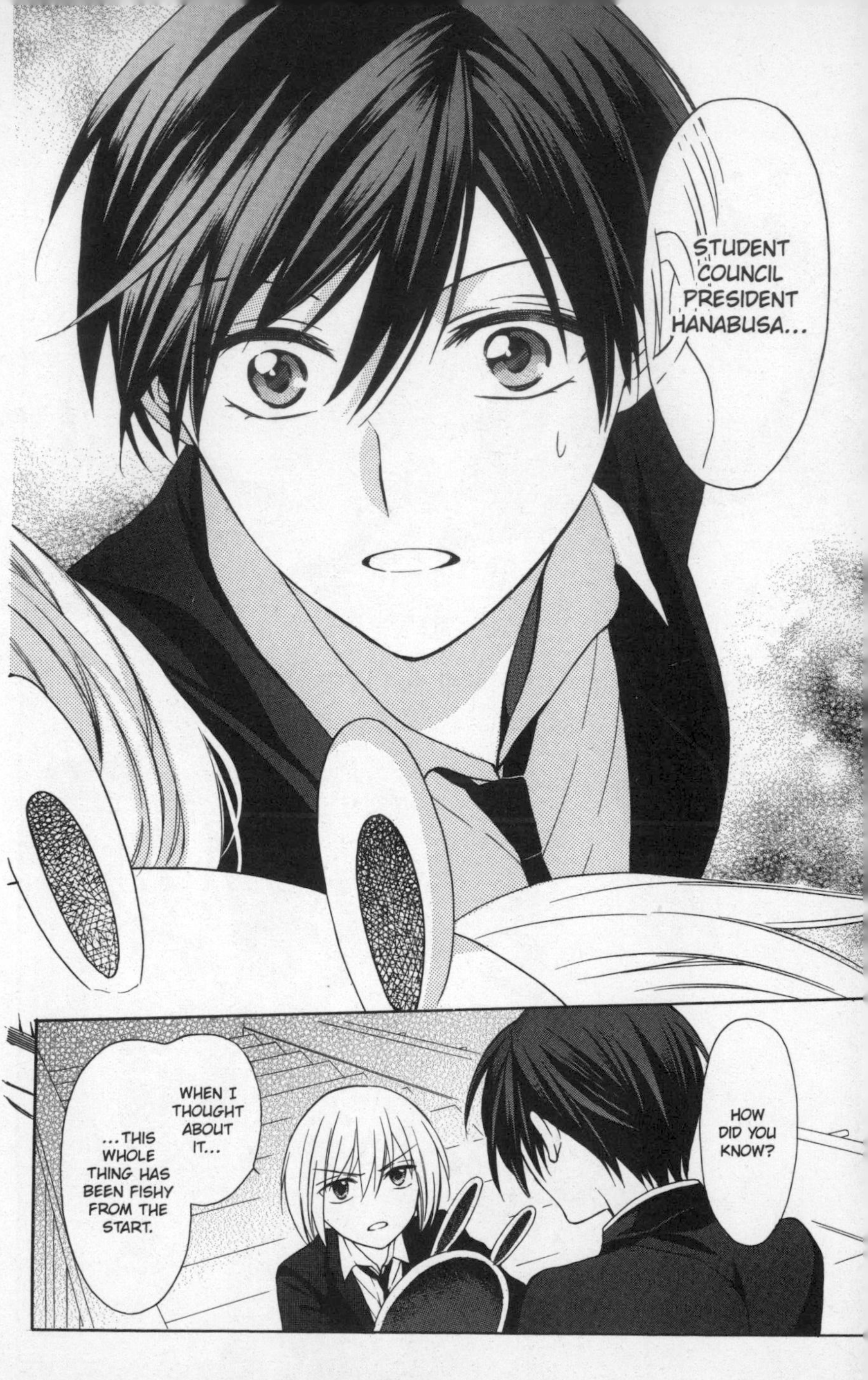
STUDENT COUNCIL PRESIDENT HANABUSA...
HOW DID YOU KNOW?
WHEN I THOUGHT ABOUT IT...
...THIS WHOLE THING HAS BEEN FISHY FROM THE START.

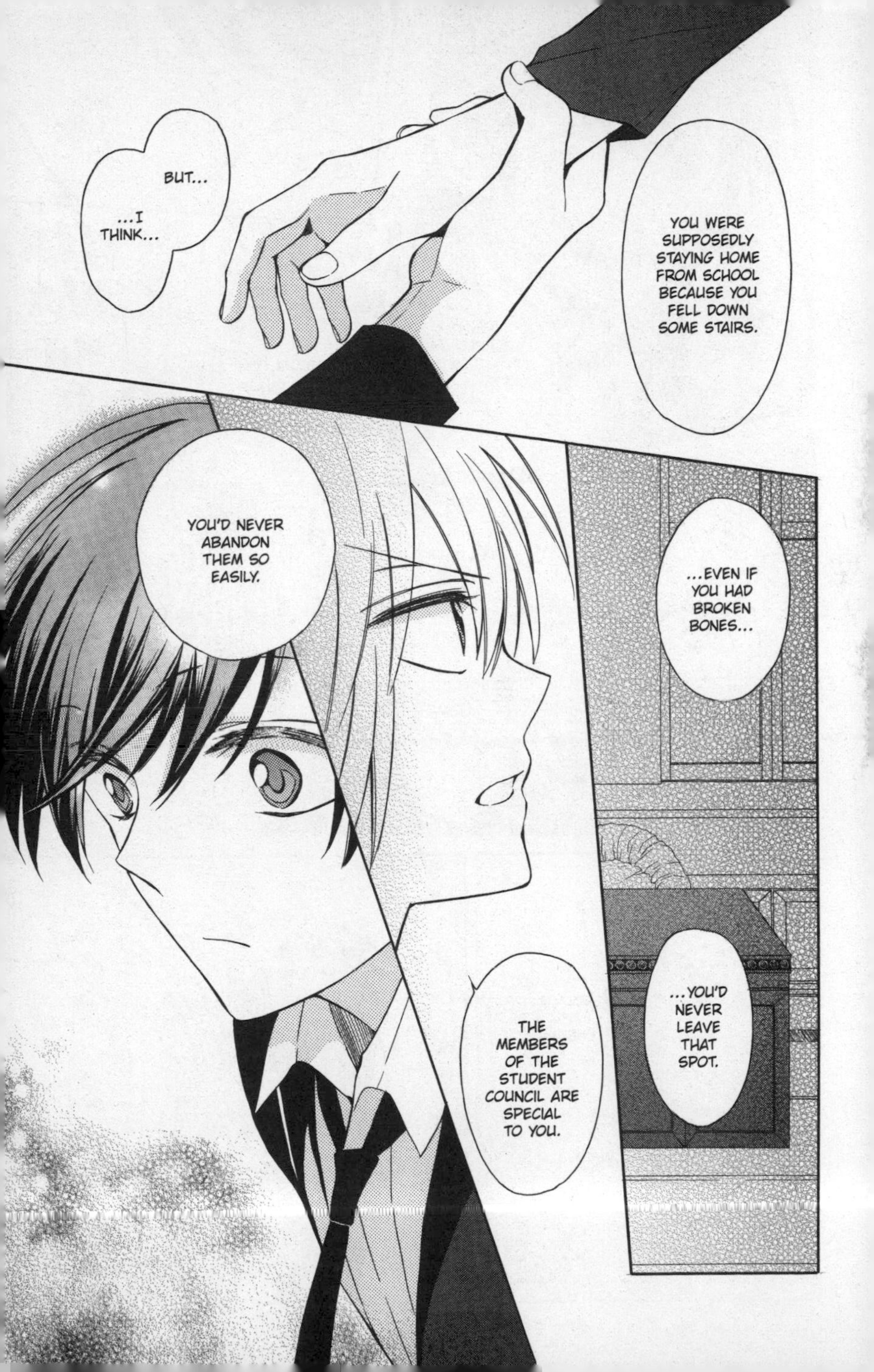

YOU WERE SUPPOSEDLY STAYING HOME FROM SCHOOL BECAUSE YOU FELL DOWN SOME STAIRS.
BUT...
...I THINK...
...EVEN IF YOU HAD BROKEN BONES...
...YOU'D NEVER LEAVE THAT SPOT.
YOU'D NEVER ABANDON THEM SO EASILY.
THE MEMBERS OF THE STUDENT COUNCIL ARE SPECIAL TO YOU.

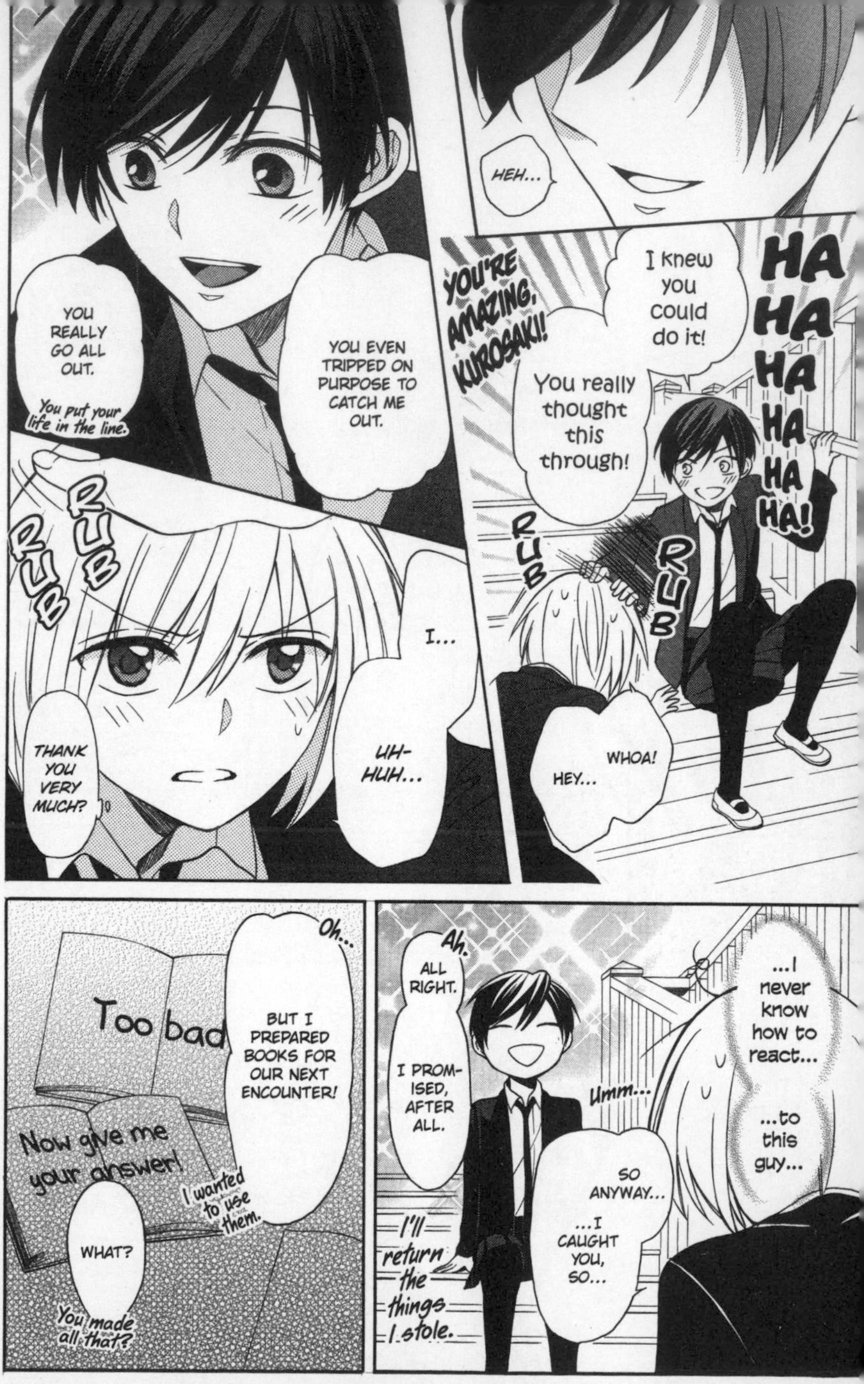
HEH...
HA HA HA HA HA HA HA!
I knew you could do it!
YOU'RE AMAZING, KUROSAKI!!
You really thought this through!
RUB
RUB
WHOA!
HEY...
YOU EVEN TRIPPED ON PURPOSE TO CATCH ME OUT.
YOU REALLY GO ALL OUT.
You put your life in the line.
RUB
RUB
I...
UH-HUH...
THANK YOU VERY MUCH?
...I never know how to react...
...to this guy...
Umm...
SO ANYWAY...
...I CAUGHT YOU, SO...
Ah.
ALL RIGHT.
I PROMISED, AFTER ALL.
I'll return the things I stole.
Oh...
BUT I PREPARED BOOKS FOR OUR NEXT ENCOUNTER!
I wanted to use them.
Too bad
Now give me your answer!
WHAT?
You made all that?

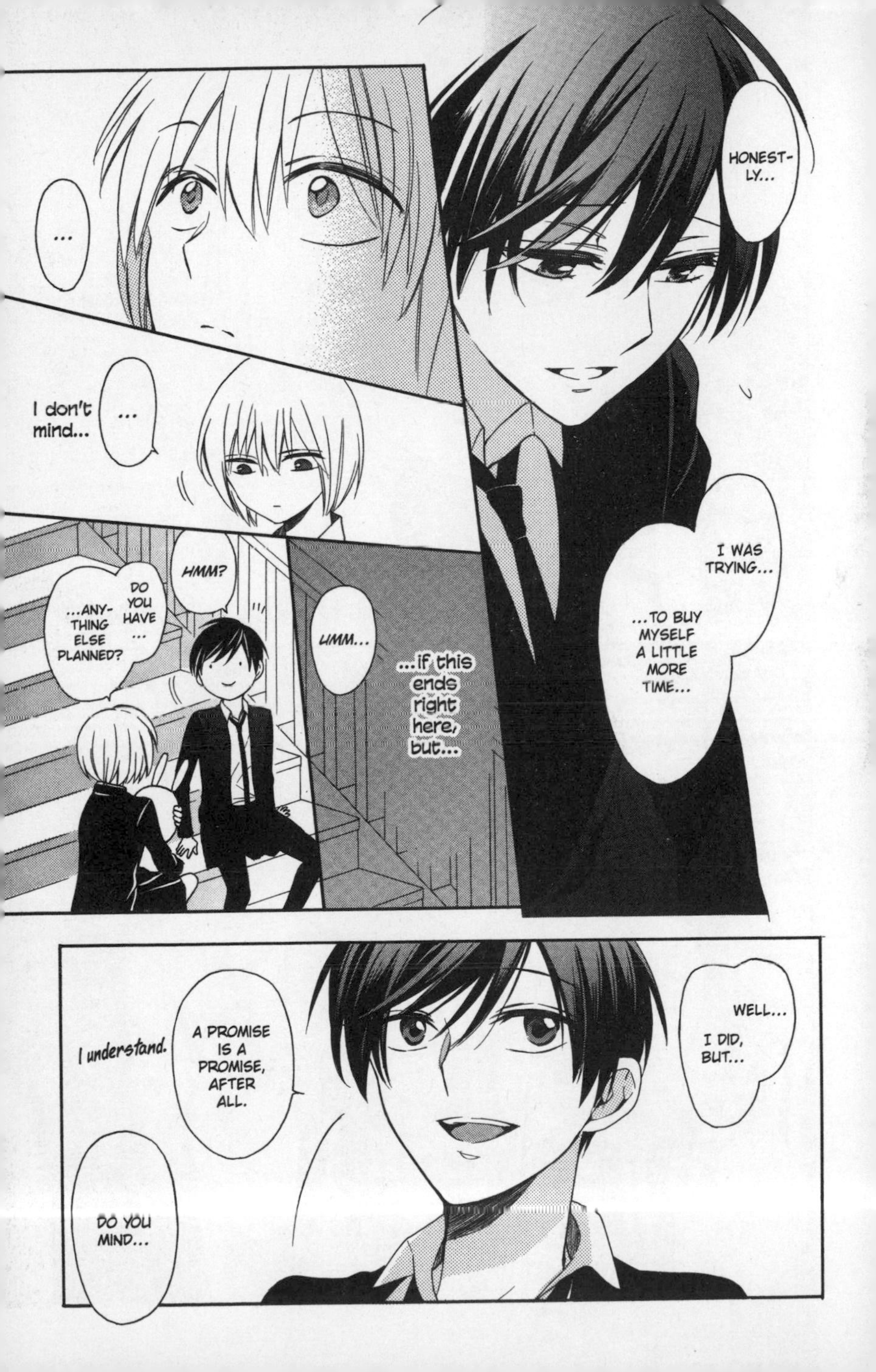
HONESTLY...
I WAS TRYING...
...TO BUY MYSELF A LITTLE MORE TIME...
...
...
I don't mind...
UMM...
...if this ends right here, but...
HMM?
DO YOU HAVE ...
...ANYTHING ELSE PLANNED?
WELL... I DID, BUT...
A PROMISE IS A PROMISE, AFTER ALL.
I understand.
DO YOU MIND...

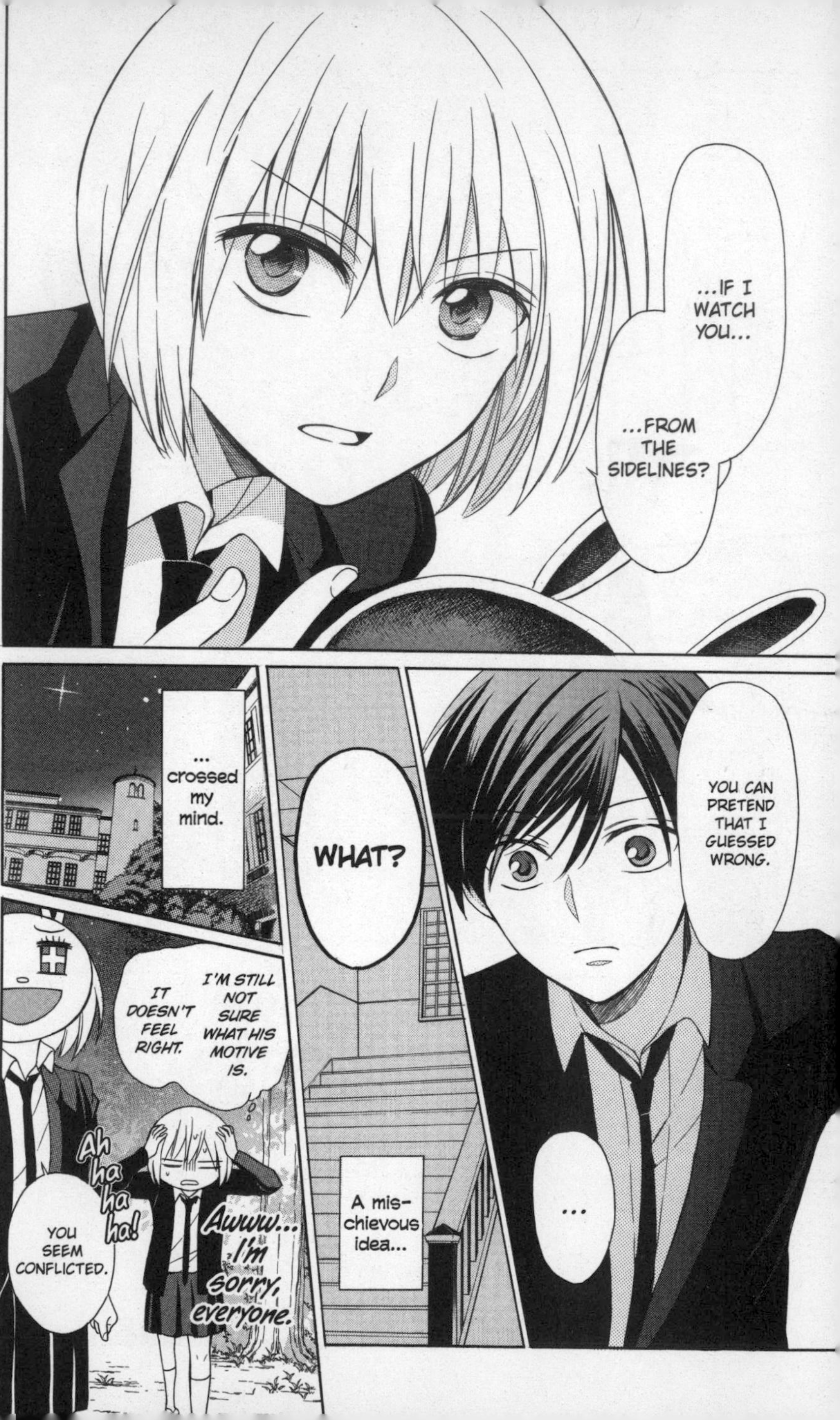

...IF I WATCH YOU...
...FROM THE SIDELINES?
YOU CAN PRETEND THAT I GUESSED WRONG.
WHAT?
...
A mis-chievous idea...
... crossed my mind.
I'M STILL NOT SURE WHAT HIS MOTIVE IS.
IT DOESN'T FEEL RIGHT.
Awww... I'm sorry, everyone.
Ah ha ha ha!
YOU SEEM CONFLICTED.

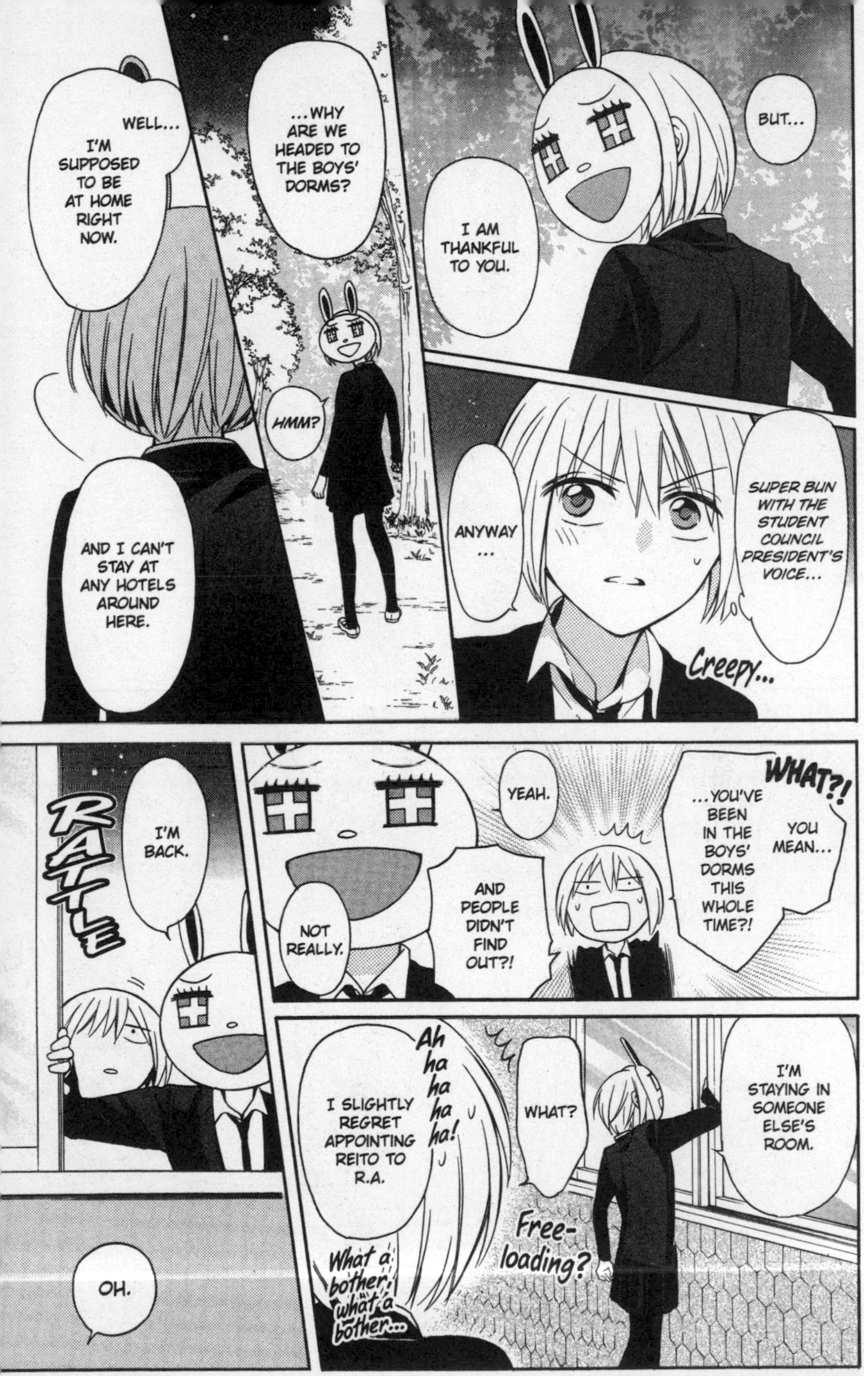

...WHY ARE WE HEADED TO THE BOYS' DORMS?
HMM?
WELL... I'M SUPPOSED TO BE AT HOME RIGHT NOW.
AND I CAN'T STAY AT ANY HOTELS AROUND HERE.
BUT...
I AM THANKFUL TO YOU.
ANYWAY...
SUPER BUN WITH THE STUDENT COUNCIL PRESIDENT'S VOICE...
Creepy...
RATTLE
I'M BACK.
OH.
WHAT?!
YOU MEAN...
...YOU'VE BEEN IN THE BOYS' DORMS THIS WHOLE TIME?!
YEAH.
AND PEOPLE DIDN'T FIND OUT?!
NOT REALLY.
I'M STAYING IN SOMEONE ELSE'S ROOM.
WHAT?
Free-loading?
Ah ha ha ha ha!
I SLIGHTLY REGRET APPOINTING REITO TO R.A.
What a bother, what a bother...

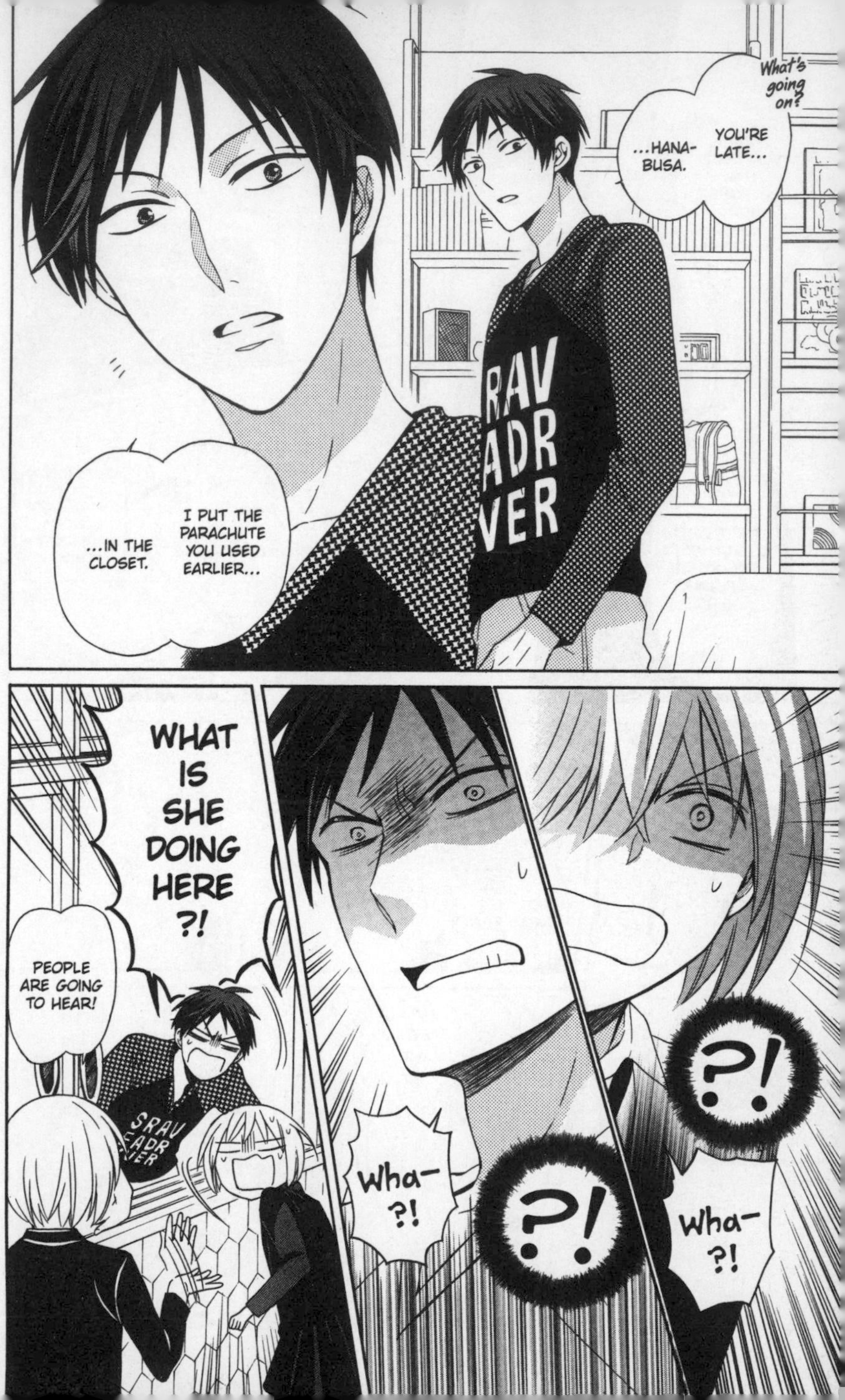
What's going on?
YOU'RE LATE... ...HANA-BUSA.
I PUT THE PARACHUTE YOU USED EARLIER... ...IN THE CLOSET.
?!
Wha- ?!
?!
Wha- ?!
WHAT IS SHE DOING HERE ?!
PEOPLE ARE GOING TO HEAR!

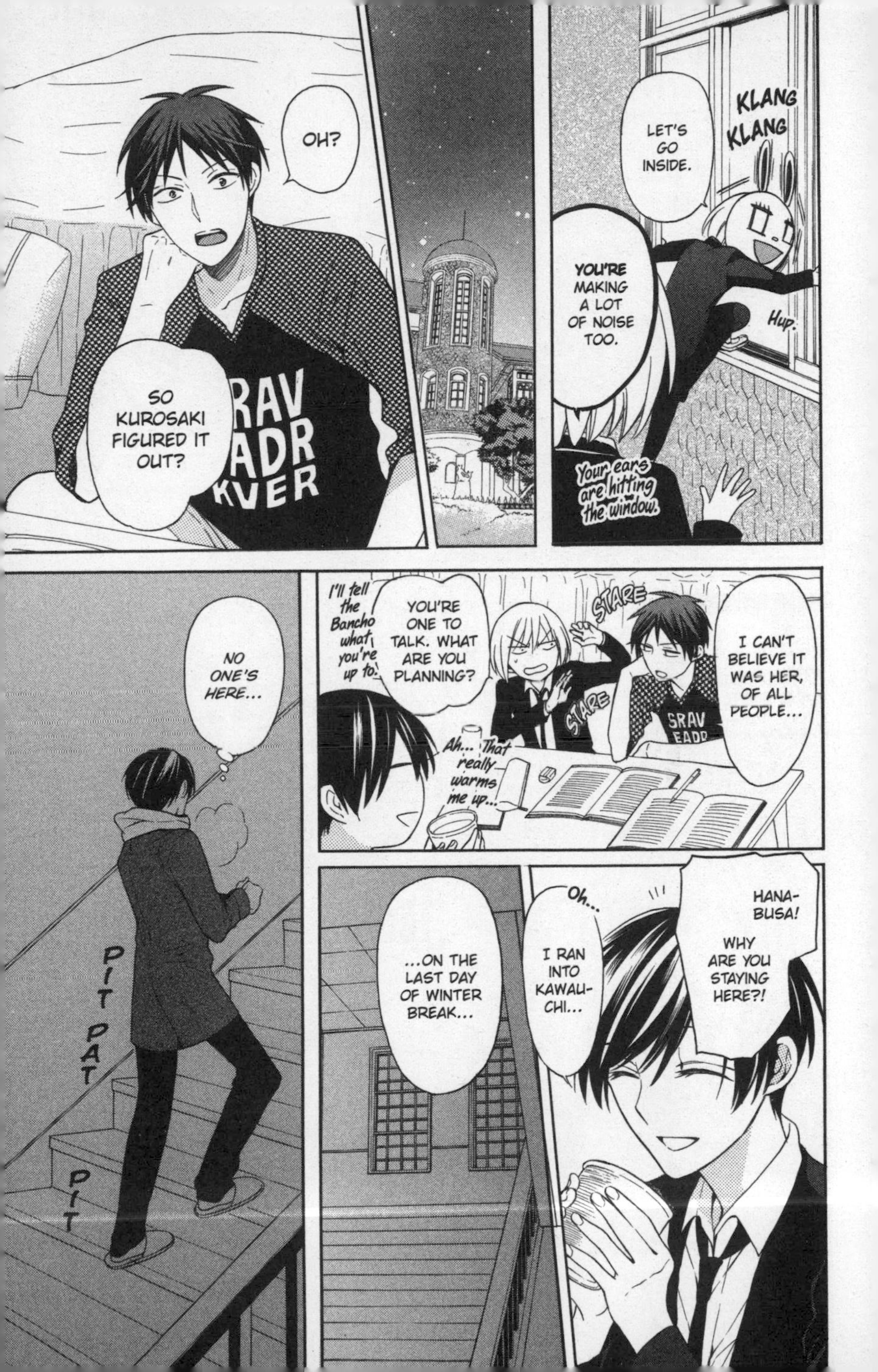
KLANG KLANG
LET'S GO INSIDE.
Hup.
YOU'RE MAKING A LOT OF NOISE TOO.
Your ears are hitting the window.
OH?
SO KUROSAKI FIGURED IT OUT?
STARE
I CAN'T BELIEVE IT WAS HER, OF ALL PEOPLE...
STARE
YOU'RE ONE TO TALK. WHAT ARE YOU PLANNING?
I'll tell the Bancho what you're up to!
Ah... That really warms me up...
HANA-BUSA!
WHY ARE YOU STAYING HERE?!
Oh...
I RAN INTO KAWAU-CHI...
...ON THE LAST DAY OF WINTER BREAK...
NO ONE'S HERE...
PIT PAT
PIT PIT

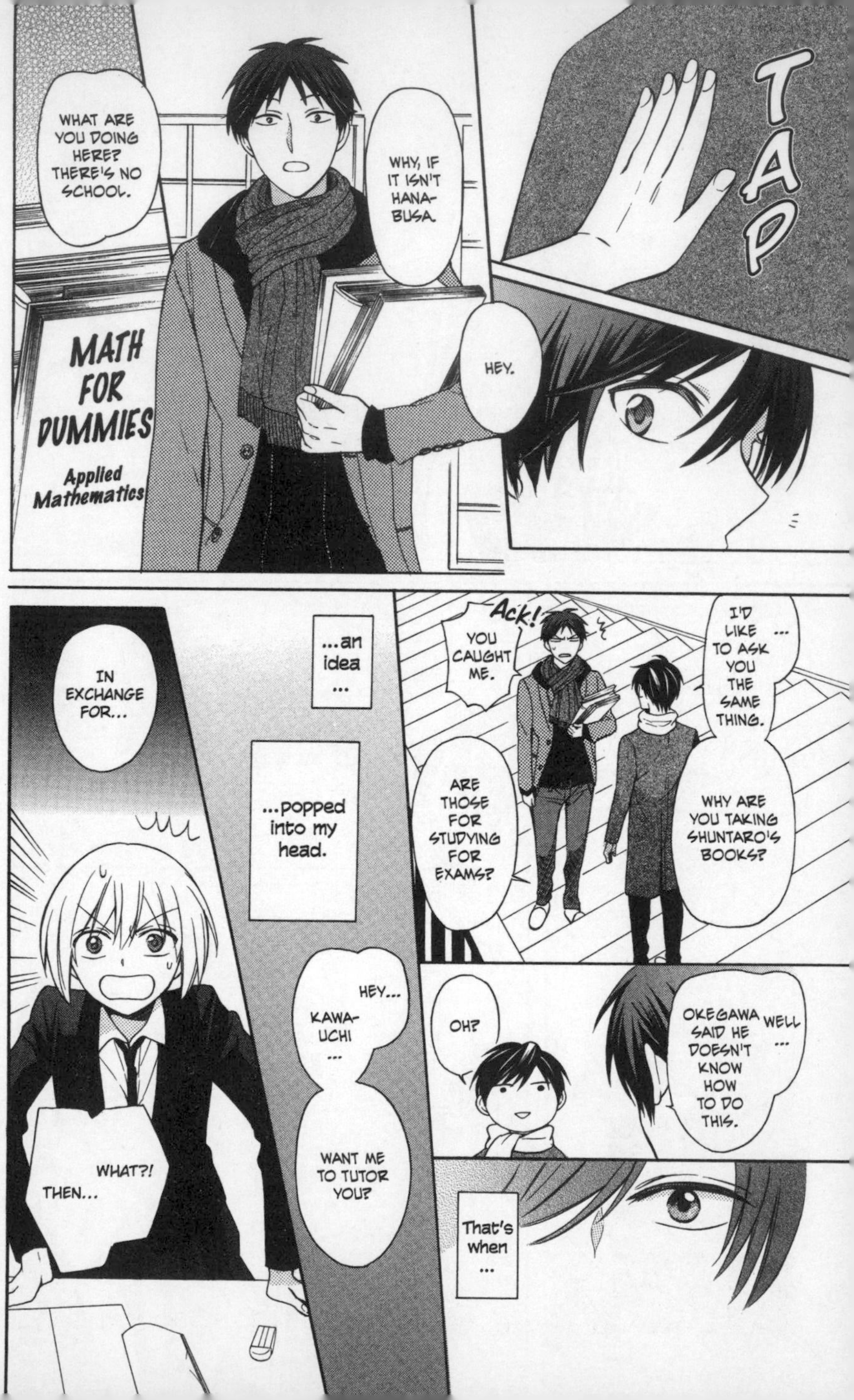
TAP
HEY.
WHY, IF IT ISN'T HANA-BUSA.
WHAT ARE YOU DOING HERE? THERE'S NO SCHOOL.
MATH FOR DUMMIES
Applied Mathematics
I'D LIKE TO ASK YOU THE SAME THING...
Ack!
YOU CAUGHT ME.
WHY ARE YOU TAKING SHUNTARO'S BOOKS?
ARE THOSE FOR STUDYING FOR EXAMS?
WELL...
OKEGAWA SAID HE DOESN'T KNOW HOW TO DO THIS.
OH?
That's when...
...an idea...
...popped into my head.
HEY... KAWA-UCHI...
WANT ME TO TUTOR YOU?
IN EXCHANGE FOR...
WHAT?! THEN...

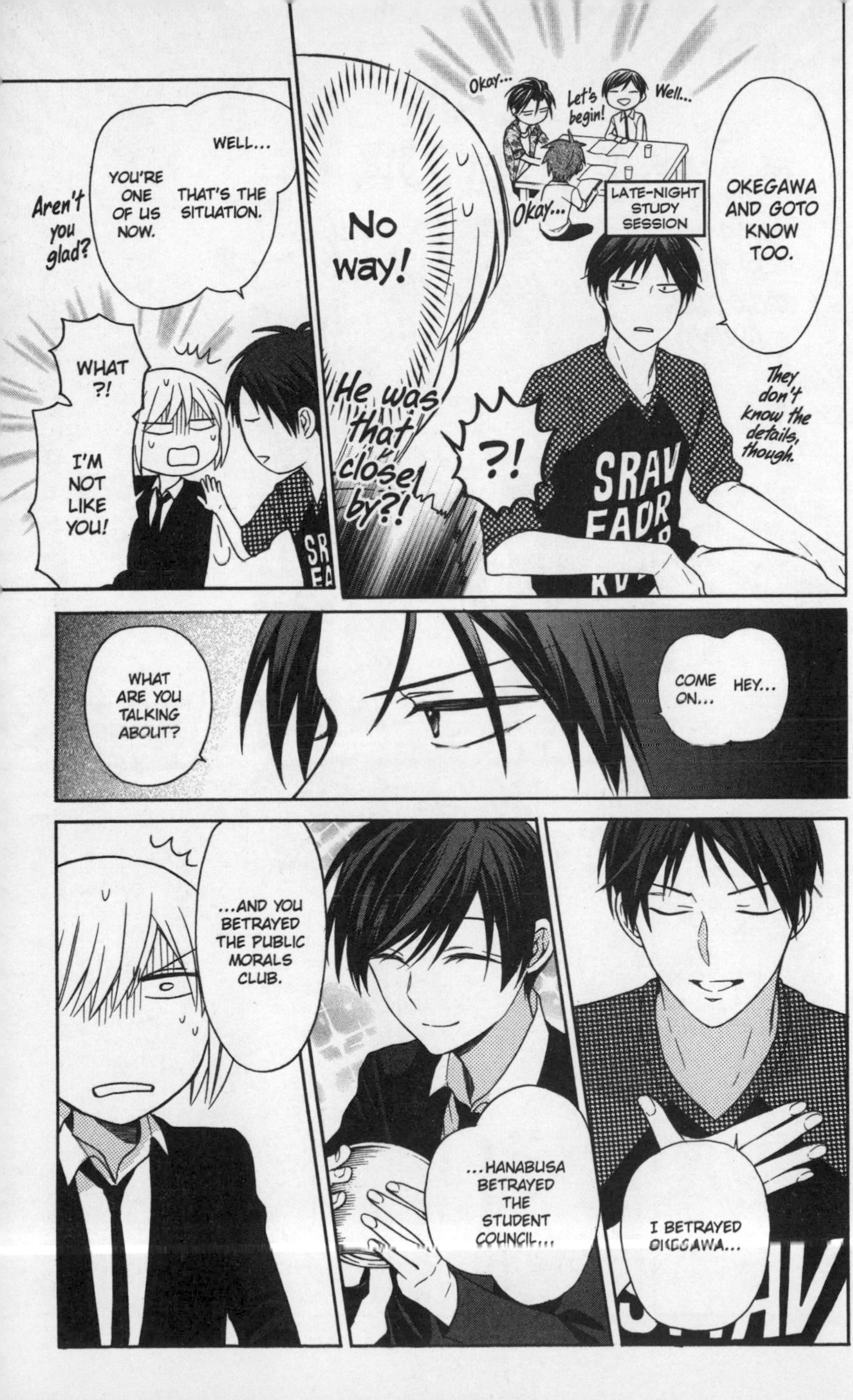
OKEGAWA AND GOTO KNOW TOO.
Well...
Let's begin!
Okay...
Okay...
LATE-NIGHT STUDY SESSION
They don't know the details, though.
?!
No way!
He was that close by?!
WELL...
THAT'S THE SITUATION.
YOU'RE ONE OF US NOW.
Aren't you glad?
WHAT?!
I'M NOT LIKE YOU!
HEY...
COME ON...
WHAT ARE YOU TALKING ABOUT?
I BETRAYED OKEGAWA...
...HANABUSA BETRAYED THE STUDENT COUNCIL...
...AND YOU BETRAYED THE PUBLIC MORALS CLUB.

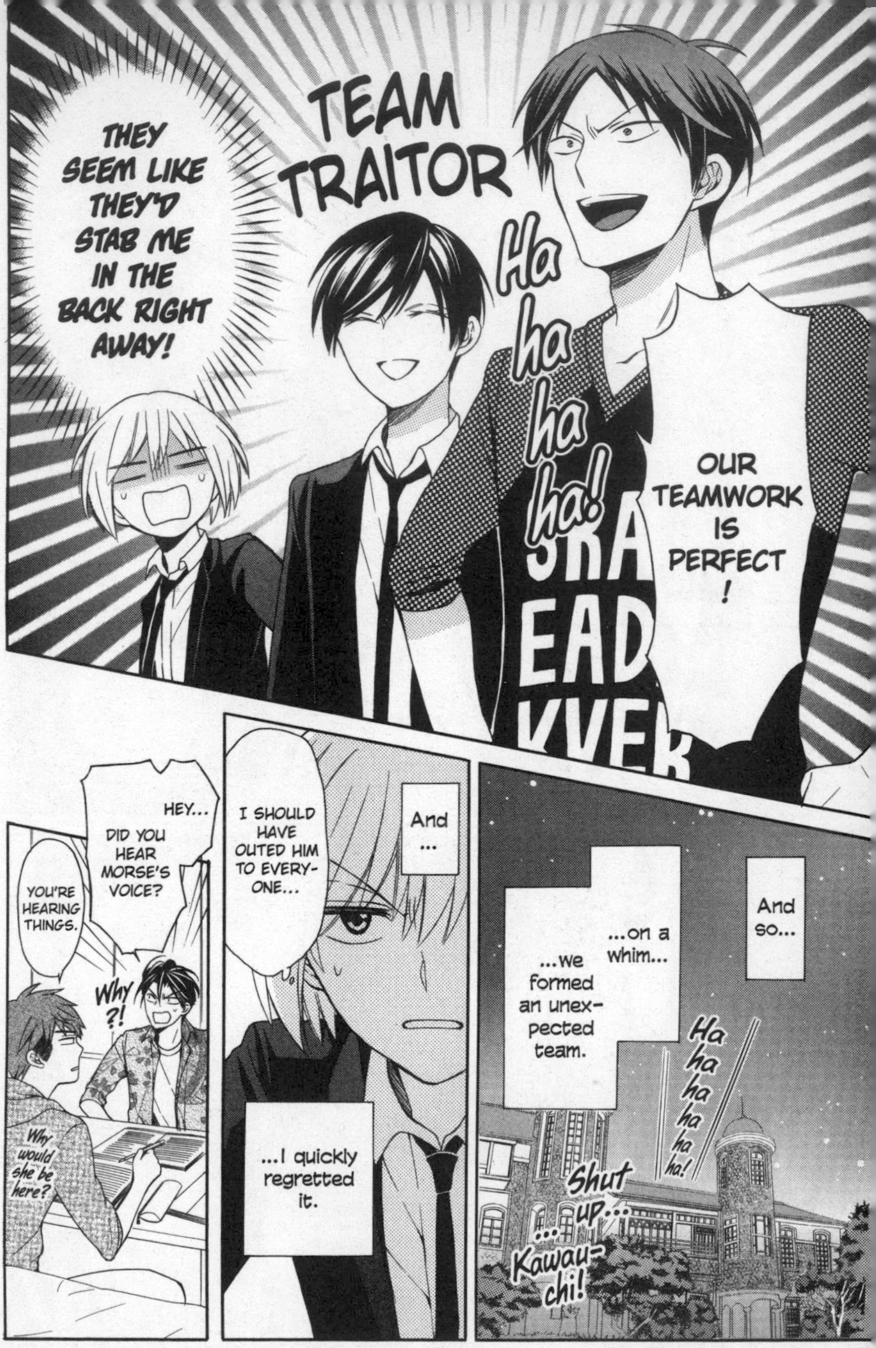
TEAM TRAITOR
Ha ha ha ha!
OUR TEAMWORK IS PERFECT!
THEY SEEM LIKE THEY'D STAB ME IN THE BACK RIGHT AWAY!
And so...
...on a whim...
...we formed an unexpected team.
Ha ha ha ha ha ha ha!
Shut up... ...Kawauchi!
And ...
I SHOULD HAVE OUTED HIM TO EVERY-ONE...
...I quickly regretted it.
HEY... DID YOU HEAR MORSE'S VOICE?
YOU'RE HEARING THINGS.
Why?!
Why would she be here?

Chapter 124

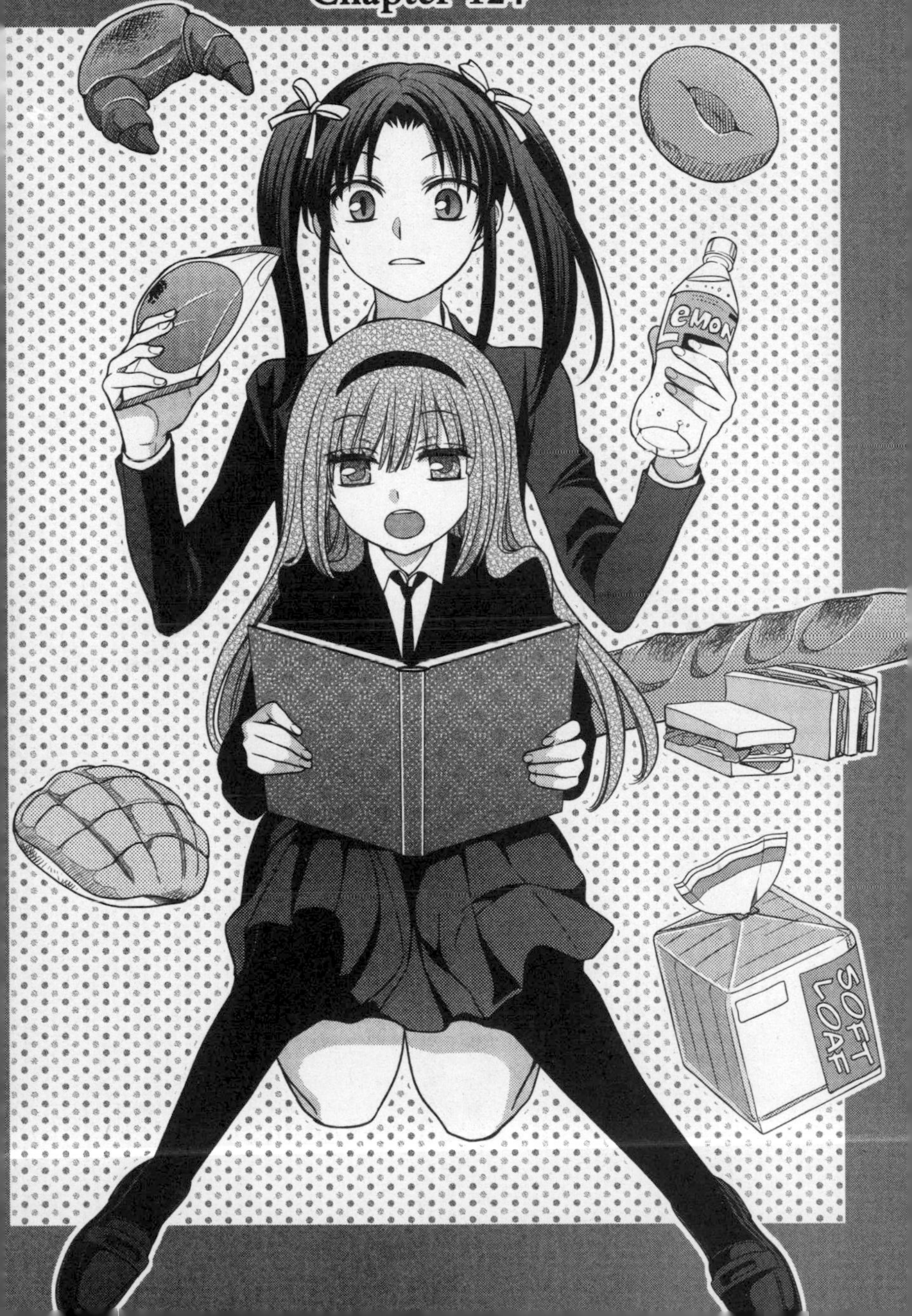
eMON
SOFT LOAF

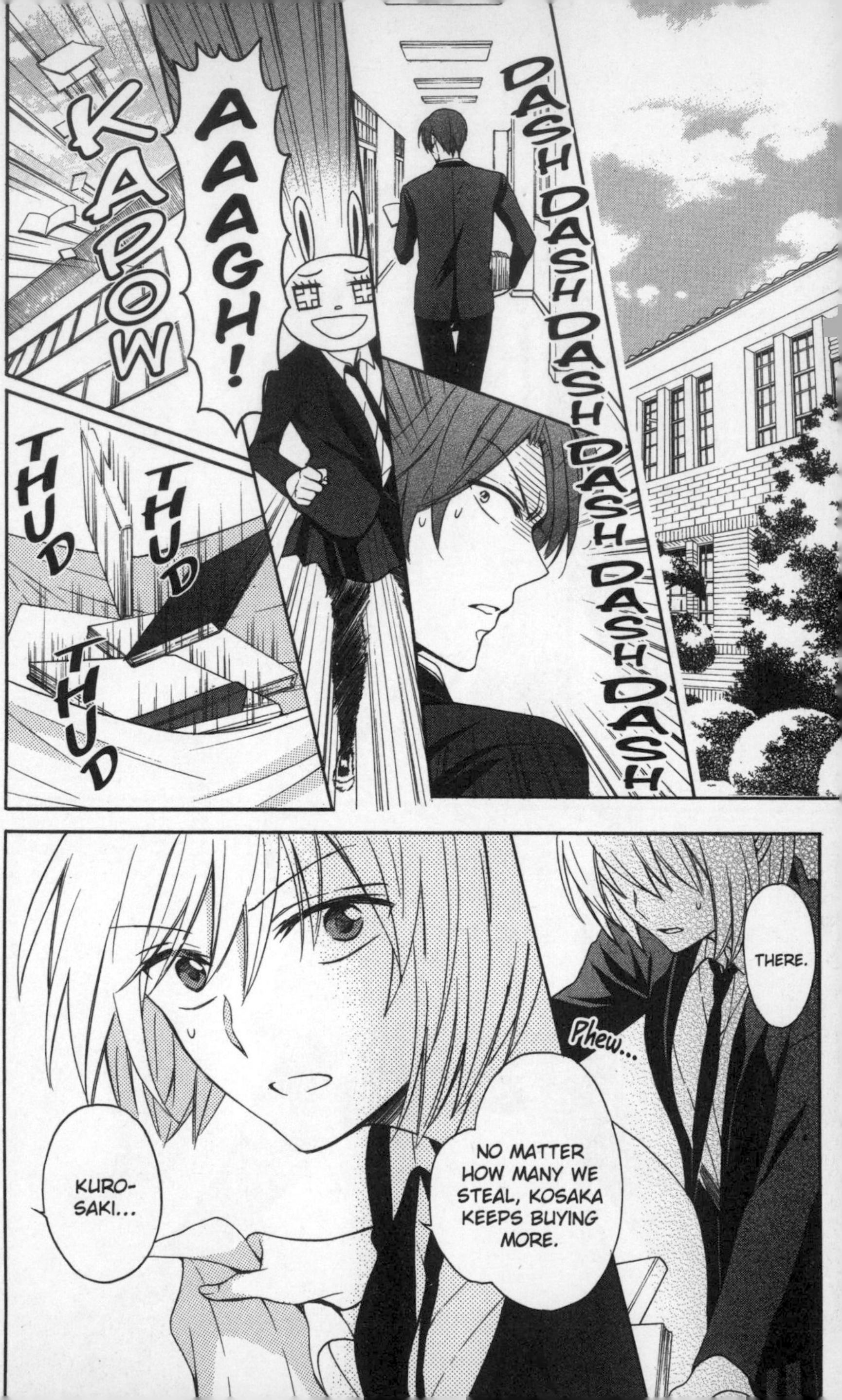
DASH DASH DASH DASH DASH DASH DASH
AAAGH!
KAPOW
THUD THUD THUD
THERE.
Phew...
NO MATTER HOW MANY WE STEAL, KOSAKA KEEPS BUYING MORE.
KURO-SAKI...

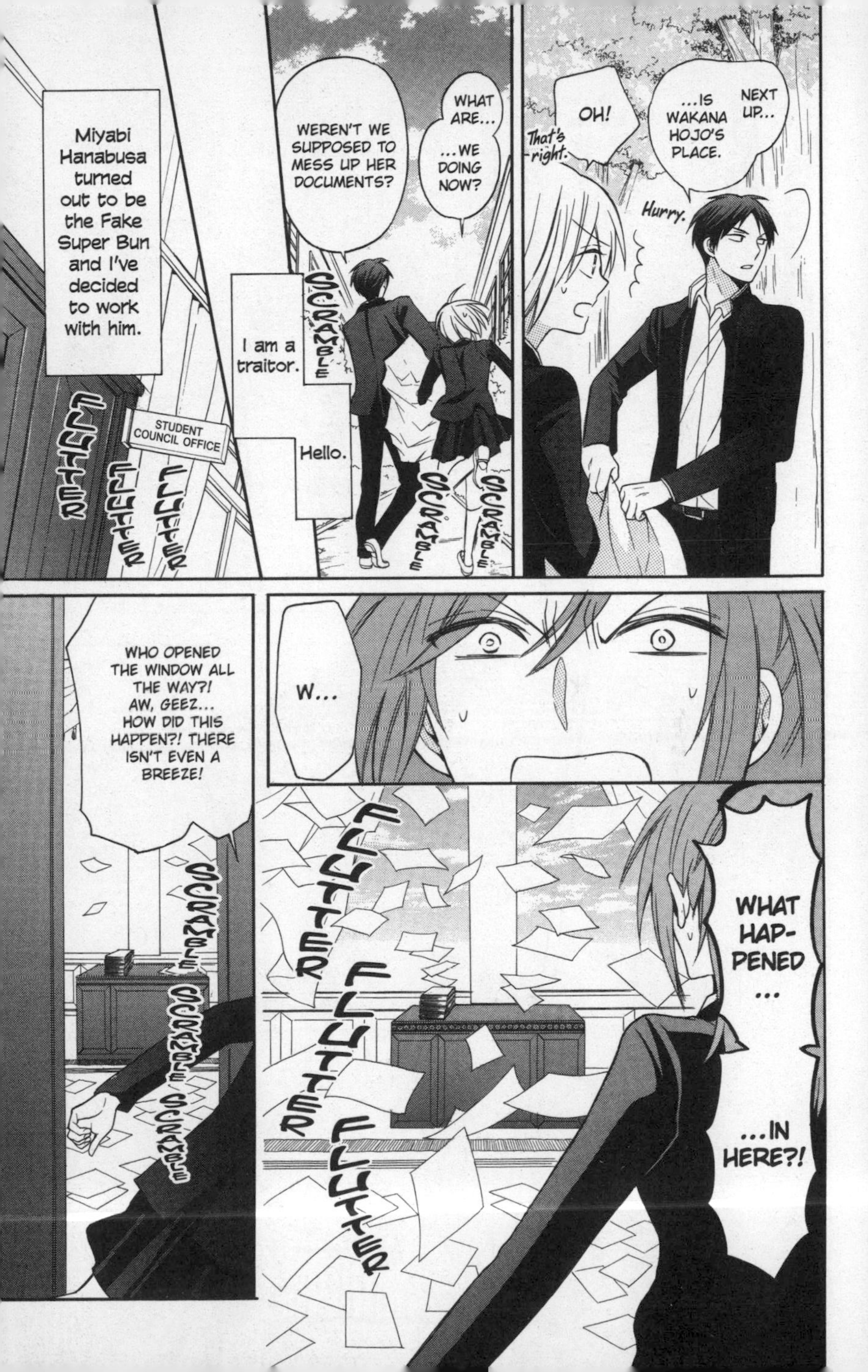
NEXT UP...
...IS WAKANA HOJO'S PLACE.
OH!
That's right.
Hurry.
WHAT ARE...
...WE DOING NOW?
WEREN'T WE SUPPOSED TO MESS UP HER DOCUMENTS?
SCRAMBLE
I am a traitor.
Hello.
SCRAMBLE
SCRAMBLE
Miyabi Hanabusa turned out to be the Fake Super Bun and I've decided to work with him.
STUDENT COUNCIL OFFICE
FLUTTER
FLUTTER
FLUTTER
W...
WHAT HAP-PENED...
...IN HERE?!
FLUTTER
FLUTTER
FLUTTER
WHO OPENED THE WINDOW ALL THE WAY?! AW, GEEZ... HOW DID THIS HAPPEN?! THERE ISN'T EVEN A BREEZE!
SCRAMBLE
SCRAMBLE
SCRAMBLE

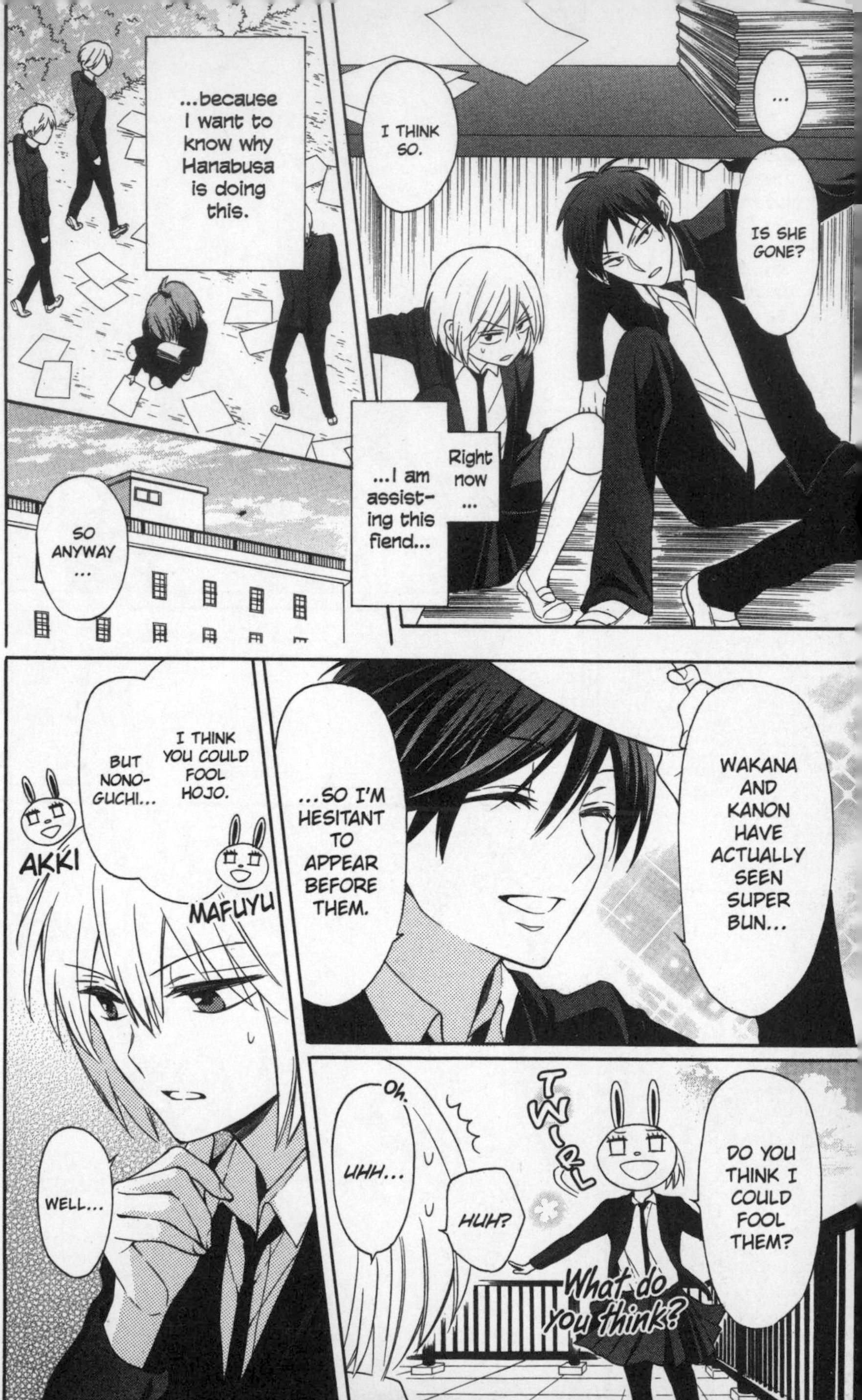
...
IS SHE GONE?
I THINK SO.
Right now...
...I am assisting this fiend...
...because I want to know why Hanabusa is doing this.
SO ANYWAY...
WAKANA AND KANON HAVE ACTUALLY SEEN SUPER BUN...
...SO I'M HESITANT TO APPEAR BEFORE THEM.
DO YOU THINK I COULD FOOL THEM?
TWIRL
What do you think?
Oh.
UHH...
HUH?
I THINK YOU COULD FOOL HOJO.
BUT NONOGUCHI...
MAFUYU
AKKI
WELL...

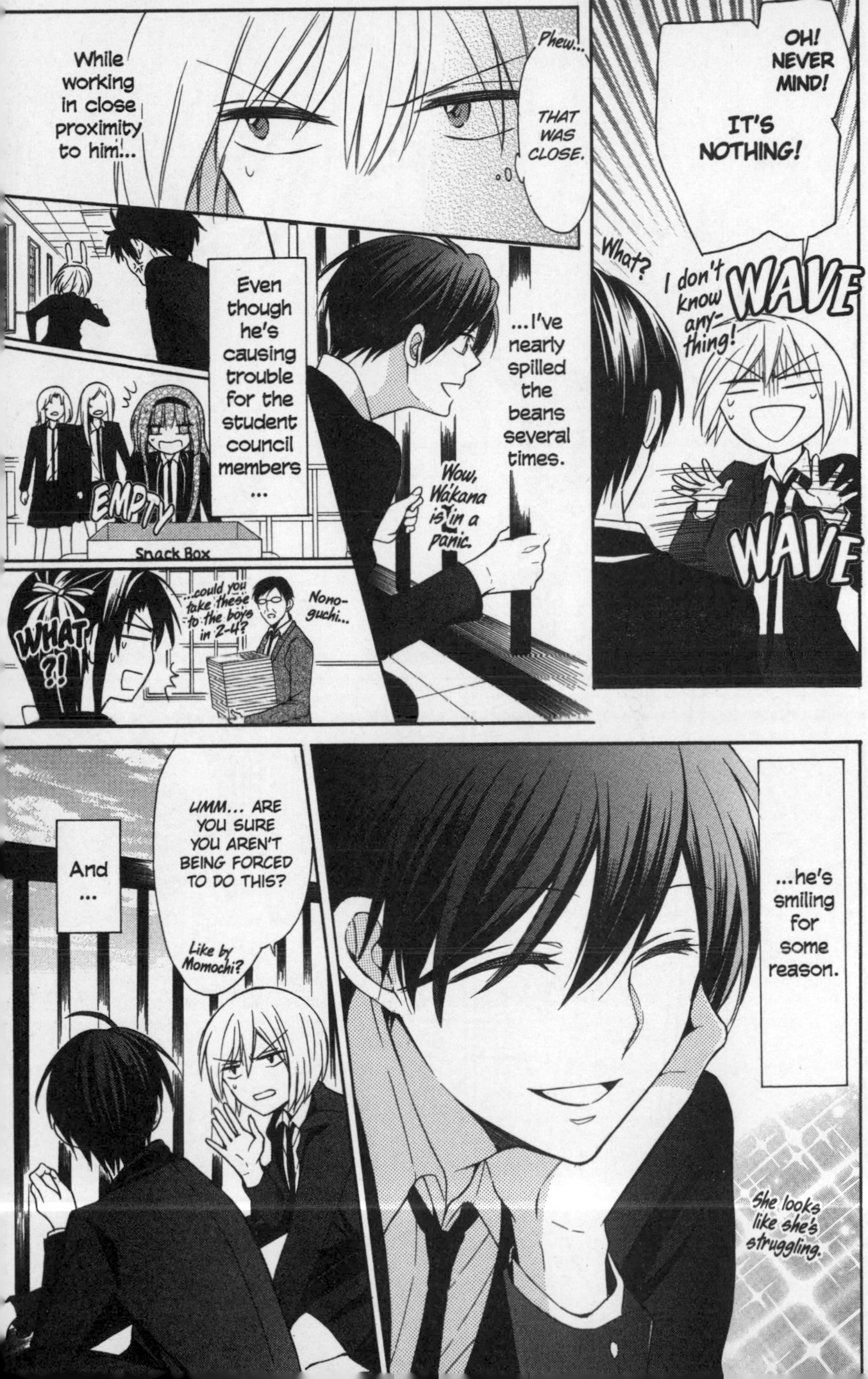
OH! NEVER MIND!
IT'S NOTHING!
What?
I don't know any-thing!
WAVE
WAVE
Phew...
THAT WAS CLOSE.
While working in close proximity to him...
...I've nearly spilled the beans several times.
Even though he's causing trouble for the student council members ...
Wow, Wakana is in a panic.
EMPTY
Snack Box
Nono-guchi...
...could you take these to the boys in 2-4?
WHAT ?!
...he's smiling for some reason.
She looks like she's struggling.
UMM... ARE YOU SURE YOU AREN'T BEING FORCED TO DO THIS?
Like by Momochi?
And ...

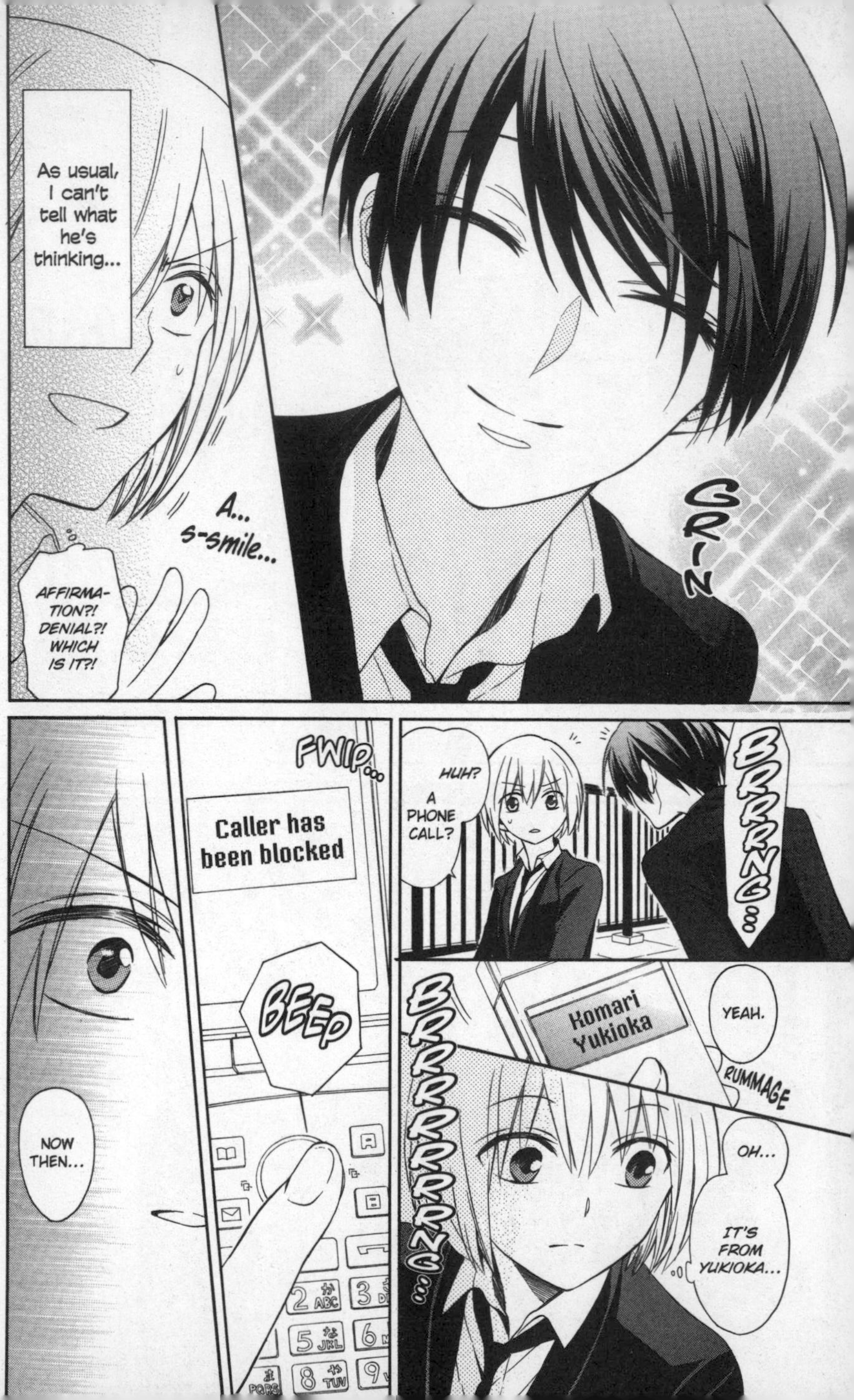
As usual, I can't tell what he's thinking...
GRIN
A... s-smile...
AFFIRMATION?! DENIAL?! WHICH IS IT?!
BRRRRNG...
HUH? A PHONE CALL?
Komari Yukioka
YEAH.
RUMMAGE
BRRRRRRRRRNG...
OH...
IT'S FROM YUKIOKA...
FWIP...
Caller has been blocked
BEEP
NOW THEN...

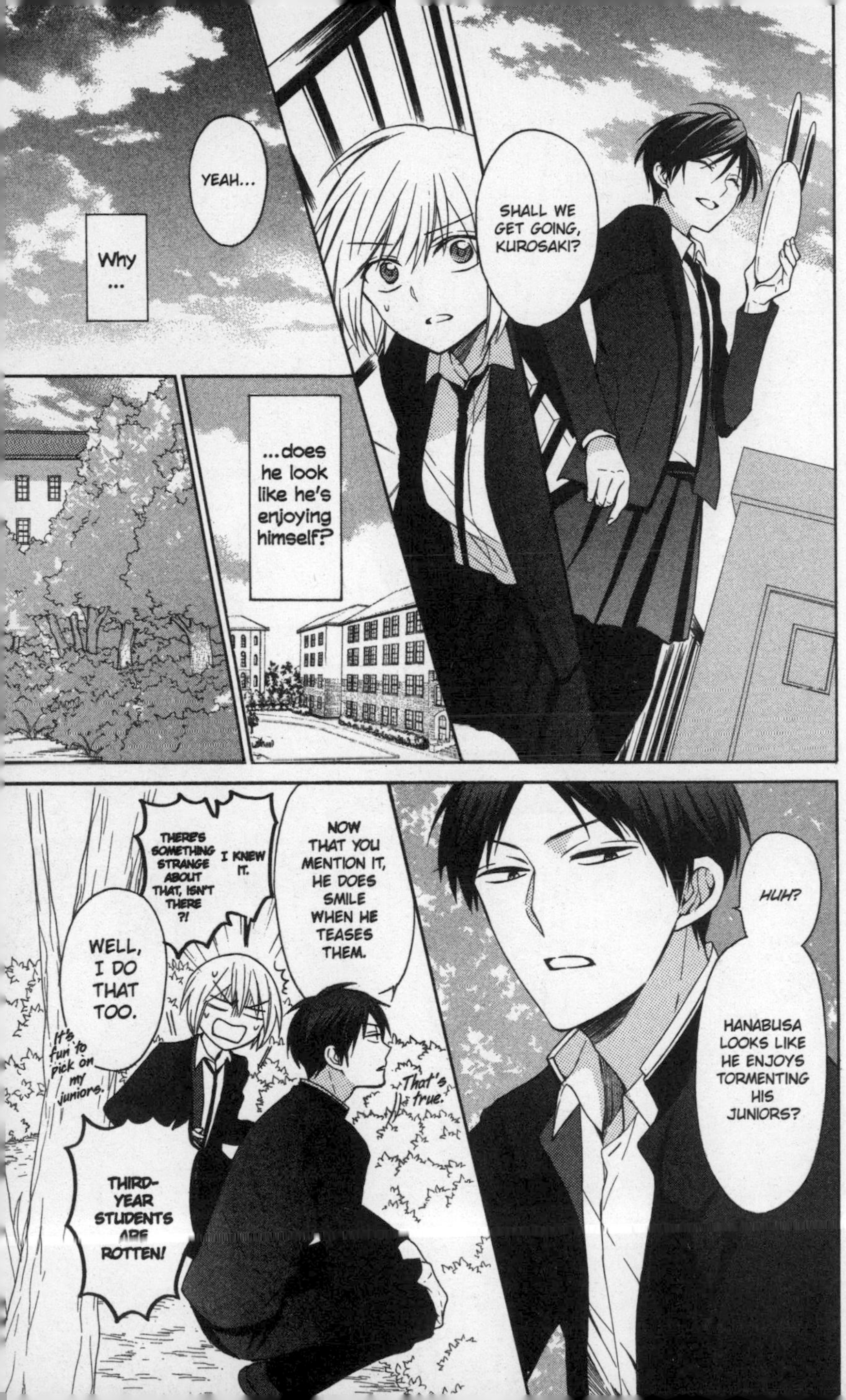
SHALL WE GET GOING, KUROSAKI?
YEAH...
Why ...
...does he look like he's enjoying himself?
HUH?
HANABUSA LOOKS LIKE HE ENJOYS TORMENTING HIS JUNIORS?
NOW THAT YOU MENTION IT, HE DOES SMILE WHEN HE TEASES THEM.
I KNEW IT.
THERE'S SOMETHING STRANGE ABOUT THAT, ISN'T THERE ?!
WELL, I DO THAT TOO.
That's true.
It's fun to pick on my juniors.
THIRD-YEAR STUDENTS ARE ROTTEN!

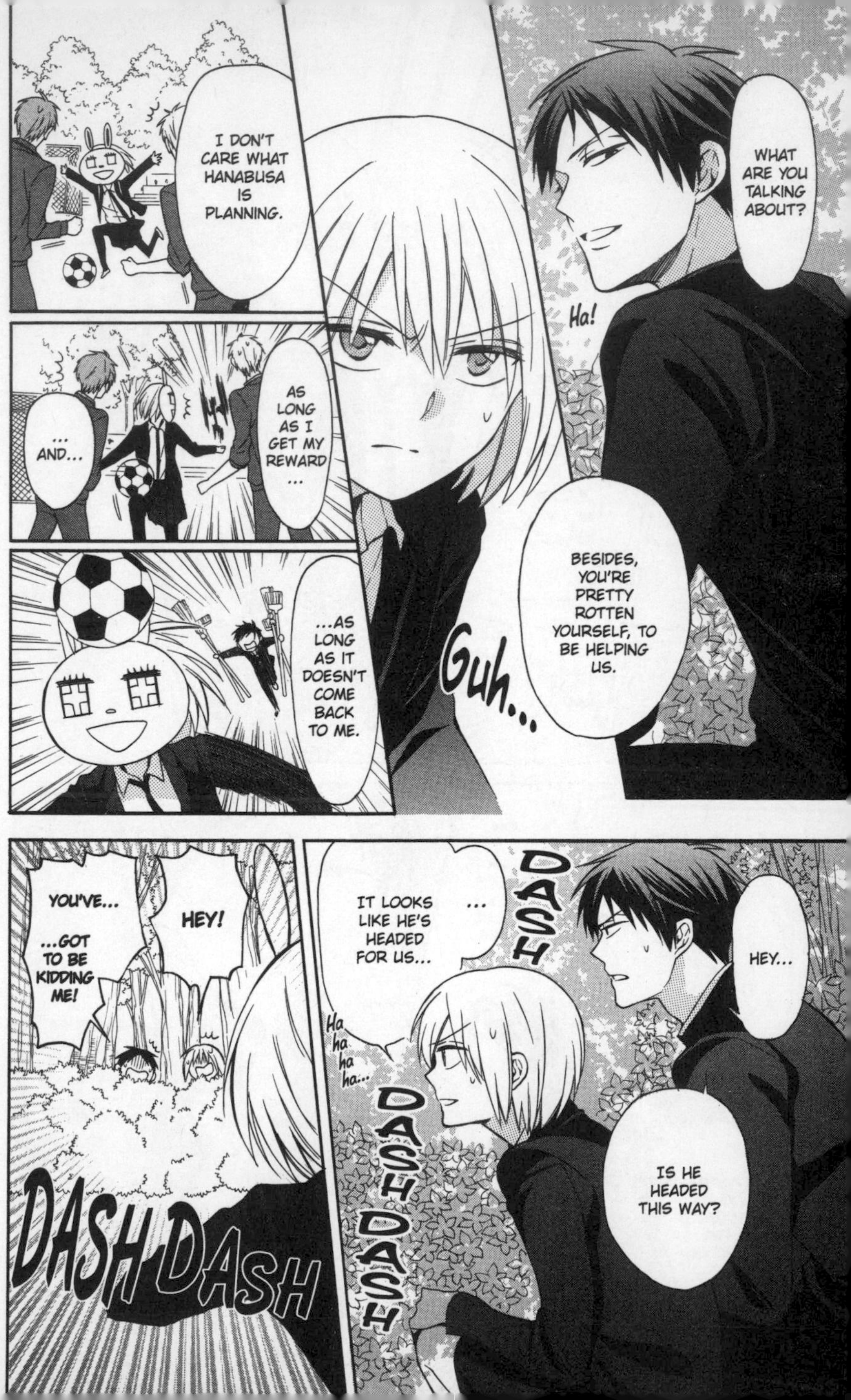
WHAT ARE YOU TALKING ABOUT?
Ha!
BESIDES, YOU'RE PRETTY ROTTEN YOURSELF, TO BE HELPING US.
Guh...
I DON'T CARE WHAT HANABUSA IS PLANNING.
AS LONG AS I GET MY REWARD ...
... AND...
...AS LONG AS IT DOESN'T COME BACK TO ME.
HEY...
IS HE HEADED THIS WAY?
...
IT LOOKS LIKE HE'S HEADED FOR US...
DASH DASH
Ha ha ha ha...
DASH DASH
HEY!
YOU'VE...
...GOT TO BE KIDDING ME!
DASH DASH

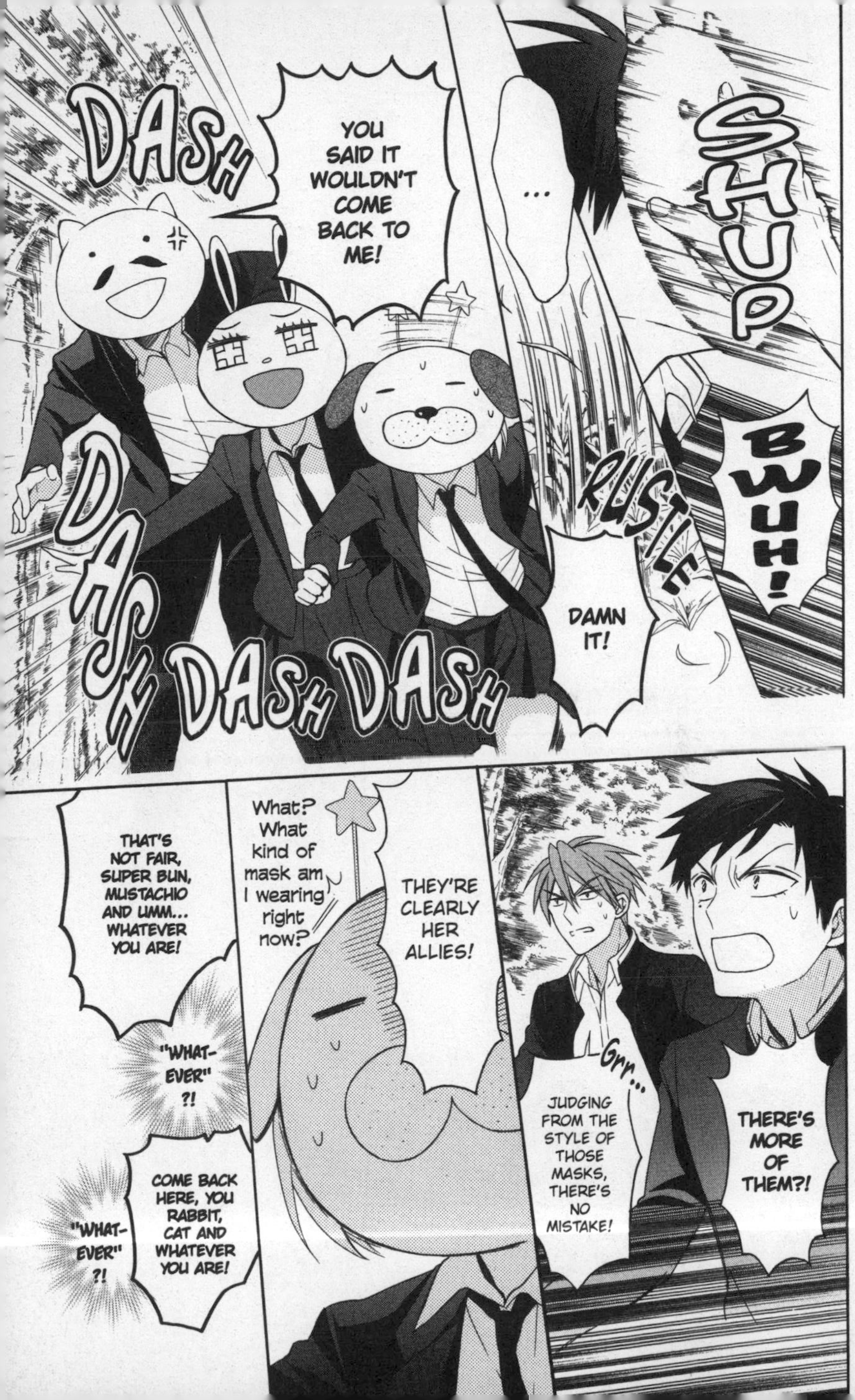
SHUP
...
BWUH!
RUSTLE
DAMN IT!
YOU SAID IT WOULDN'T COME BACK TO ME!
DASH
DASH DASH DASH
THERE'S MORE OF THEM?!
Grr...
JUDGING FROM THE STYLE OF THOSE MASKS, THERE'S NO MISTAKE!
THEY'RE CLEARLY HER ALLIES!
What? What kind of mask am I wearing right now?
THAT'S NOT FAIR, SUPER BUN, MUSTACHIO AND UMM... WHATEVER YOU ARE!
"WHAT-EVER" ?!
COME BACK HERE, YOU RABBIT, CAT AND WHATEVER YOU ARE!
"WHAT-EVER" ?!

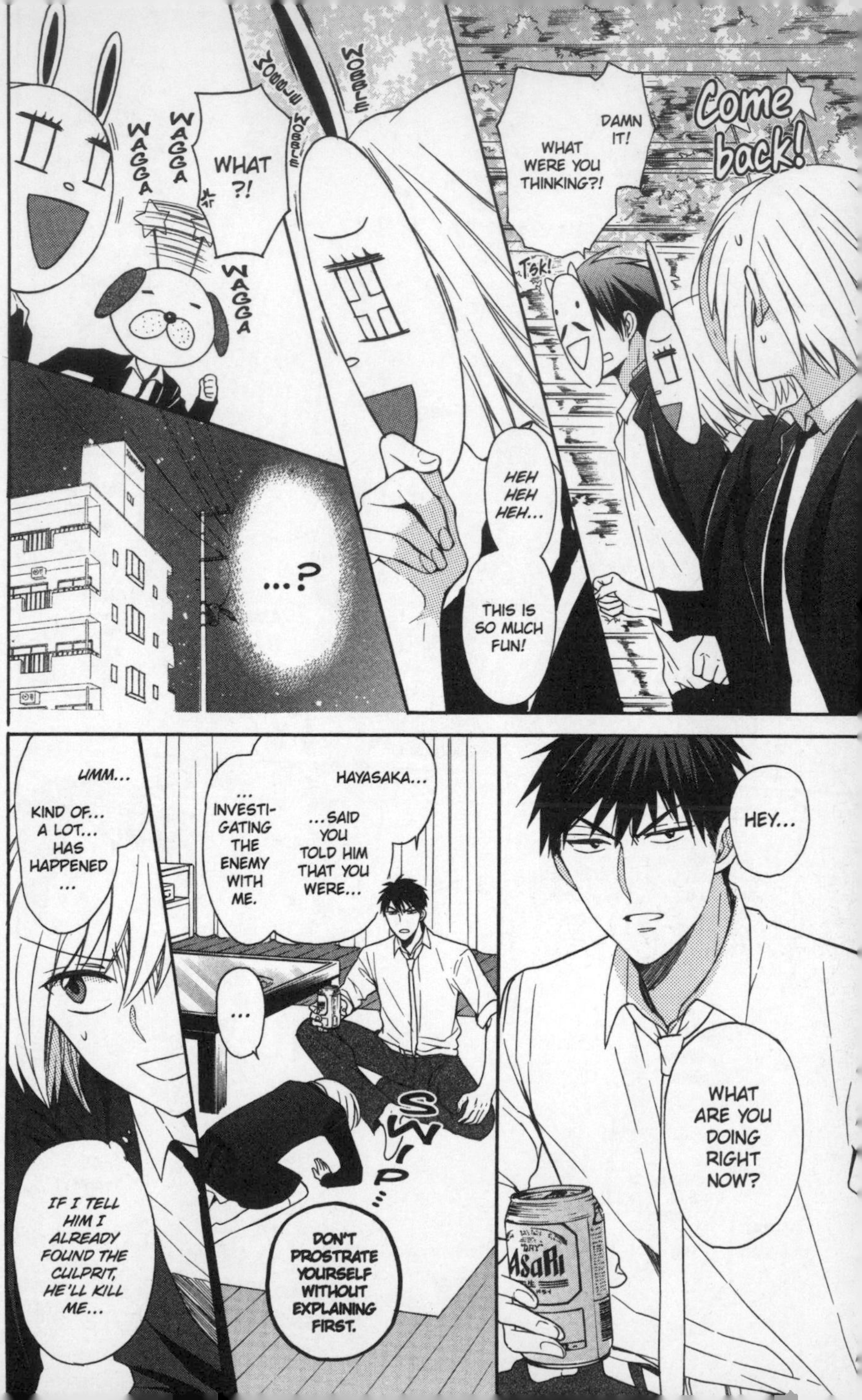
Come back!
DAMN IT!
WHAT WERE YOU THINKING?!
TSK!
HEH HEH HEH...
THIS IS SO MUCH FUN!
WOBBLE
WOBBLE WOBBLE
WAGGA WAGGA
WHAT ?!
WAGGA WAGGA
...?
HEY...
WHAT ARE YOU DOING RIGHT NOW?
HAYASAKA...
...SAID YOU TOLD HIM THAT YOU WERE...
...INVESTIGATING THE ENEMY WITH ME.
...
SWIP...
DON'T PROSTRATE YOURSELF WITHOUT EXPLAINING FIRST.
UMM...
KIND OF... A LOT... HAS HAPPENED...
IF I TELL HIM I ALREADY FOUND THE CULPRIT, HE'LL KILL ME...

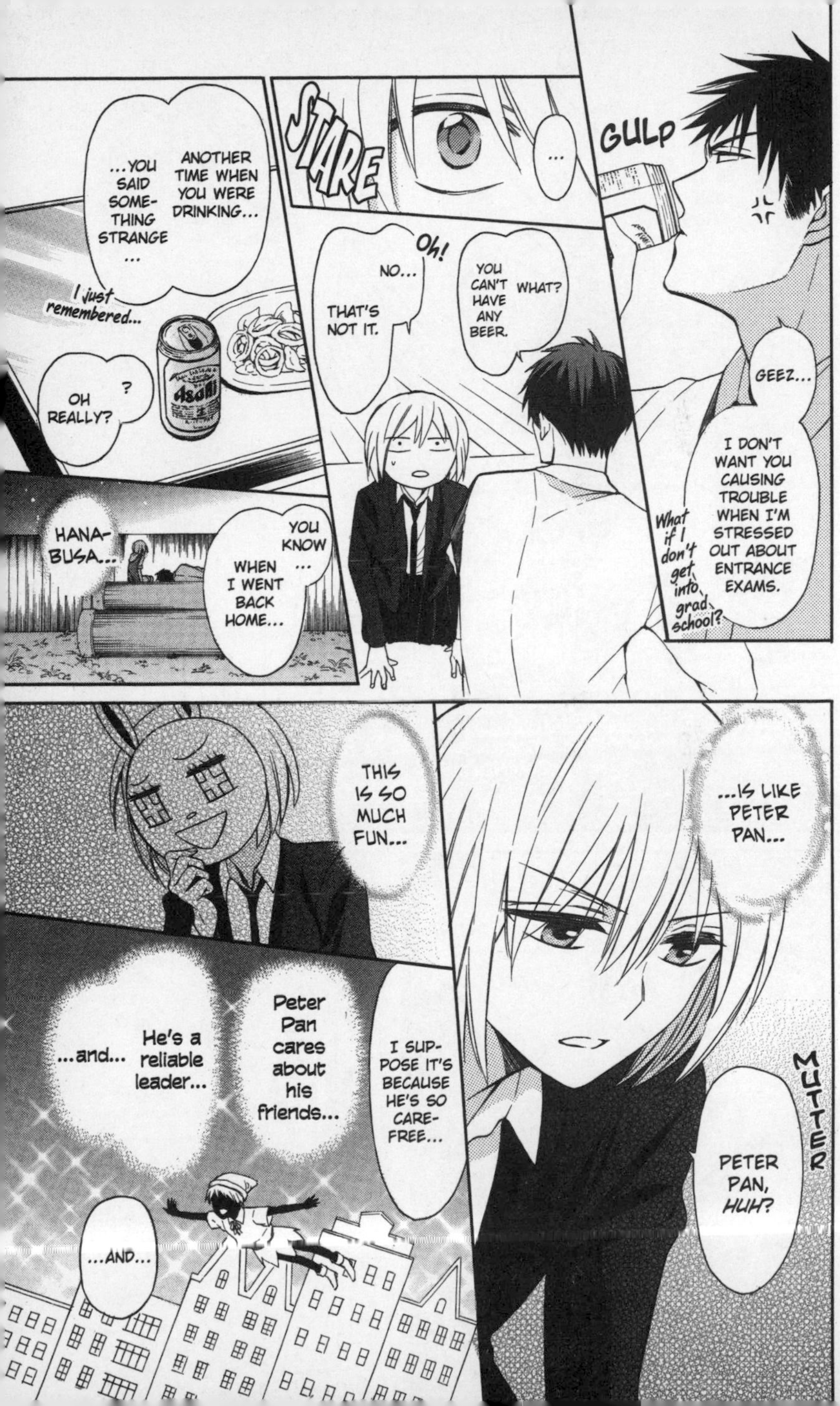
GULP
GEEZ...
I DON'T WANT YOU CAUSING TROUBLE WHEN I'M STRESSED OUT ABOUT ENTRANCE EXAMS.
What if I don't get into grad school?
STARE
...
YOU CAN'T HAVE ANY BEER.
WHAT?
Oh!
NO... THAT'S NOT IT.
ANOTHER TIME WHEN YOU WERE DRINKING...
...YOU SAID SOMETHING STRANGE...
I just remembered...
?
OH REALLY?
YOU KNOW... WHEN I WENT BACK HOME...
HANABUSA...
...IS LIKE PETER PAN...
THIS IS SO MUCH FUN...
MUTTER
PETER PAN, HUH?
I SUPPOSE IT'S BECAUSE HE'S SO CAREFREE...
Peter Pan cares about his friends...
He's a reliable leader...
...and...
...AND...

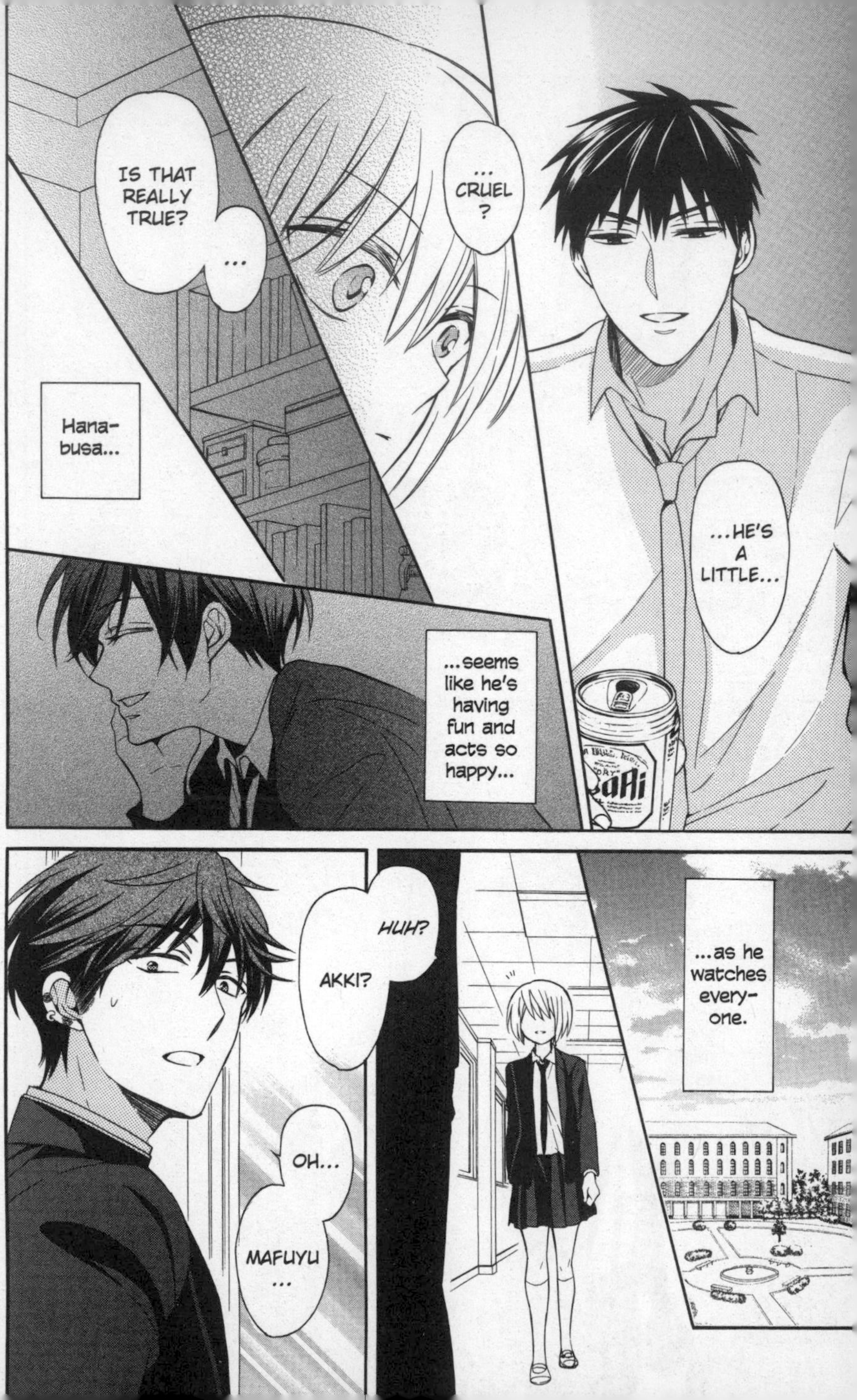
...HE'S A LITTLE...
...CRUEL?
IS THAT REALLY TRUE?
...
Hana-busa...
...seems like he's having fun and acts so happy...
...as he watches every-one.
HUH?
AKKI?
OH...
MAFUYU ...

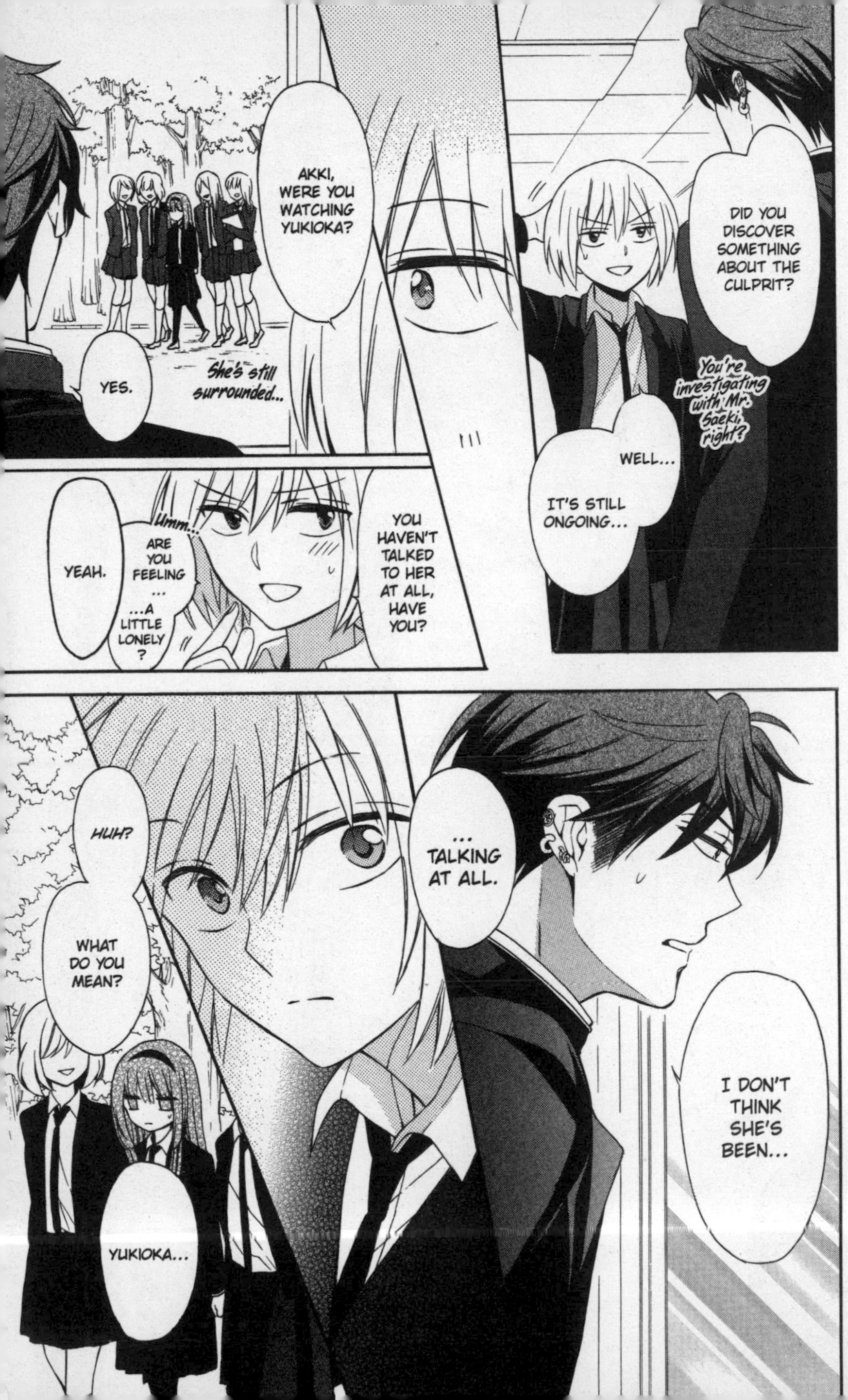
DID YOU DISCOVER SOMETHING ABOUT THE CULPRIT?
You're investigating with Mr. Saeki, right?
WELL...
IT'S STILL ONGOING...
AKKI, WERE YOU WATCHING YUKIOKA?
YES.
She's still surrounded...
YOU HAVEN'T TALKED TO HER AT ALL, HAVE YOU?
Umm...
ARE YOU FEELING ... ...A LITTLE LONELY?
YEAH.
I DON'T THINK SHE'S BEEN...
... TALKING AT ALL.
HUH?
WHAT DO YOU MEAN?
YUKIOKA...

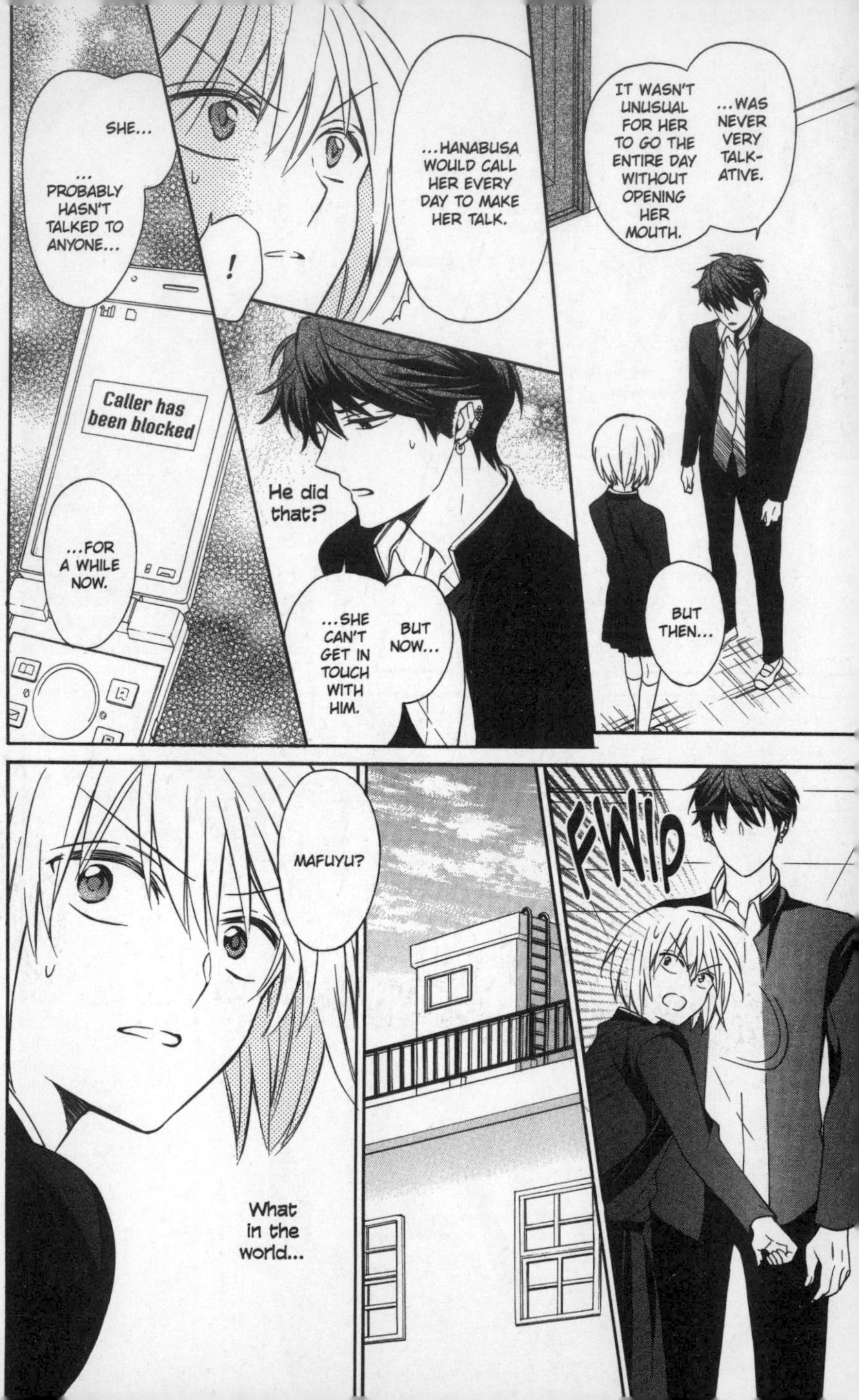
...WAS NEVER VERY TALK-ATIVE.
IT WASN'T UNUSUAL FOR HER TO GO THE ENTIRE DAY WITHOUT OPENING HER MOUTH.
BUT THEN...
...HANABUSA WOULD CALL HER EVERY DAY TO MAKE HER TALK.
!
He did that?
BUT NOW...
...SHE CAN'T GET IN TOUCH WITH HIM.
SHE...
...PROBABLY HASN'T TALKED TO ANYONE...
Caller has been blocked
...FOR A WHILE NOW.
FWIP
MAFUYU?
What in the world...

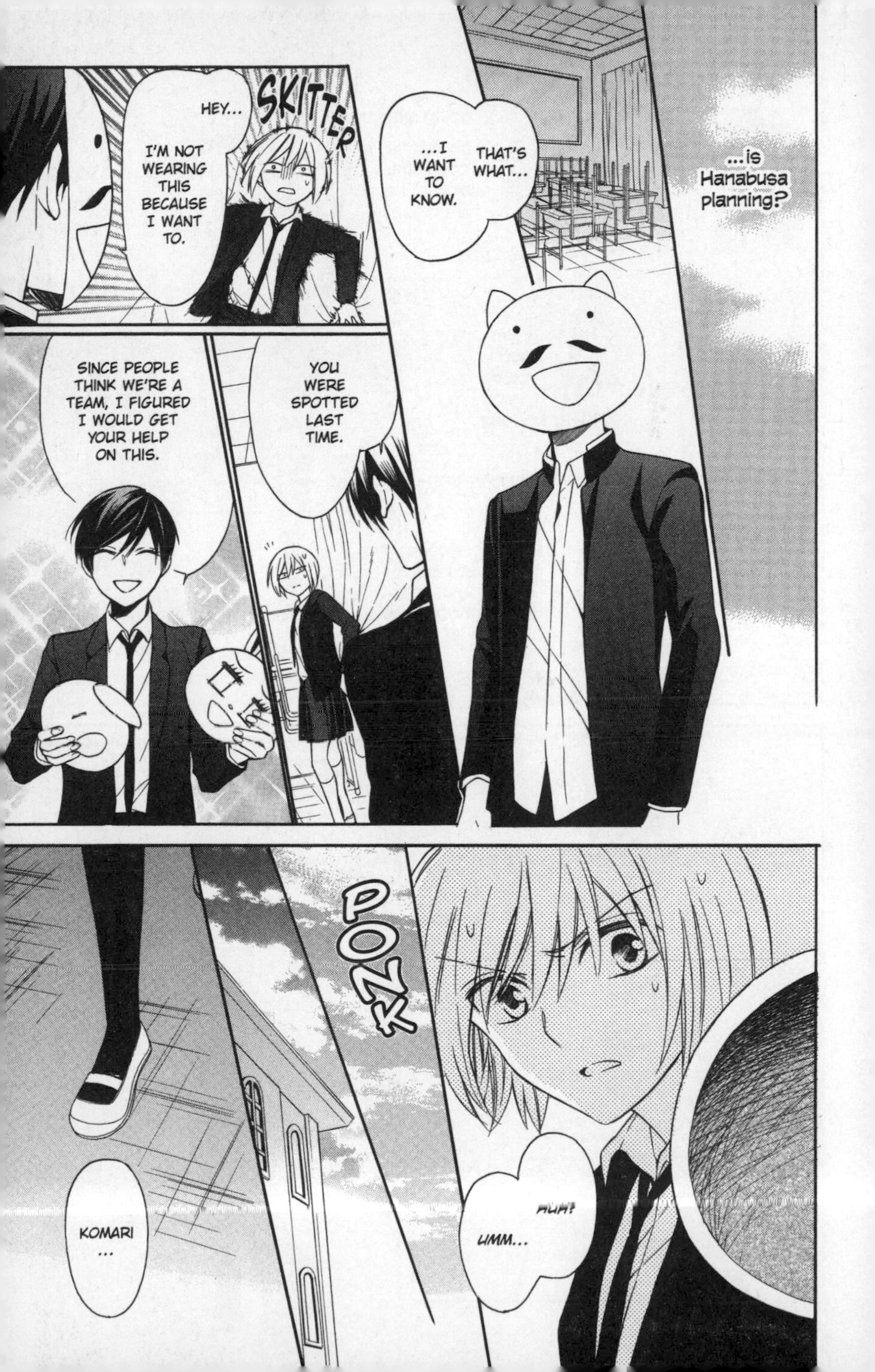
THAT'S WHAT... ...I WANT TO KNOW.
...is Hanabusa planning?
SKITTER
HEY... I'M NOT WEARING THIS BECAUSE I WANT TO.
YOU WERE SPOTTED LAST TIME.
SINCE PEOPLE THINK WE'RE A TEAM, I FIGURED I WOULD GET YOUR HELP ON THIS.
PONK
UMM... HUH?
KOMARI ...

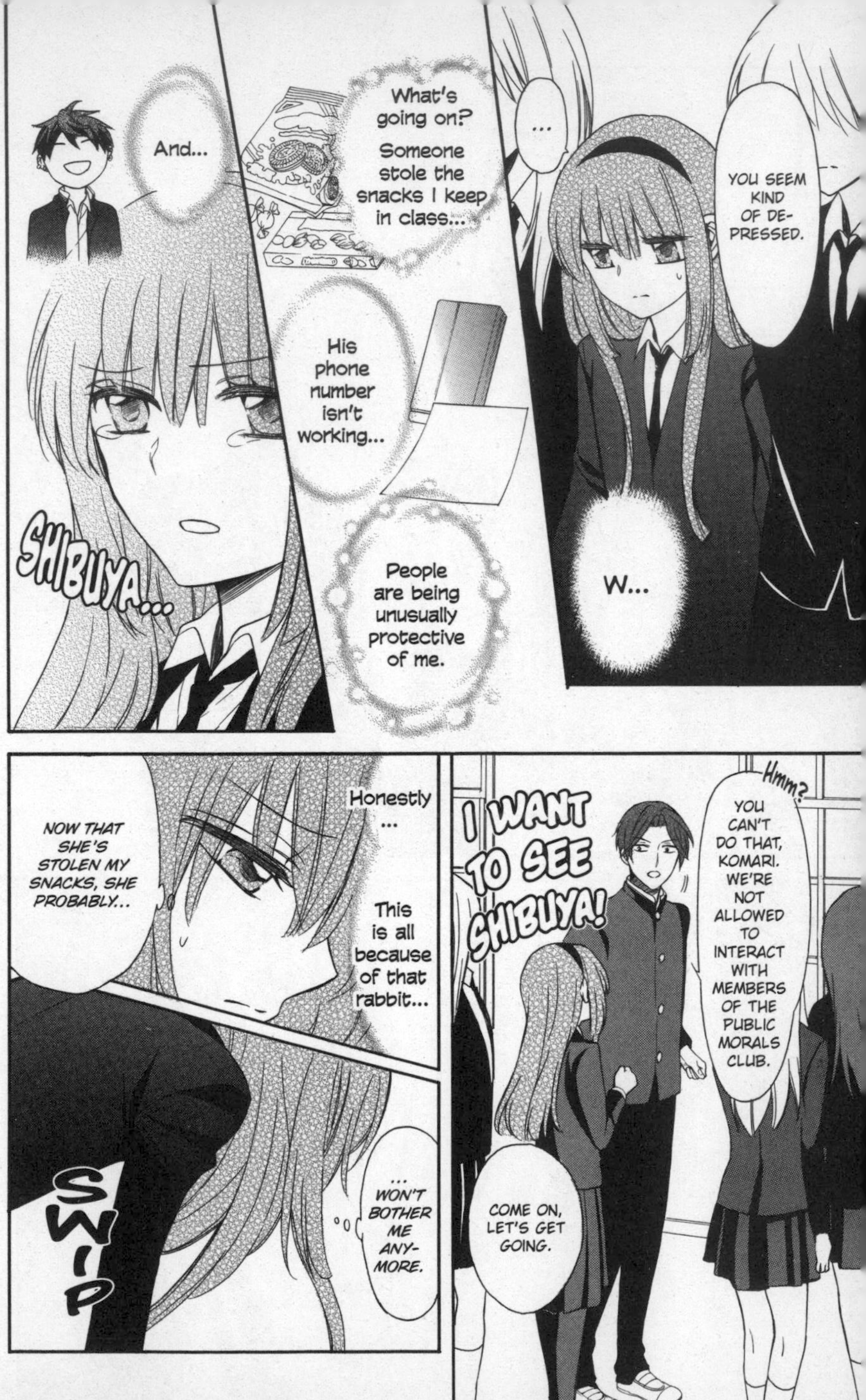
YOU SEEM KIND OF DE-PRESSED.
...
W...
What's going on?
Someone stole the snacks I keep in class...
His phone number isn't working...
People are being unusually protective of me.
And...
SHIBUYA...
Hmm?
YOU CAN'T DO THAT, KOMARI. WE'RE NOT ALLOWED TO INTERACT WITH MEMBERS OF THE PUBLIC MORALS CLUB.
I WANT TO SEE SHIBUYA!
COME ON, LET'S GET GOING.
Honestly...
This is all because of that rabbit...
NOW THAT SHE'S STOLEN MY SNACKS, SHE PROBABLY...
...WON'T BOTHER ME ANYMORE.
SWIP

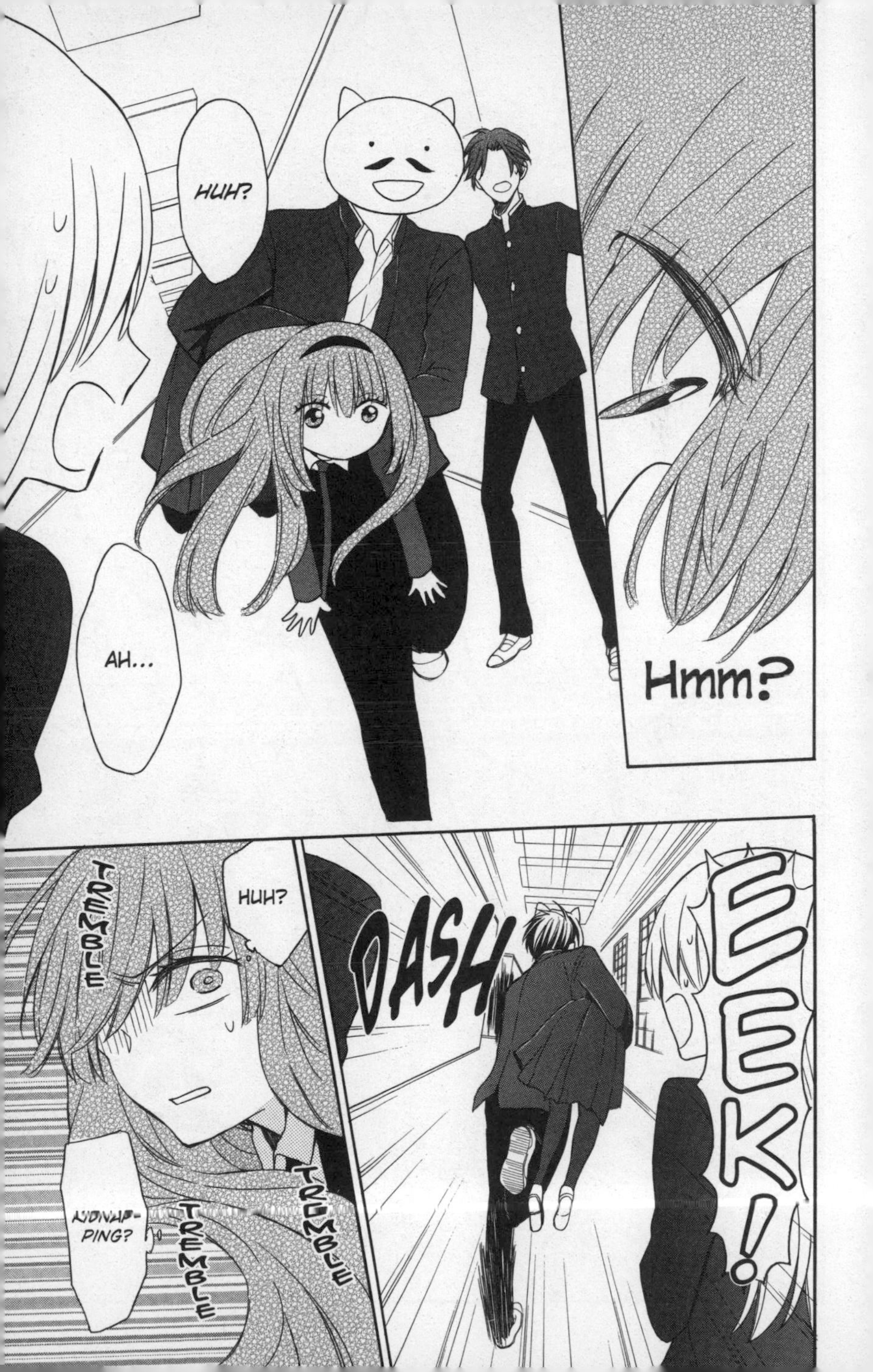
Hmm?
HUH?
AH...
EEEK!
DASH
HUH?
TREMBLE
KIDNAP-PING?
TREMBLE
TREMBLE

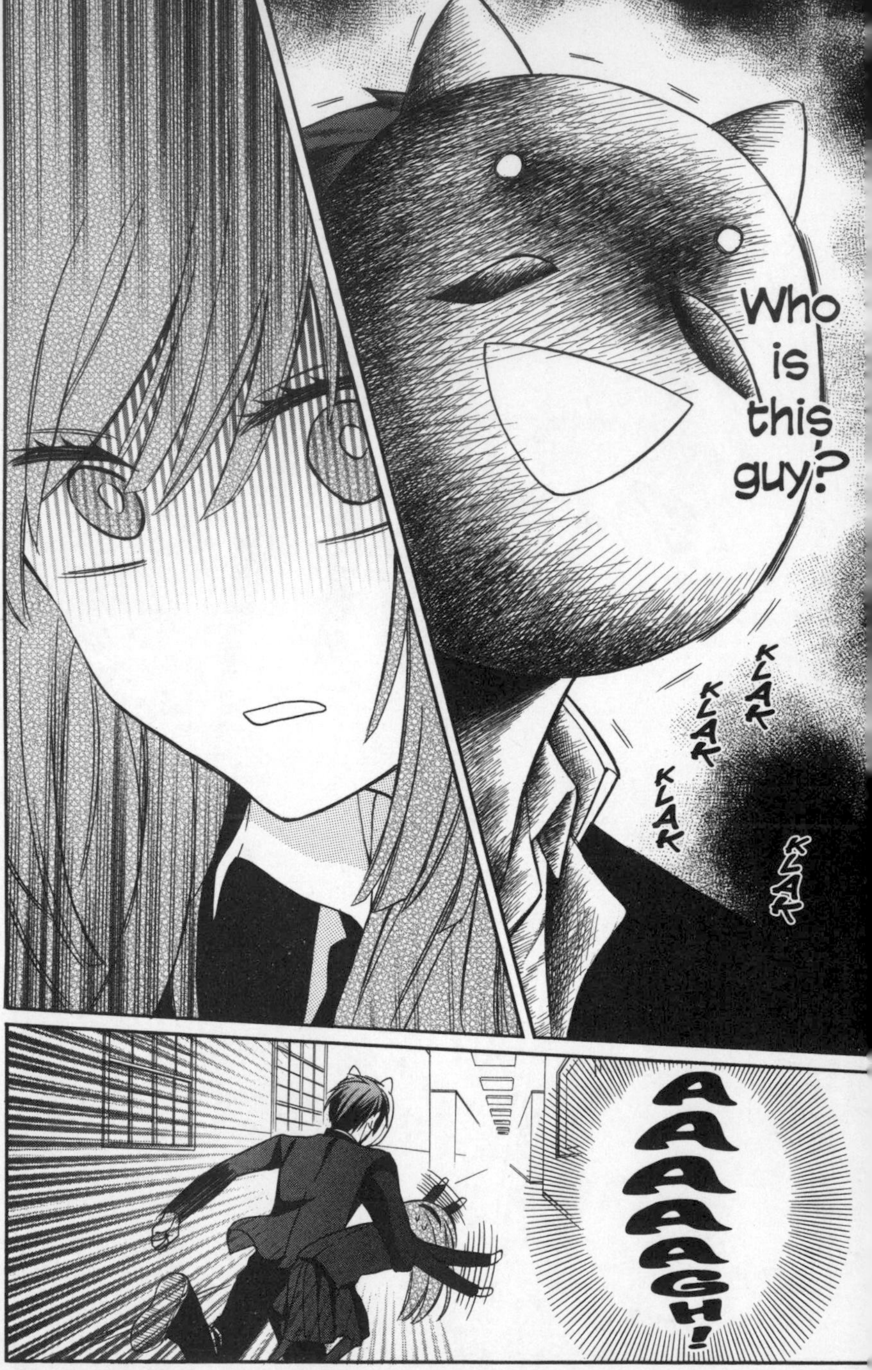
Who is this guy?
KLAK
KLAK
KLAK
KLAK
AAAAAGH!

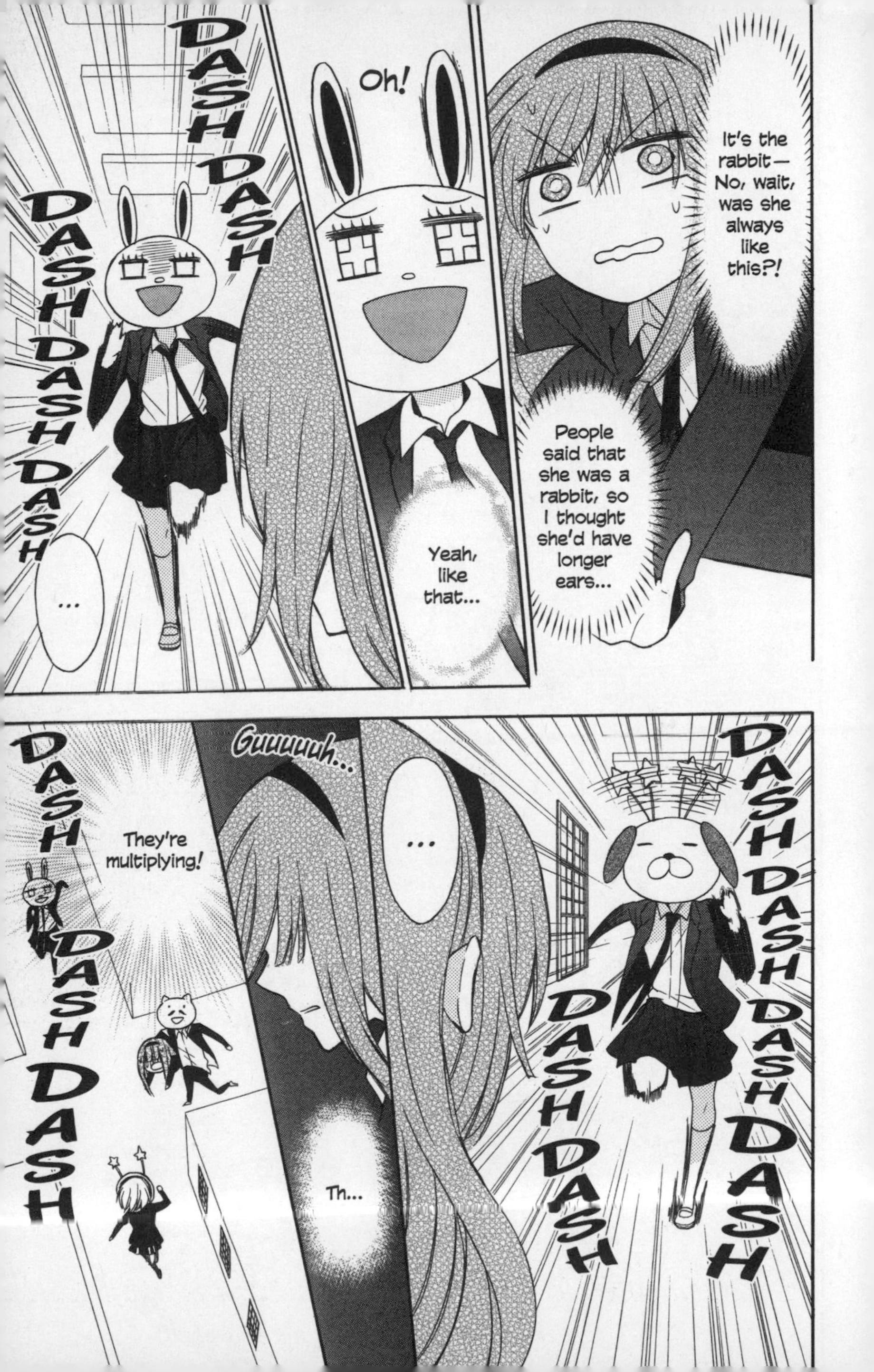
It's the rabbit— No, wait, was she always like this?!
Oh!
DASH DASH
DASH DASH DASH DASH
People said that she was a rabbit, so I thought she'd have longer ears...
Yeah, like that...
...
DASH DASH DASH DASH DASH
DASH DASH
Guuuuuh...
...
Th...
They're multiplying!
DASH DASH DASH DASH

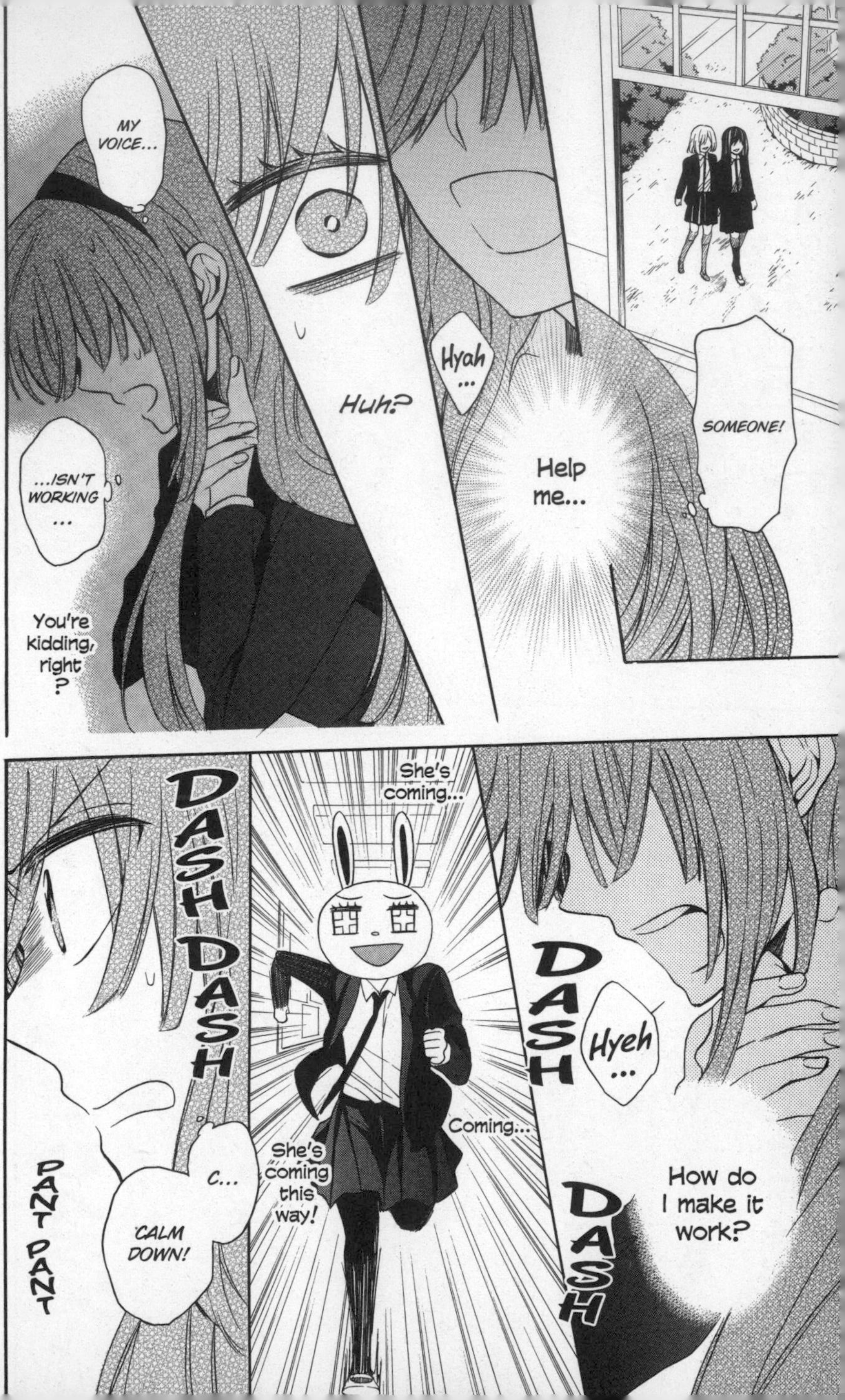
SOMEONE!
Hyah...
Help me...
Huh?
MY VOICE...
...ISN'T WORKING...
You're kidding, right?
Hyeh...
DASH
DASH
How do I make it work?
She's coming...
Coming...
She's coming this way!
DASH DASH
C...
CALM DOWN!
PANT PANT

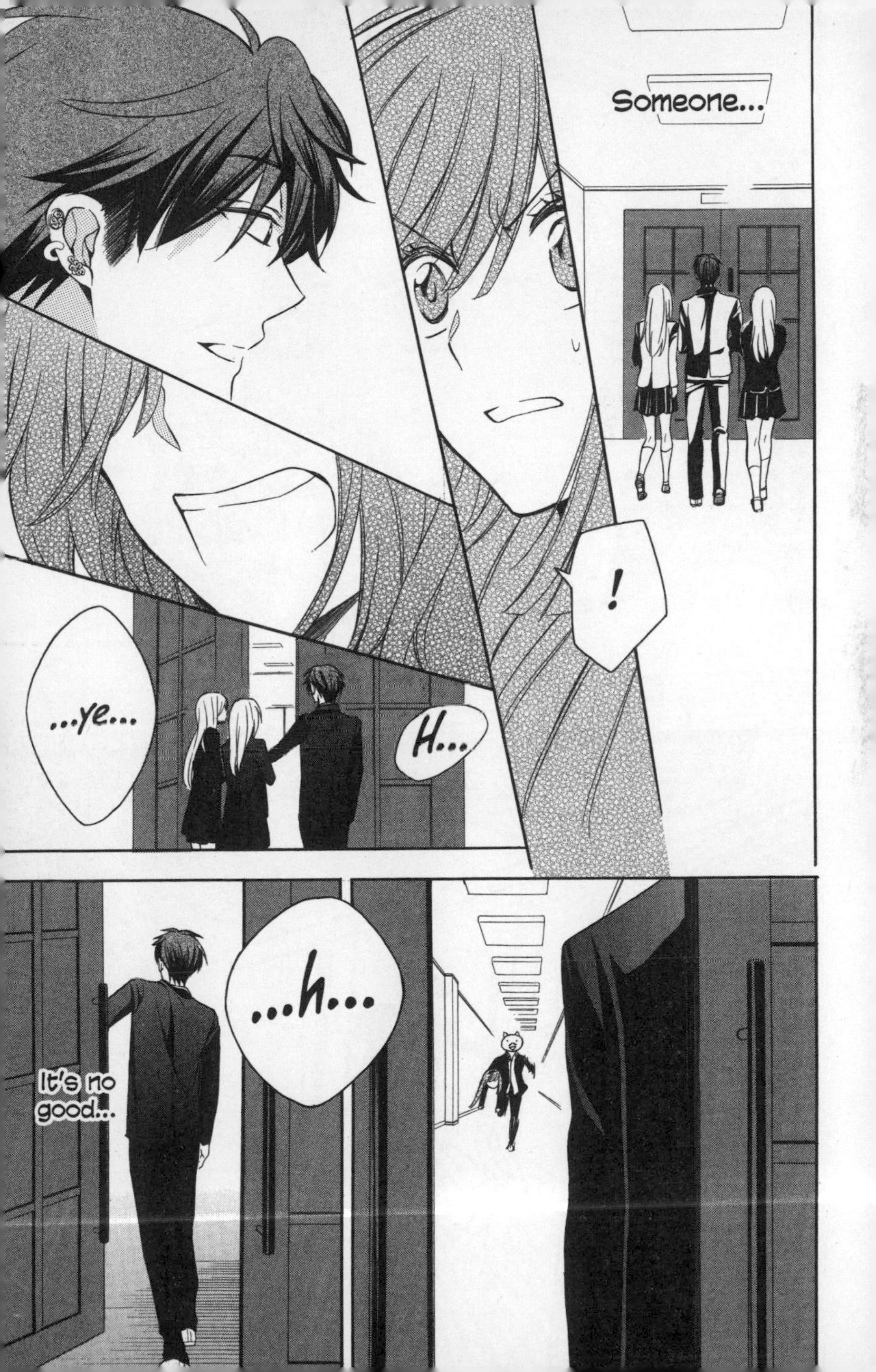
Someone...
!
H...
...ye...
...h...
It's no good...

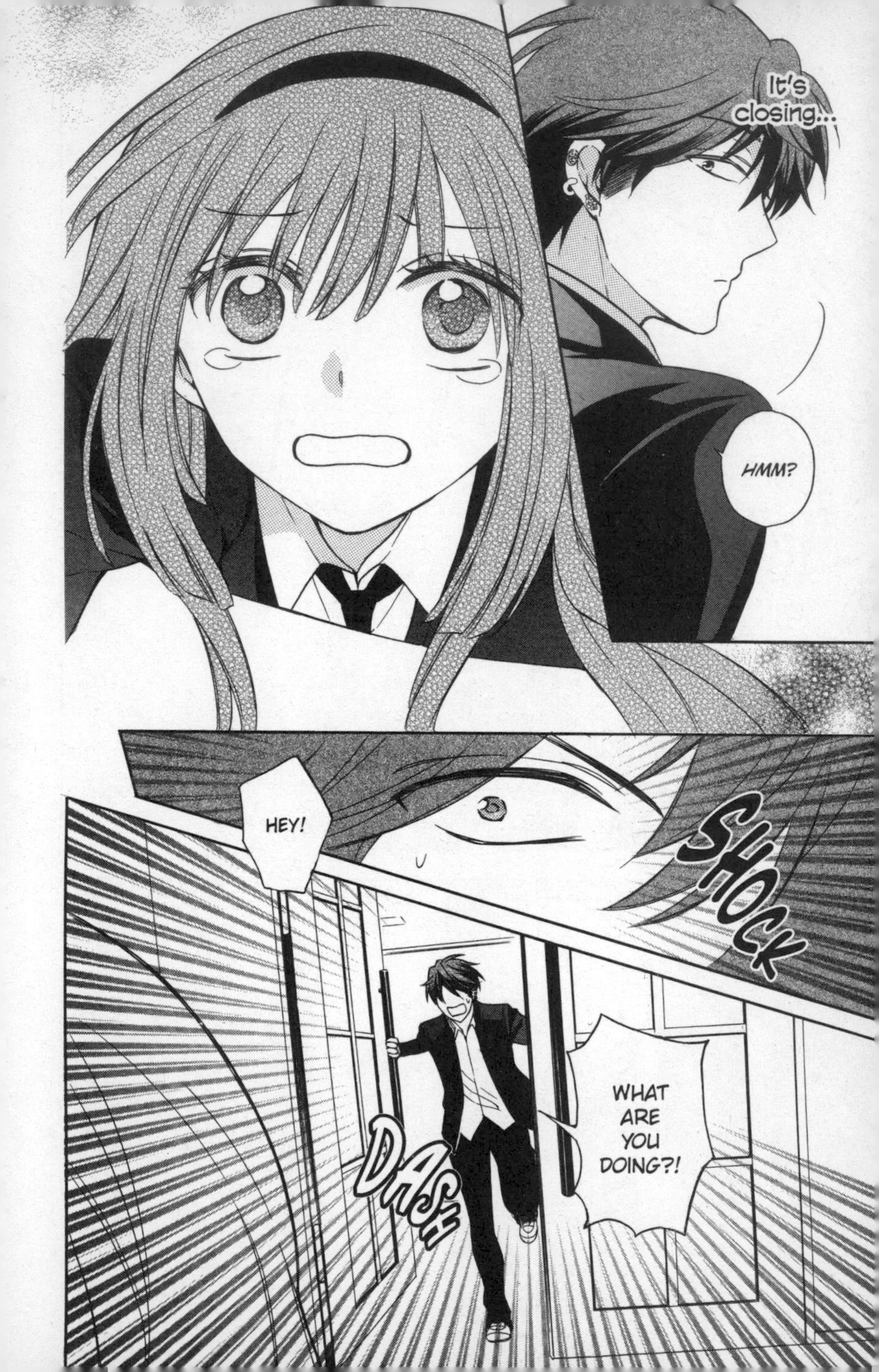
It's closing...
HMM?
SHOCK
HEY!
WHAT ARE YOU DOING?!
DASH

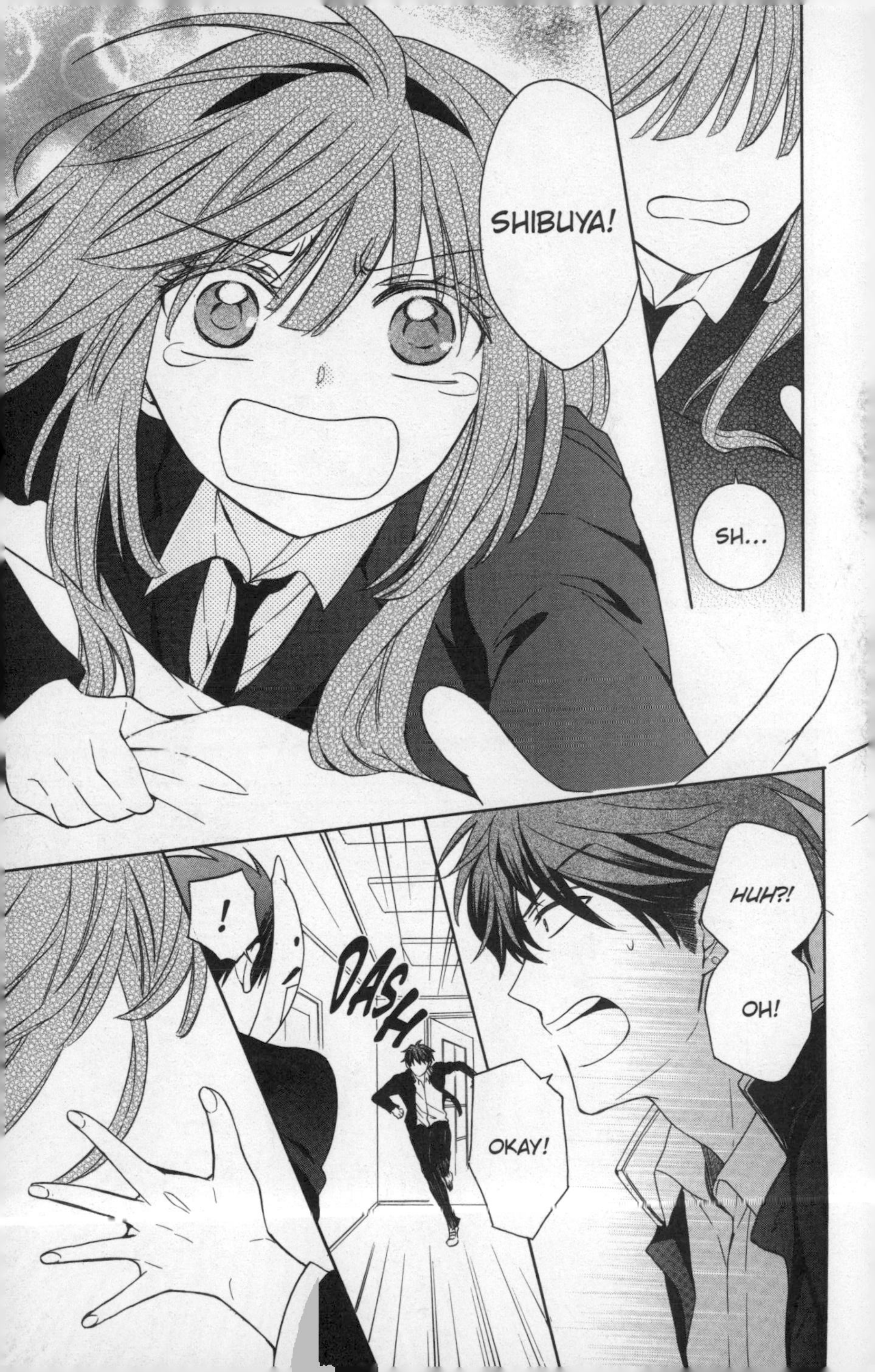
SHIBUYA!
SH...
HUH?!
OH!
OKAY!
!
DASH

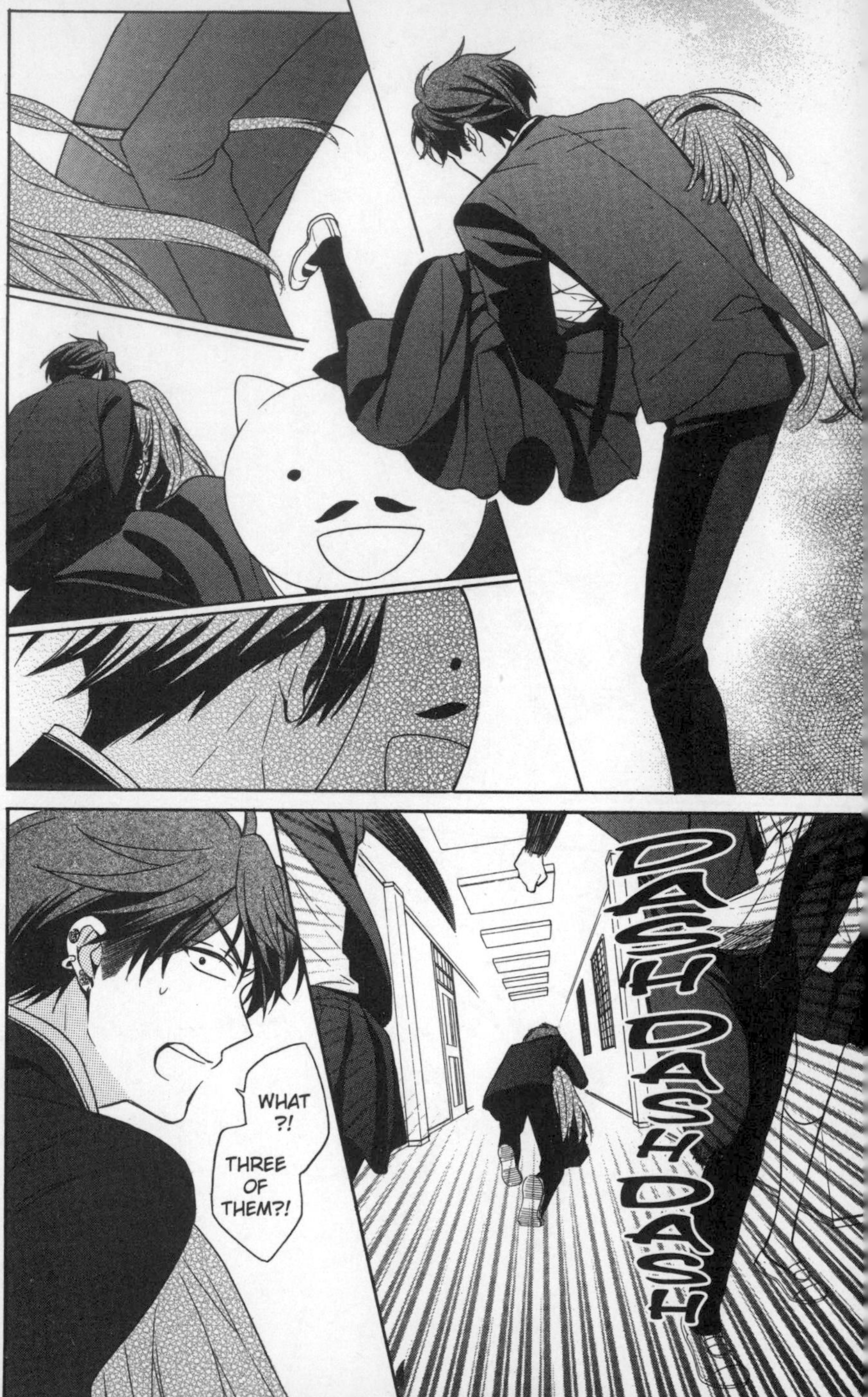
DASH DASH DASH
WHAT?!
THREE OF THEM?!

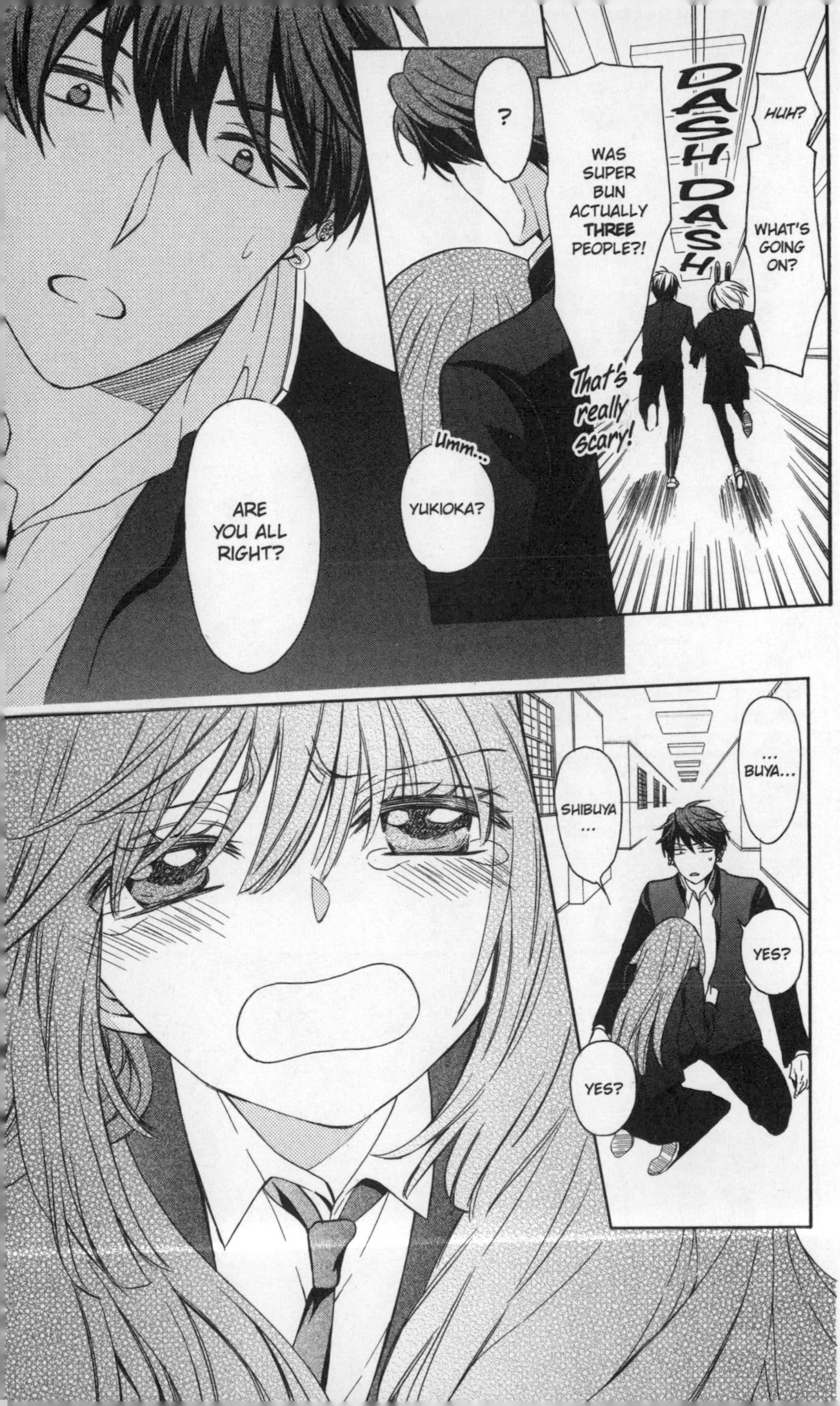
HUH?
WHAT'S GOING ON?
DASH DASH
WAS SUPER BUN ACTUALLY **THREE** PEOPLE?!
That's really scary!
?
Umm...
YUKIOKA?
ARE YOU ALL RIGHT?
...BUYA...
SHIBUYA...
YES?
YES?

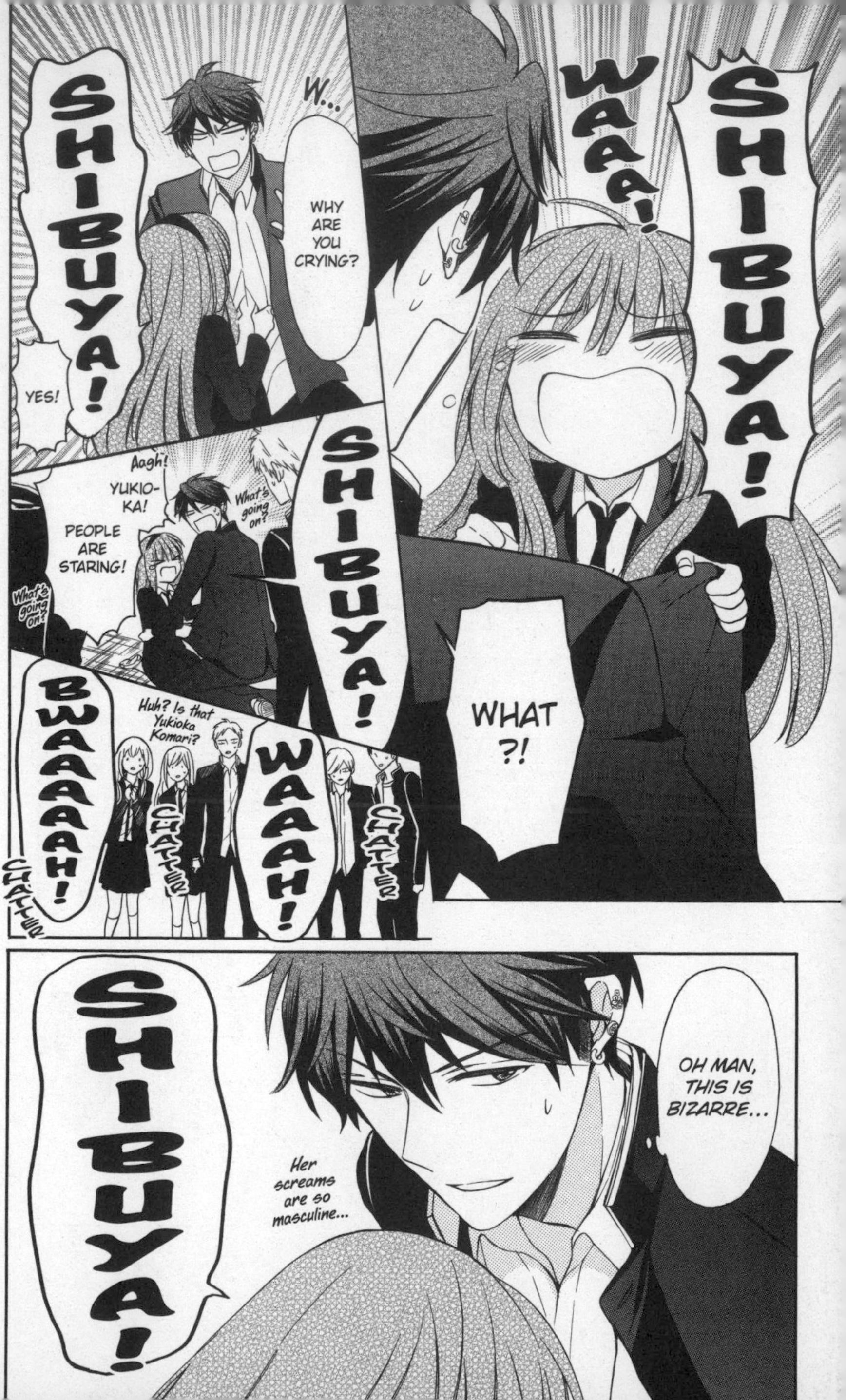
SHIBUYA!
WAAA!
WHAT?!
W...
WHY ARE YOU CRYING?
SHIBUYA!
YES!
SHIBUYA!
What's going on?
Aagh!
YUKIOKA!
PEOPLE ARE STARING!
What's going on?
CHATTER
WAAAH!
Huh? Is that Yukioka Komari?
CHATTER
BWAAAAAAH!
CHATTER
OH MAN, THIS IS BIZARRE...
SHIBUYA!
Her screams are so masculine...

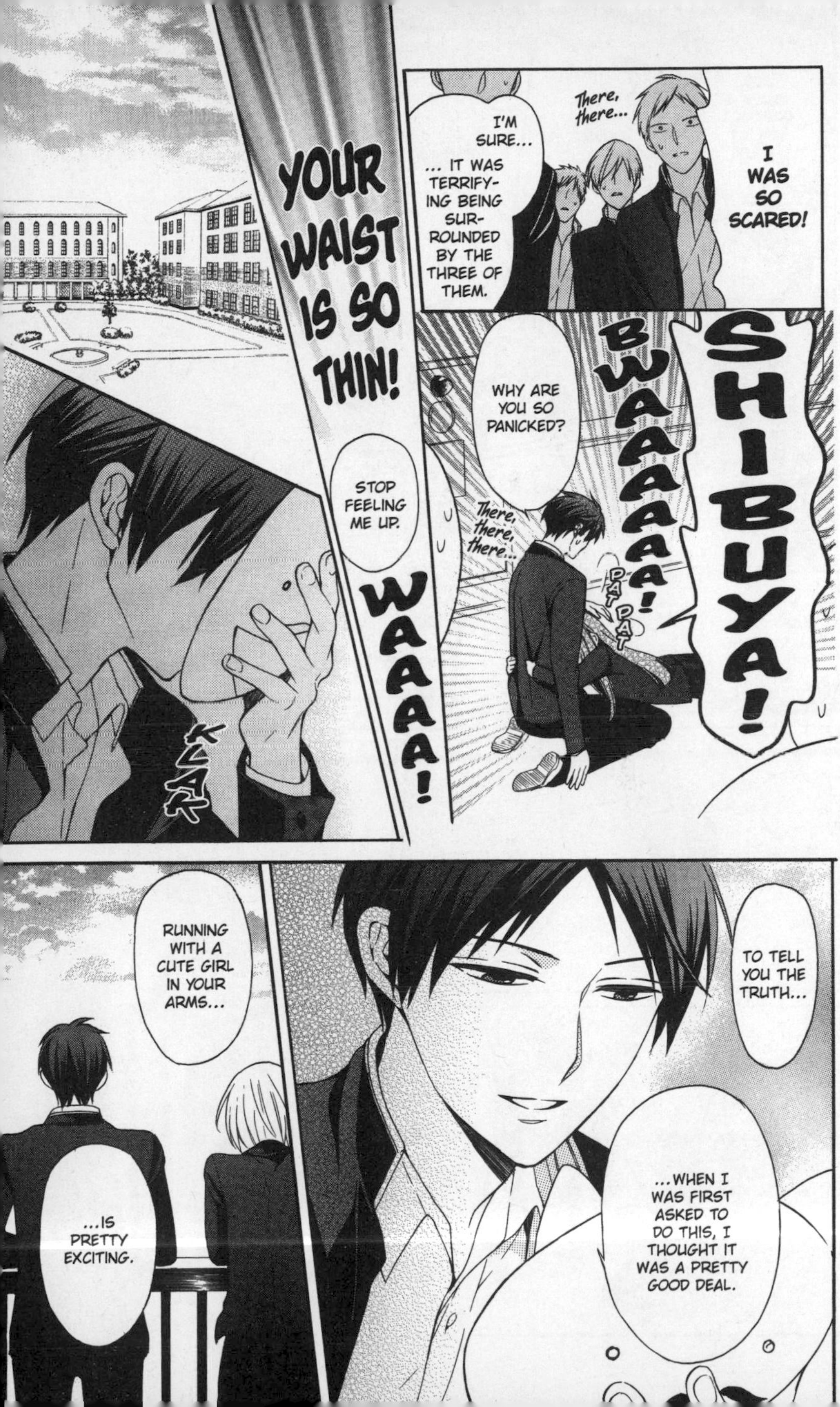
I WAS SO SCARED!
There, there...
I'M SURE... ... IT WAS TERRIFYING BEING SURROUNDED BY THE THREE OF THEM.
SHIBUYA!
BWAAAAAAA!
PAT PAT
WHY ARE YOU SO PANICKED?
There, there, there...
YOUR WAIST IS SO THIN!
STOP FEELING ME UP.
WAAAAA!
KLAK
TO TELL YOU THE TRUTH...
...WHEN I WAS FIRST ASKED TO DO THIS, I THOUGHT IT WAS A PRETTY GOOD DEAL.
RUNNING WITH A CUTE GIRL IN YOUR ARMS...
...IS PRETTY EXCITING.

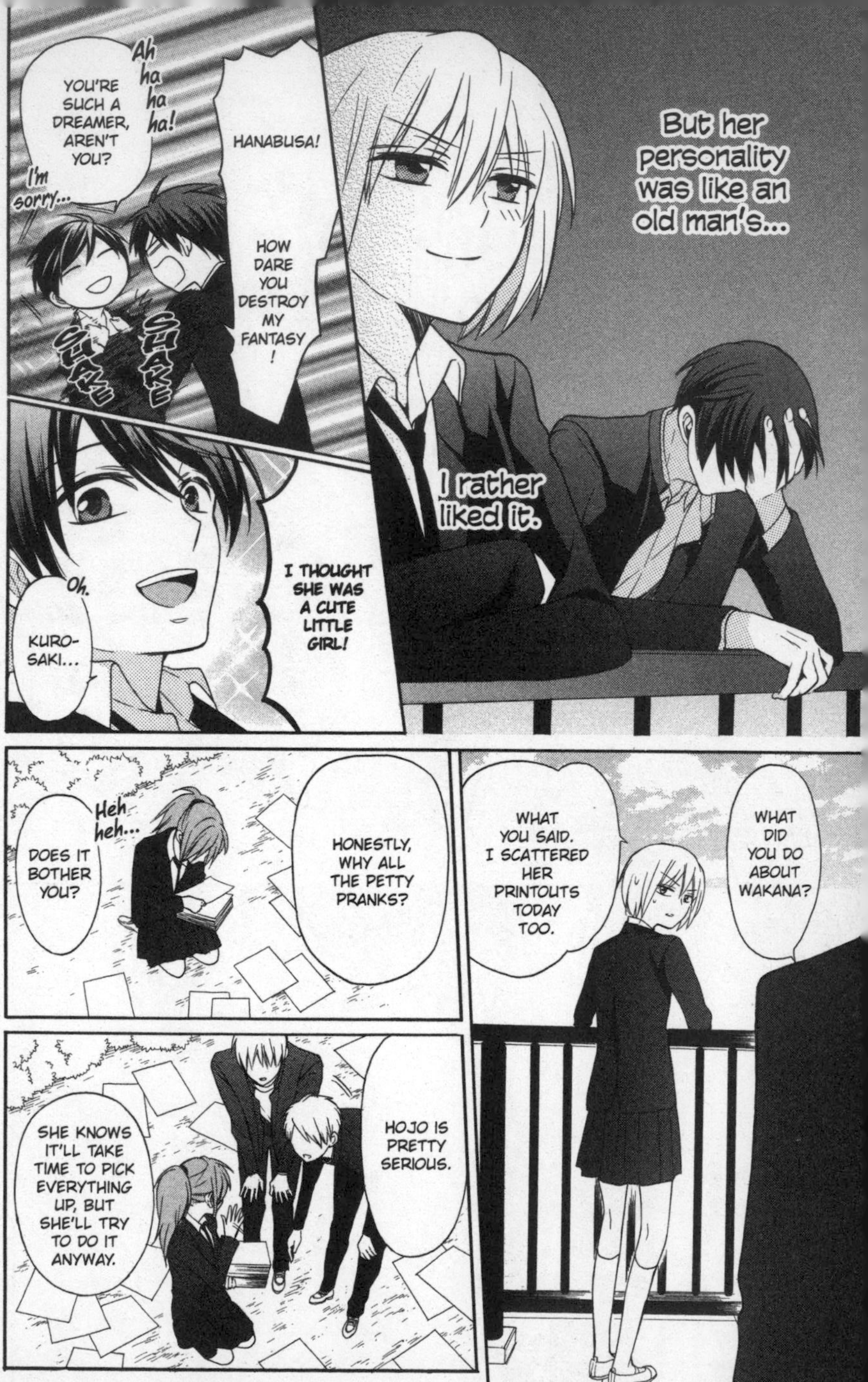

But her personality was like an old man's...
I rather liked it.
HANABUSA!
HOW DARE YOU DESTROY MY FANTASY!
Ah ha ha ha!
YOU'RE SUCH A DREAMER, AREN'T YOU?
I'm sorry...
SHAKE
SHAKE
I THOUGHT SHE WAS A CUTE LITTLE GIRL!
Oh.
KURO-SAKI...
WHAT DID YOU DO ABOUT WAKANA?
WHAT YOU SAID. I SCATTERED HER PRINTOUTS TODAY TOO.
HONESTLY, WHY ALL THE PETTY PRANKS?
Heh heh...
DOES IT BOTHER YOU?
HOJO IS PRETTY SERIOUS.
SHE KNOWS IT'LL TAKE TIME TO PICK EVERYTHING UP, BUT SHE'LL TRY TO DO IT ANYWAY.

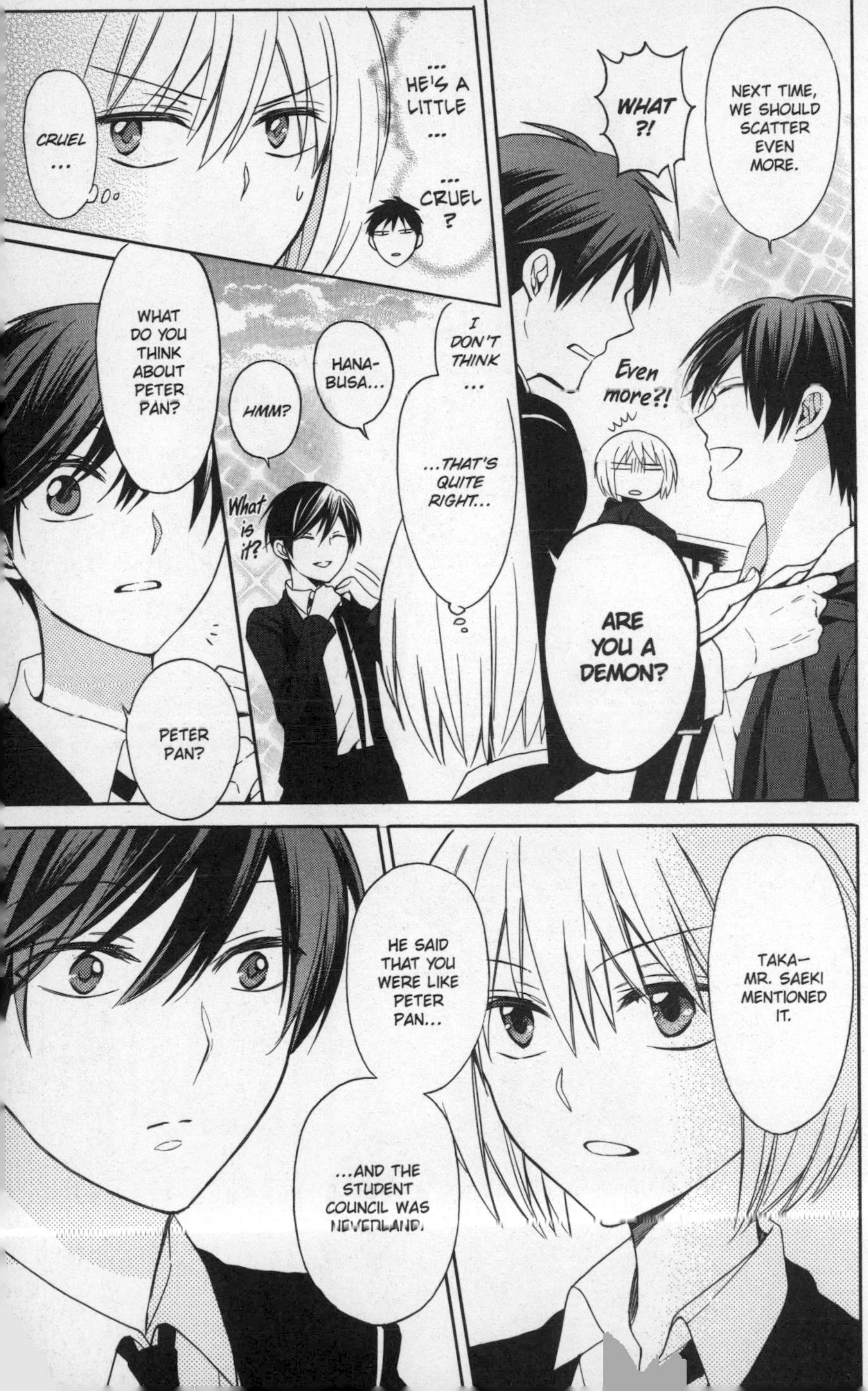
NEXT TIME, WE SHOULD SCATTER EVEN MORE.
WHAT ?!
Even more?!
ARE YOU A DEMON?
... HE'S A LITTLE ...
... CRUEL ?
CRUEL ...
I DON'T THINK ...
...THAT'S QUITE RIGHT...
HANA-BUSA...
HMM?
What is it?
WHAT DO YOU THINK ABOUT PETER PAN?
PETER PAN?
TAKA— MR. SAEKI MENTIONED IT.
HE SAID THAT YOU WERE LIKE PETER PAN...
...AND THE STUDENT COUNCIL WAS NEVERLAND.

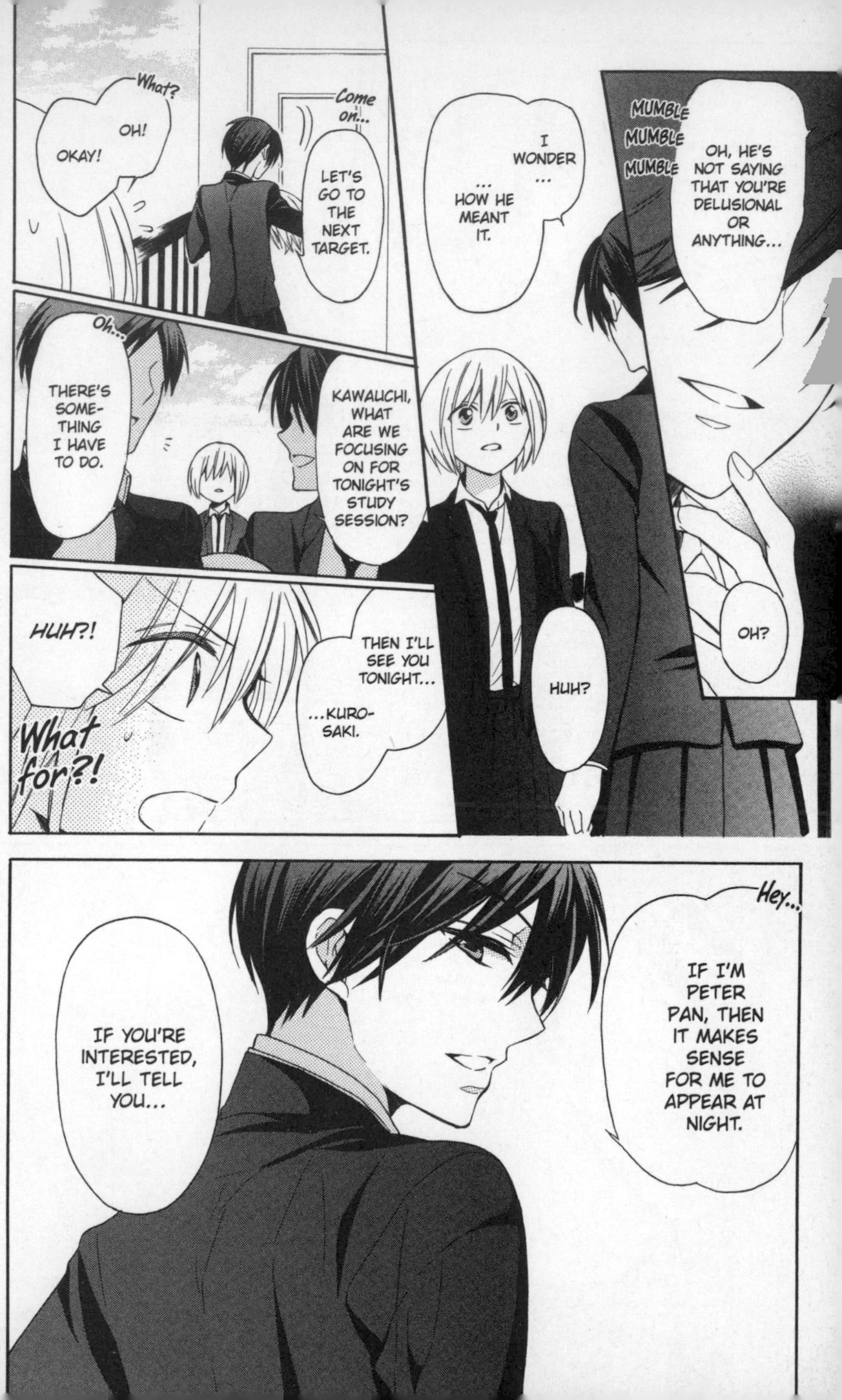
MUMBLE MUMBLE MUMBLE
OH, HE'S NOT SAYING THAT YOU'RE DELUSIONAL OR ANYTHING...
OH?
I WONDER... ...HOW HE MEANT IT.
HUH?
Come on...
LET'S GO TO THE NEXT TARGET.
What?
OH! OKAY!
KAWAUCHI, WHAT ARE WE FOCUSING ON FOR TONIGHT'S STUDY SESSION?
Oh...
THERE'S SOME-THING I HAVE TO DO.
THEN I'LL SEE YOU TONIGHT...
...KURO-SAKI.
HUH?!
What for?!
Hey...
IF I'M PETER PAN, THEN IT MAKES SENSE FOR ME TO APPEAR AT NIGHT.
IF YOU'RE INTERESTED, I'LL TELL YOU...

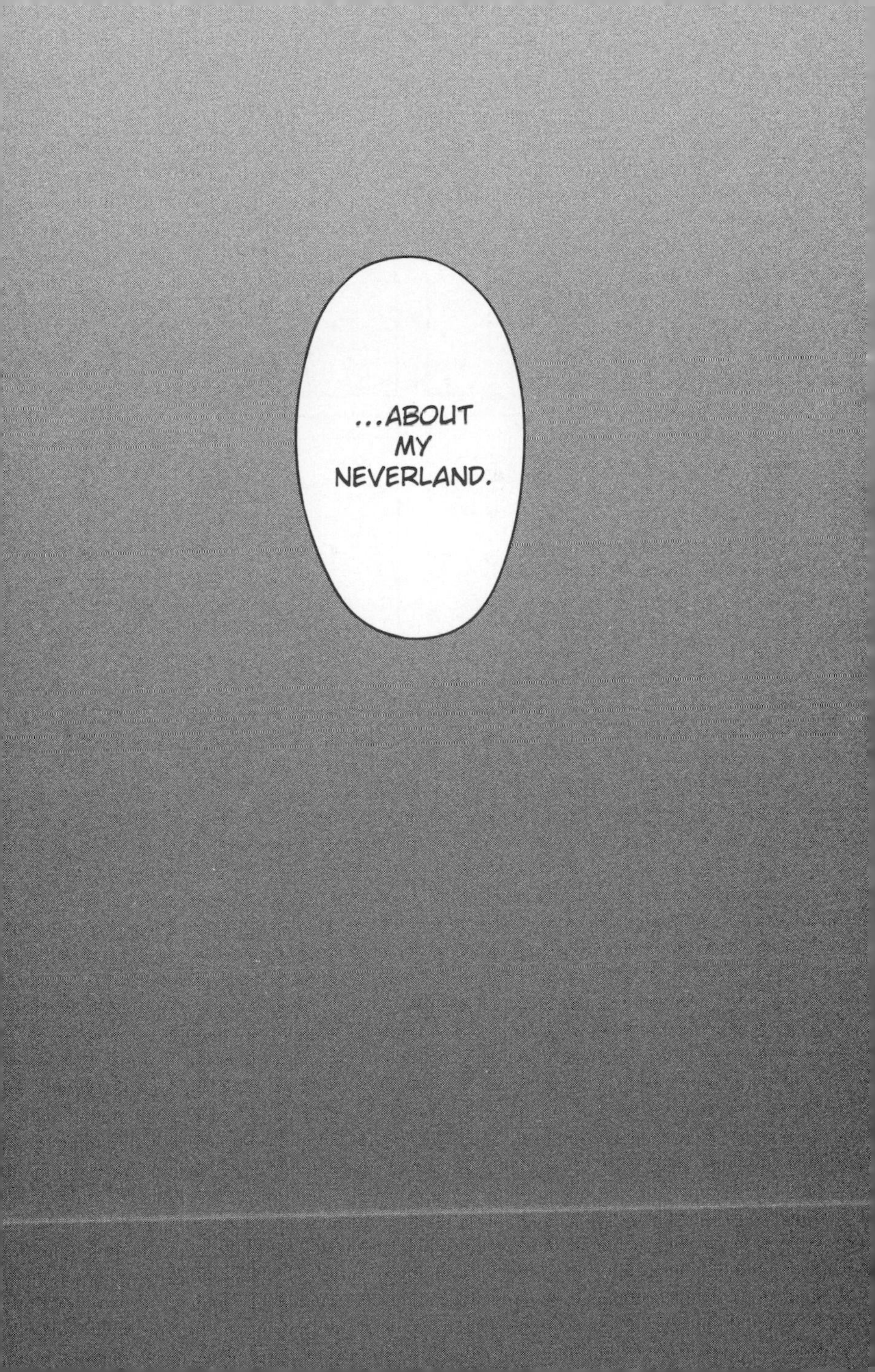
...ABOUT MY NEVERLAND.

SIMILAR MINDS

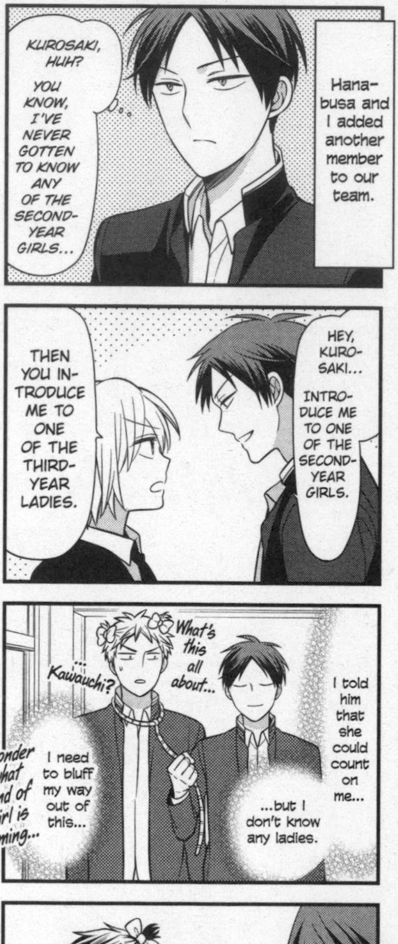
Hanabusa and I added another member to our team.
KUROSAKI, HUH?
YOU KNOW, I'VE NEVER GOTTEN TO KNOW ANY OF THE SECOND-YEAR GIRLS...
HEY, KUROSAKI...
INTRODUCE ME TO ONE OF THE SECOND-YEAR GIRLS.
THEN YOU INTRODUCE ME TO ONE OF THE THIRD-YEAR LADIES.
I told him that she could count on me...
...but I don't know any ladies.
What's this all about...
...Kawauchi?
I need to bluff my way out of this...
I wonder what kind of girl is coming...

LOVE RATING

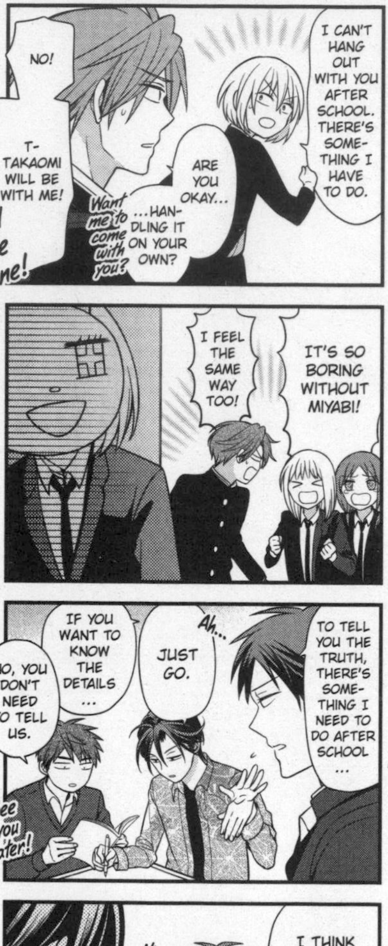
I CAN'T HANG OUT WITH YOU AFTER SCHOOL. THERE'S SOMETHING I HAVE TO DO.
ARE YOU OKAY...
...HANDLING IT ON YOUR OWN?
Want me to come with you?
NO!
T-TAKAOMI WILL BE WITH ME!
I'll be fine!
IT'S SO BORING WITHOUT MIYABI!
I FEEL THE SAME WAY TOO!
TO TELL YOU THE TRUTH, THERE'S SOMETHING I NEED TO DO AFTER SCHOOL...
Ah...
JUST GO.
IF YOU WANT TO KNOW THE DETAILS...
NO, YOU DON'T NEED TO TELL US.
See you later!
I THINK IT MEANS THEY HAVE THE UTMOST FAITH IN ME.
It must be love.

Chapter 125

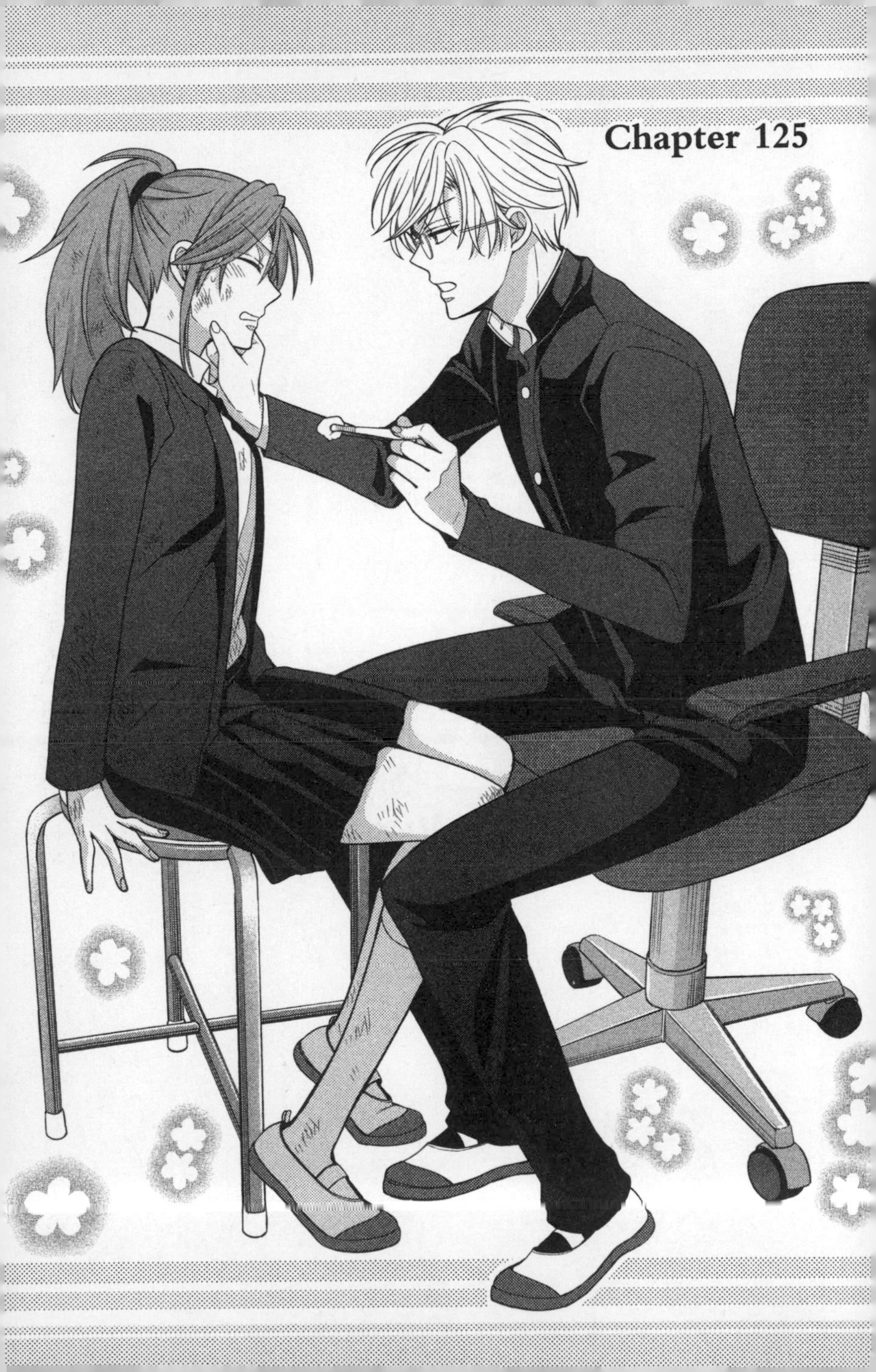

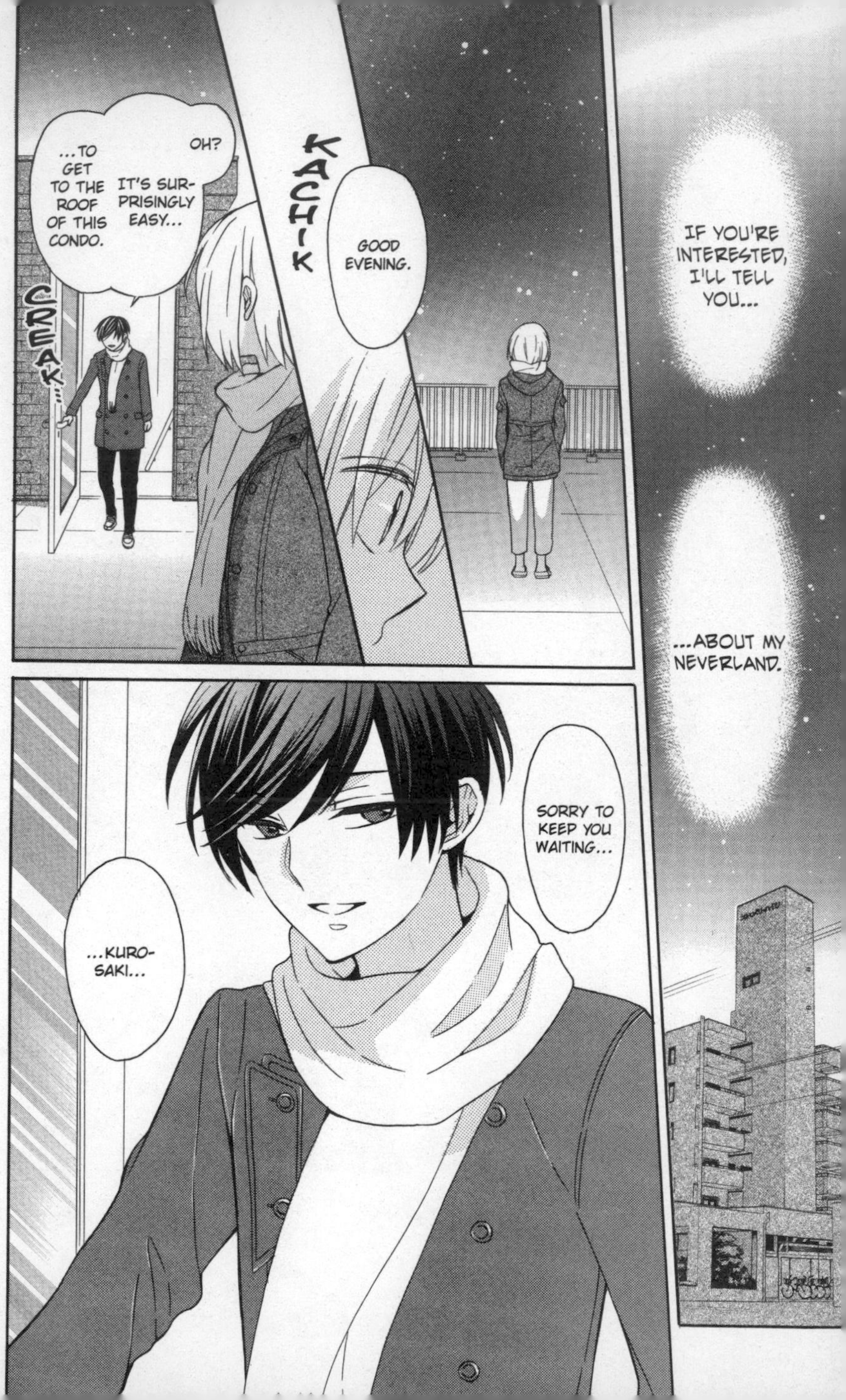
IF YOU'RE INTERESTED, I'LL TELL YOU...
...ABOUT MY NEVERLAND.
KACHIK
GOOD EVENING.
OH? IT'S SURPRISINGLY EASY...
...TO GET TO THE ROOF OF THIS CONDO.
CREAK...
SORRY TO KEEP YOU WAITING...
...KURO-SAKI...

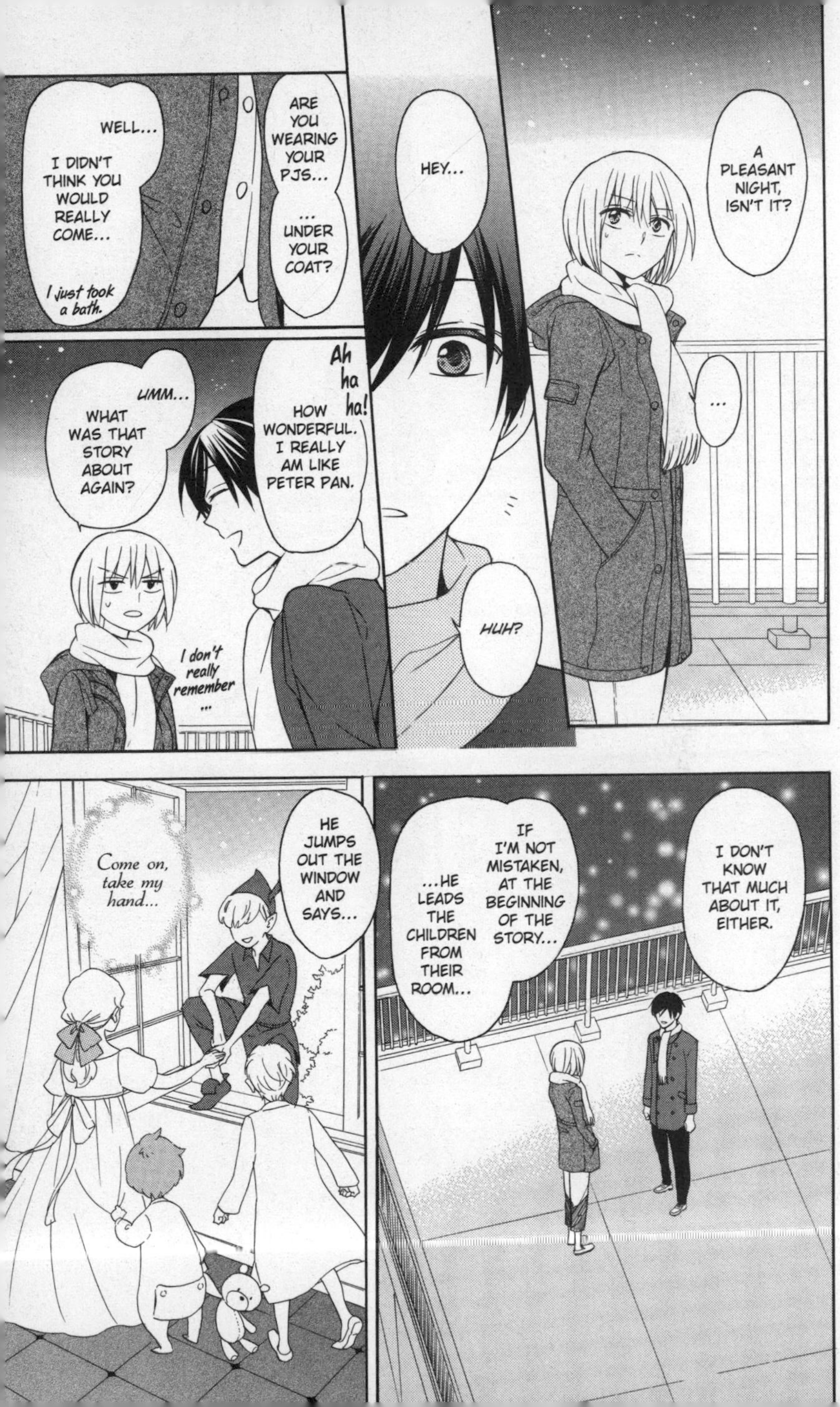
A PLEASANT NIGHT, ISN'T IT?
...
HEY...
HUH?
ARE YOU WEARING YOUR PJS...
... UNDER YOUR COAT?
WELL...
I DIDN'T THINK YOU WOULD REALLY COME...
I just took a bath.
Ah ha ha!
HOW WONDERFUL. I REALLY AM LIKE PETER PAN.
UMM... WHAT WAS THAT STORY ABOUT AGAIN?
I don't really remember...
I DON'T KNOW THAT MUCH ABOUT IT, EITHER.
IF I'M NOT MISTAKEN, AT THE BEGINNING OF THE STORY...
...HE LEADS THE CHILDREN FROM THEIR ROOM...
HE JUMPS OUT THE WINDOW AND SAYS...
Come on, take my hand...

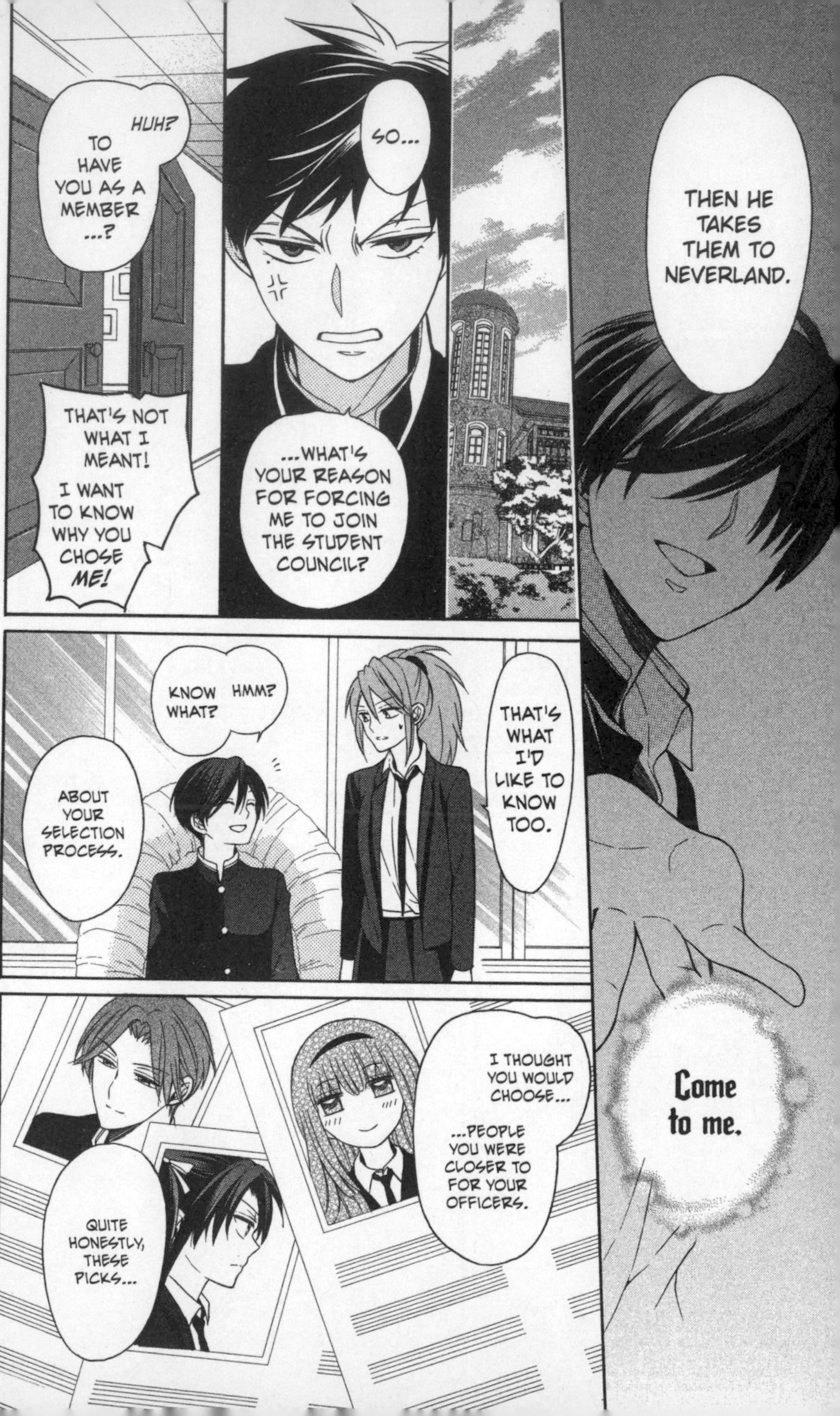
THEN HE TAKES THEM TO NEVERLAND.
Come to me.
SO...
...WHAT'S YOUR REASON FOR FORCING ME TO JOIN THE STUDENT COUNCIL?
HUH? TO HAVE YOU AS A MEMBER ...?
THAT'S NOT WHAT I MEANT! I WANT TO KNOW WHY YOU CHOSE *ME!*
THAT'S WHAT I'D LIKE TO KNOW TOO.
HMM? KNOW WHAT?
ABOUT YOUR SELECTION PROCESS.
I THOUGHT YOU WOULD CHOOSE...
...PEOPLE YOU WERE CLOSER TO FOR YOUR OFFICERS.
QUITE HONESTLY, THESE PICKS...

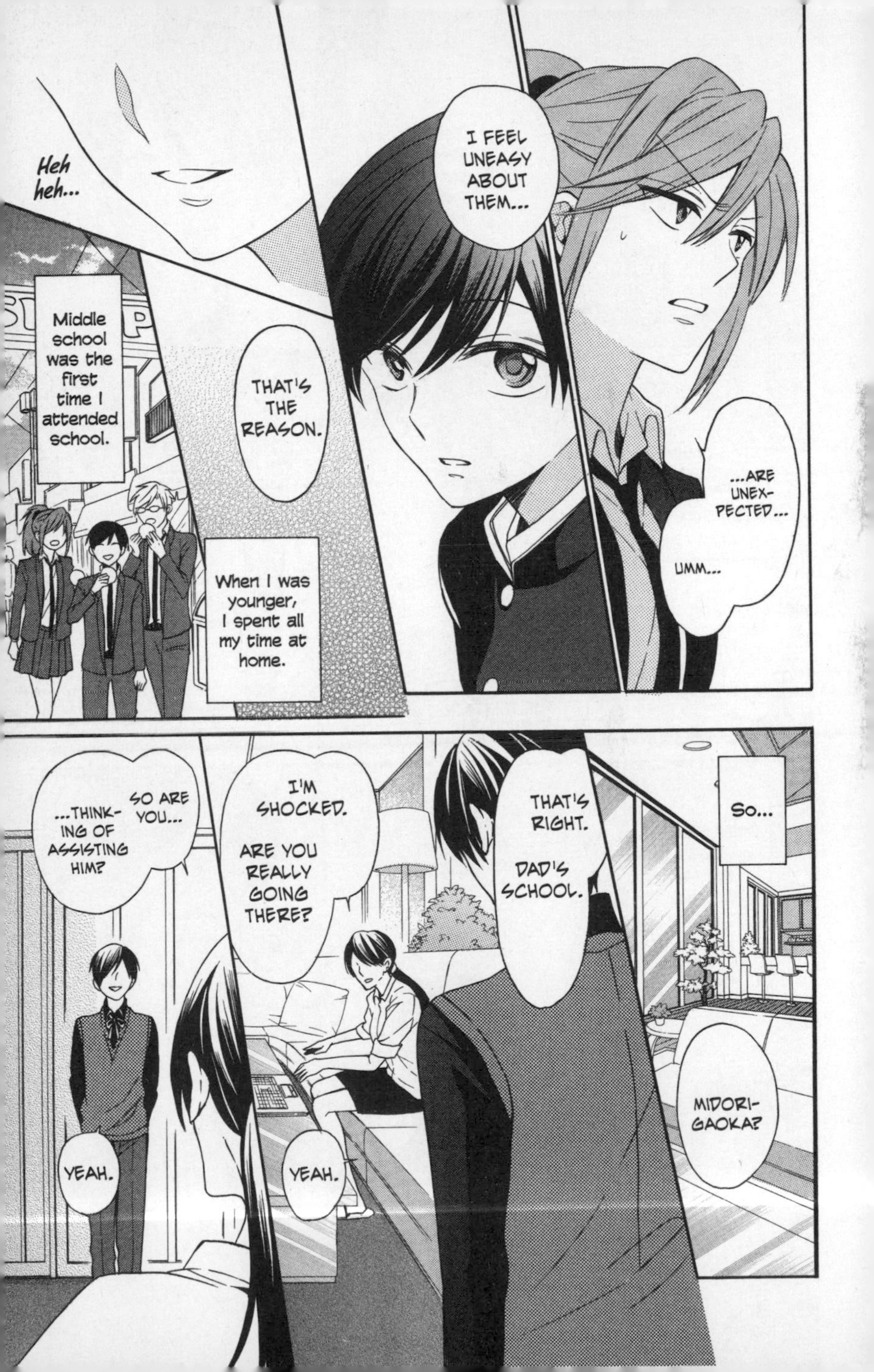
...ARE UNEXPECTED...
UMM...
I FEEL UNEASY ABOUT THEM...
THAT'S THE REASON.
Heh heh...
When I was younger, I spent all my time at home.
Middle school was the first time I attended school.
So...
MIDORI-GAOKA?
THAT'S RIGHT.
DAD'S SCHOOL.
I'M SHOCKED.
ARE YOU REALLY GOING THERE?
YEAH.
SO ARE YOU...
...THINKING OF ASSISTING HIM?
YEAH.

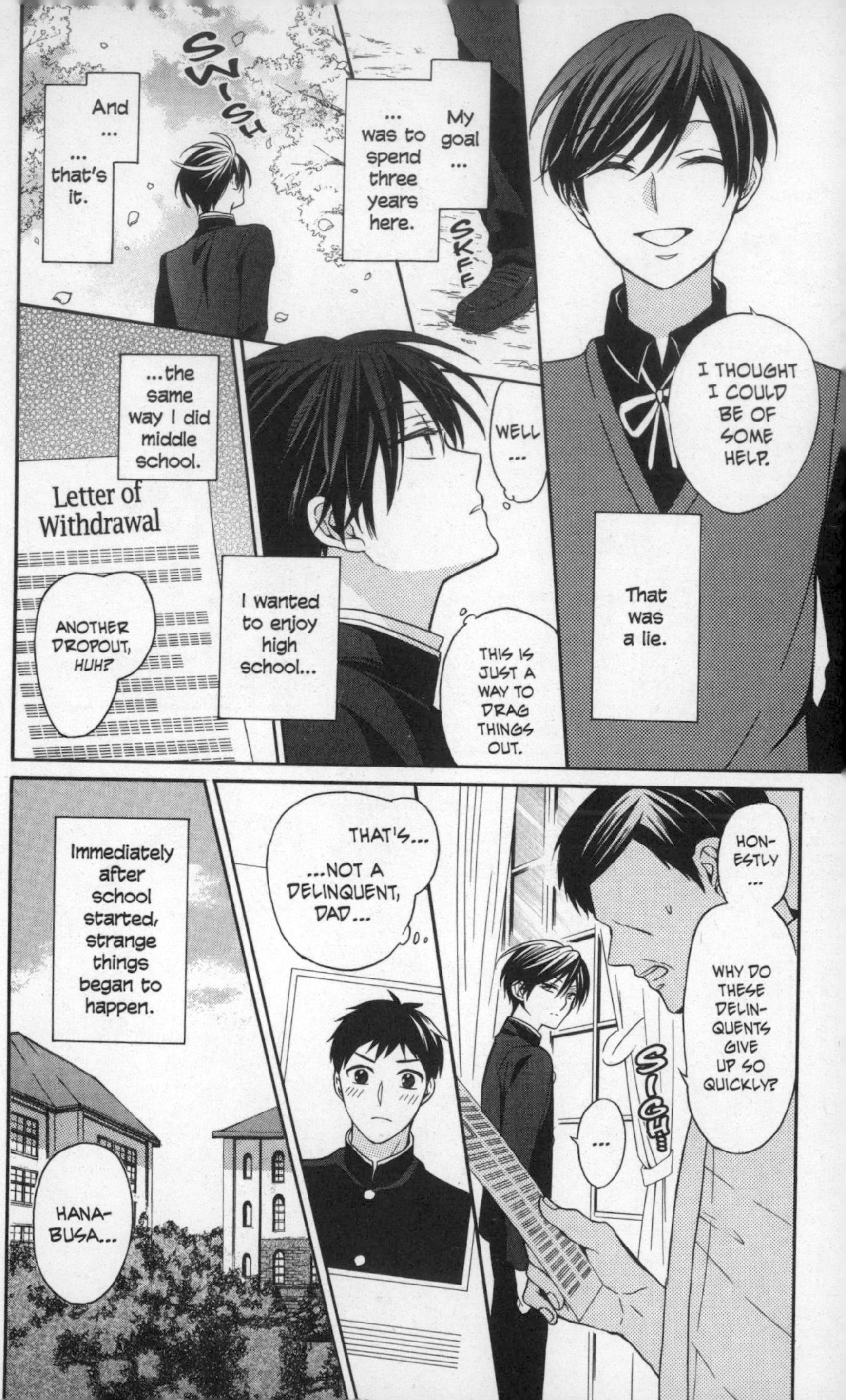
I THOUGHT I COULD BE OF SOME HELP.
That was a lie.
My goal ...
... was to spend three years here.
SKFF
SWISH
And ...
... that's it.
WELL ...
I wanted to enjoy high school...
THIS IS JUST A WAY TO DRAG THINGS OUT.
...the same way I did middle school.
Letter of Withdrawal
ANOTHER DROPOUT, HUH?
HON-ESTLY ...
WHY DO THESE DELIN-QUENTS GIVE UP SO QUICKLY?
SIGH
...
THAT'S...
...NOT A DELINQUENT, DAD...
Immediately after school started, strange things began to happen.
HANA-BUSA...

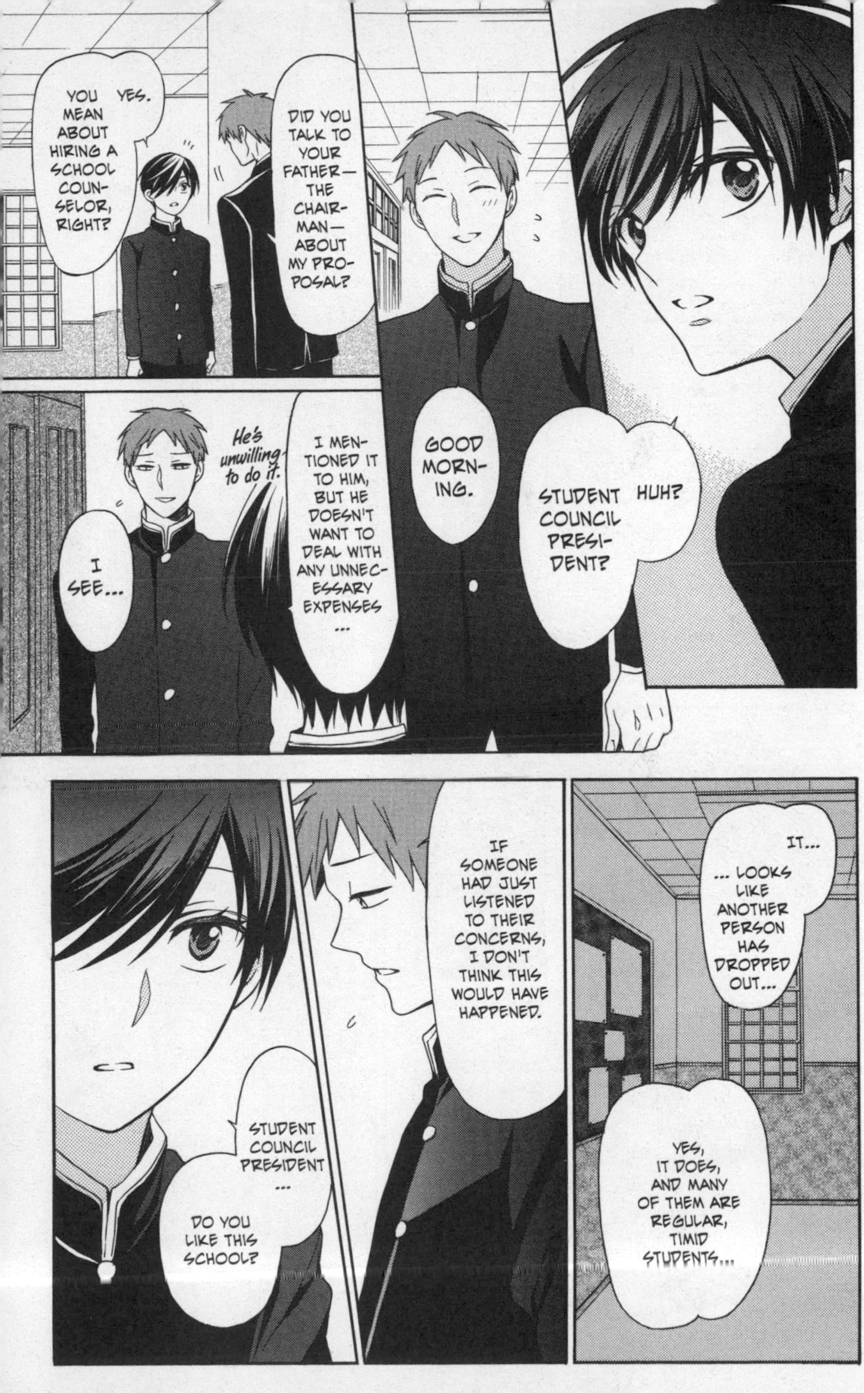
HUH? STUDENT COUNCIL PRESIDENT?
GOOD MORNING.
DID YOU TALK TO YOUR FATHER—THE CHAIRMAN—ABOUT MY PROPOSAL?
YES. YOU MEAN ABOUT HIRING A SCHOOL COUNSELOR, RIGHT?
I MENTIONED IT TO HIM, BUT HE DOESN'T WANT TO DEAL WITH ANY UNNECESSARY EXPENSES...
He's unwilling to do it.
I SEE...
IT...
... LOOKS LIKE ANOTHER PERSON HAS DROPPED OUT...
YES, IT DOES, AND MANY OF THEM ARE REGULAR, TIMID STUDENTS...
IF SOMEONE HAD JUST LISTENED TO THEIR CONCERNS, I DON'T THINK THIS WOULD HAVE HAPPENED.
STUDENT COUNCIL PRESIDENT...
DO YOU LIKE THIS SCHOOL?

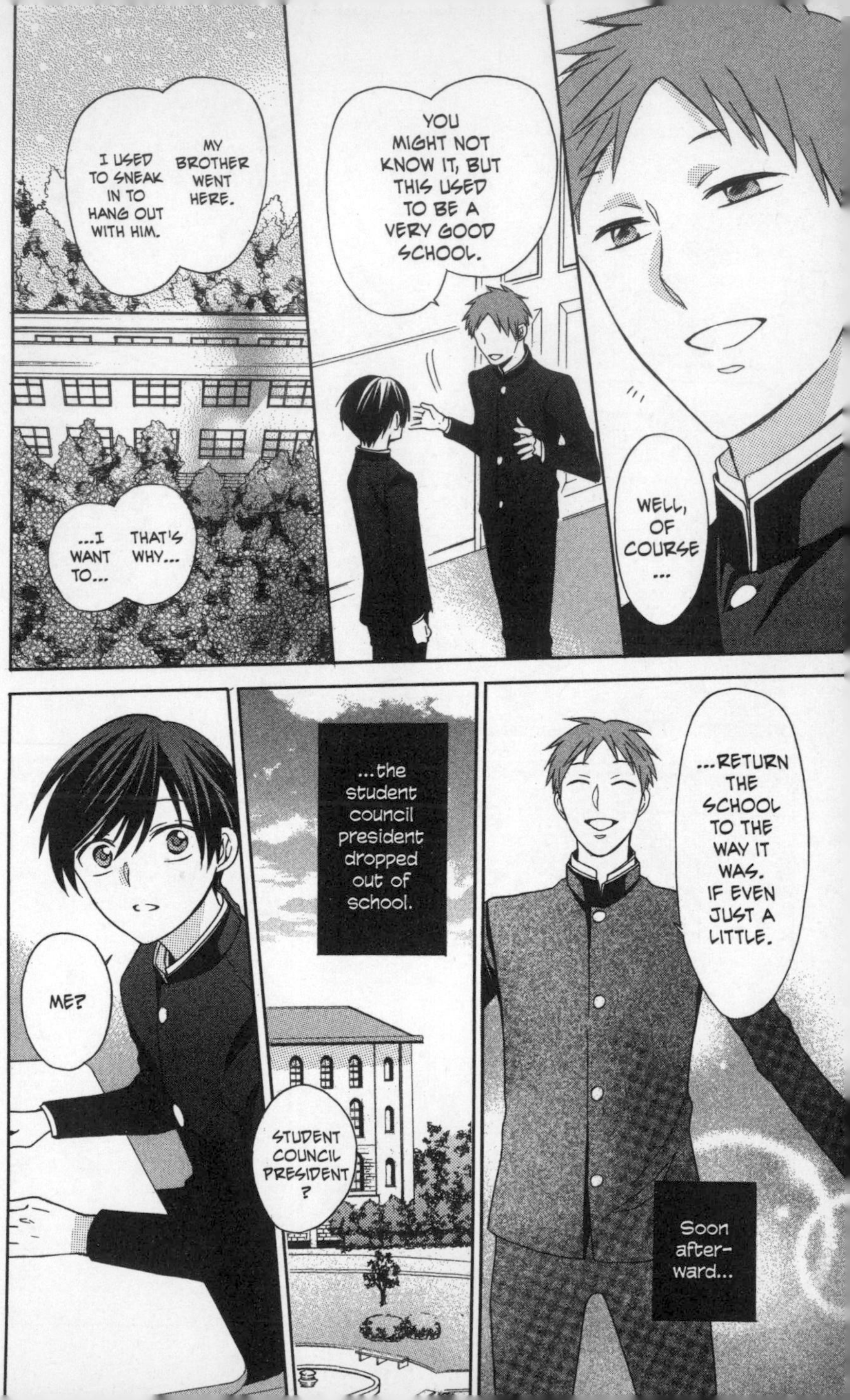
WELL, OF COURSE...
YOU MIGHT NOT KNOW IT, BUT THIS USED TO BE A VERY GOOD SCHOOL.
MY BROTHER WENT HERE.
I USED TO SNEAK IN TO HANG OUT WITH HIM.
THAT'S WHY...
...I WANT TO...
...RETURN THE SCHOOL TO THE WAY IT WAS. IF EVEN JUST A LITTLE.
Soon afterward...
...the student council president dropped out of school.
STUDENT COUNCIL PRESIDENT?
ME?

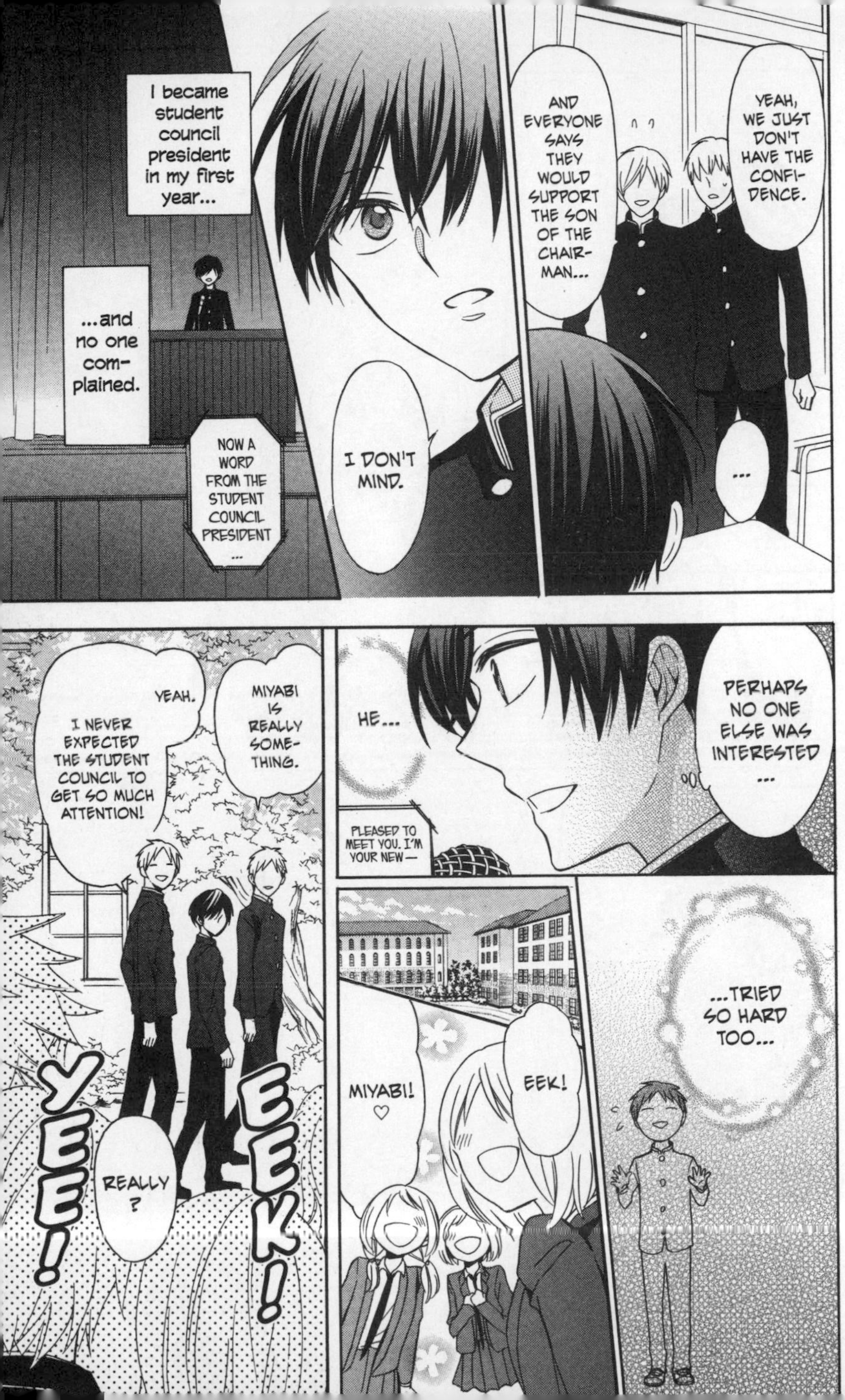
YEAH, WE JUST DON'T HAVE THE CONFIDENCE.
AND EVERYONE SAYS THEY WOULD SUPPORT THE SON OF THE CHAIRMAN...
...
I DON'T MIND.
I became student council president in my first year...
...and no one complained.
NOW A WORD FROM THE STUDENT COUNCIL PRESIDENT...
PERHAPS NO ONE ELSE WAS INTERESTED...
HE...
PLEASED TO MEET YOU. I'M YOUR NEW—
...TRIED SO HARD TOO...
EEK!
MIYABI! ♡
MIYABI IS REALLY SOMETHING.
YEAH.
I NEVER EXPECTED THE STUDENT COUNCIL TO GET SO MUCH ATTENTION!
EEK!
YEE!
REALLY?

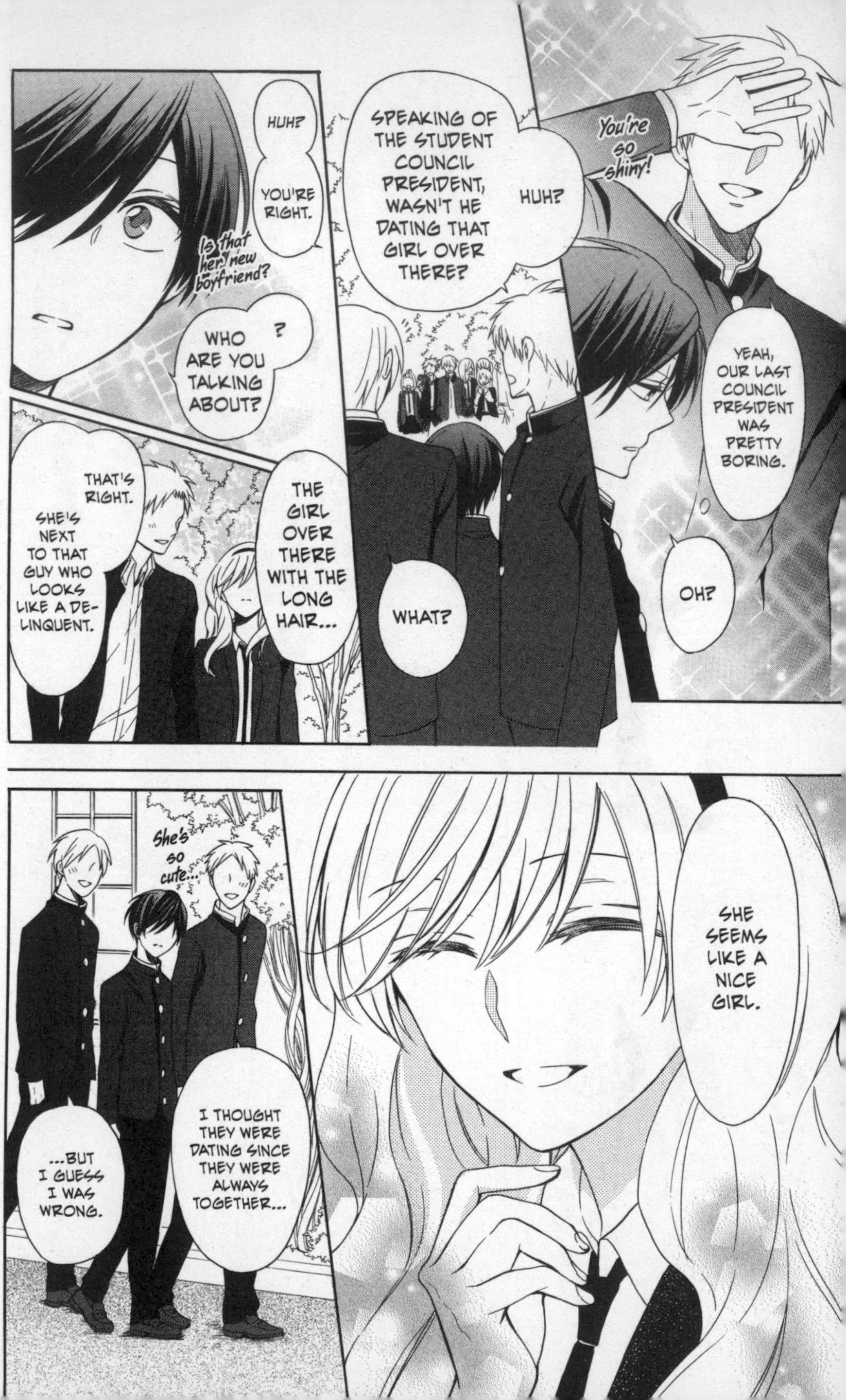
You're so shiny!
YEAH, OUR LAST COUNCIL PRESIDENT WAS PRETTY BORING.
OH?
SPEAKING OF THE STUDENT COUNCIL PRESIDENT, WASN'T HE DATING THAT GIRL OVER THERE?
HUH?
WHAT?
HUH?
YOU'RE RIGHT.
Is that her new boyfriend?
?
WHO ARE YOU TALKING ABOUT?
THE GIRL OVER THERE WITH THE LONG HAIR...
THAT'S RIGHT.
SHE'S NEXT TO THAT GUY WHO LOOKS LIKE A DE-LINQUENT.
SHE SEEMS LIKE A NICE GIRL.
She's so cute...
I THOUGHT THEY WERE DATING SINCE THEY WERE ALWAYS TOGETHER...
...BUT I GUESS I WAS WRONG.

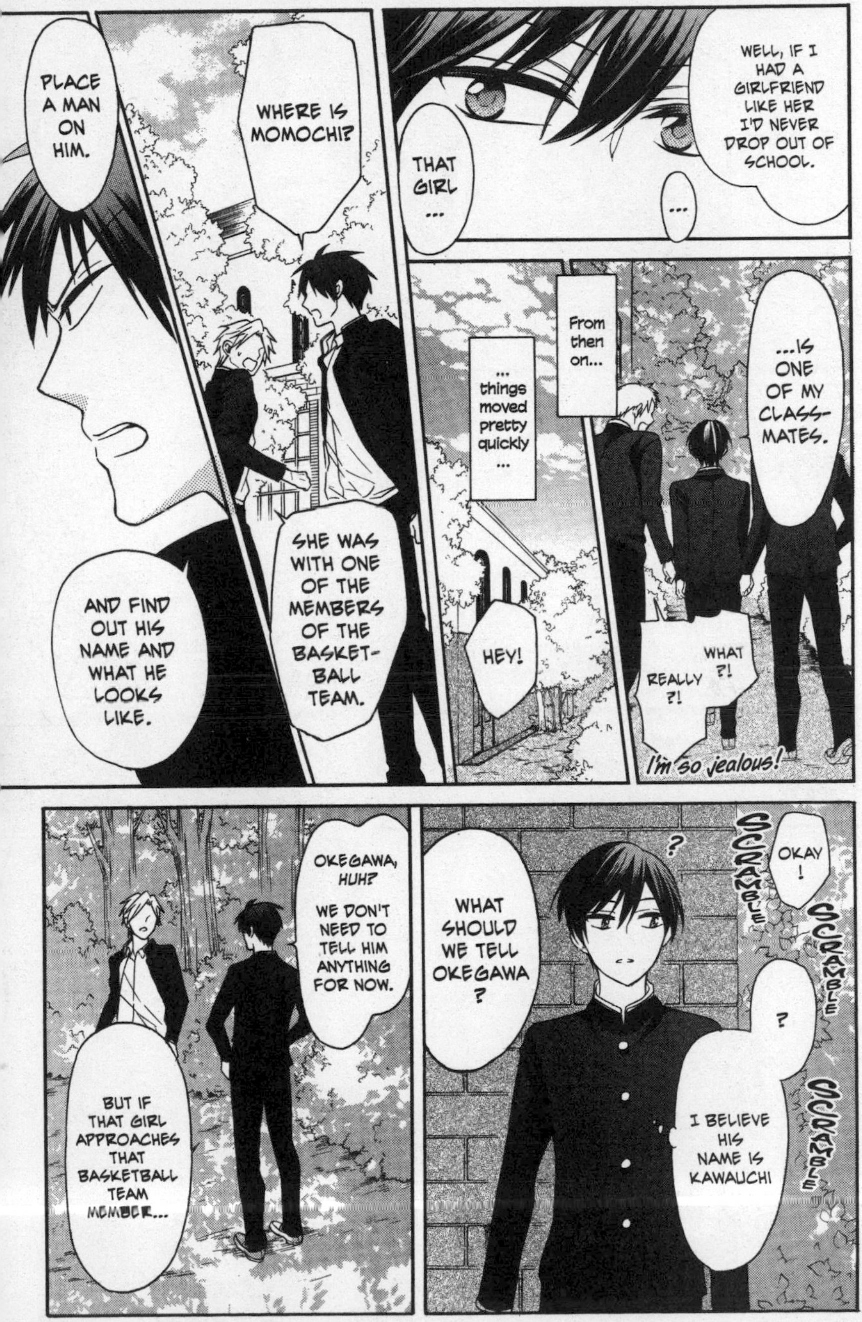
WELL, IF I HAD A GIRLFRIEND LIKE HER I'D NEVER DROP OUT OF SCHOOL.
...
THAT GIRL ...
...IS ONE OF MY CLASSMATES.
From then on...
... things moved pretty quickly ...
WHAT ?!
REALLY ?!
I'm so jealous!
HEY!
WHERE IS MOMOCHI?
SHE WAS WITH ONE OF THE MEMBERS OF THE BASKETBALL TEAM.
PLACE A MAN ON HIM.
AND FIND OUT HIS NAME AND WHAT HE LOOKS LIKE.
SCRAMBLE
OKAY !
SCRAMBLE
?
WHAT SHOULD WE TELL OKEGAWA ?
?
SCRAMBLE
I BELIEVE HIS NAME IS KAWAUCHI
OKEGAWA, HUH?
WE DON'T NEED TO TELL HIM ANYTHING FOR NOW.
BUT IF THAT GIRL APPROACHES THAT BASKETBALL TEAM MEMBER...

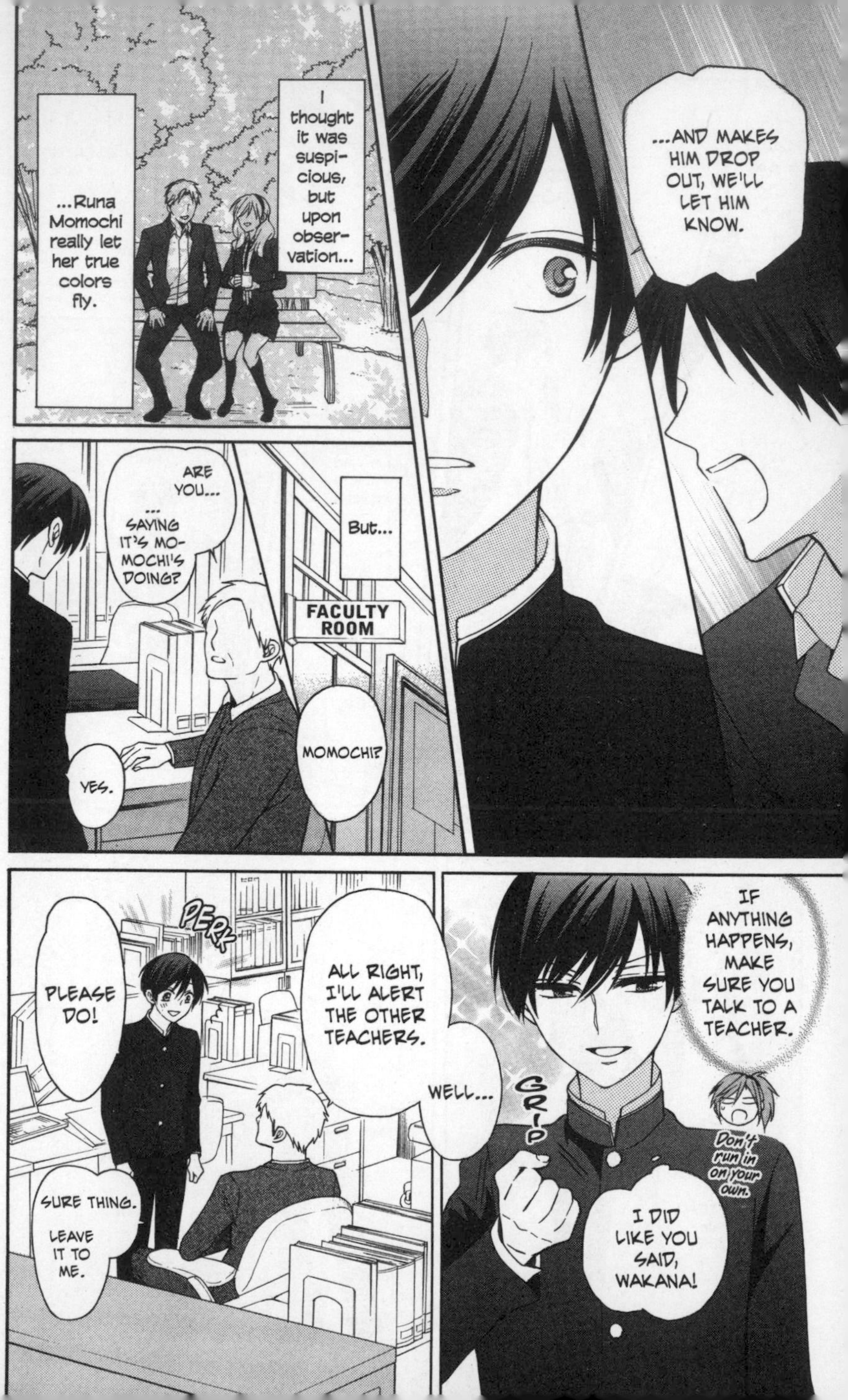
...AND MAKES HIM DROP OUT, WE'LL LET HIM KNOW.
I thought it was suspicious, but upon observation...
...Runa Momochi really let her true colors fly.
But...
ARE YOU...
...SAYING IT'S MOMOCHI'S DOING?
FACULTY ROOM
MOMOCHI?
YES.
IF ANYTHING HAPPENS, MAKE SURE YOU TALK TO A TEACHER.
Don't run in on your own.
GRIP
I DID LIKE YOU SAID, WAKANA!
WELL...
ALL RIGHT, I'LL ALERT THE OTHER TEACHERS.
PERK
PLEASE DO!
SURE THING.
LEAVE IT TO ME.

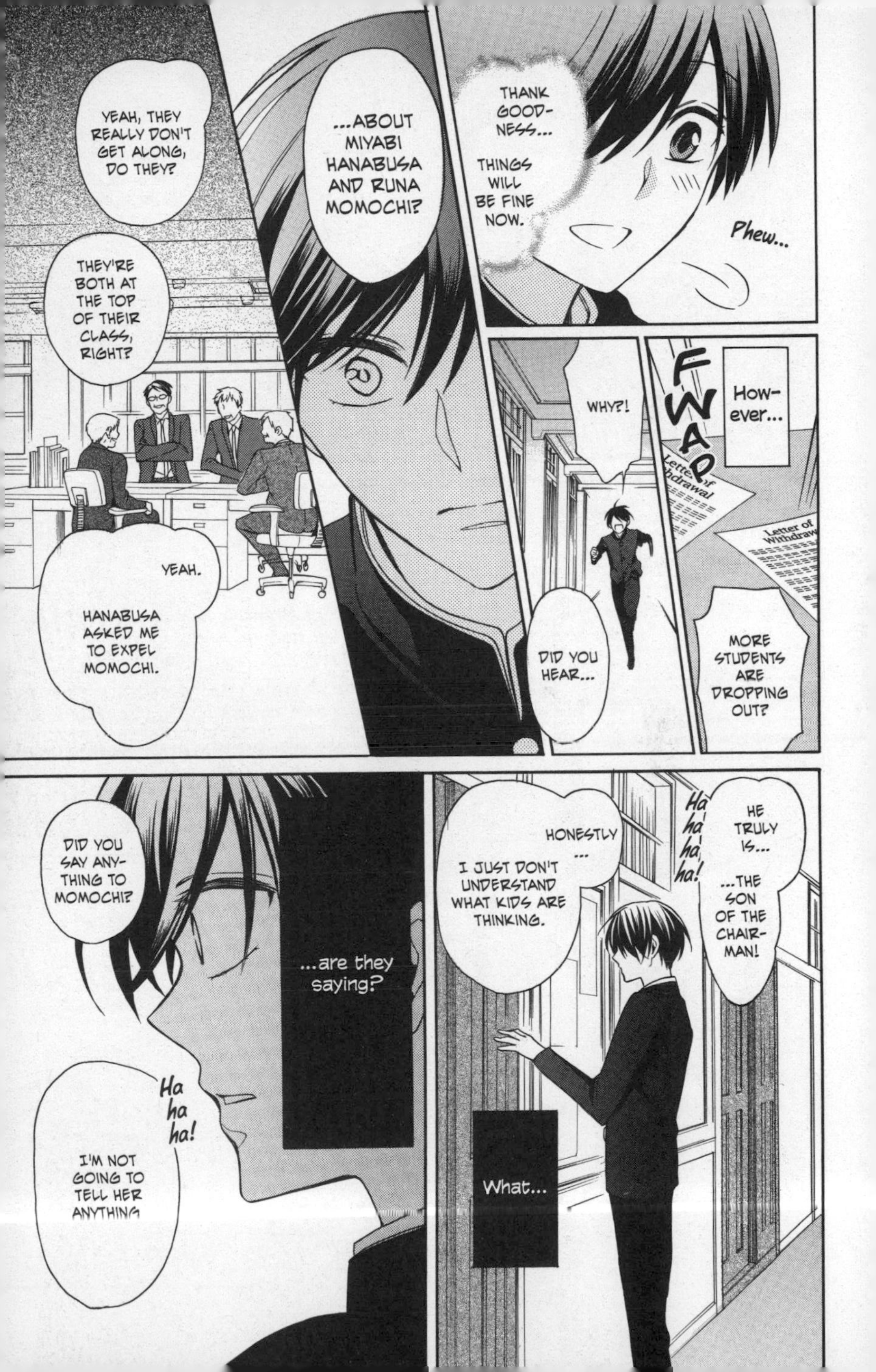
THANK GOODNESS...
THINGS WILL BE FINE NOW.
Phew...
However...
FWAP
Letter of Withdrawal
Letter of Withdraw
MORE STUDENTS ARE DROPPING OUT?
WHY?!
DID YOU HEAR...
...ABOUT MIYABI HANABUSA AND RUNA MOMOCHI?
YEAH, THEY REALLY DON'T GET ALONG, DO THEY?
THEY'RE BOTH AT THE TOP OF THEIR CLASS, RIGHT?
YEAH.
HANABUSA ASKED ME TO EXPEL MOMOCHI.
HE TRULY IS...
...THE SON OF THE CHAIRMAN!
Ha ha ha ha!
HONESTLY...
I JUST DON'T UNDERSTAND WHAT KIDS ARE THINKING.
What...
...are they saying?
DID YOU SAY ANYTHING TO MOMOCHI?
Ha ha ha!
I'M NOT GOING TO TELL HER ANYTHING

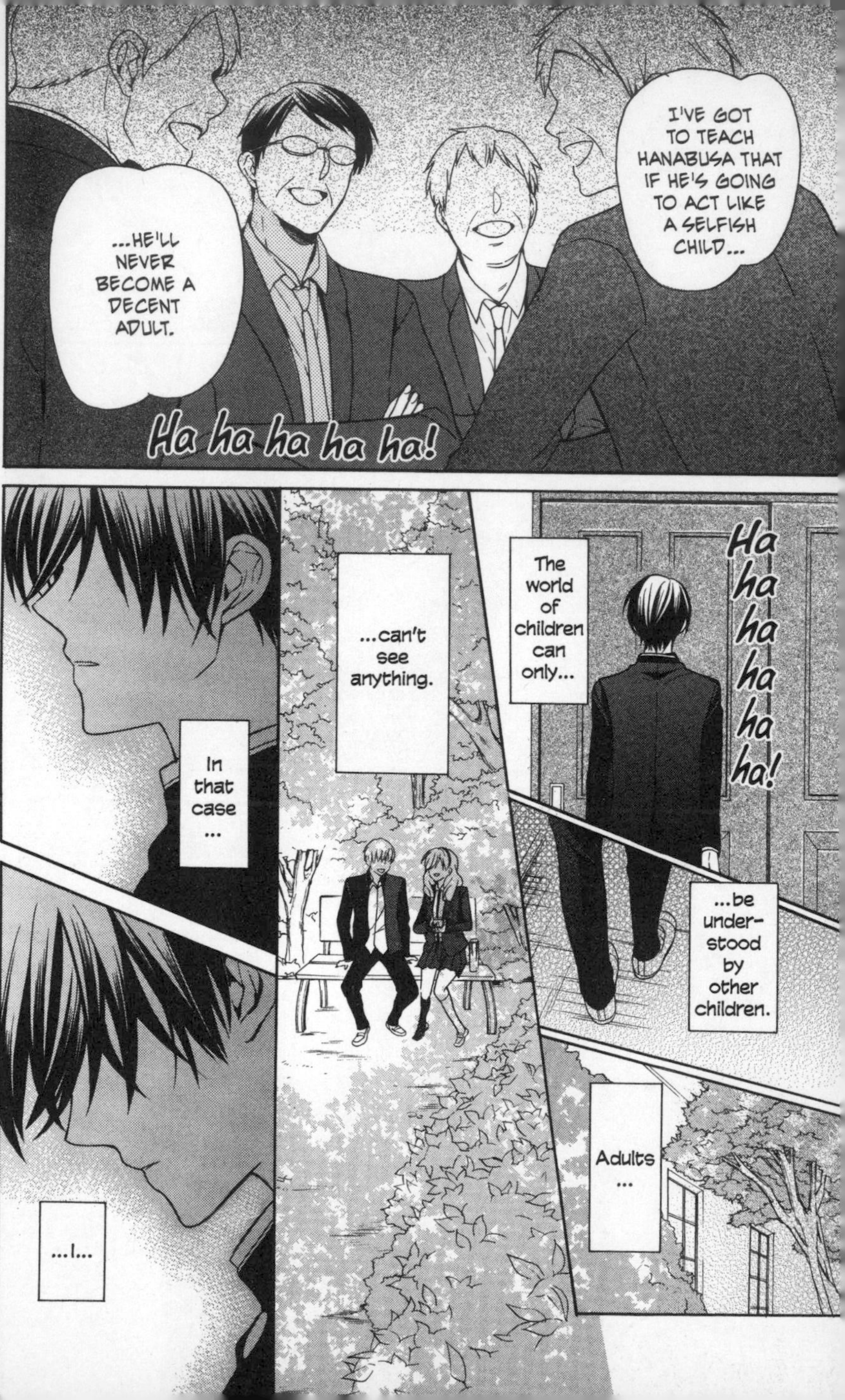
I'VE GOT TO TEACH HANABUSA THAT IF HE'S GOING TO ACT LIKE A SELFISH CHILD...
...HE'LL NEVER BECOME A DECENT ADULT.
Ha ha ha ha ha!
Ha ha ha ha ha ha ha!
The world of children can only...
...be understood by other children.
Adults...
...can't see anything.
In that case...
...I...

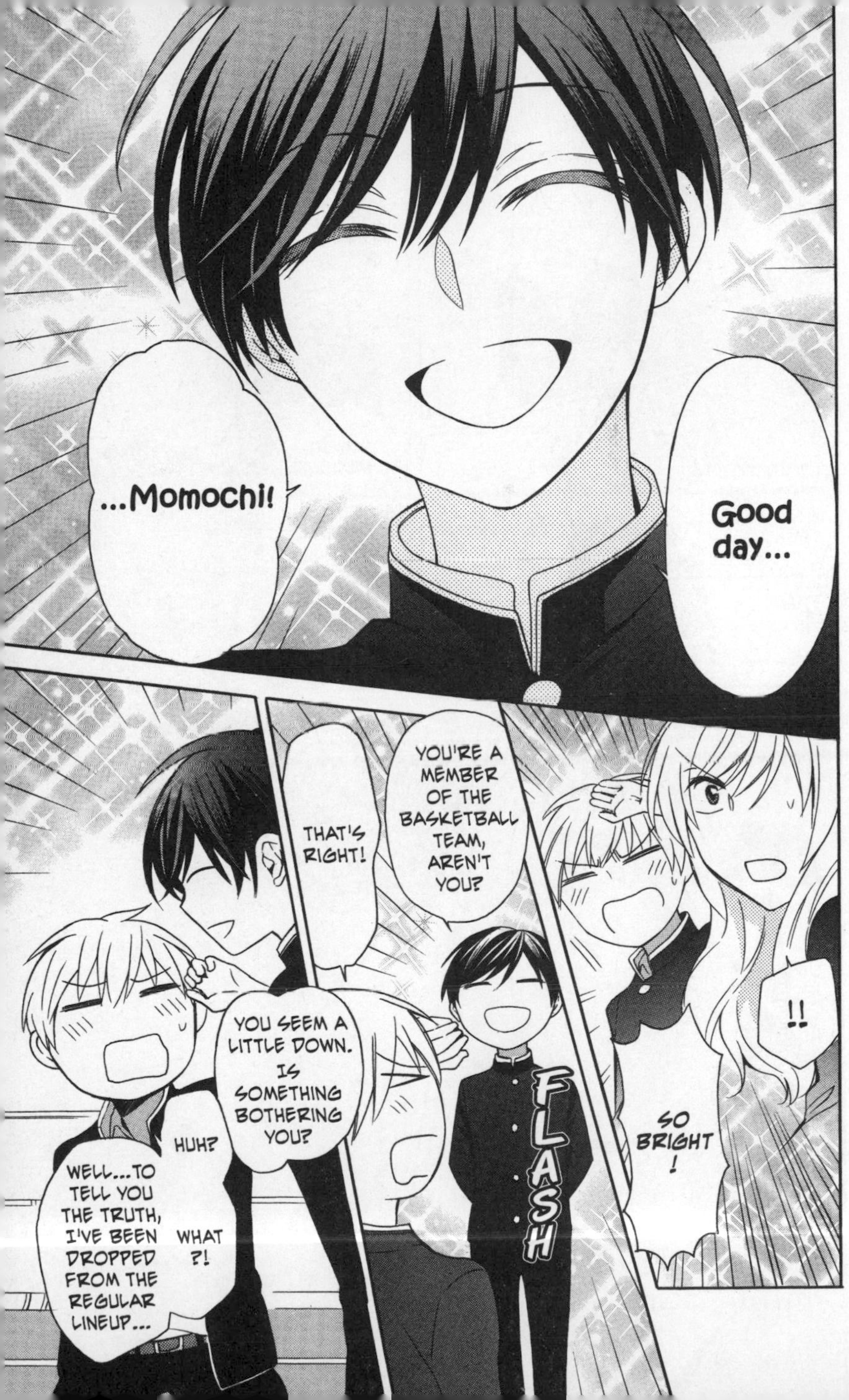
Good day...
...Momochi!
!!
SO BRIGHT!
YOU'RE A MEMBER OF THE BASKETBALL TEAM, AREN'T YOU?
THAT'S RIGHT!
FLASH
YOU SEEM A LITTLE DOWN. IS SOMETHING BOTHERING YOU?
HUH?
WELL...TO TELL YOU THE TRUTH, I'VE BEEN DROPPED FROM THE REGULAR LINEUP...
WHAT?!

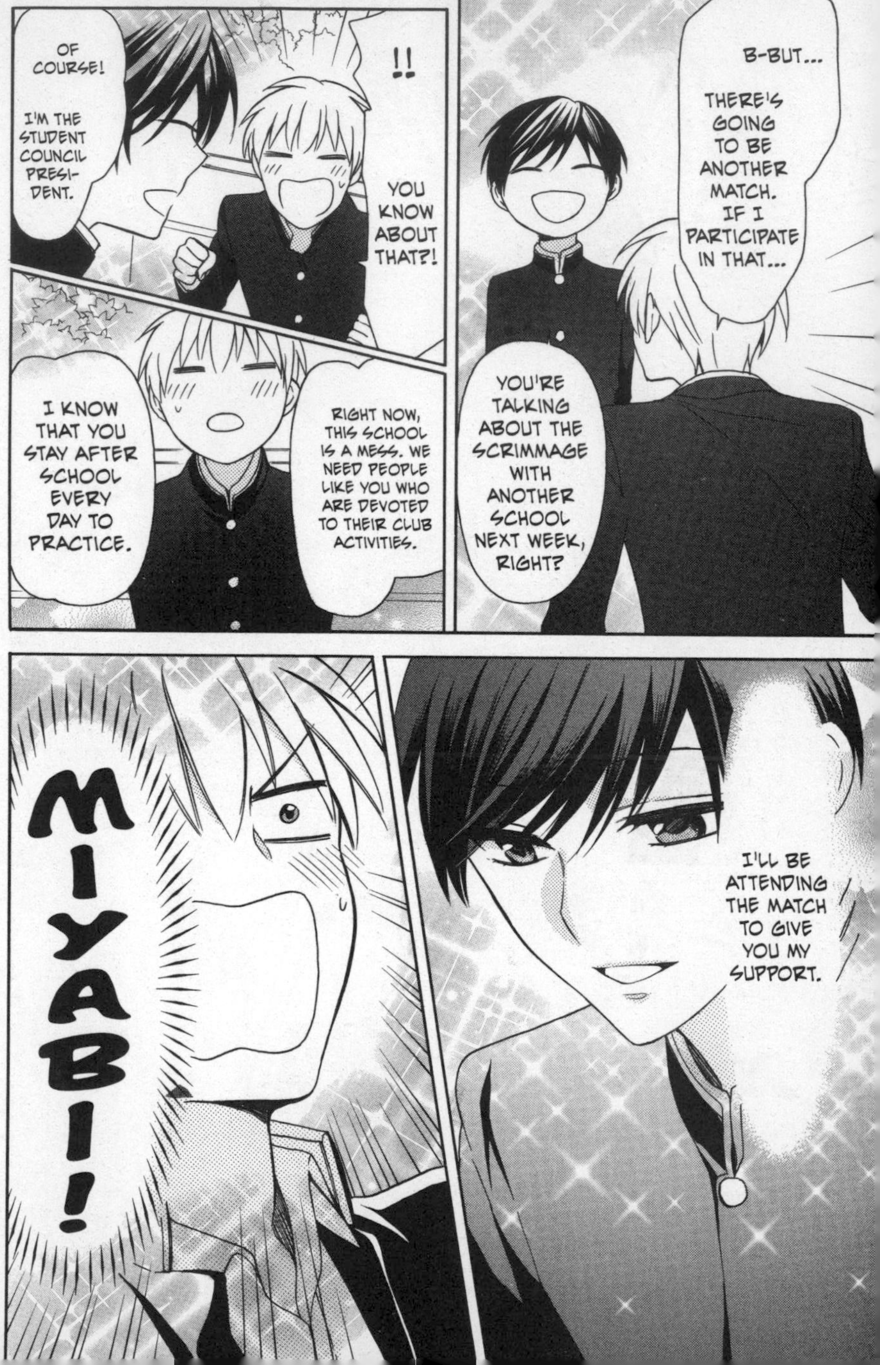
B-BUT...
THERE'S GOING TO BE ANOTHER MATCH. IF I PARTICIPATE IN THAT...
YOU'RE TALKING ABOUT THE SCRIMMAGE WITH ANOTHER SCHOOL NEXT WEEK, RIGHT?
!!
YOU KNOW ABOUT THAT?!
OF COURSE!
I'M THE STUDENT COUNCIL PRESI-DENT.
RIGHT NOW, THIS SCHOOL IS A MESS. WE NEED PEOPLE LIKE YOU WHO ARE DEVOTED TO THEIR CLUB ACTIVITIES.
I KNOW THAT YOU STAY AFTER SCHOOL EVERY DAY TO PRACTICE.
I'LL BE ATTENDING THE MATCH TO GIVE YOU MY SUPPORT.
MIYABI!

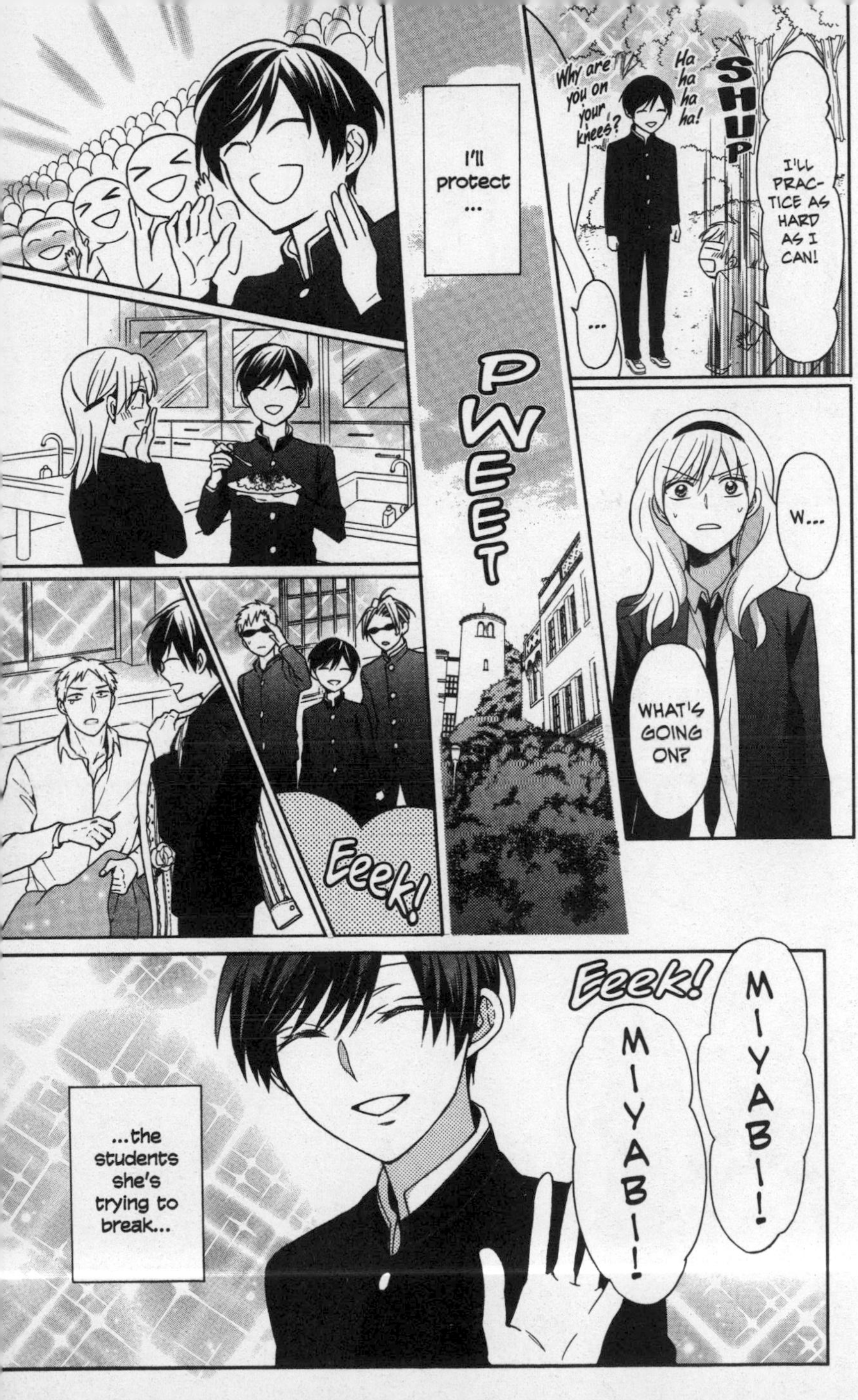
SHUP
I'LL PRACTICE AS HARD AS I CAN!
Ha ha ha ha!
Why are you on your knees?
...
W...
WHAT'S GOING ON?
I'll protect...
PWEET
Eeek!
Eeek!
MIYABI!!
MIYABI!!
...the students she's trying to break...

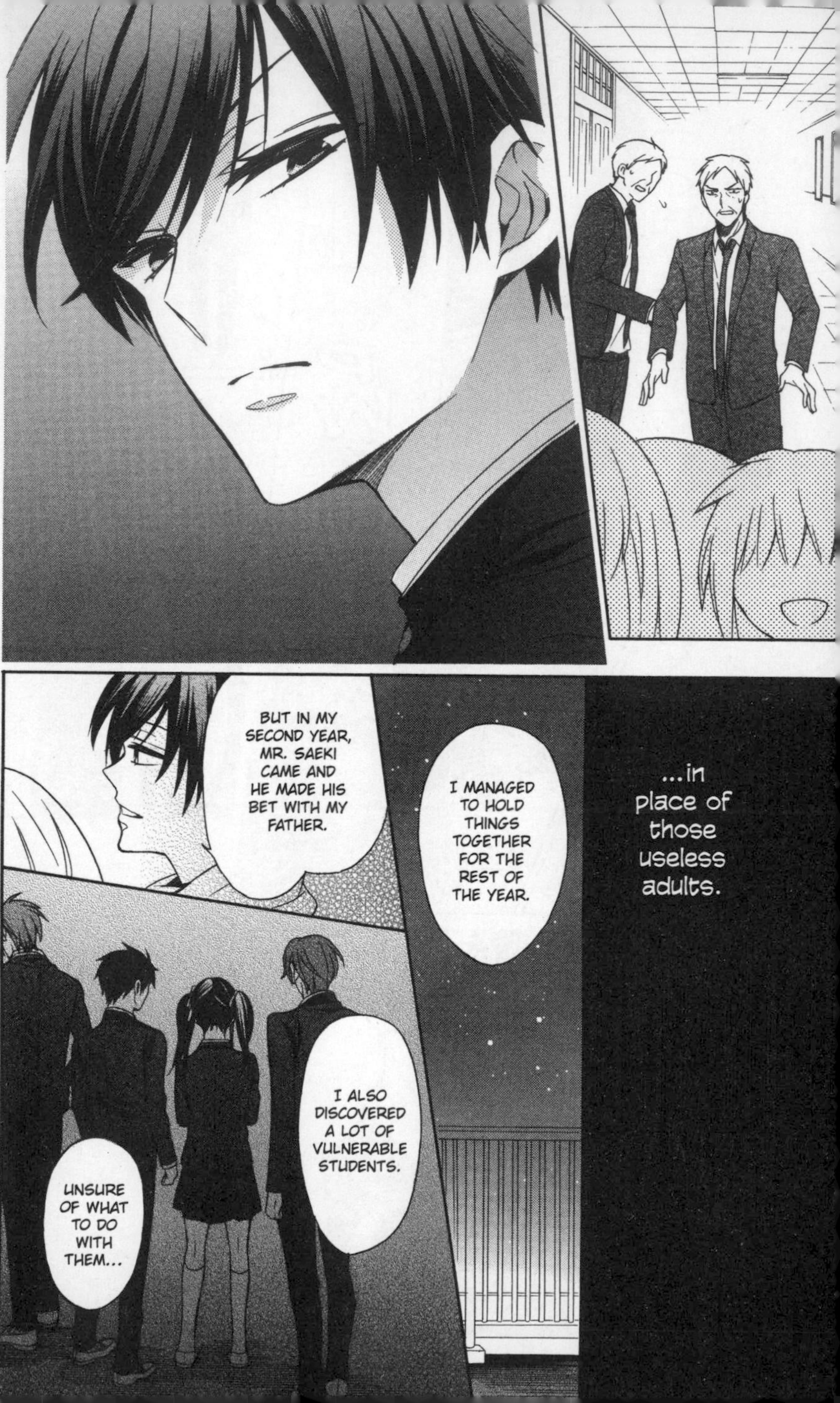
...in place of those useless adults.
I MANAGED TO HOLD THINGS TOGETHER FOR THE REST OF THE YEAR.
BUT IN MY SECOND YEAR, MR. SAEKI CAME AND HE MADE HIS BET WITH MY FATHER.
I ALSO DISCOVERED A LOT OF VULNERABLE STUDENTS.
UNSURE OF WHAT TO DO WITH THEM...

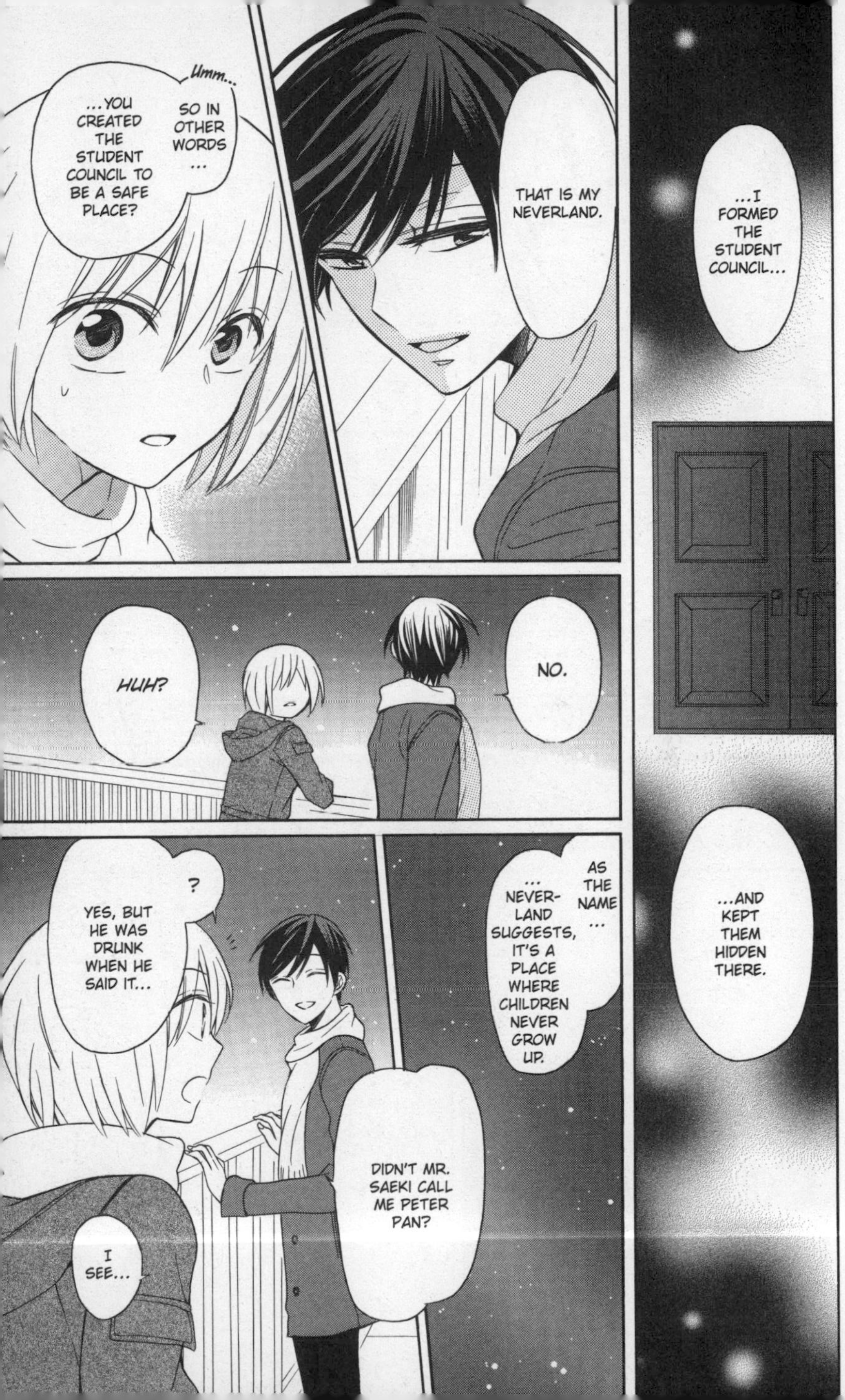
...I FORMED THE STUDENT COUNCIL...
...AND KEPT THEM HIDDEN THERE.
THAT IS MY NEVERLAND.
Umm...
SO IN OTHER WORDS...
...YOU CREATED THE STUDENT COUNCIL TO BE A SAFE PLACE?
NO.
HUH?
AS THE NAME...
...NEVERLAND SUGGESTS, IT'S A PLACE WHERE CHILDREN NEVER GROW UP.
?
DIDN'T MR. SAEKI CALL ME PETER PAN?
YES, BUT HE WAS DRUNK WHEN HE SAID IT...
I SEE...

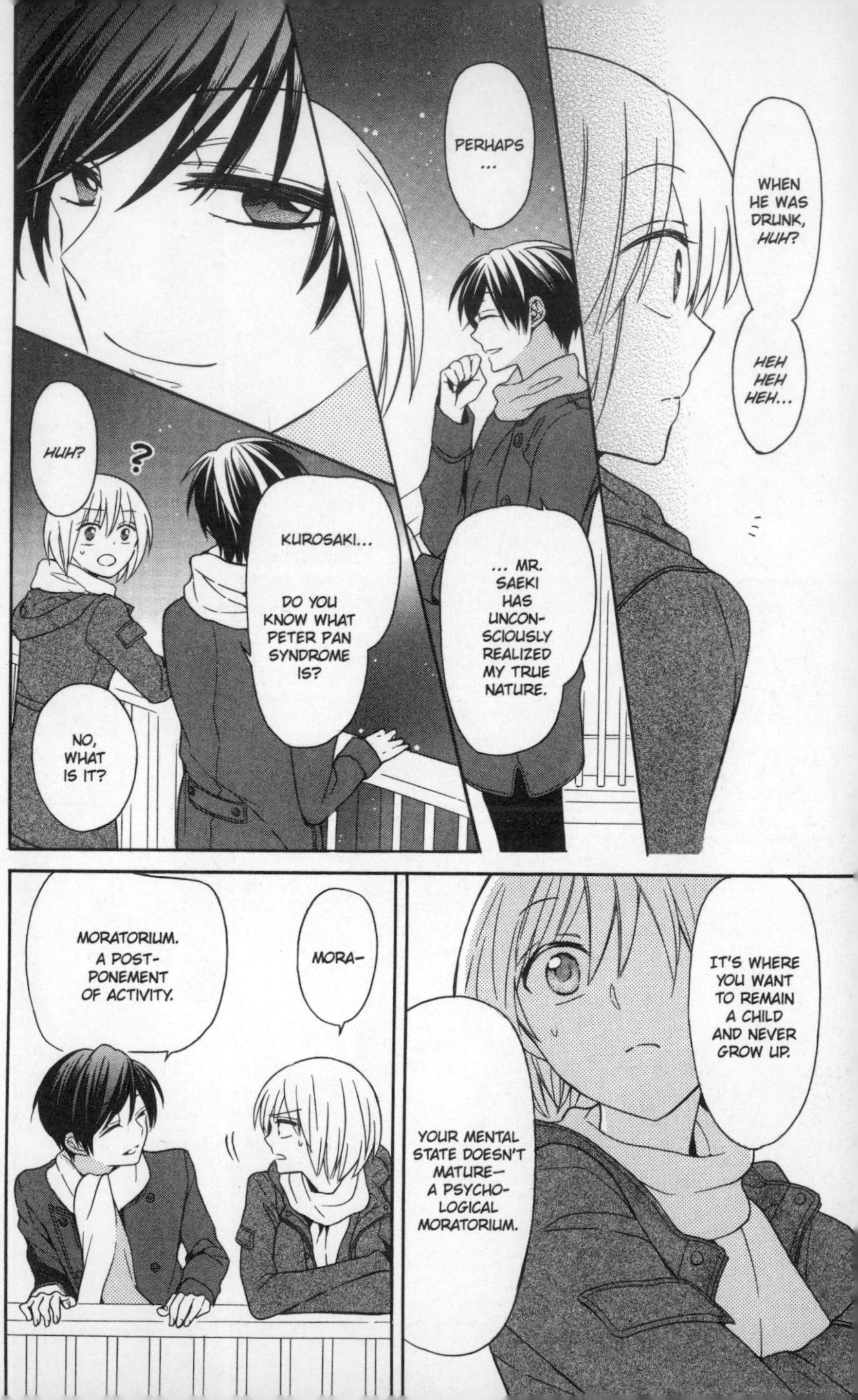
WHEN HE WAS DRUNK, *HUH?*
HEH HEH HEH...
PERHAPS ...
... MR. SAEKI HAS UNCONSCIOUSLY REALIZED MY TRUE NATURE.
KUROSAKI... DO YOU KNOW WHAT PETER PAN SYNDROME IS?
HUH?
NO, WHAT IS IT?
IT'S WHERE YOU WANT TO REMAIN A CHILD AND NEVER GROW UP.
YOUR MENTAL STATE DOESN'T MATURE—A PSYCHOLOGICAL MORATORIUM.
MORA-
MORATORIUM. A POSTPONEMENT OF ACTIVITY.

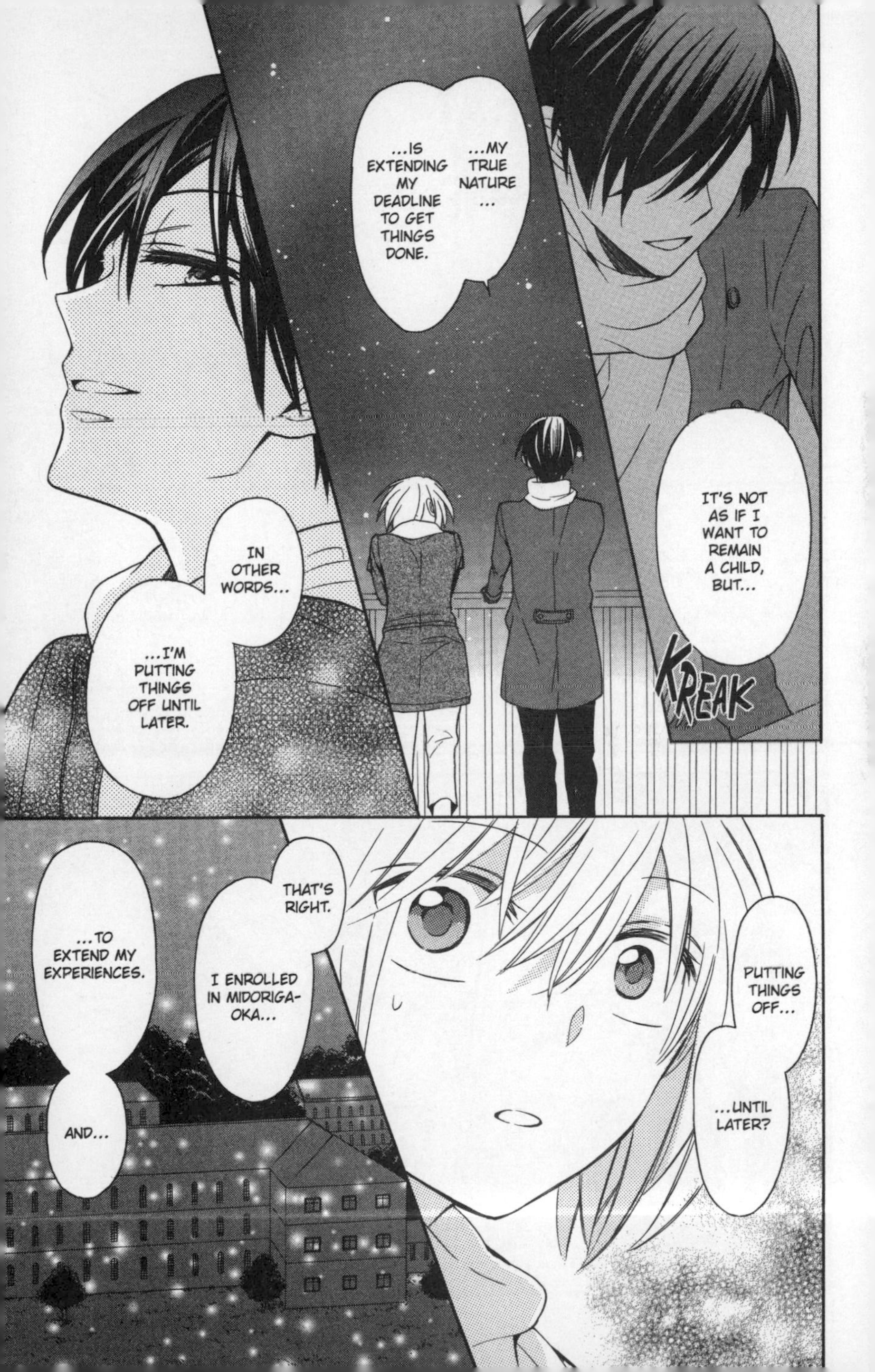
IT'S NOT AS IF I WANT TO REMAIN A CHILD, BUT...
KREAK
...MY TRUE NATURE...
...IS EXTENDING MY DEADLINE TO GET THINGS DONE.
IN OTHER WORDS...
...I'M PUTTING THINGS OFF UNTIL LATER.
PUTTING THINGS OFF...
...UNTIL LATER?
THAT'S RIGHT.
I ENROLLED IN MIDORIGA-OKA...
...TO EXTEND MY EXPERIENCES.
AND...

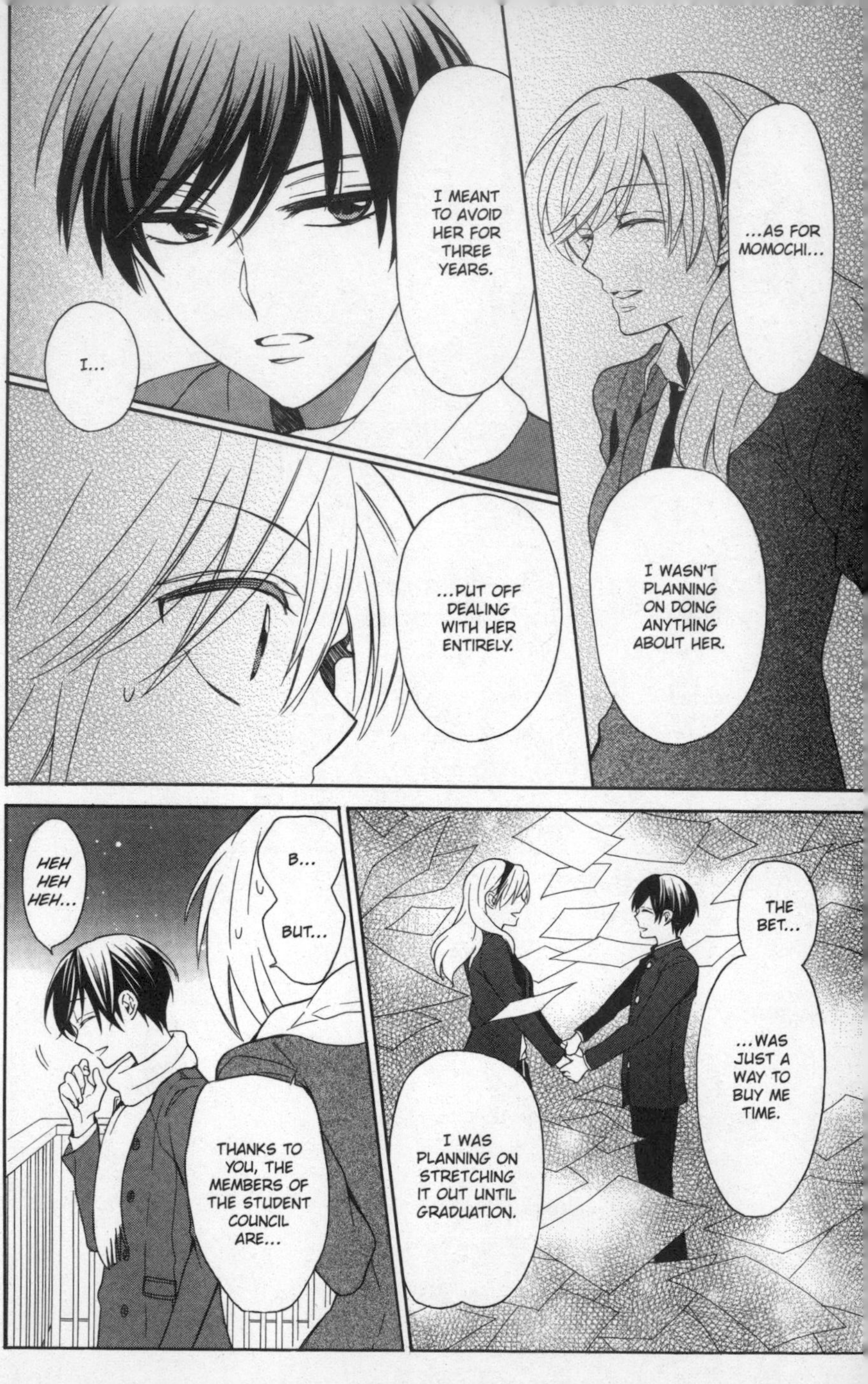
...AS FOR MOMOCHI...
I WASN'T PLANNING ON DOING ANYTHING ABOUT HER.
I MEANT TO AVOID HER FOR THREE YEARS.
I...
...PUT OFF DEALING WITH HER ENTIRELY.
THE BET...
...WAS JUST A WAY TO BUY ME TIME.
I WAS PLANNING ON STRETCHING IT OUT UNTIL GRADUATION.
B...
BUT...
HEH HEH HEH...
THANKS TO YOU, THE MEMBERS OF THE STUDENT COUNCIL ARE...

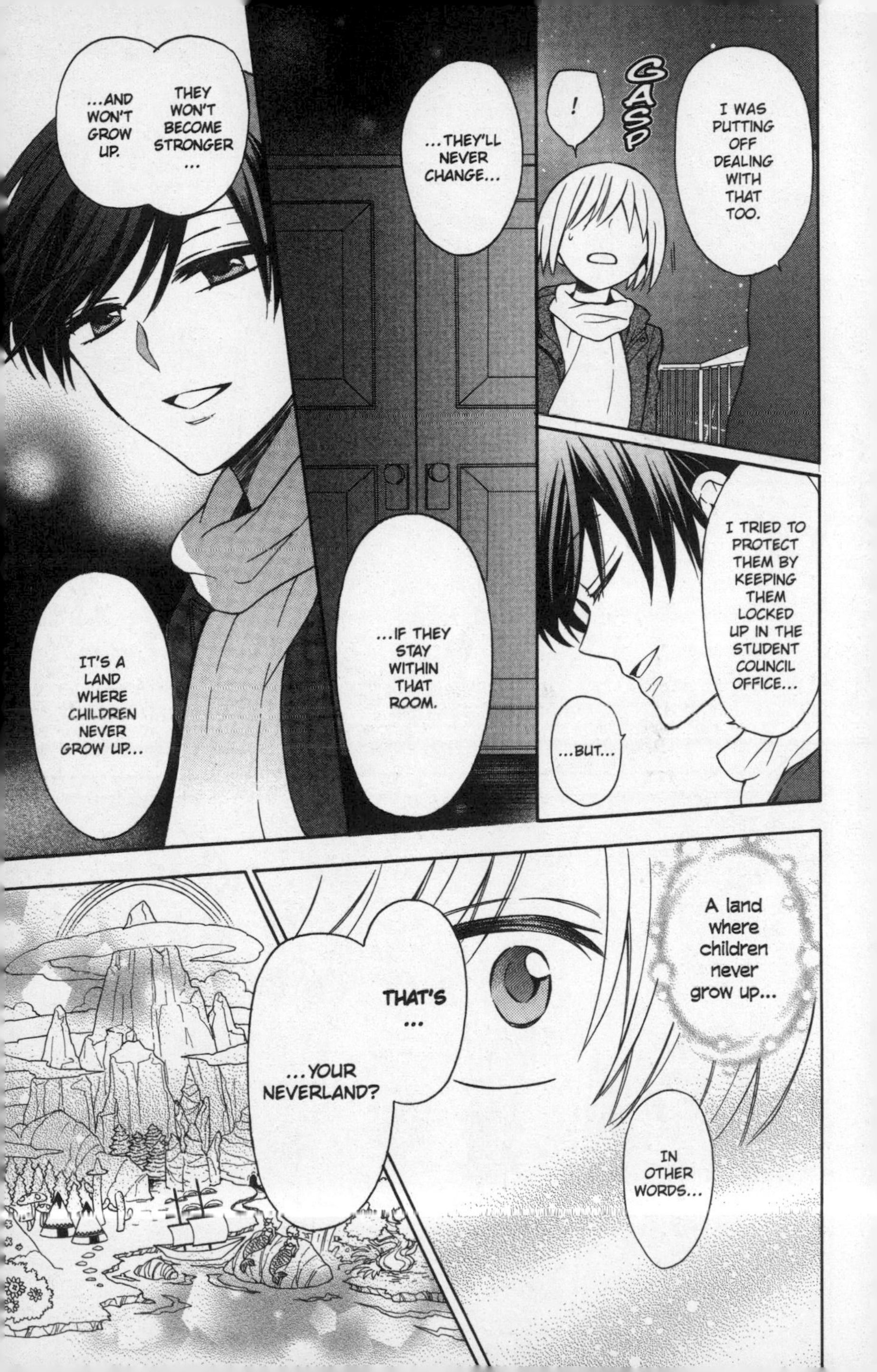
I WAS PUTTING OFF DEALING WITH THAT TOO.
GASP
!
I TRIED TO PROTECT THEM BY KEEPING THEM LOCKED UP IN THE STUDENT COUNCIL OFFICE...
...BUT...
...THEY'LL NEVER CHANGE...
...IF THEY STAY WITHIN THAT ROOM.
THEY WON'T BECOME STRONGER...
...AND WON'T GROW UP.
IT'S A LAND WHERE CHILDREN NEVER GROW UP...
A land where children never grow up...
IN OTHER WORDS...
THAT'S...
...YOUR NEVERLAND?

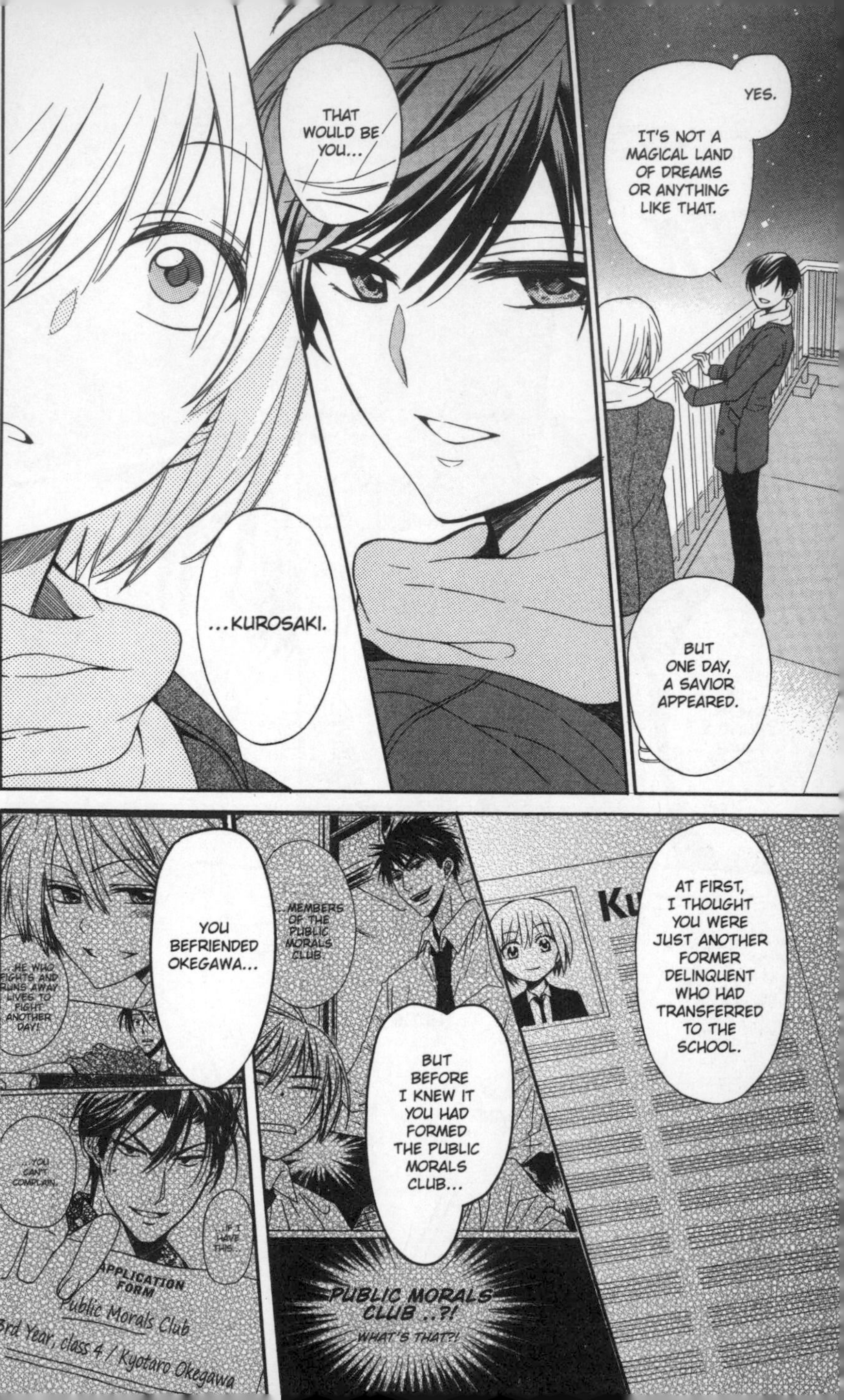
YES.
IT'S NOT A MAGICAL LAND OF DREAMS OR ANYTHING LIKE THAT.
BUT ONE DAY, A SAVIOR APPEARED.
THAT WOULD BE YOU...
...KUROSAKI.
AT FIRST, I THOUGHT YOU WERE JUST ANOTHER FORMER DELINQUENT WHO HAD TRANSFERRED TO THE SCHOOL.
BUT BEFORE I KNEW IT YOU HAD FORMED THE PUBLIC MORALS CLUB...
PUBLIC MORALS CLUB ..?!
WHAT'S THAT?!
YOU BEFRIENDED OKEGAWA...
...MEMBERS OF THE PUBLIC MORALS CLUB.
...HE WHO FIGHTS AND RUNS AWAY LIVES TO FIGHT ANOTHER DAY!
...YOU CAN'T COMPLAIN.
...IF I HAVE THIS...
APPLICATION FORM
Public Morals Club
3rd Year, class 4 / Kyotaro Okegawa

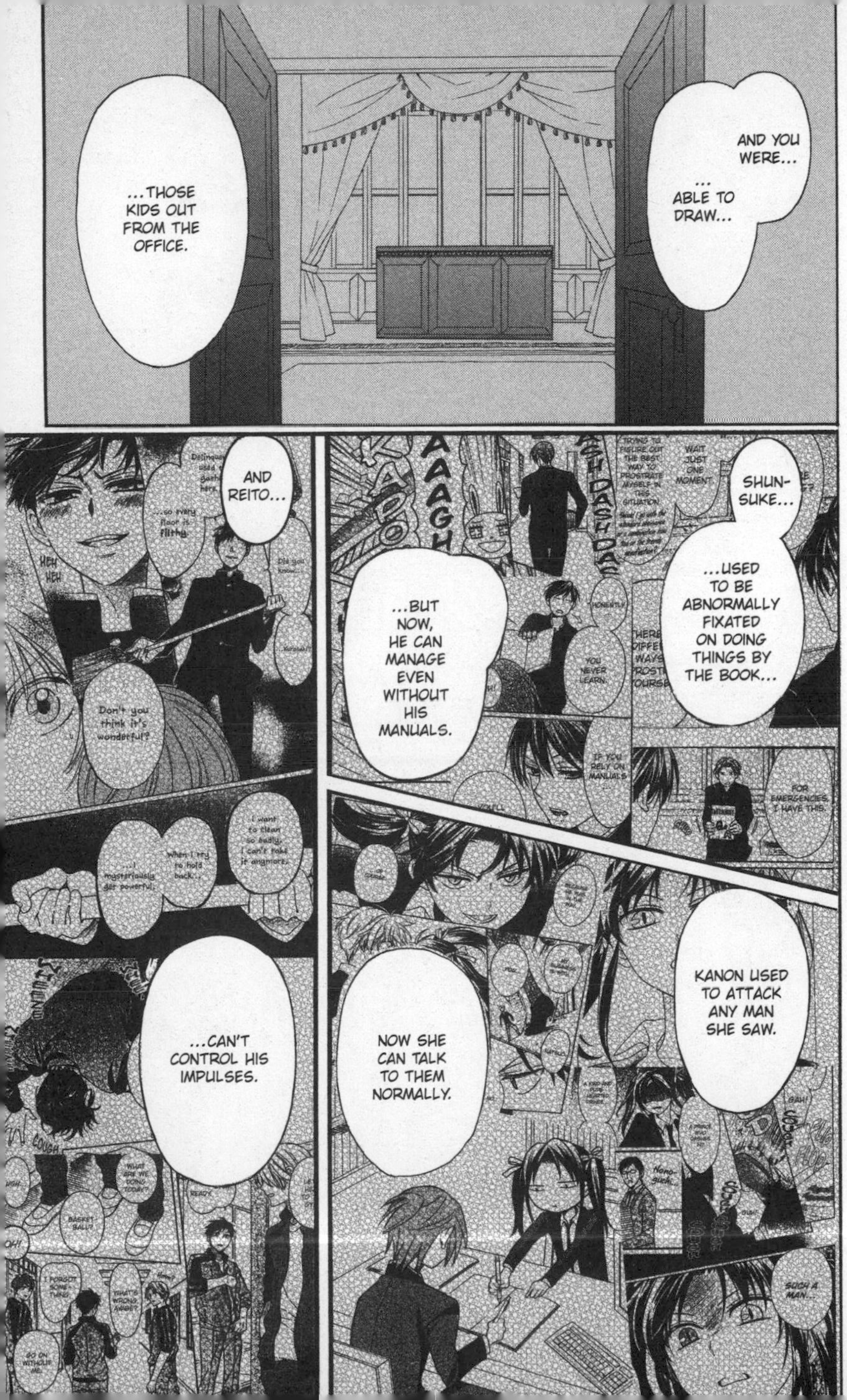
AND YOU WERE...
...ABLE TO DRAW...
...THOSE KIDS OUT FROM THE OFFICE.
SHUN-SUKE...
...USED TO BE ABNORMALLY FIXATED ON DOING THINGS BY THE BOOK...
WAIT JUST ONE MOMENT.
TRYING TO FIGURE OUT THE BEST WAY TO PROSTRATE MYSELF IN THIS SITUATION.
DASH DASH
AAAGH
FOR EMERGENCIES, I HAVE THIS.
HONESTLY.
YOU NEVER LEARN.
IF YOU RELY ON MANUALS...
...BUT NOW, HE CAN MANAGE EVEN WITHOUT HIS MANUALS.
AND REITO...
...so every floor is filthy.
Did you know...
HEH HEH
Don't you think it's wonderful?
KANON USED TO ATTACK ANY MAN SHE SAW.
GAH!
Nono-guchi...
Such a man...
NOW SHE CAN TALK TO THEM NORMALLY.
I want to clean so badly, I can't take it anymore.
When I try to hold back...
...I mysteriously get powerful.
...CAN'T CONTROL HIS IMPULSES.
COUGH
WHAT ARE WE DOING TODAY?
BASKET-BALL?
READY
WHAT'S WRONG, AMANE?
I FORGOT SOME-THING!
GO ON WITHOUT ME.

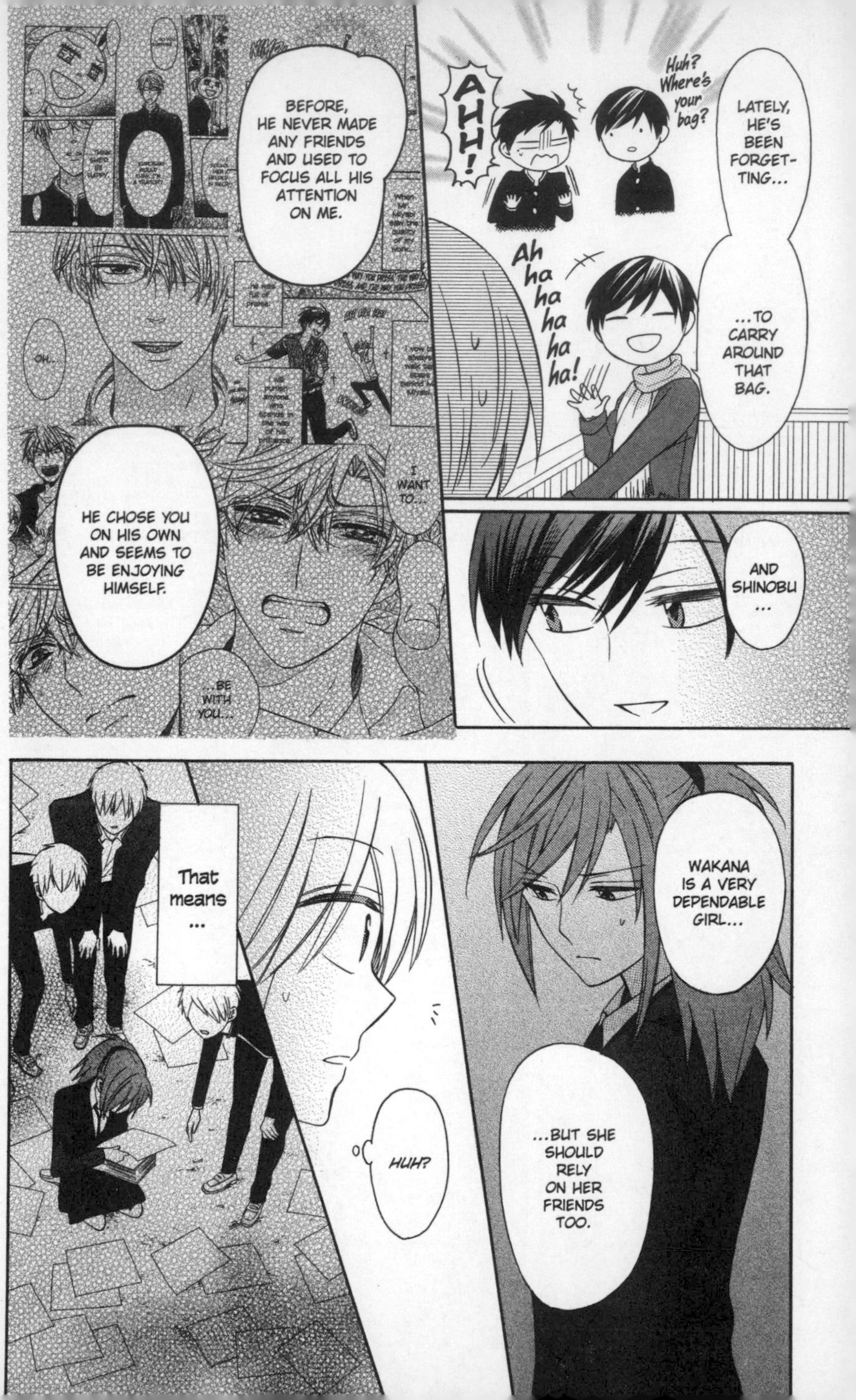
LATELY, HE'S BEEN FORGET-TING...
Huh? Where's your bag?
AHH!
...TO CARRY AROUND THAT BAG.
Ah ha ha ha ha ha!
AND SHINOBU...
BEFORE, HE NEVER MADE ANY FRIENDS AND USED TO FOCUS ALL HIS ATTENTION ON ME.
OH...
I WANT TO...
HE CHOSE YOU ON HIS OWN AND SEEMS TO BE ENJOYING HIMSELF.
...BE WITH YOU...
WAKANA IS A VERY DEPENDABLE GIRL...
...BUT SHE SHOULD RELY ON HER FRIENDS TOO.
HUH?
That means...

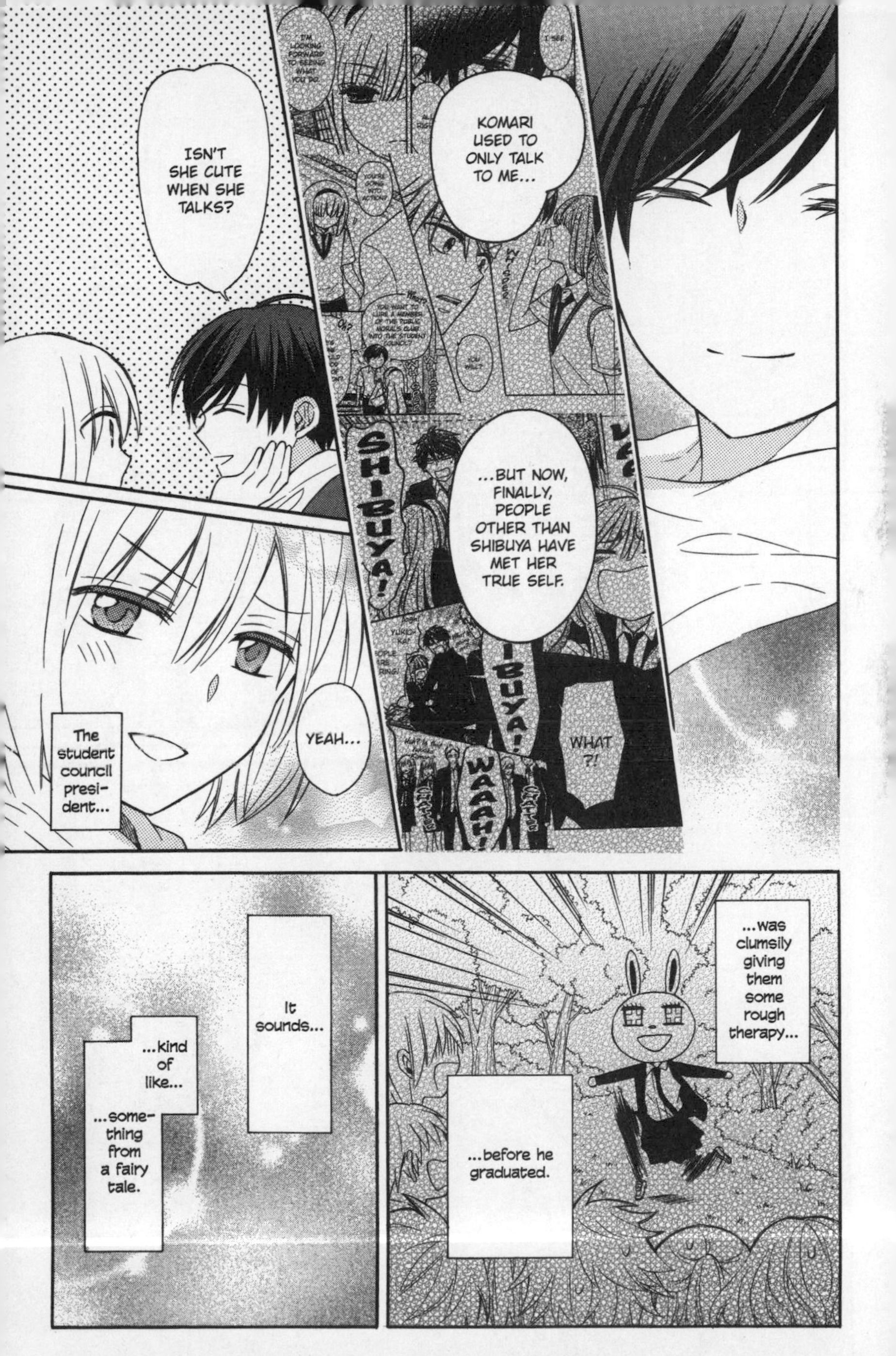
I SEE.
I'M LOOKING FORWARD TO SEEING WHAT YOU DO.
KOMARI USED TO ONLY TALK TO ME...
YOU WANT TO LURE A MEMBER OF THE PUBLIC MORALS CLUB INTO THE STUDENT COUNCIL?
SHIBUYA!
...BUT NOW, FINALLY, PEOPLE OTHER THAN SHIBUYA HAVE MET HER TRUE SELF.
SHIBUYA!
WHAT?!
WAAAH!
ISN'T SHE CUTE WHEN SHE TALKS?
YEAH...
The student council president...
...was clumsily giving them some rough therapy...
...before he graduated.
It sounds...
...kind of like...
...something from a fairy tale.

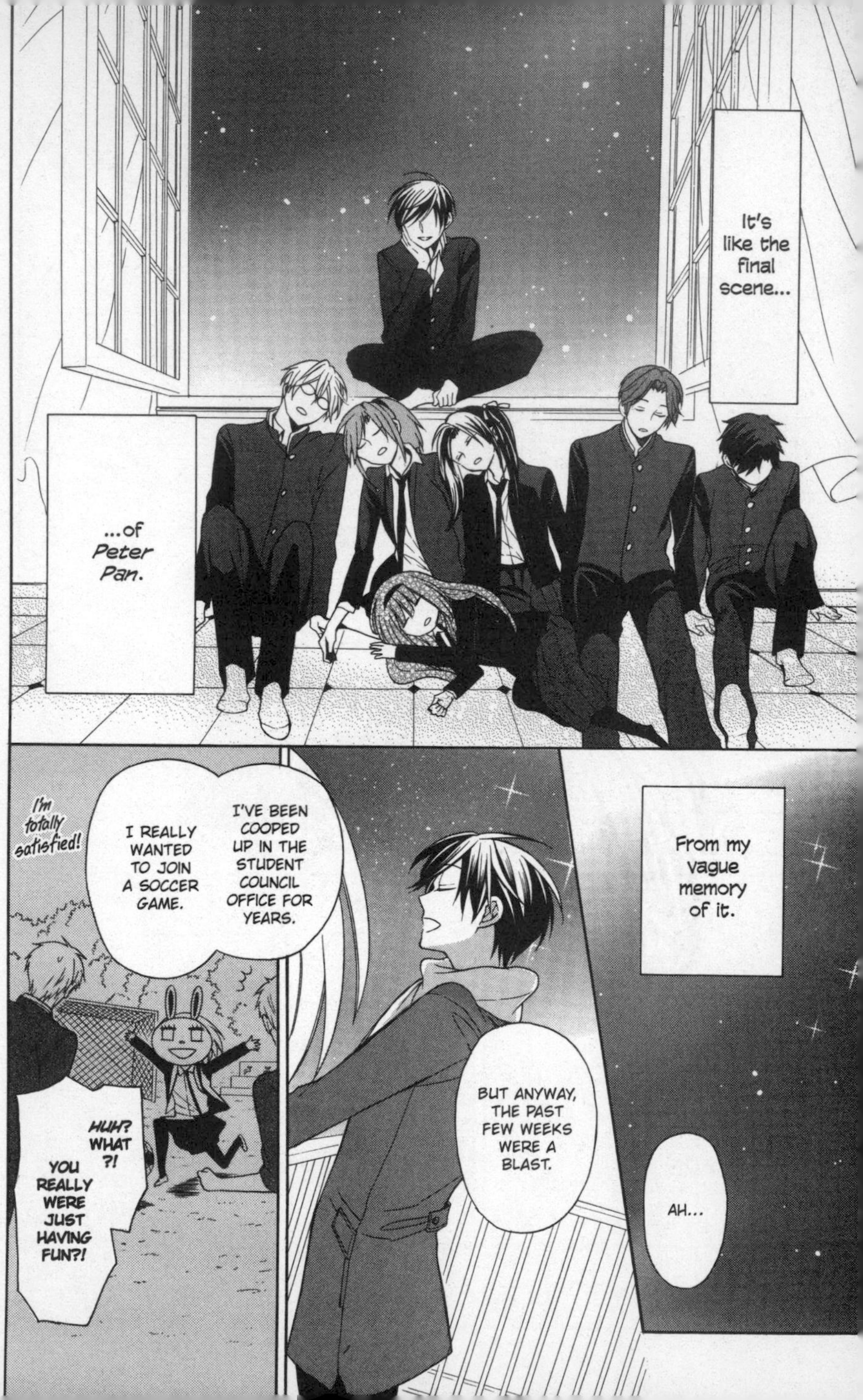
It's like the final scene...
...of *Peter Pan*.
From my vague memory of it.
AH...
BUT ANYWAY, THE PAST FEW WEEKS WERE A BLAST.
I'VE BEEN COOPED UP IN THE STUDENT COUNCIL OFFICE FOR YEARS.
I REALLY WANTED TO JOIN A SOCCER GAME.
I'm totally satisfied!
HUH? WHAT?!
YOU REALLY WERE JUST HAVING FUN?!

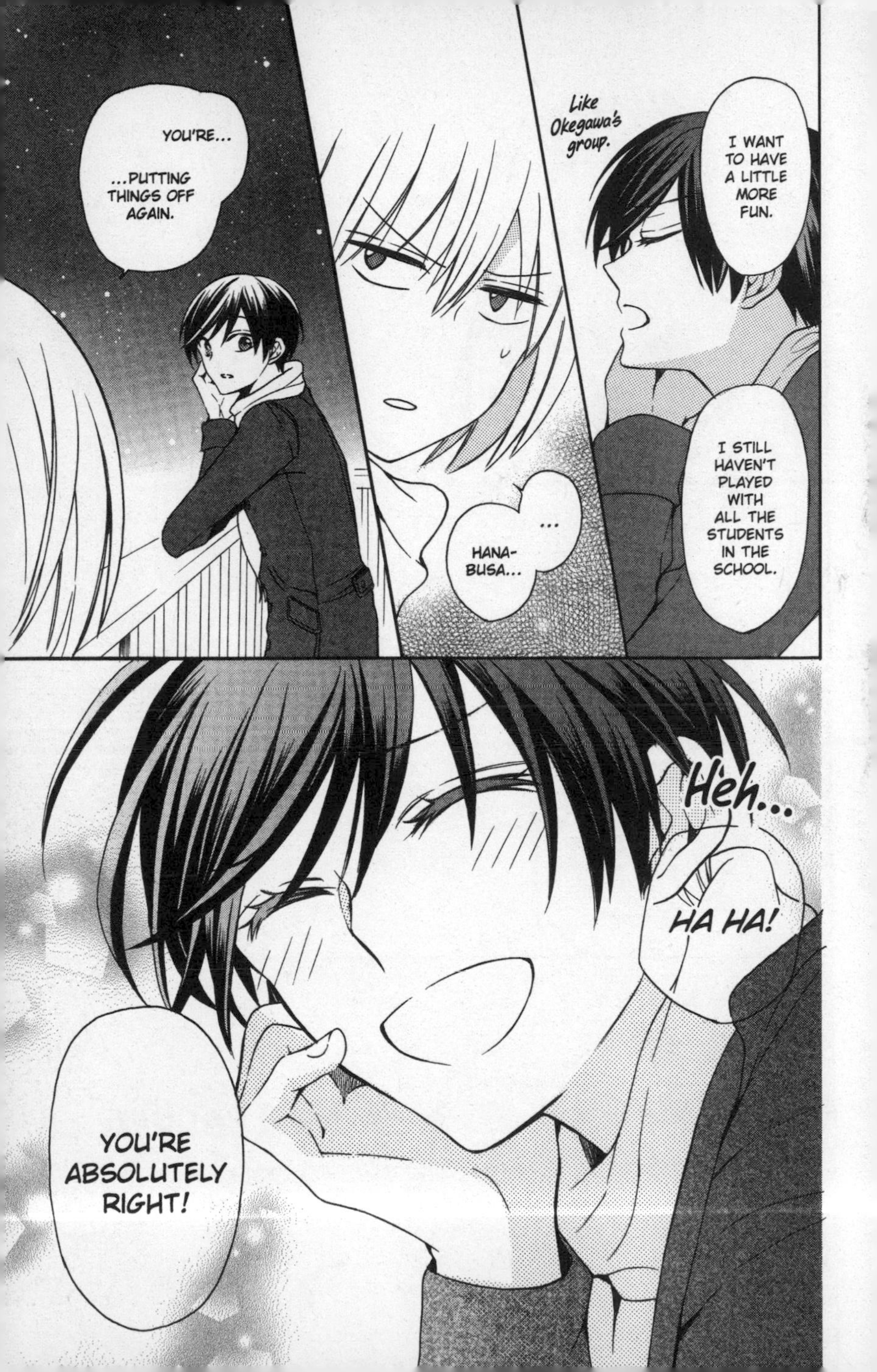
I WANT TO HAVE A LITTLE MORE FUN.
Like Okegawa's group.
I STILL HAVEN'T PLAYED WITH ALL THE STUDENTS IN THE SCHOOL.
... HANA-BUSA...
YOU'RE...
...PUTTING THINGS OFF AGAIN.
Heh...
HA HA!
YOU'RE ABSOLUTELY RIGHT!

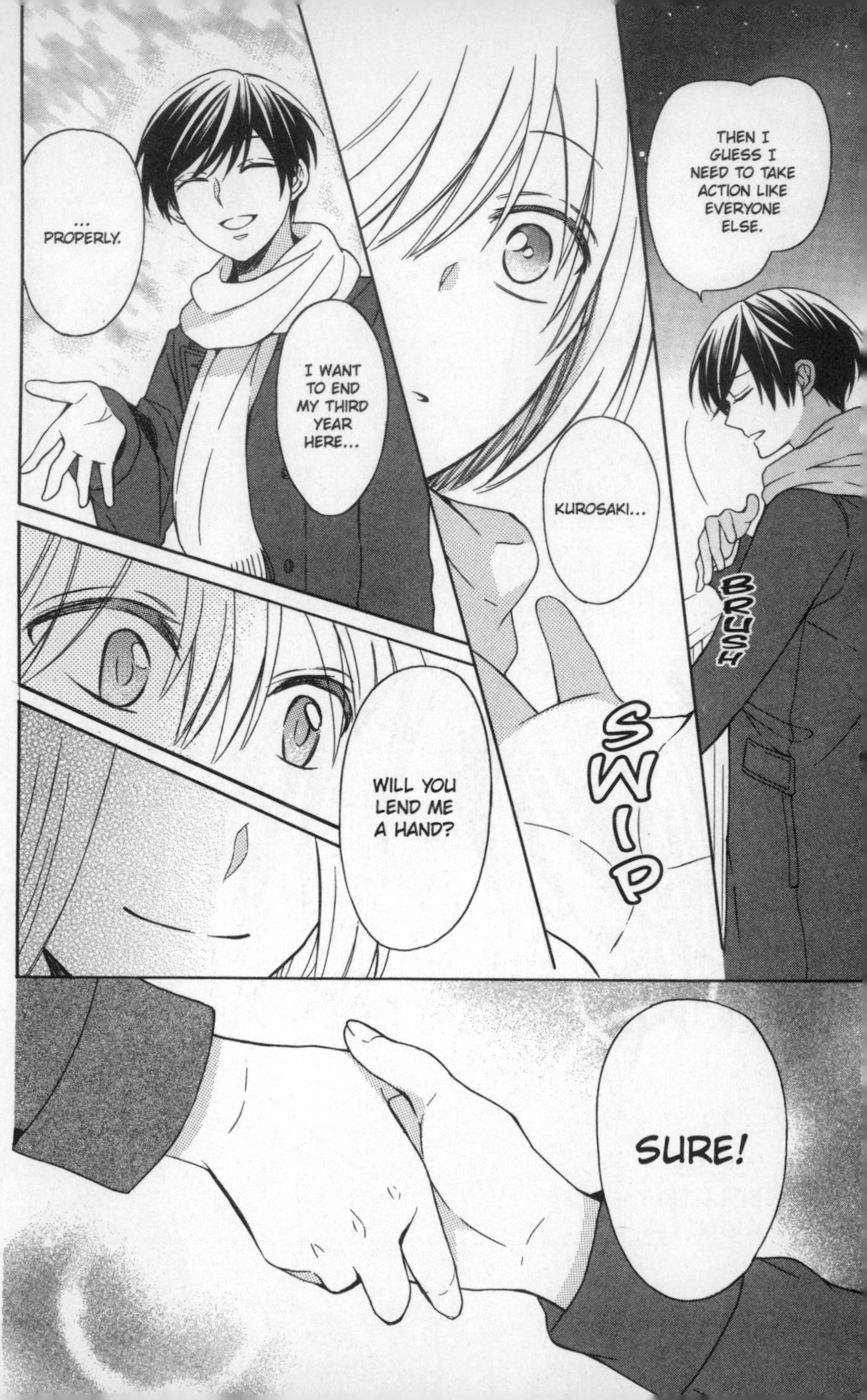
THEN I GUESS I NEED TO TAKE ACTION LIKE EVERYONE ELSE.
BRUSH
KUROSAKI...
SWIP
I WANT TO END MY THIRD YEAR HERE...
...PROPERLY.
WILL YOU LEND ME A HAND?
SURE!

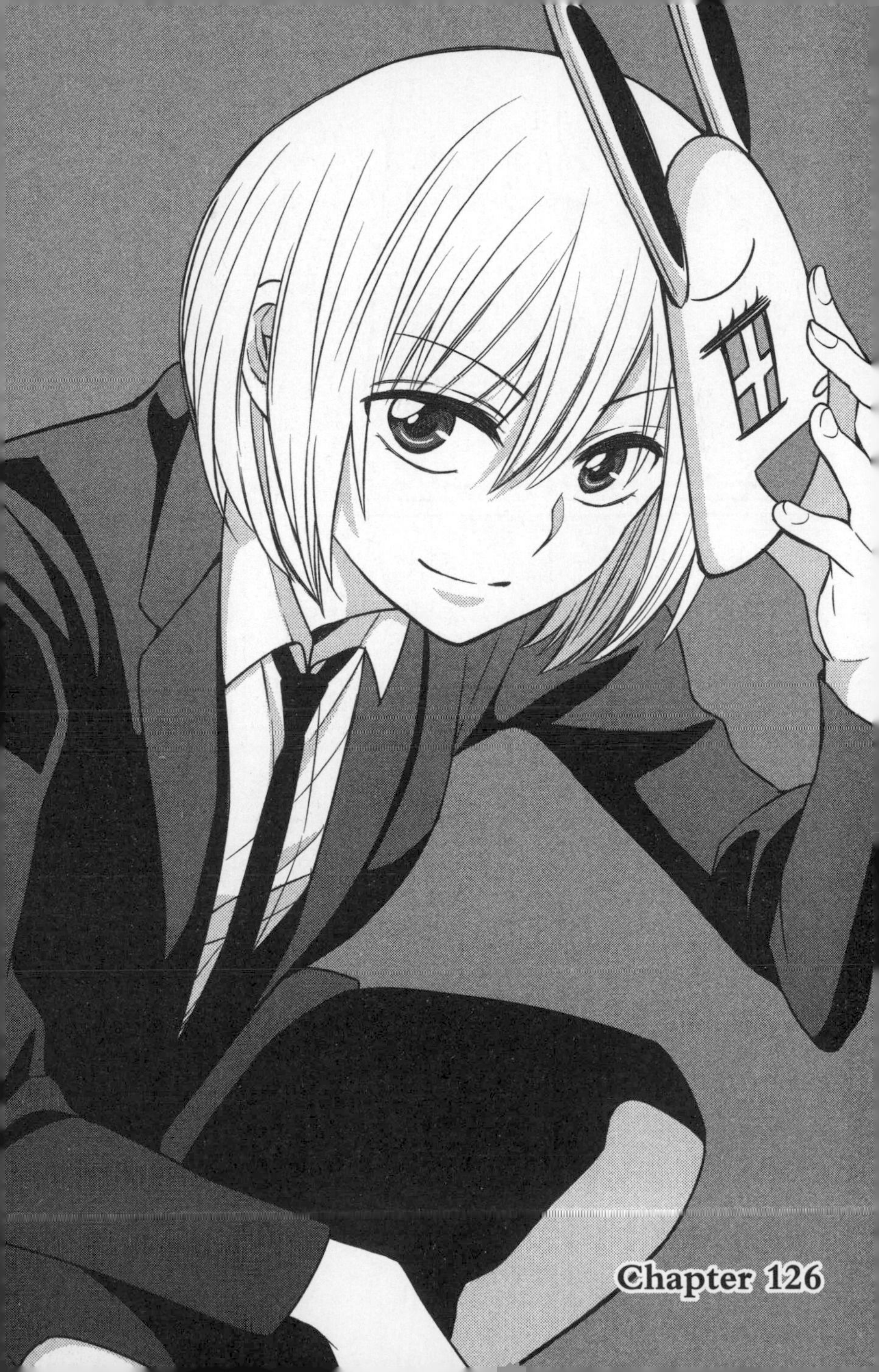
Chapter 126

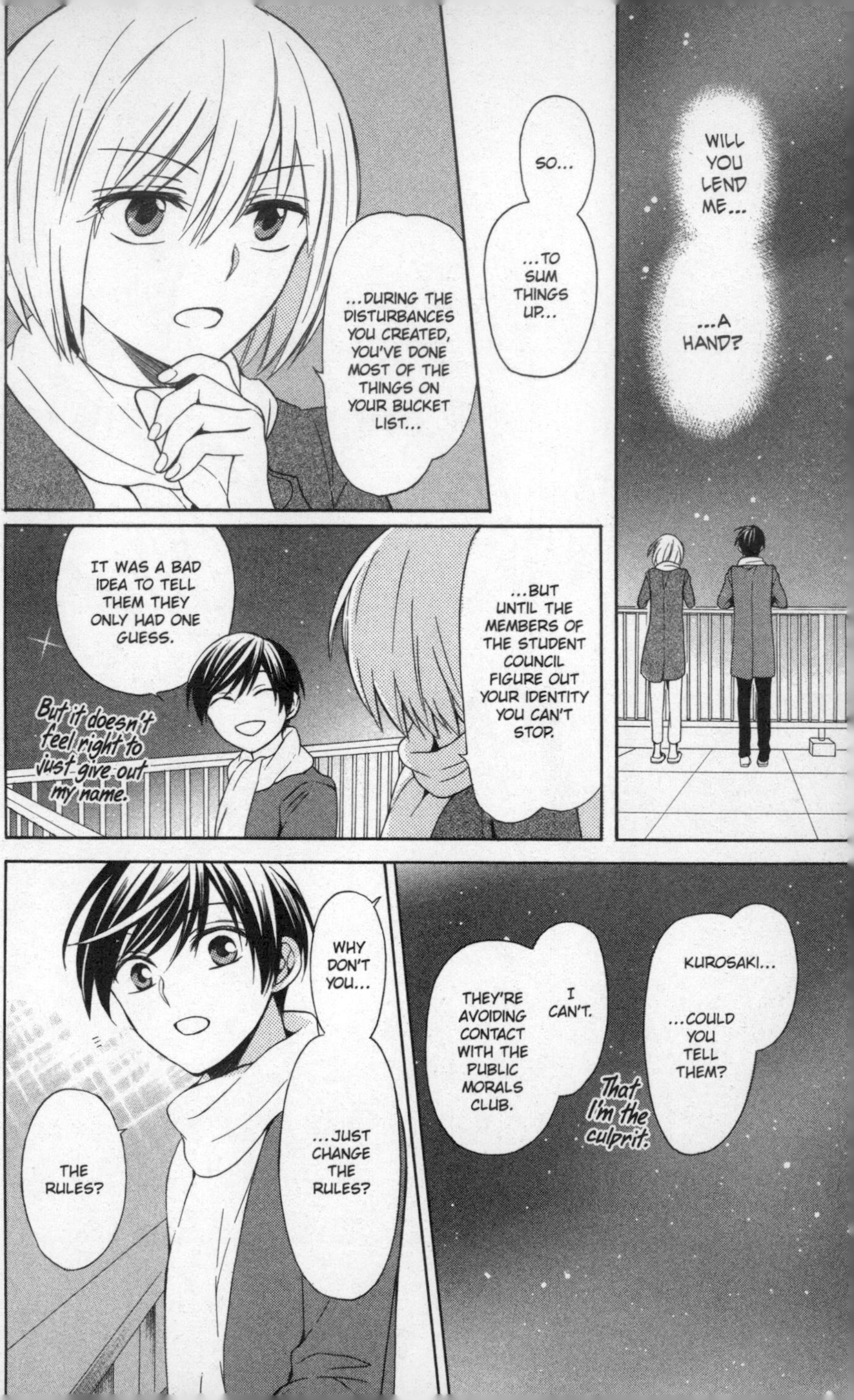
WILL YOU LEND ME...
...A HAND?
SO...
...TO SUM THINGS UP...
...DURING THE DISTURBANCES YOU CREATED, YOU'VE DONE MOST OF THE THINGS ON YOUR BUCKET LIST...
...BUT UNTIL THE MEMBERS OF THE STUDENT COUNCIL FIGURE OUT YOUR IDENTITY YOU CAN'T STOP.
IT WAS A BAD IDEA TO TELL THEM THEY ONLY HAD ONE GUESS.
But it doesn't feel right to just give out my name.
KUROSAKI...
...COULD YOU TELL THEM?
That I'm the culprit.
I CAN'T.
THEY'RE AVOIDING CONTACT WITH THE PUBLIC MORALS CLUB.
WHY DON'T YOU...
...JUST CHANGE THE RULES?
THE RULES?

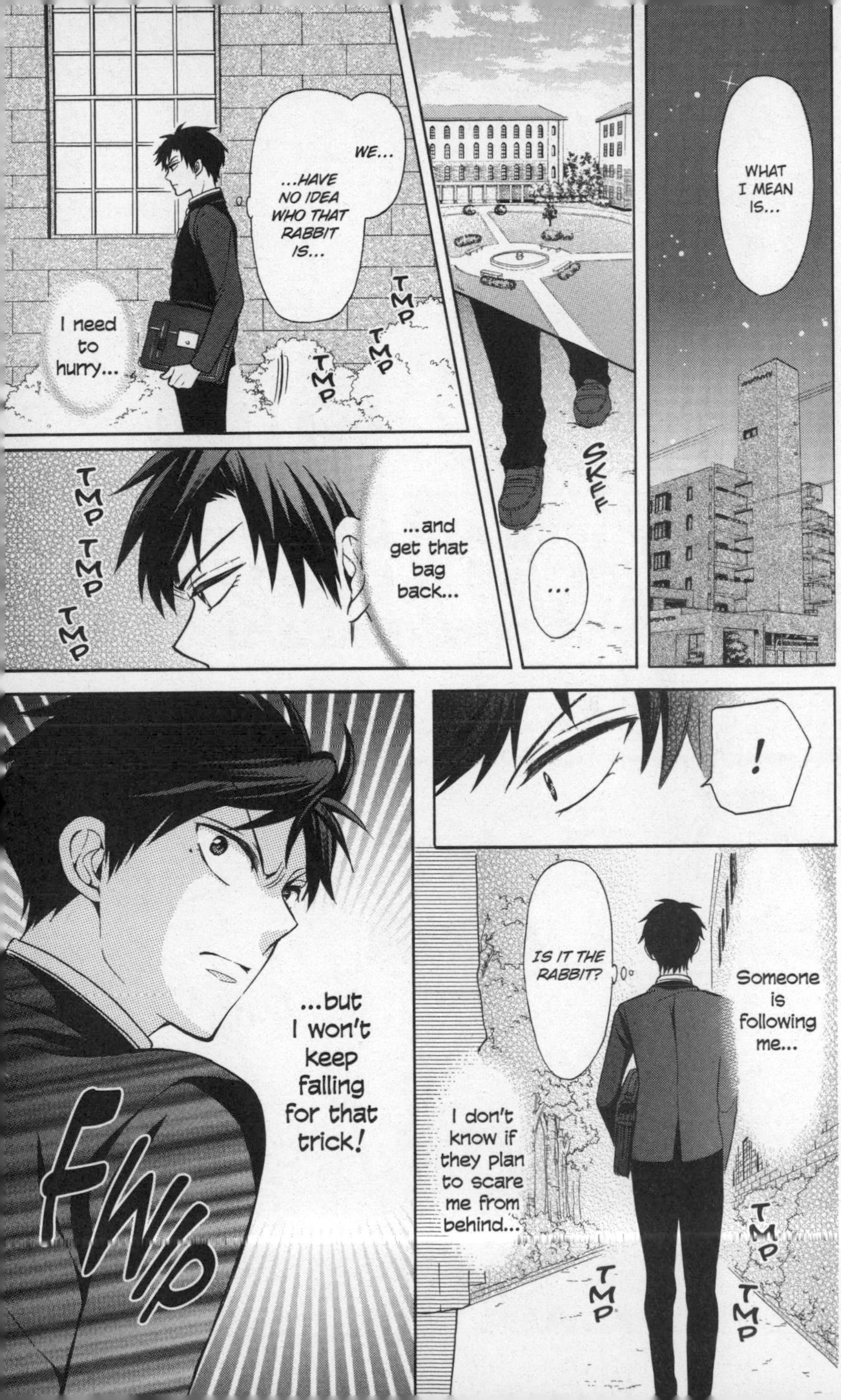
WHAT I MEAN IS...
...
SKFF
WE...
...HAVE NO IDEA WHO THAT RABBIT IS...
I need to hurry...
TMP TMP TMP
TMP TMP TMP
...and get that bag back...
!
Someone is following me...
IS IT THE RABBIT?
I don't know if they plan to scare me from behind...
TMP TMP TMP
...but I won't keep falling for that trick!
FWIP

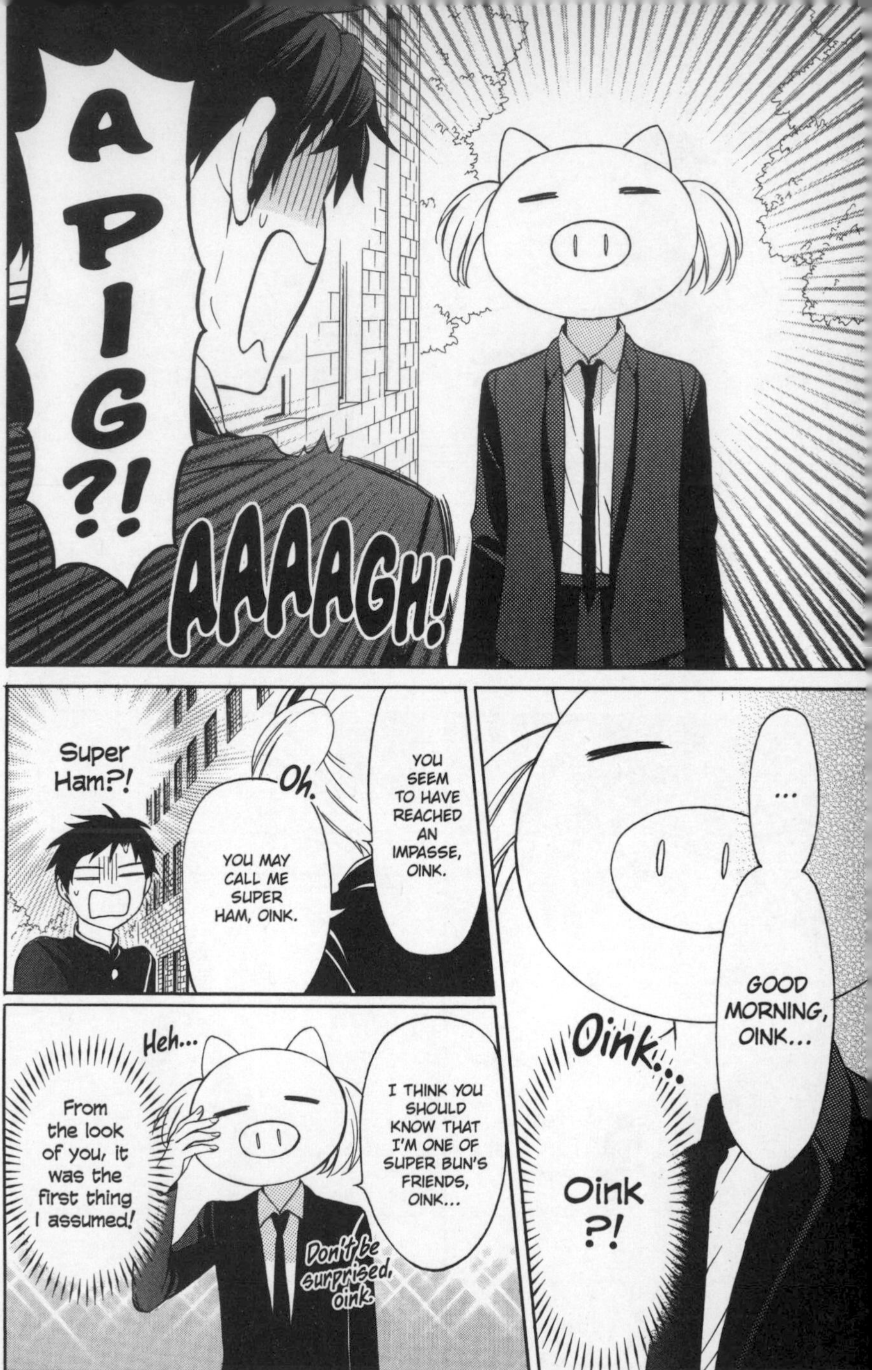
A PIG?!
AAAAGH!
...
GOOD MORNING, OINK...
Oink...
Oink ?!
YOU SEEM TO HAVE REACHED AN IMPASSE, OINK.
Oh.
YOU MAY CALL ME SUPER HAM, OINK.
Super Ham?!
I THINK YOU SHOULD KNOW THAT I'M ONE OF SUPER BUN'S FRIENDS, OINK...
Heh...
From the look of you, it was the first thing I assumed!
Don't be surprised, oink

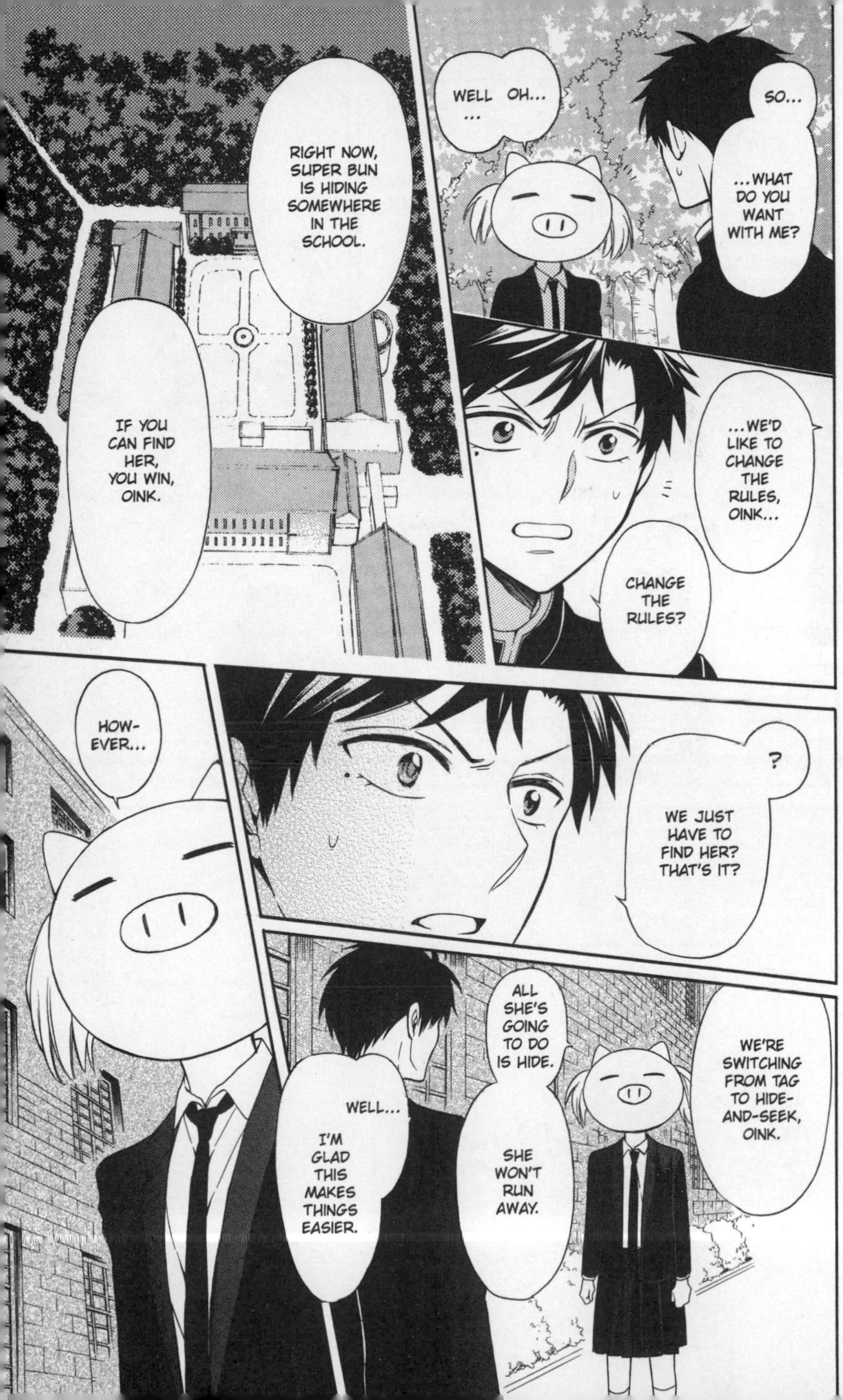
SO...
...WHAT DO YOU WANT WITH ME?
WELL OH... ...
...WE'D LIKE TO CHANGE THE RULES, OINK...
CHANGE THE RULES?
RIGHT NOW, SUPER BUN IS HIDING SOMEWHERE IN THE SCHOOL.
IF YOU CAN FIND HER, YOU WIN, OINK.
?
WE JUST HAVE TO FIND HER? THAT'S IT?
WE'RE SWITCHING FROM TAG TO HIDE-AND-SEEK, OINK.
ALL SHE'S GOING TO DO IS HIDE.
SHE WON'T RUN AWAY.
WELL...
I'M GLAD THIS MAKES THINGS EASIER.
HOW-EVER...

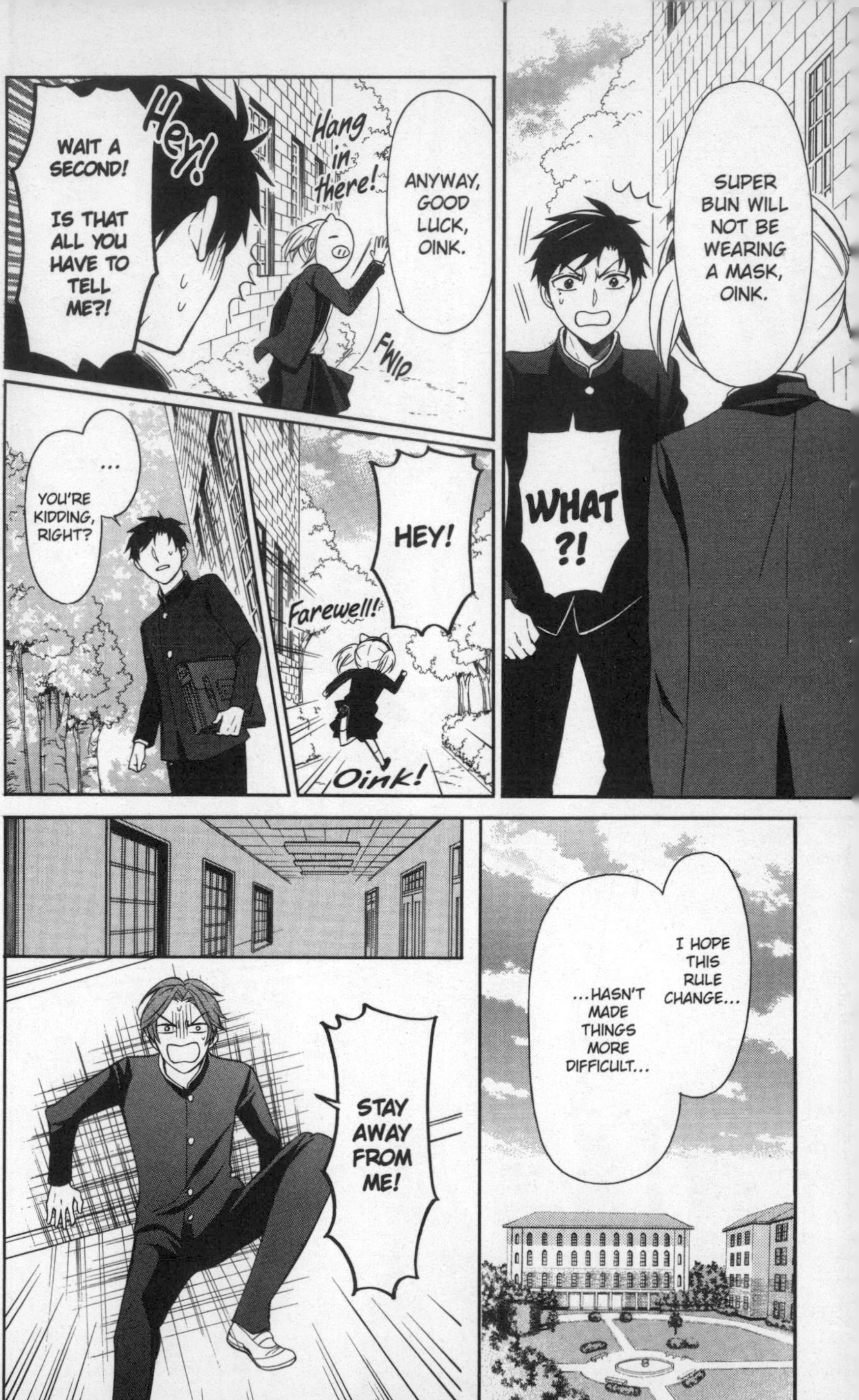

SUPER BUN WILL NOT BE WEARING A MASK, OINK.
WHAT?!
ANYWAY, GOOD LUCK, OINK.
Hang in there!
Hey!
WAIT A SECOND!
IS THAT ALL YOU HAVE TO TELL ME?!
FWIP
HEY!
Farewell!
Oink!
...
YOU'RE KIDDING, RIGHT?
I HOPE THIS RULE CHANGE...
...HASN'T MADE THINGS MORE DIFFICULT...
STAY AWAY FROM ME!

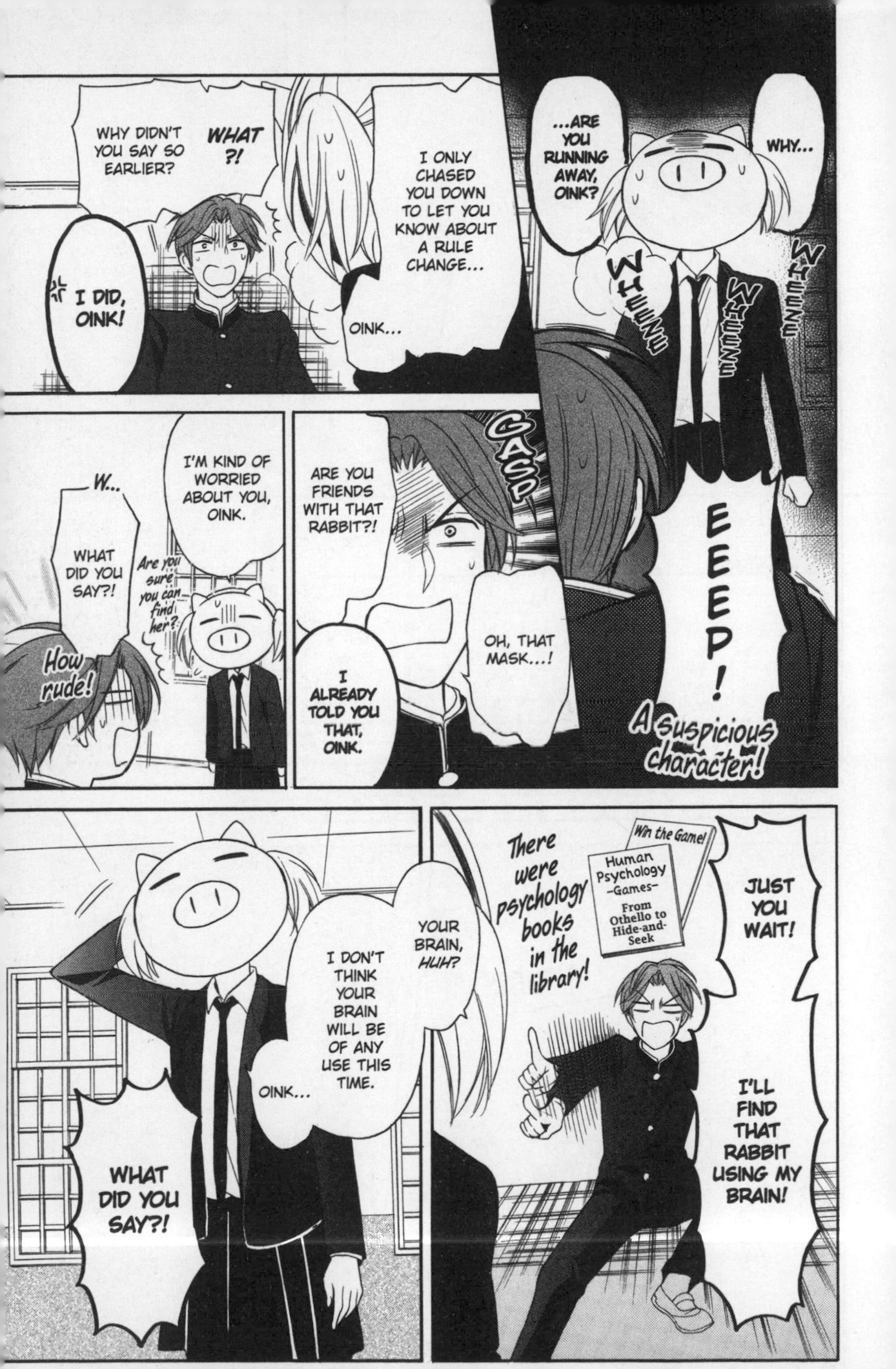
WHY...
...ARE YOU RUNNING AWAY, OINK?
WHEEZE
WHEEZE
WHEEZE
GASP
EEEP!
A suspicious character!
I ONLY CHASED YOU DOWN TO LET YOU KNOW ABOUT A RULE CHANGE...
OINK...
WHAT?!
WHY DIDN'T YOU SAY SO EARLIER?
I DID, OINK!
OH, THAT MASK...!
ARE YOU FRIENDS WITH THAT RABBIT?!
I ALREADY TOLD YOU THAT, OINK.
I'M KIND OF WORRIED ABOUT YOU, OINK.
W...
WHAT DID YOU SAY?!
Are you sure you can find her?
How rude!
There were psychology books in the library!
Win the Game!
Human Psychology -Games- From Othello to Hide-and-Seek
JUST YOU WAIT!
I'LL FIND THAT RABBIT USING MY BRAIN!
YOUR BRAIN, HUH?
I DON'T THINK YOUR BRAIN WILL BE OF ANY USE THIS TIME.
OINK...
WHAT DID YOU SAY?!

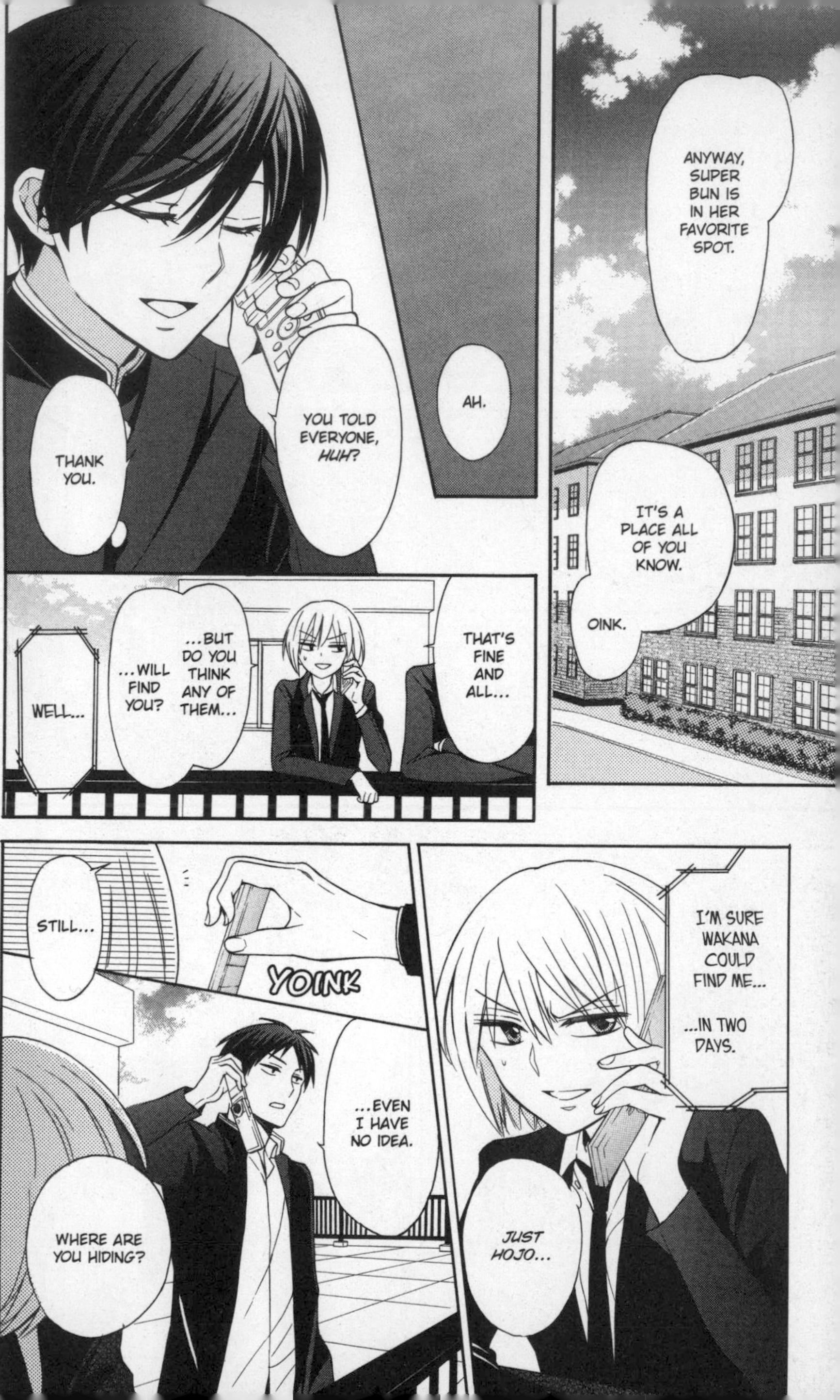
ANYWAY, SUPER BUN IS IN HER FAVORITE SPOT.
IT'S A PLACE ALL OF YOU KNOW.
OINK.
AH.
YOU TOLD EVERYONE, *HUH?*
THANK YOU.
THAT'S FINE AND ALL...
...BUT DO YOU THINK ANY OF THEM...
...WILL FIND YOU?
WELL...
I'M SURE WAKANA COULD FIND ME...
...IN TWO DAYS.
JUST HOJO...
YOINK
STILL...
...EVEN I HAVE NO IDEA.
WHERE ARE YOU HIDING?

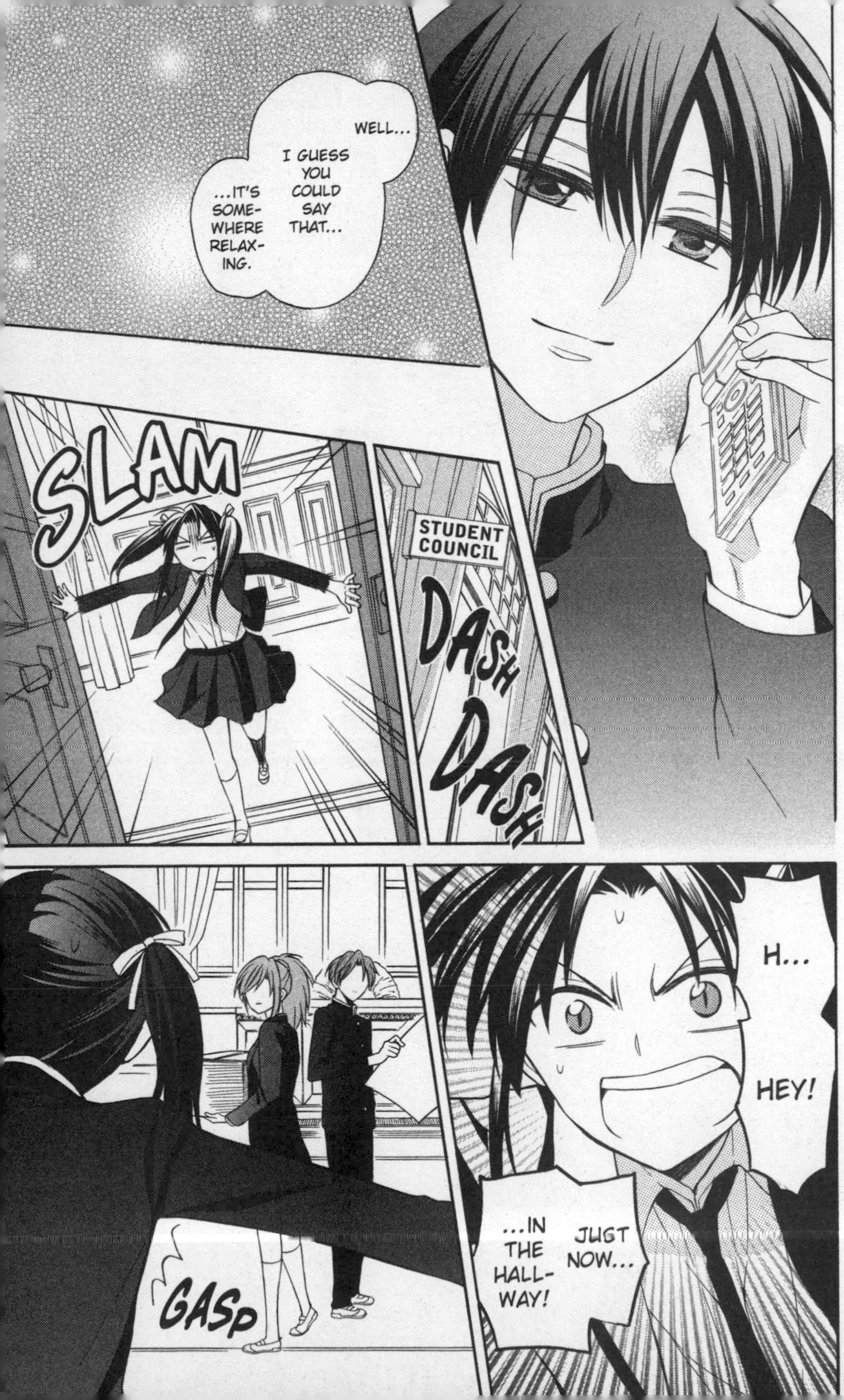

WELL...
I GUESS YOU COULD SAY THAT...
...IT'S SOMEWHERE RELAXING.
STUDENT COUNCIL
DASH DASH DASH
SLAM
H...
HEY!
JUST NOW...
...IN THE HALLWAY!
GASP

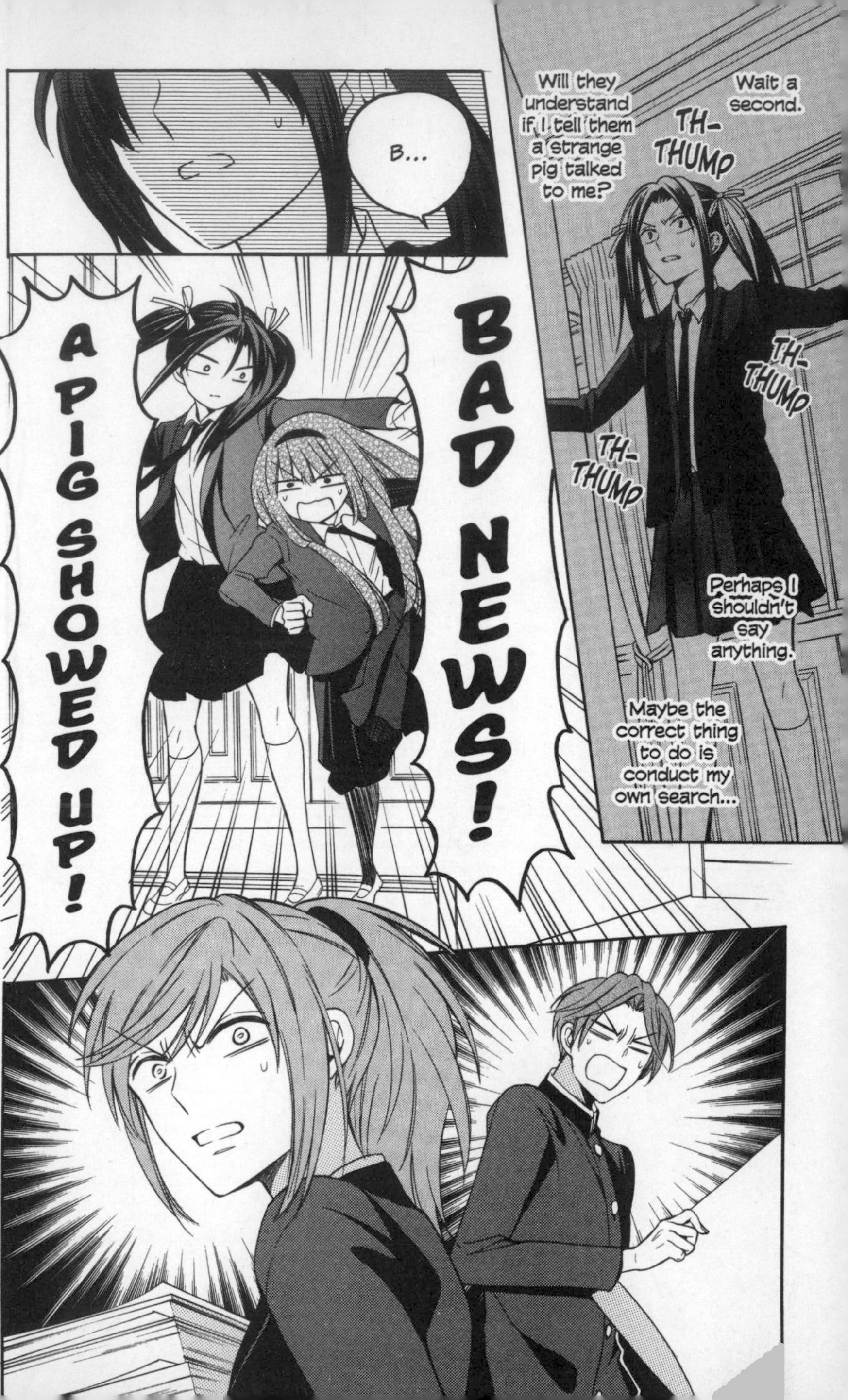
Wait a second.
TH-THUMP
Will they understand if I tell them a strange pig talked to me?
TH-THUMP
TH-THUMP
Perhaps I shouldn't say anything.
Maybe the correct thing to do is conduct my own search...
B...
BAD NEWS!
A PIG SHOWED UP!

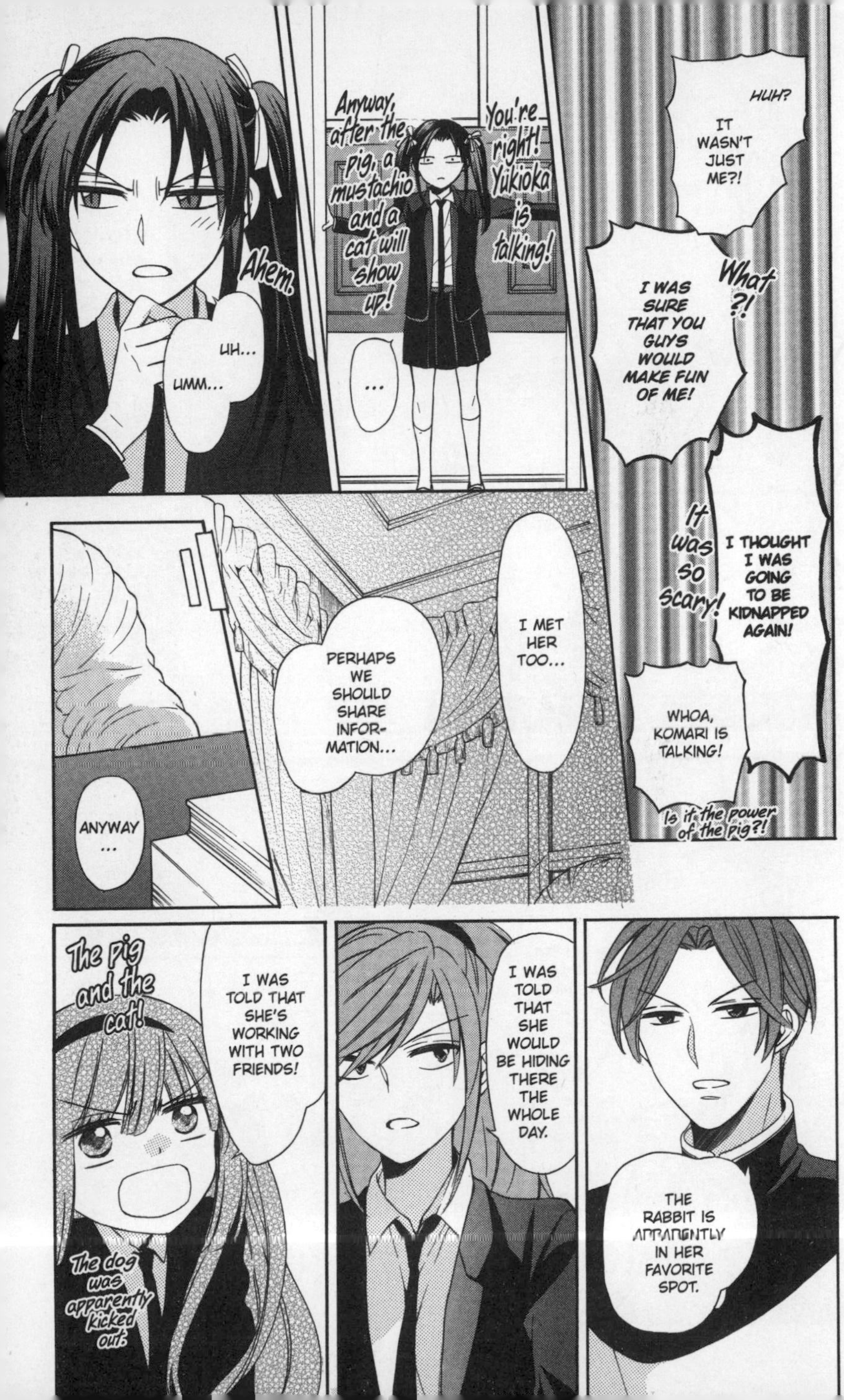

HUH?
IT WASN'T JUST ME?!
What?!
I WAS SURE THAT YOU GUYS WOULD MAKE FUN OF ME!
It was so scary!
I THOUGHT I WAS GOING TO BE KIDNAPPED AGAIN!
WHOA, KOMARI IS TALKING!
Is it the power of the pig?!
You're right! Yukioka is talking!
Anyway, after the pig, a mustachio and a cat will show up!
...
Ahem.
UH... UMM...
I MET HER TOO...
PERHAPS WE SHOULD SHARE INFORMATION...
ANYWAY...
THE RABBIT IS APPARENTLY IN HER FAVORITE SPOT.
I WAS TOLD THAT SHE WOULD BE HIDING THERE THE WHOLE DAY.
The pig and the cat!
I WAS TOLD THAT SHE'S WORKING WITH TWO FRIENDS!
The dog was apparently kicked out.

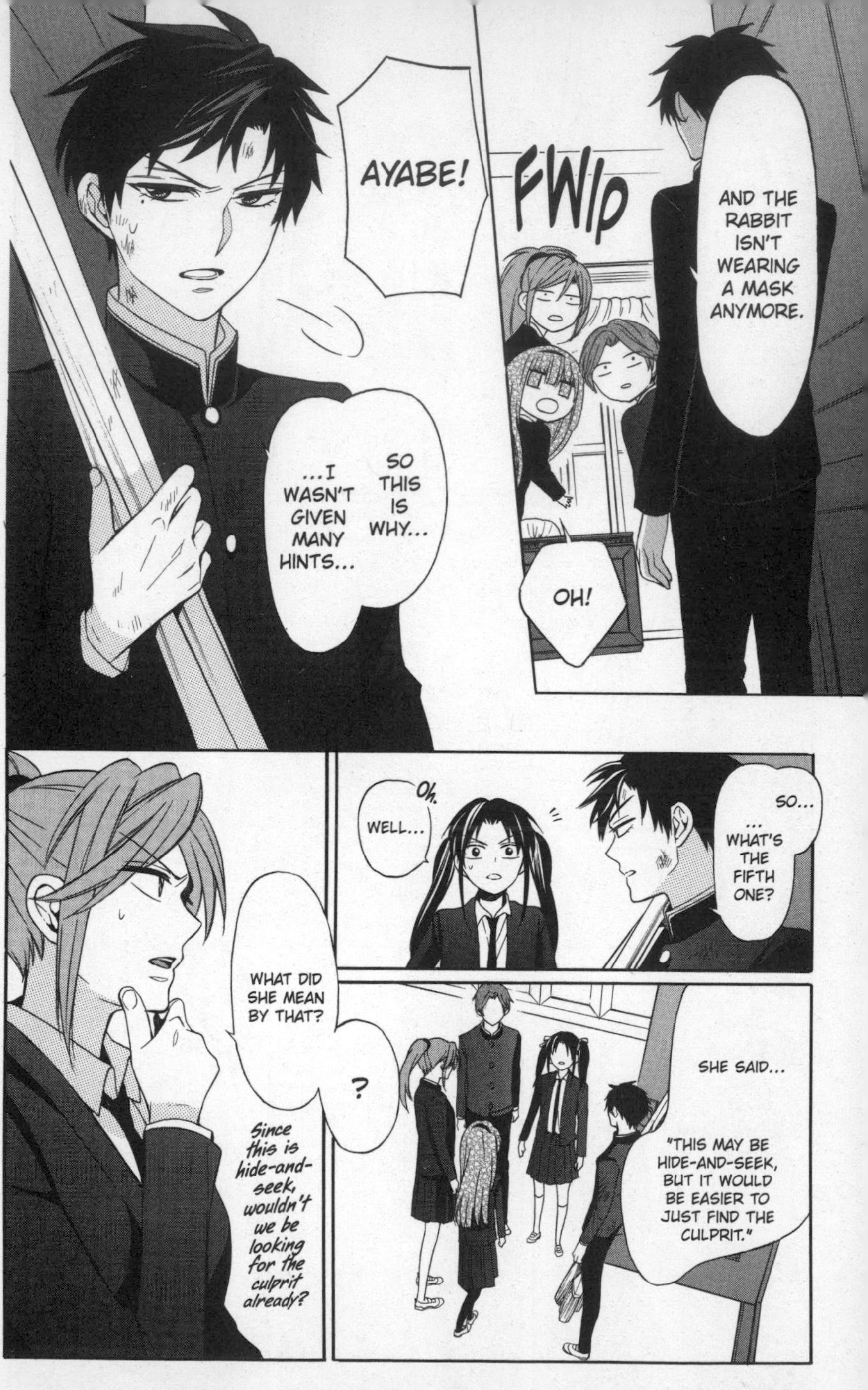
AND THE RABBIT ISN'T WEARING A MASK ANYMORE.
FWIP
OH!
AYABE!
SO THIS IS WHY...
...I WASN'T GIVEN MANY HINTS...
SO... ...WHAT'S THE FIFTH ONE?
Oh.
WELL...
SHE SAID...
"THIS MAY BE HIDE-AND-SEEK, BUT IT WOULD BE EASIER TO JUST FIND THE CULPRIT."
WHAT DID SHE MEAN BY THAT?
?
Since this is hide-and-seek, wouldn't we be looking for the culprit already?

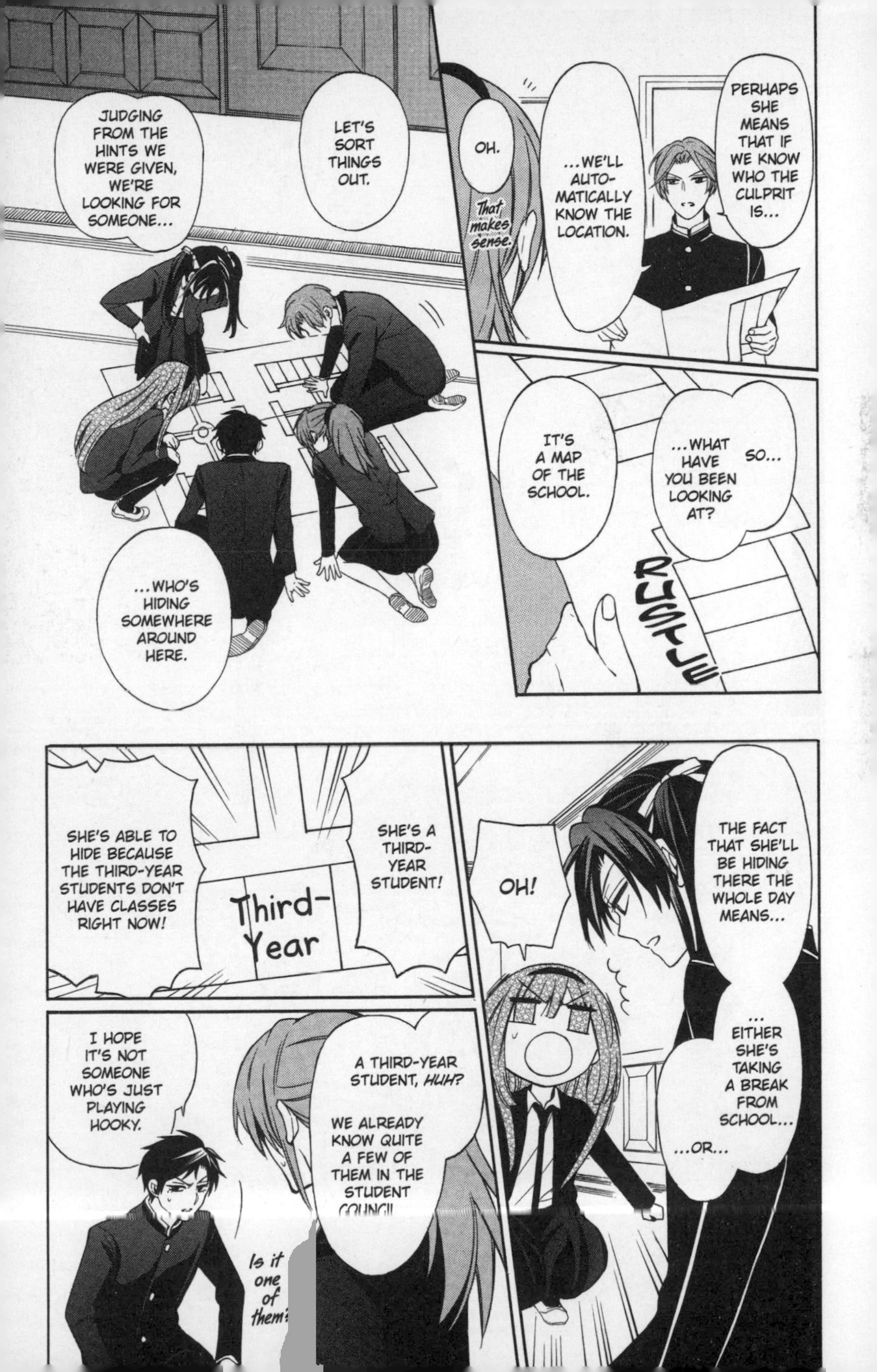
PERHAPS SHE MEANS THAT IF WE KNOW WHO THE CULPRIT IS...
...WE'LL AUTOMATICALLY KNOW THE LOCATION.
OH.
That makes sense.
SO...
...WHAT HAVE YOU BEEN LOOKING AT?
IT'S A MAP OF THE SCHOOL.
RUSTLE
LET'S SORT THINGS OUT.
JUDGING FROM THE HINTS WE WERE GIVEN, WE'RE LOOKING FOR SOMEONE...
...WHO'S HIDING SOMEWHERE AROUND HERE.
THE FACT THAT SHE'LL BE HIDING THERE THE WHOLE DAY MEANS...
OH!
...EITHER SHE'S TAKING A BREAK FROM SCHOOL...
...OR...
SHE'S A THIRD-YEAR STUDENT!
Third-Year
SHE'S ABLE TO HIDE BECAUSE THE THIRD-YEAR STUDENTS DON'T HAVE CLASSES RIGHT NOW!
A THIRD-YEAR STUDENT, *HUH?*
WE ALREADY KNOW QUITE A FEW OF THEM IN THE STUDENT COUNCIL!
I HOPE IT'S NOT SOMEONE WHO'S JUST PLAYING HOOKY.
Is it one of them?

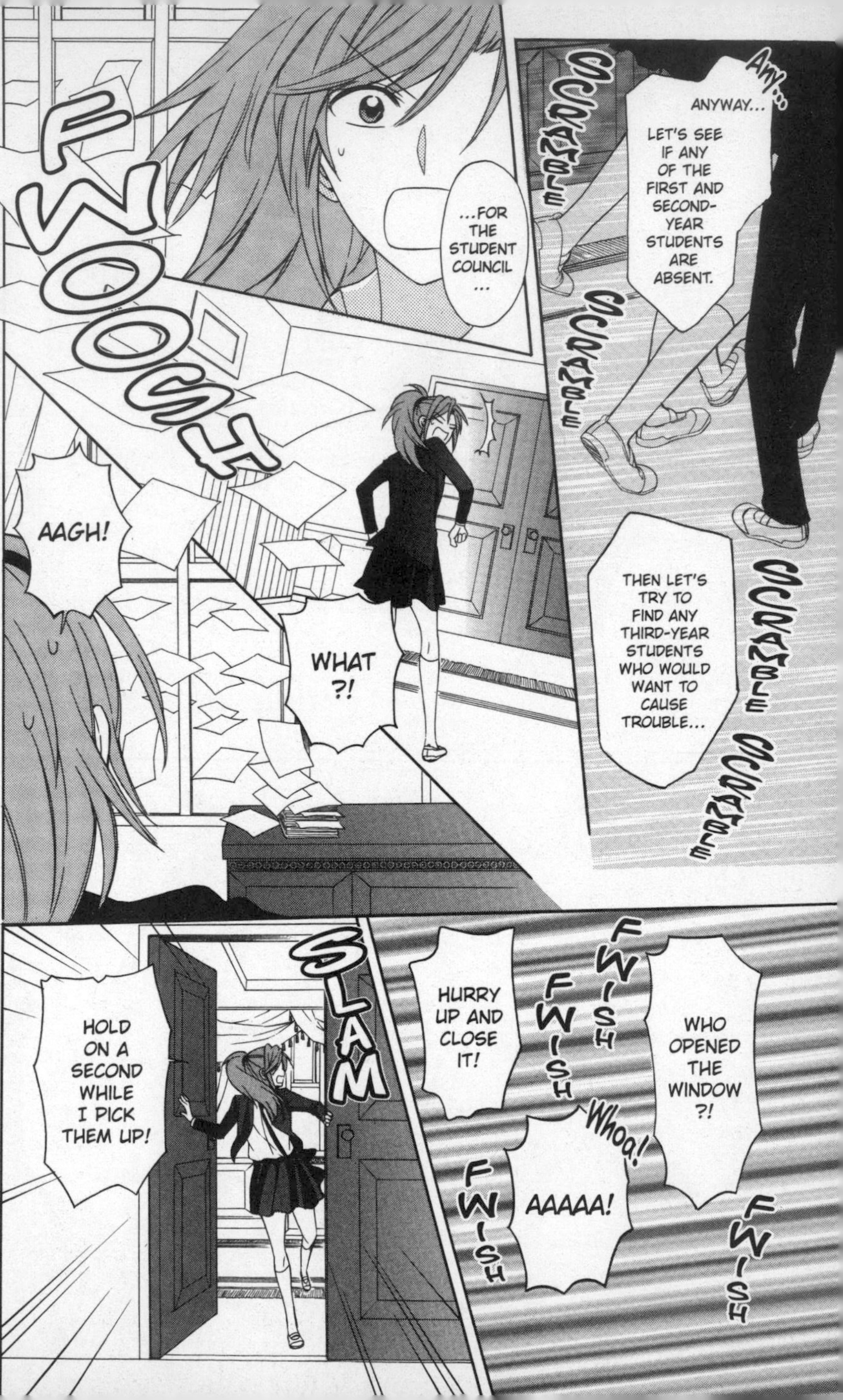

SCRAMBLE
Any...
ANYWAY...
LET'S SEE IF ANY OF THE FIRST AND SECOND-YEAR STUDENTS ARE ABSENT.
SCRAMBLE
SCRAMBLE
THEN LET'S TRY TO FIND ANY THIRD-YEAR STUDENTS WHO WOULD WANT TO CAUSE TROUBLE...
SCRAMBLE
...FOR THE STUDENT COUNCIL...
FWOOSH
AAGH!
WHAT ?!
FWISH
WHO OPENED THE WINDOW ?!
FWISH
HURRY UP AND CLOSE IT!
Whoa!
FWISH
AAAAA!
FWISH
SLAM
HOLD ON A SECOND WHILE I PICK THEM UP!

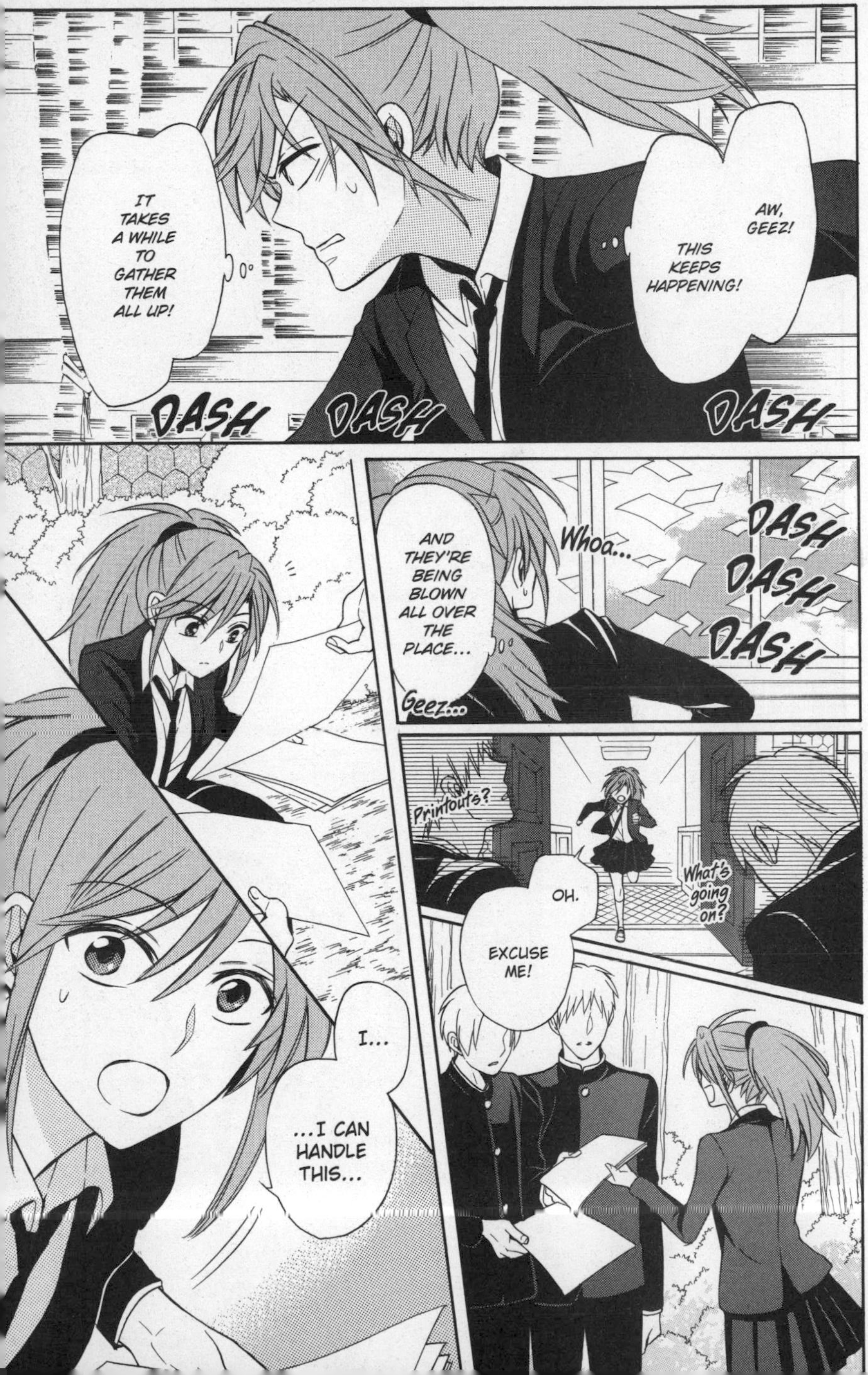
AW, GEEZ!
THIS KEEPS HAPPENING!
IT TAKES A WHILE TO GATHER THEM ALL UP!
DASH DASH DASH
DASH DASH DASH
Whoa...
AND THEY'RE BEING BLOWN ALL OVER THE PLACE...
Geez...
What's going on?
Printouts?
OH.
EXCUSE ME!
I...
...I CAN HANDLE THIS...

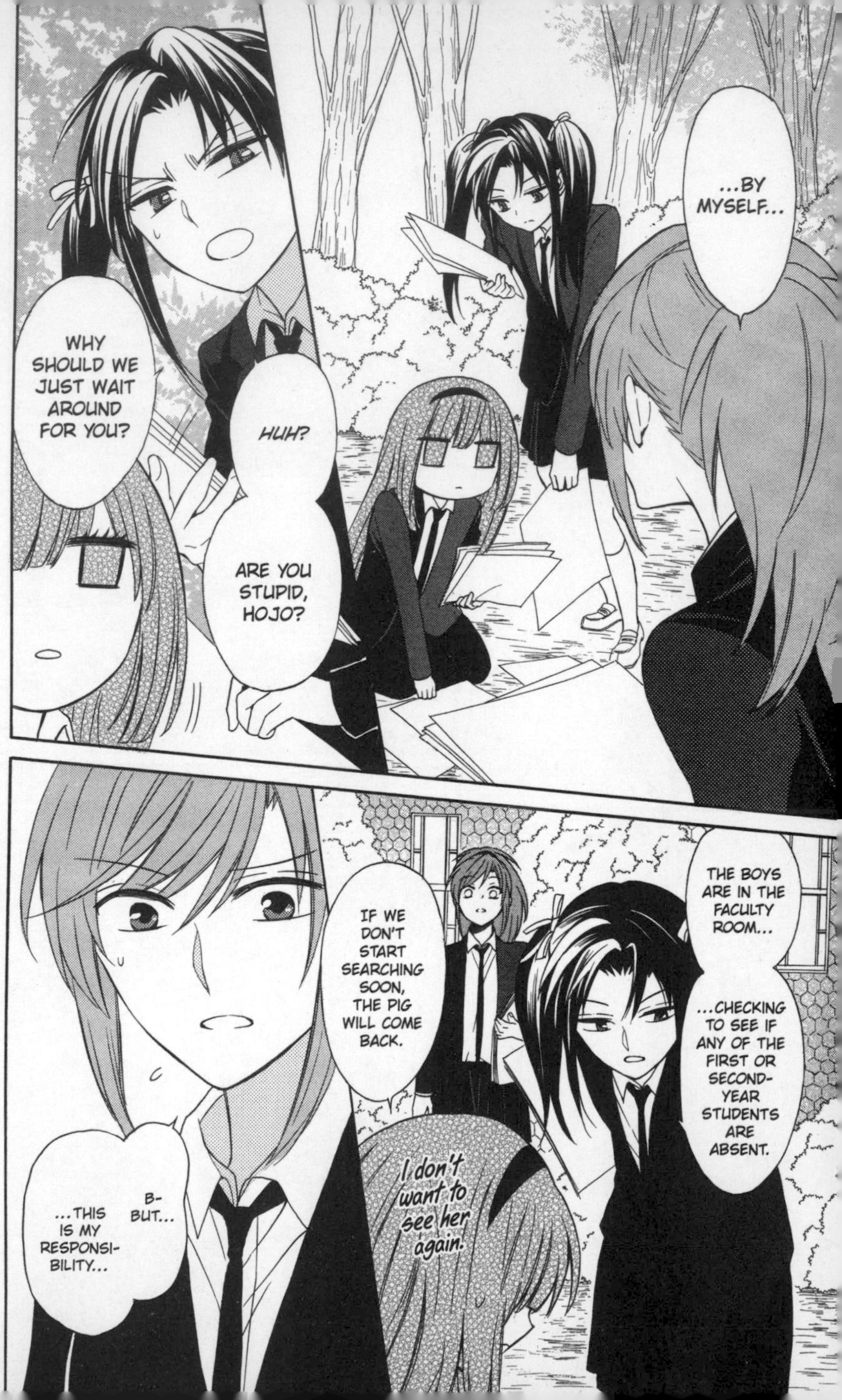
...BY MYSELF...
HUH?
ARE YOU STUPID, HOJO?
WHY SHOULD WE JUST WAIT AROUND FOR YOU?
THE BOYS ARE IN THE FACULTY ROOM...
...CHECKING TO SEE IF ANY OF THE FIRST OR SECOND-YEAR STUDENTS ARE ABSENT.
IF WE DON'T START SEARCHING SOON, THE PIG WILL COME BACK.
I don't want to see her again.
B-BUT...
...THIS IS MY RESPONSIBILITY...

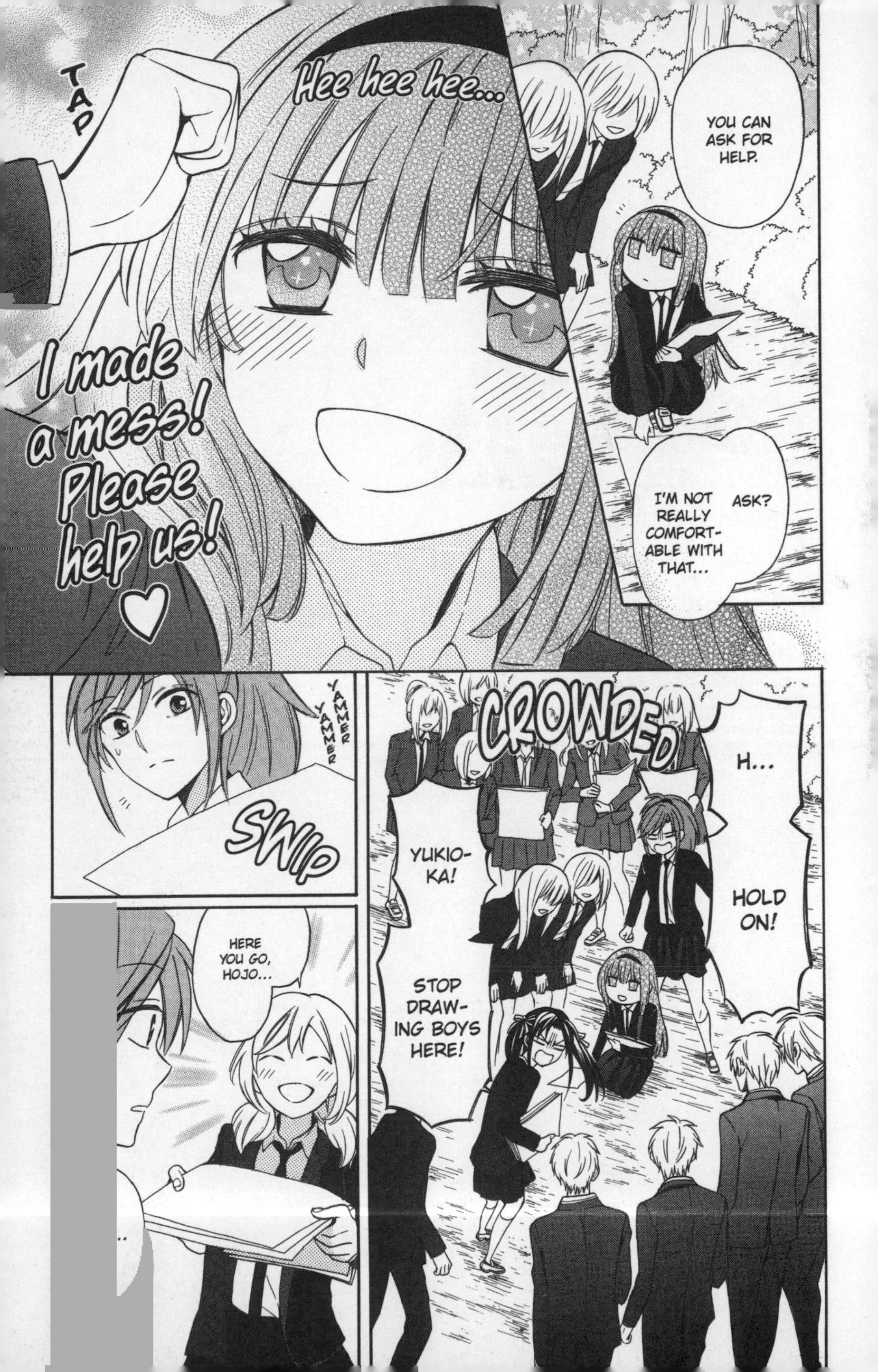
YOU CAN ASK FOR HELP.
ASK?
I'M NOT REALLY COMFORTABLE WITH THAT...
TAP
Hee hee hee...
I made a mess! Please help us! ♥
CROWDED
H...
HOLD ON!
YUKIOKA!
STOP DRAWING BOYS HERE!
YAMMER YAMMER
SWIP
HERE YOU GO, HOJO...

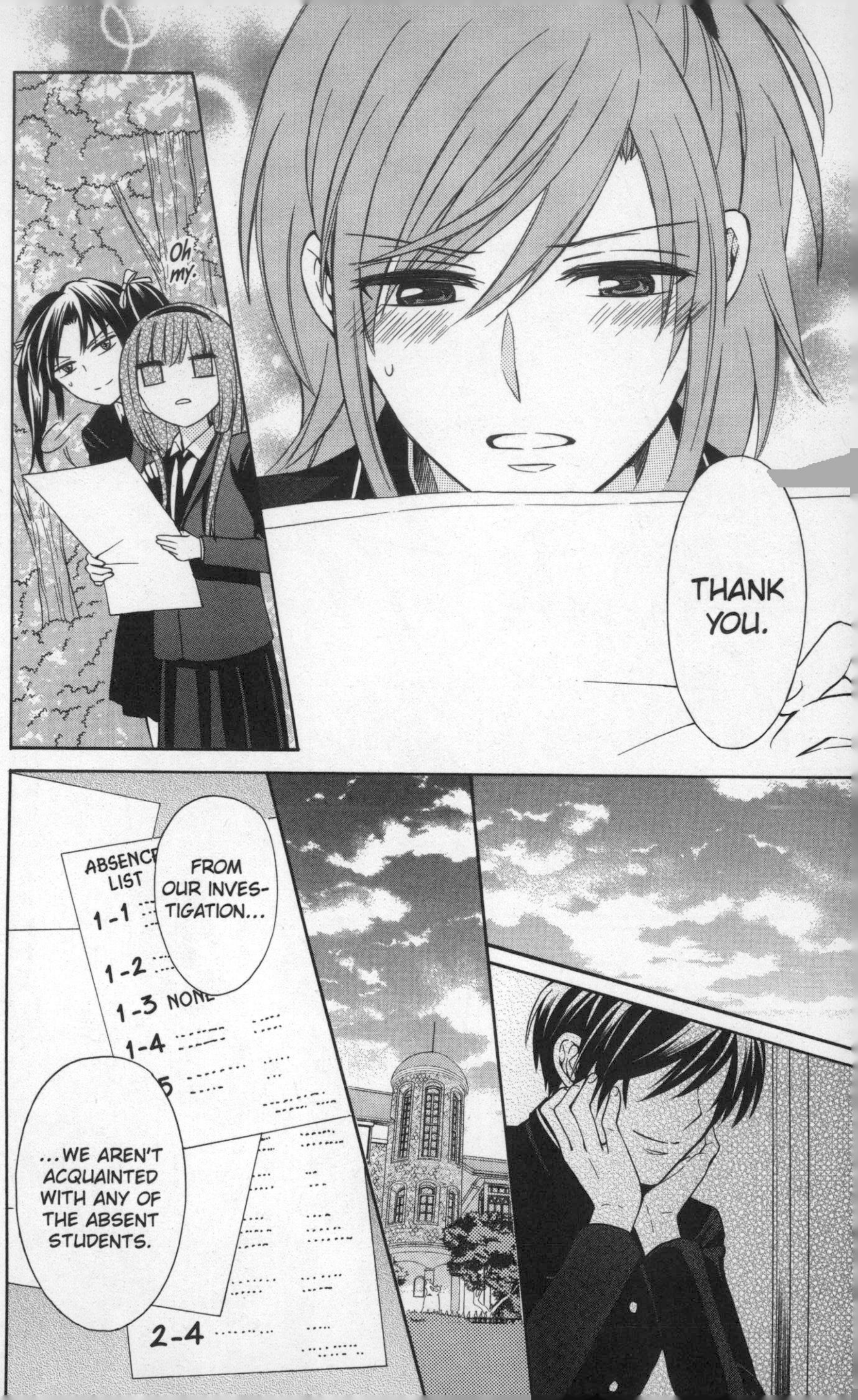
THANK YOU.
Oh my.
FROM OUR INVES-TIGATION...
ABSENC
LIST
1-1
1-2
1-3 NON
1-4
...WE AREN'T ACQUAINTED WITH ANY OF THE ABSENT STUDENTS.
2-4

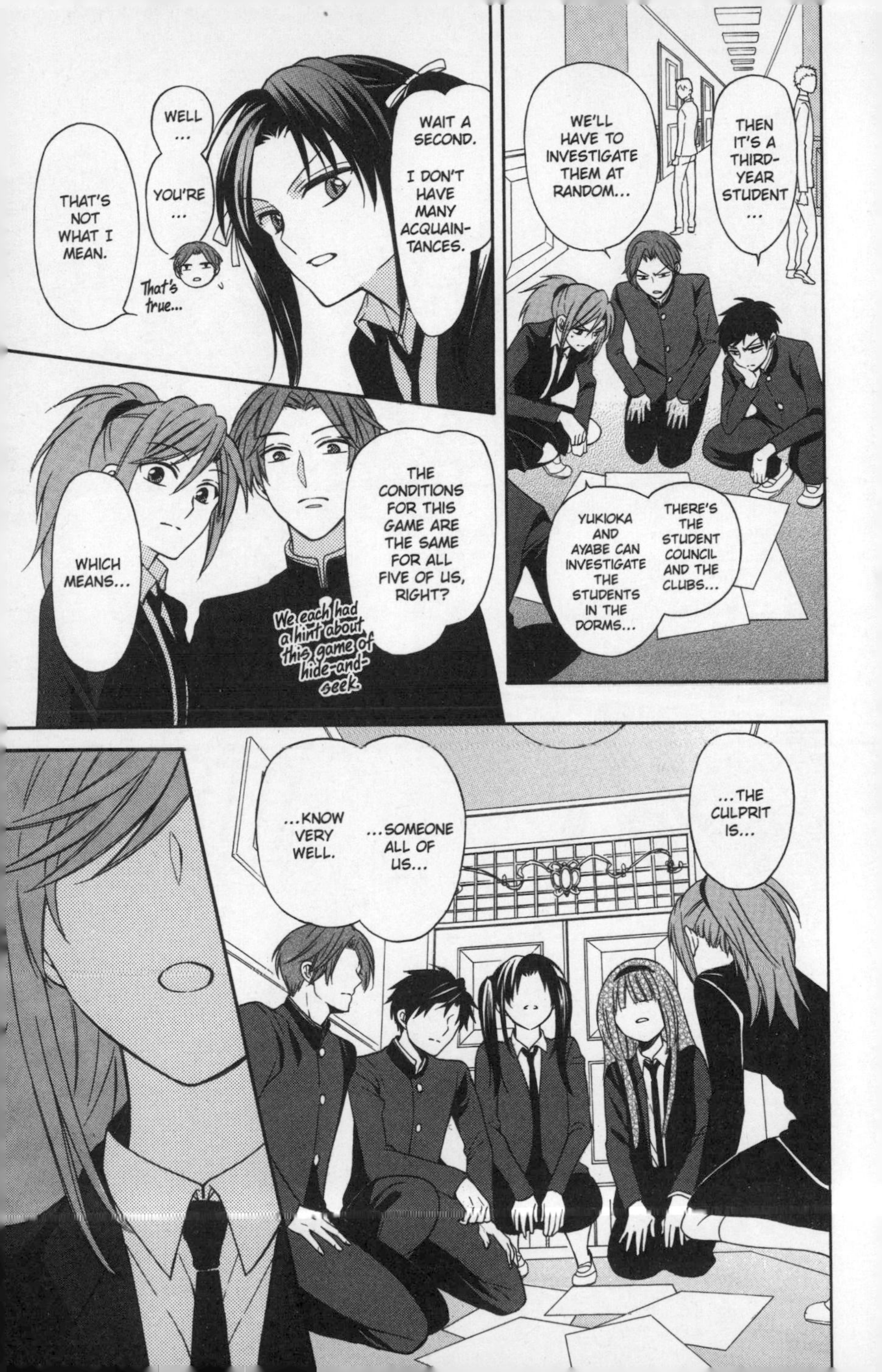
THEN IT'S A THIRD-YEAR STUDENT...
WE'LL HAVE TO INVESTIGATE THEM AT RANDOM...
THERE'S THE STUDENT COUNCIL AND THE CLUBS...
YUKIOKA AND AYABE CAN INVESTIGATE THE STUDENTS IN THE DORMS...
WAIT A SECOND.
I DON'T HAVE MANY ACQUAINTANCES.
WELL...
YOU'RE...
That's true...
THAT'S NOT WHAT I MEAN.
THE CONDITIONS FOR THIS GAME ARE THE SAME FOR ALL FIVE OF US, RIGHT?
We each had a hint about this game of hide-and-seek.
WHICH MEANS...
...THE CULPRIT IS...
...SOMEONE ALL OF US...
...KNOW VERY WELL.

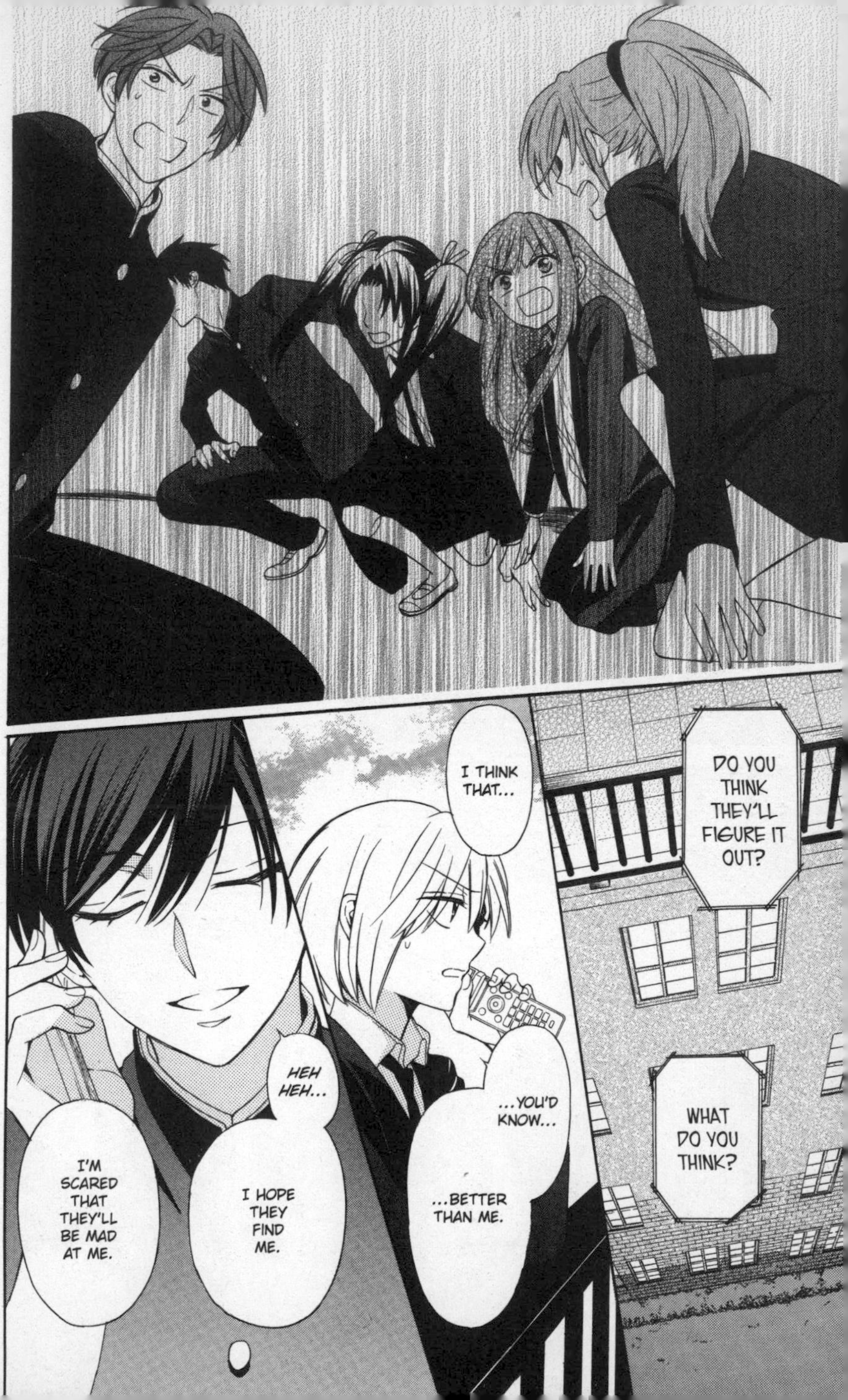
DO YOU THINK THEY'LL FIGURE IT OUT?
I THINK THAT...
WHAT DO YOU THINK?
...YOU'D KNOW...
...BETTER THAN ME.
HEH HEH...
I HOPE THEY FIND ME.
I'M SCARED THAT THEY'LL BE MAD AT ME.

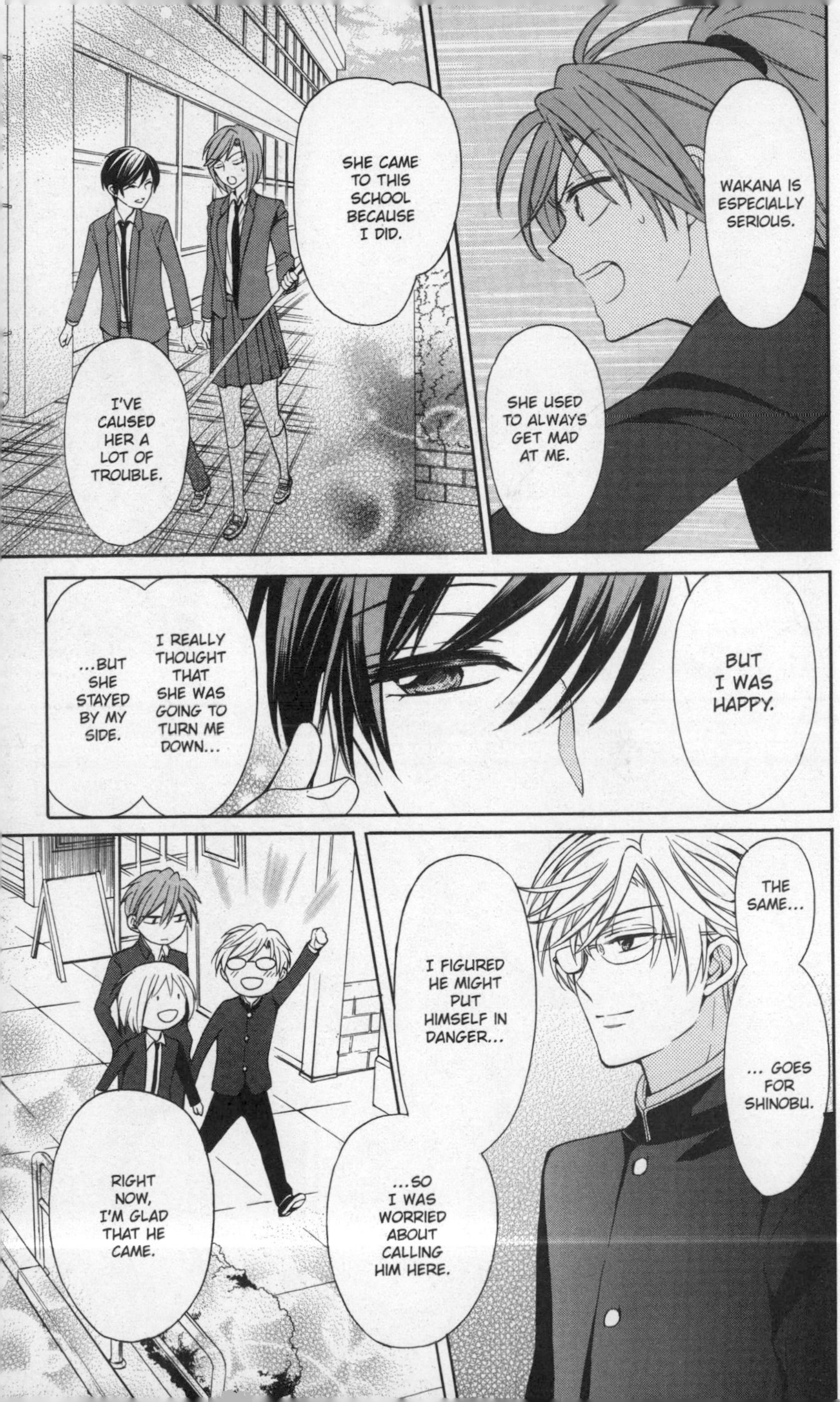
WAKANA IS ESPECIALLY SERIOUS.
SHE USED TO ALWAYS GET MAD AT ME.
SHE CAME TO THIS SCHOOL BECAUSE I DID.
I'VE CAUSED HER A LOT OF TROUBLE.
BUT I WAS HAPPY.
I REALLY THOUGHT THAT SHE WAS GOING TO TURN ME DOWN...
...BUT SHE STAYED BY MY SIDE.
THE SAME...
... GOES FOR SHINOBU.
I FIGURED HE MIGHT PUT HIMSELF IN DANGER...
...SO I WAS WORRIED ABOUT CALLING HIM HERE.
RIGHT NOW, I'M GLAD THAT HE CAME.

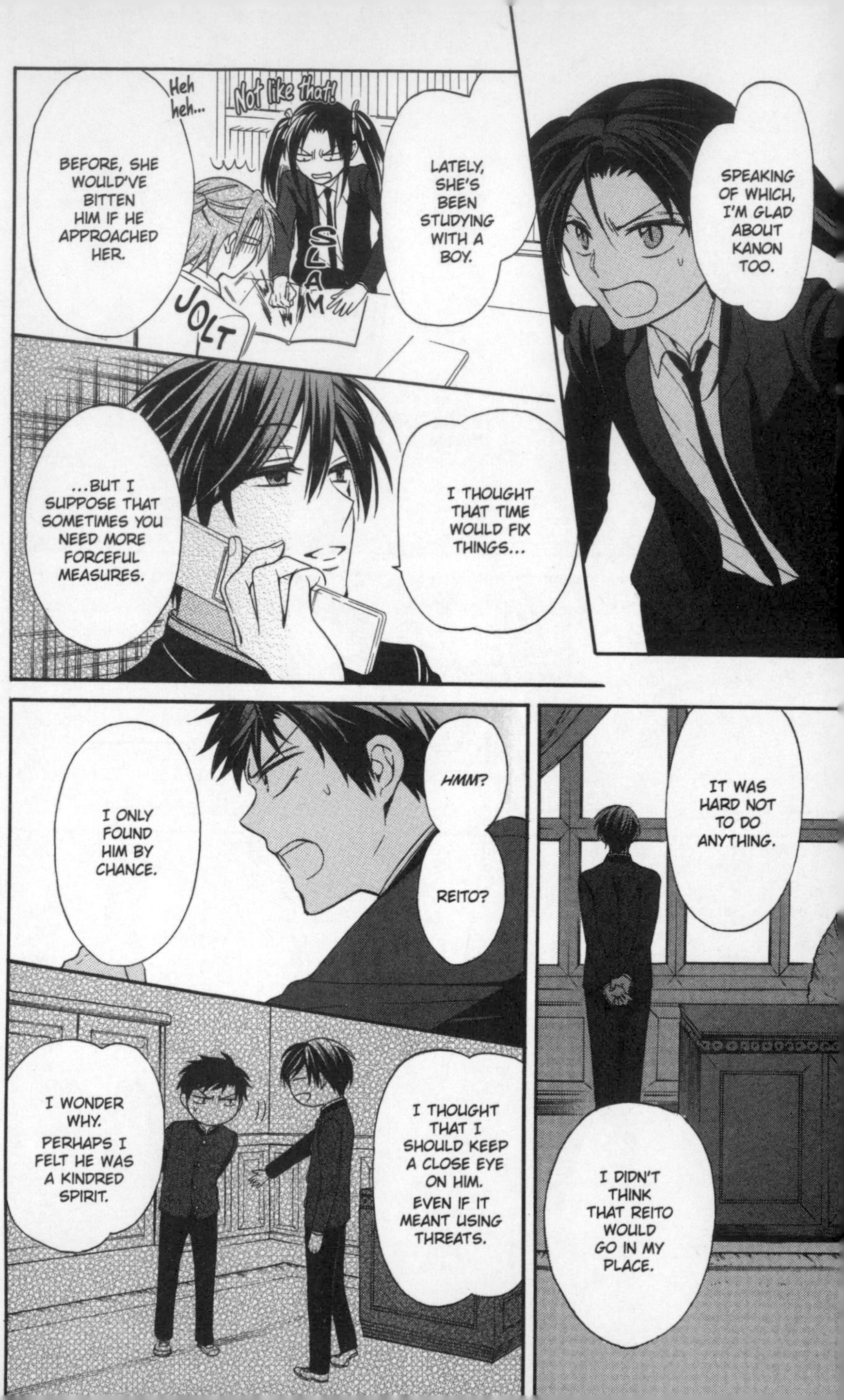
SPEAKING OF WHICH, I'M GLAD ABOUT KANON TOO.
LATELY, SHE'S BEEN STUDYING WITH A BOY.
Not like that!
Heh heh...
BEFORE, SHE WOULD'VE BITTEN HIM IF HE APPROACHED HER.
SLAM
JOLT
I THOUGHT THAT TIME WOULD FIX THINGS...
...BUT I SUPPOSE THAT SOMETIMES YOU NEED MORE FORCEFUL MEASURES.
IT WAS HARD NOT TO DO ANYTHING.
I DIDN'T THINK THAT REITO WOULD GO IN MY PLACE.
HMM?
REITO?
I ONLY FOUND HIM BY CHANCE.
I THOUGHT THAT I SHOULD KEEP A CLOSE EYE ON HIM.
EVEN IF IT MEANT USING THREATS.
I WONDER WHY. PERHAPS I FELT HE WAS A KINDRED SPIRIT.

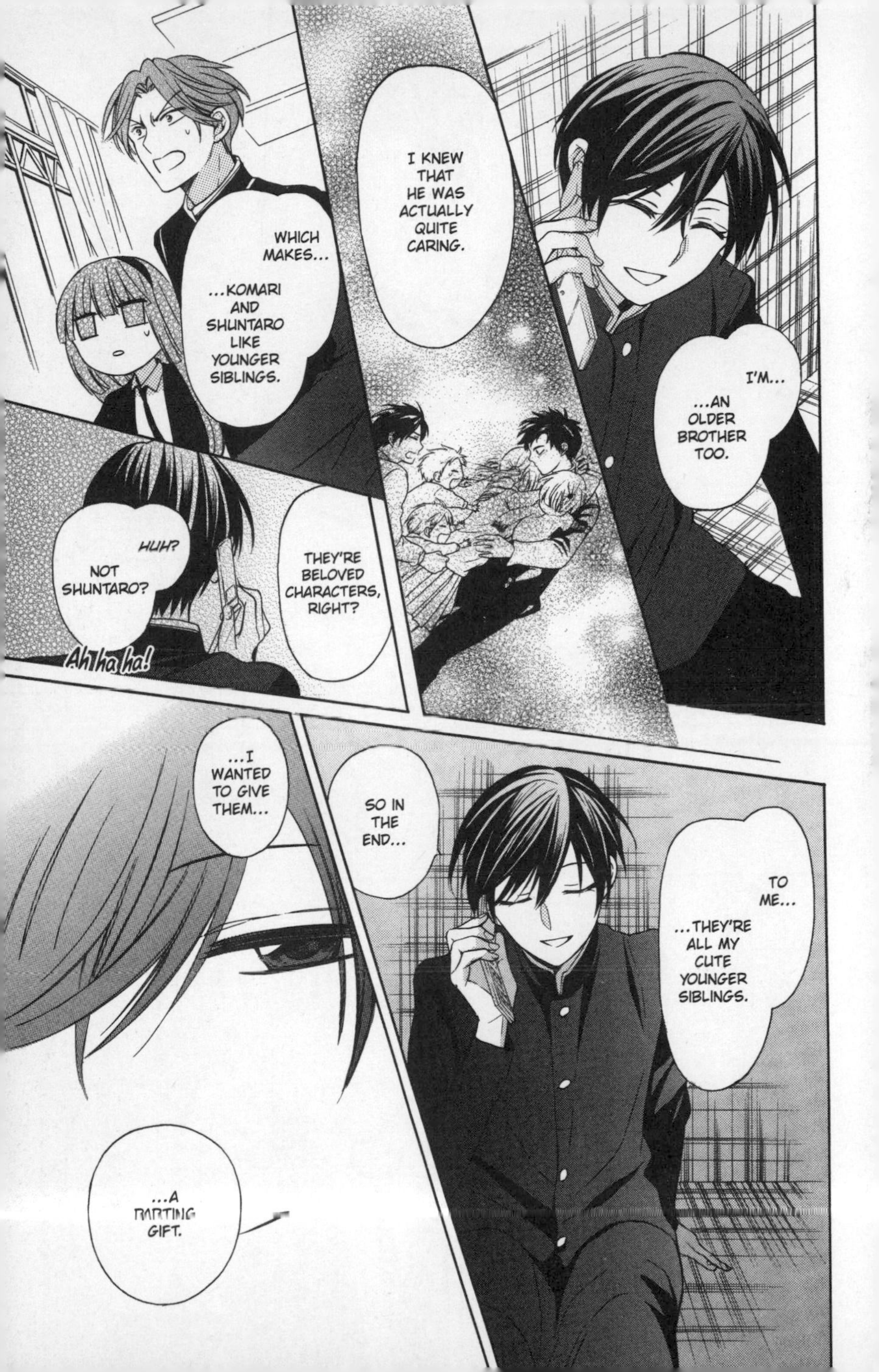
I'M...
...AN OLDER BROTHER TOO.
I KNEW THAT HE WAS ACTUALLY QUITE CARING.
WHICH MAKES...
...KOMARI AND SHUNTARO LIKE YOUNGER SIBLINGS.
THEY'RE BELOVED CHARACTERS, RIGHT?
HUH?
NOT SHUNTARO?
Ah ha ha!
TO ME...
...THEY'RE ALL MY CUTE YOUNGER SIBLINGS.
SO IN THE END...
...I WANTED TO GIVE THEM...
...A PARTING GIFT.

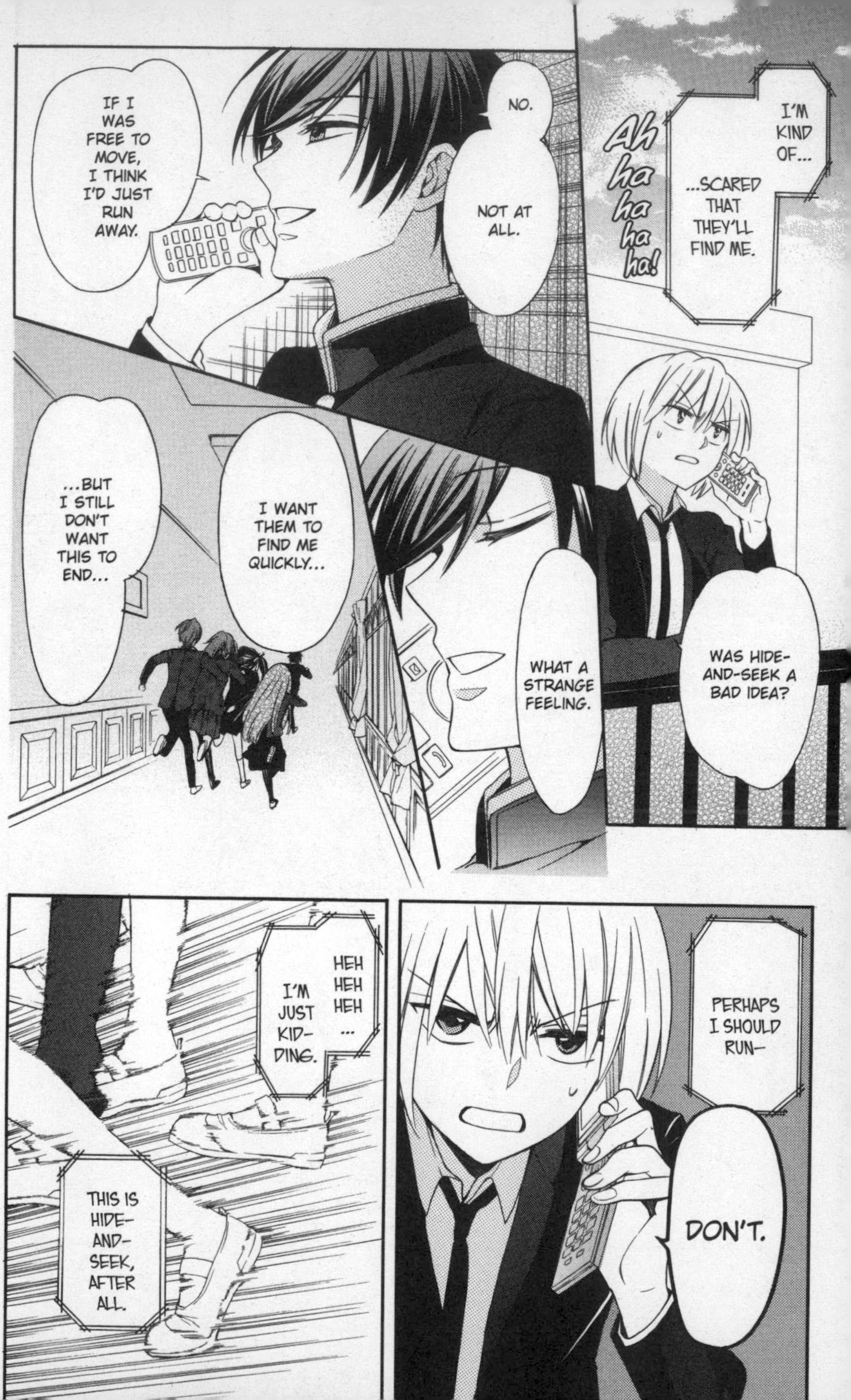

Ah ha ha ha ha!
I'M KIND OF...
...SCARED THAT THEY'LL FIND ME.
WAS HIDE-AND-SEEK A BAD IDEA?
NO.
NOT AT ALL.
IF I WAS FREE TO MOVE, I THINK I'D JUST RUN AWAY.
WHAT A STRANGE FEELING.
I WANT THEM TO FIND ME QUICKLY...
...BUT I STILL DON'T WANT THIS TO END...
PERHAPS I SHOULD RUN–
DON'T.
HEH HEH HEH...
I'M JUST KID-DING.
THIS IS HIDE-AND-SEEK, AFTER ALL.

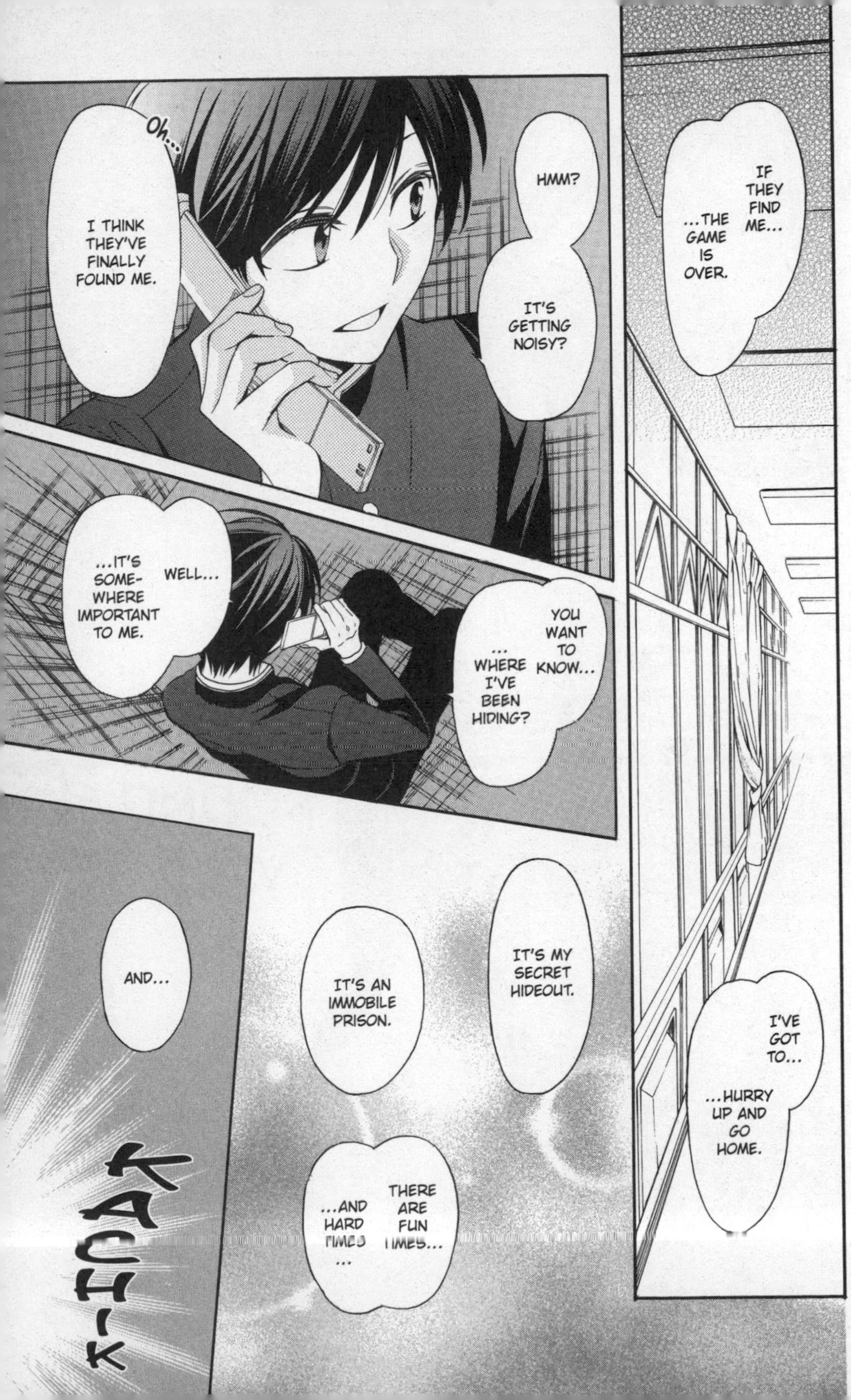
IF THEY FIND ME...
...THE GAME IS OVER.
I'VE GOT TO...
...HURRY UP AND GO HOME.
HMM?
IT'S GETTING NOISY?
Oh...
I THINK THEY'VE FINALLY FOUND ME.
YOU WANT TO KNOW...
...WHERE I'VE BEEN HIDING?
WELL...
...IT'S SOMEWHERE IMPORTANT TO ME.
IT'S MY SECRET HIDEOUT.
IT'S AN IMMOBILE PRISON.
AND...
THERE ARE FUN TIMES...
...AND HARD TIMES...
KACHIK

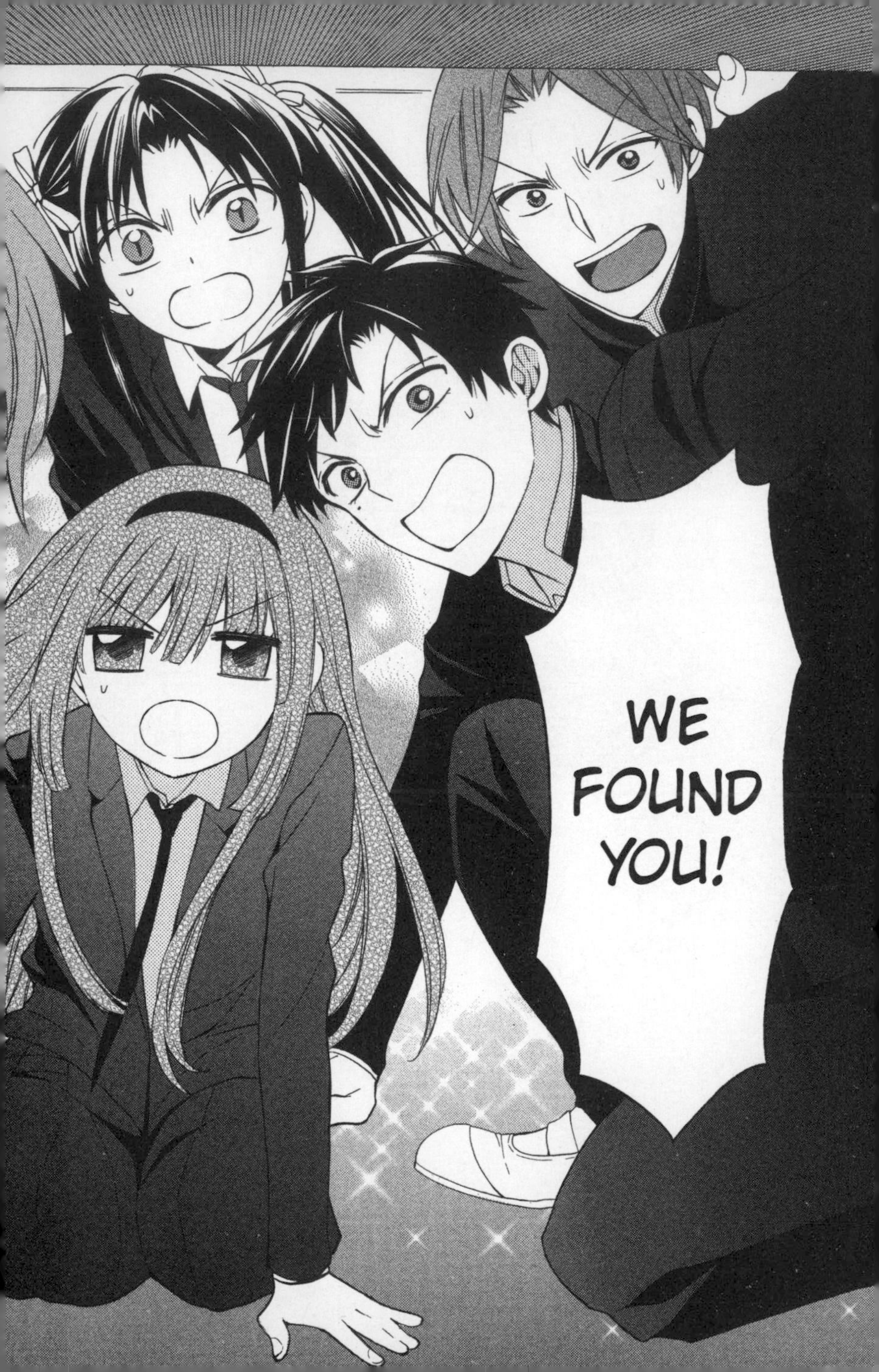
WE FOUND YOU!

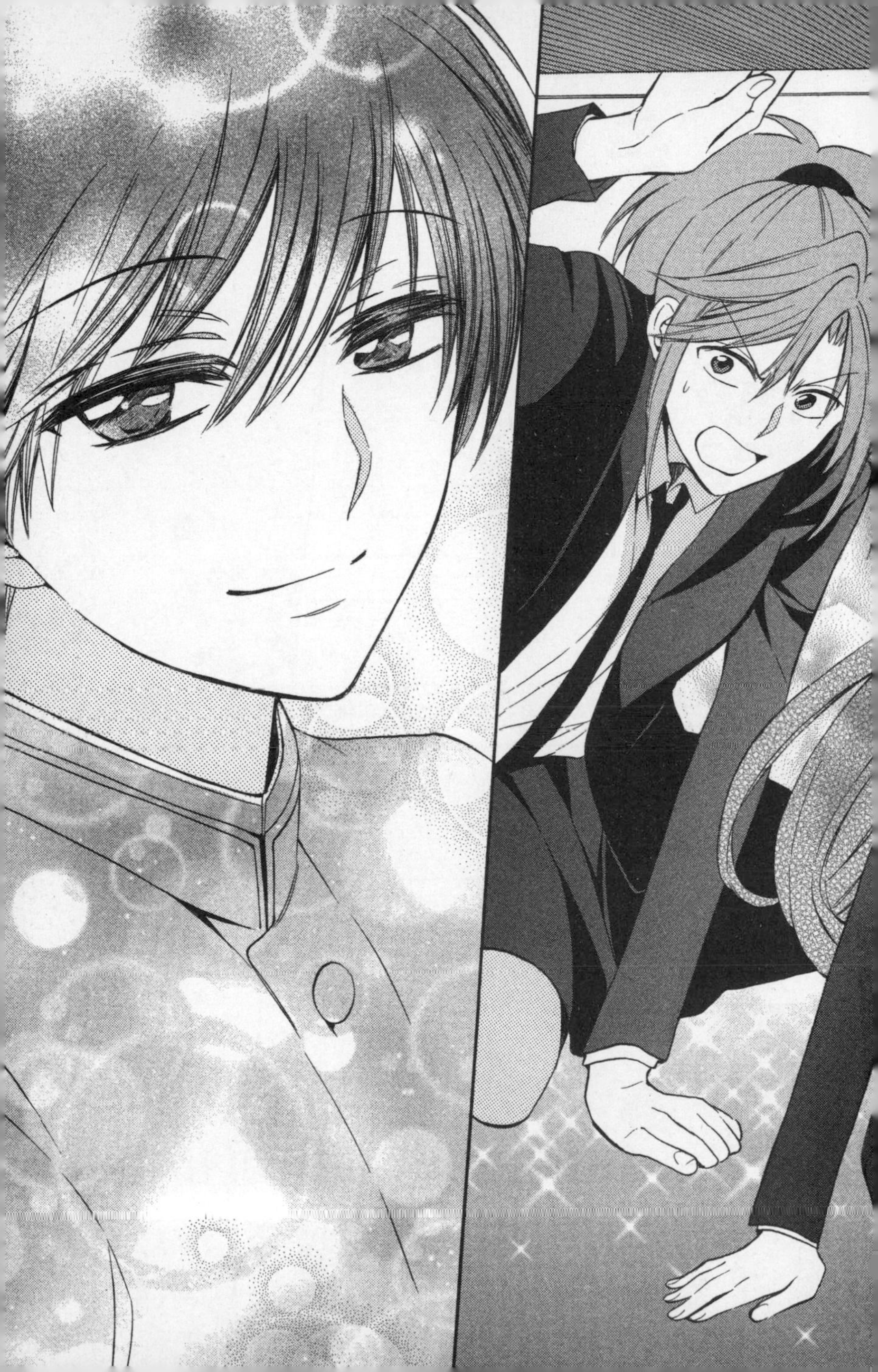

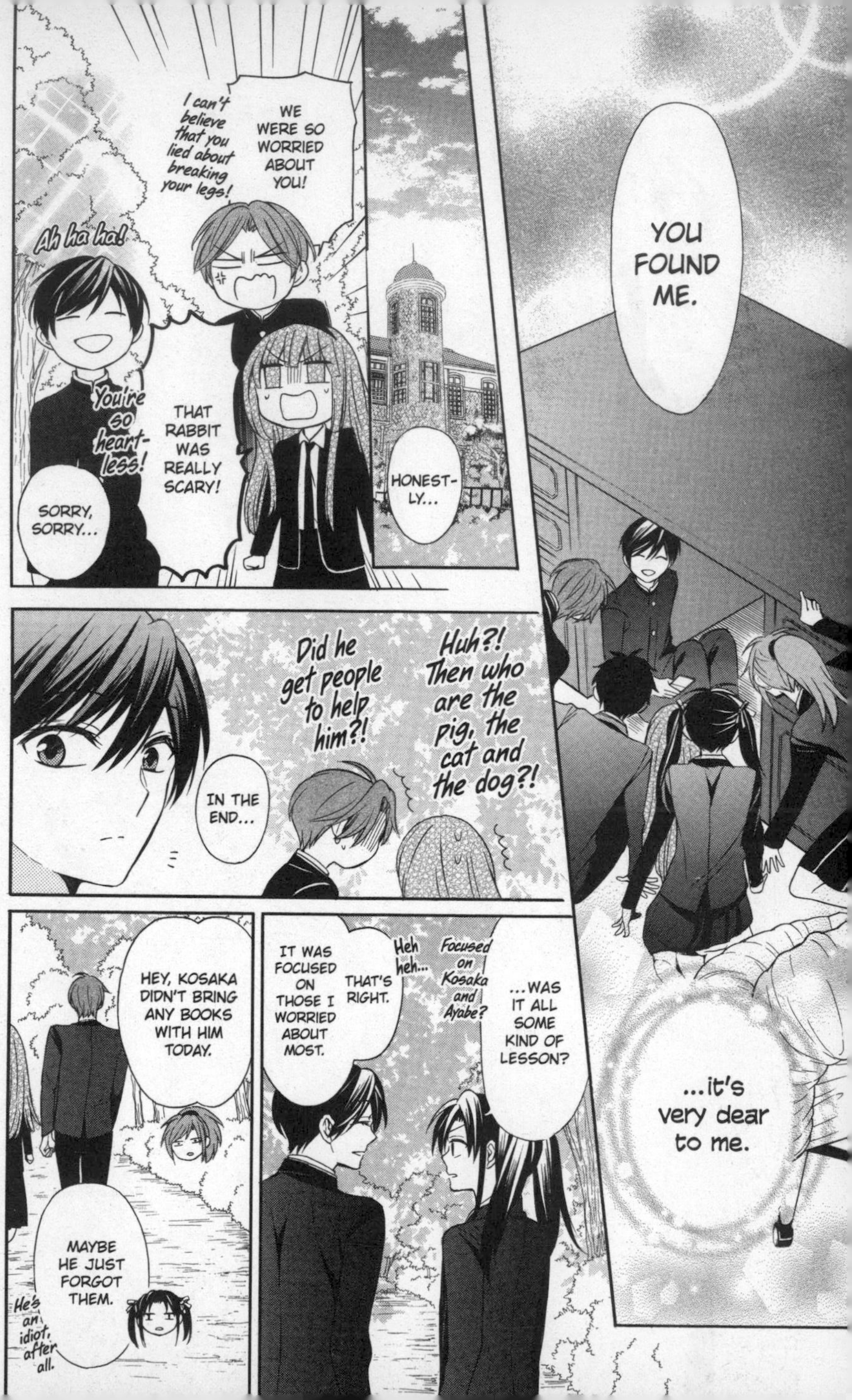
YOU FOUND ME.
...it's very dear to me.
HONEST-LY...
WE WERE SO WORRIED ABOUT YOU!
I can't believe that you lied about breaking your legs!
Ah ha ha!
THAT RABBIT WAS REALLY SCARY!
You're so heart-less!
SORRY, SORRY...
Huh?! Then who are the pig, the cat and the dog?!
Did he get people to help him?!
IN THE END...
...WAS IT ALL SOME KIND OF LESSON?
Focused on Kosaka and Ayabe?
Heh heh...
THAT'S RIGHT.
IT WAS FOCUSED ON THOSE I WORRIED ABOUT MOST.
HEY, KOSAKA DIDN'T BRING ANY BOOKS WITH HIM TODAY.
MAYBE HE JUST FORGOT THEM.
He's an idiot, after all.

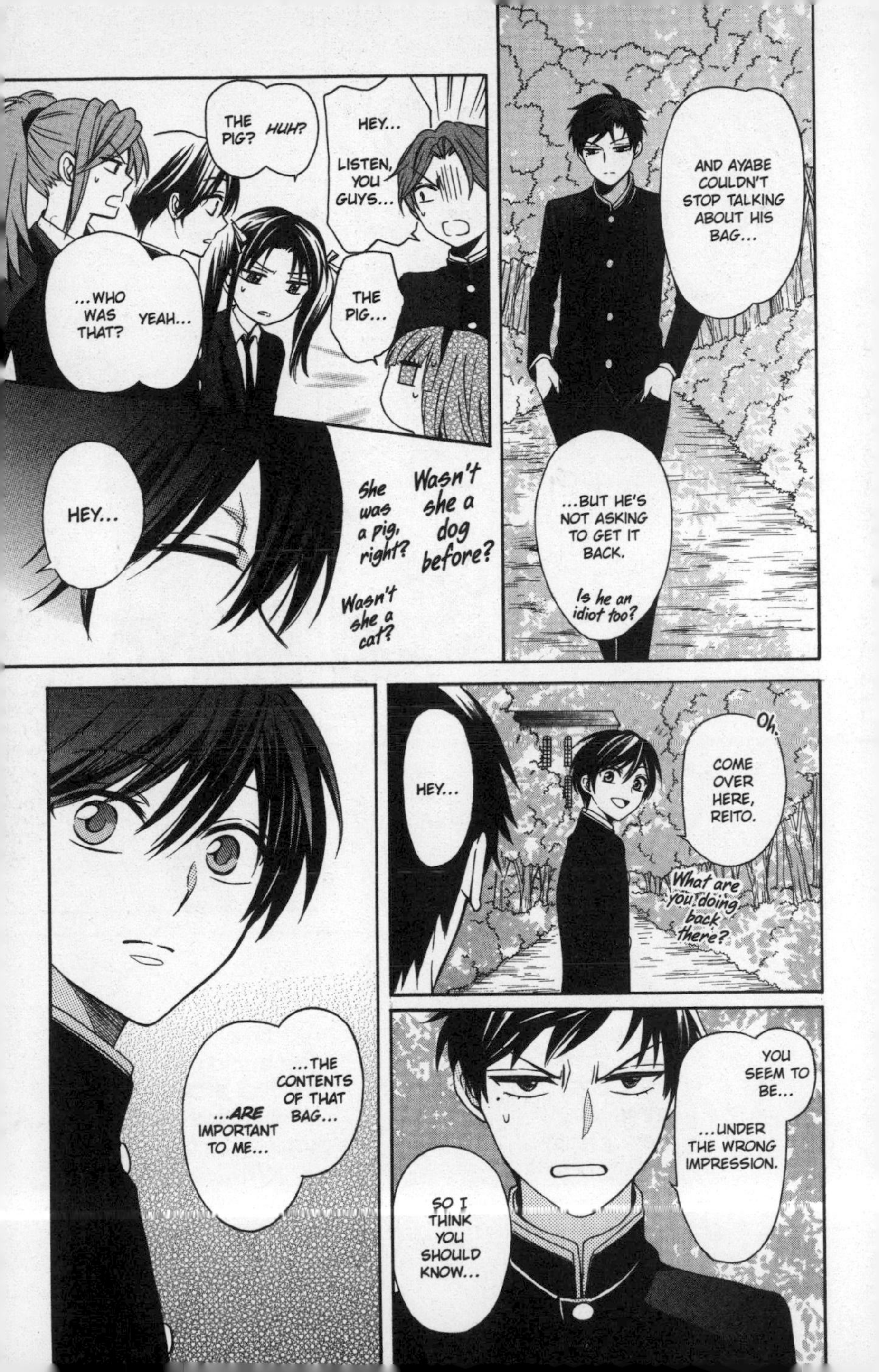
AND AYABE COULDN'T STOP TALKING ABOUT HIS BAG...
...BUT HE'S NOT ASKING TO GET IT BACK.
Is he an idiot too?
HEY...
LISTEN, YOU GUYS...
HUH?
THE PIG?
THE PIG...
YEAH...
...WHO WAS THAT?
Wasn't she a dog before?
She was a pig, right?
Wasn't she a cat?
HEY...
Oh.
COME OVER HERE, REITO.
What are you doing back there?
HEY...
YOU SEEM TO BE...
...UNDER THE WRONG IMPRESSION.
SO I THINK YOU SHOULD KNOW...
...THE CONTENTS OF THAT BAG...
...*ARE* IMPORTANT TO ME...

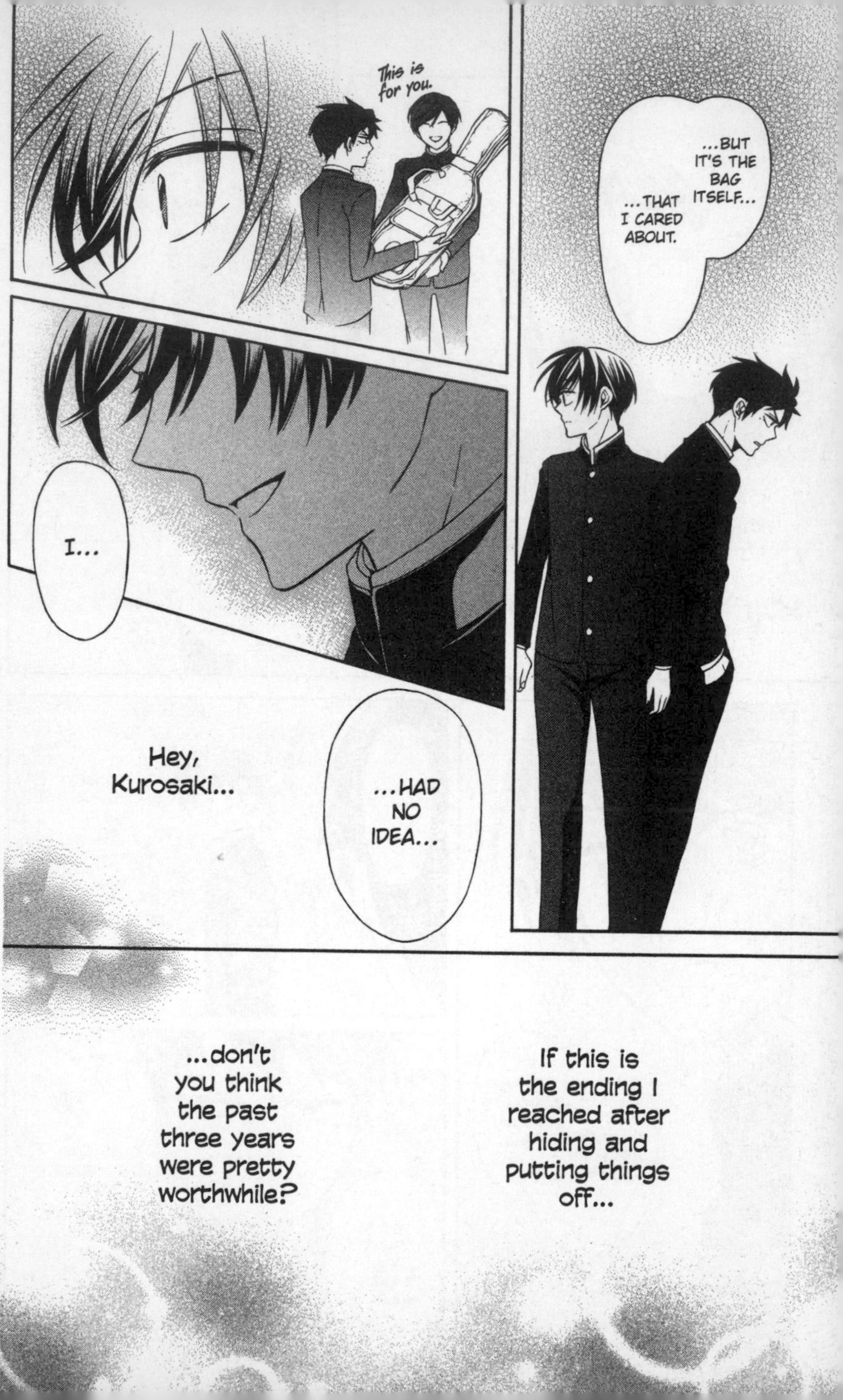
...BUT IT'S THE BAG ITSELF...
...THAT I CARED ABOUT.
This is for you.
I...
...HAD NO IDEA...
Hey, Kurosaki...
If this is the ending I reached after hiding and putting things off...
...don't you think the past three years were pretty worthwhile?

Chapter 127

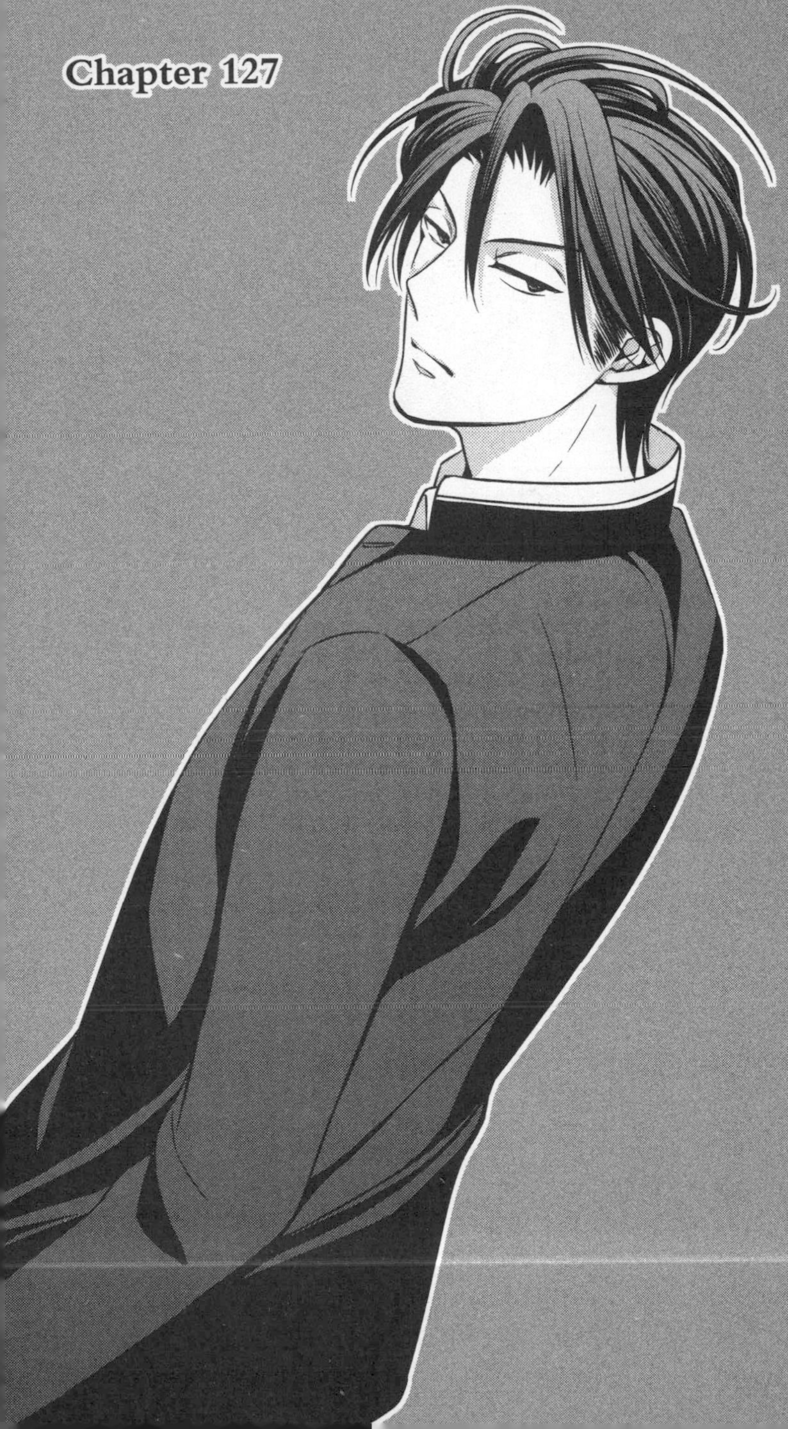

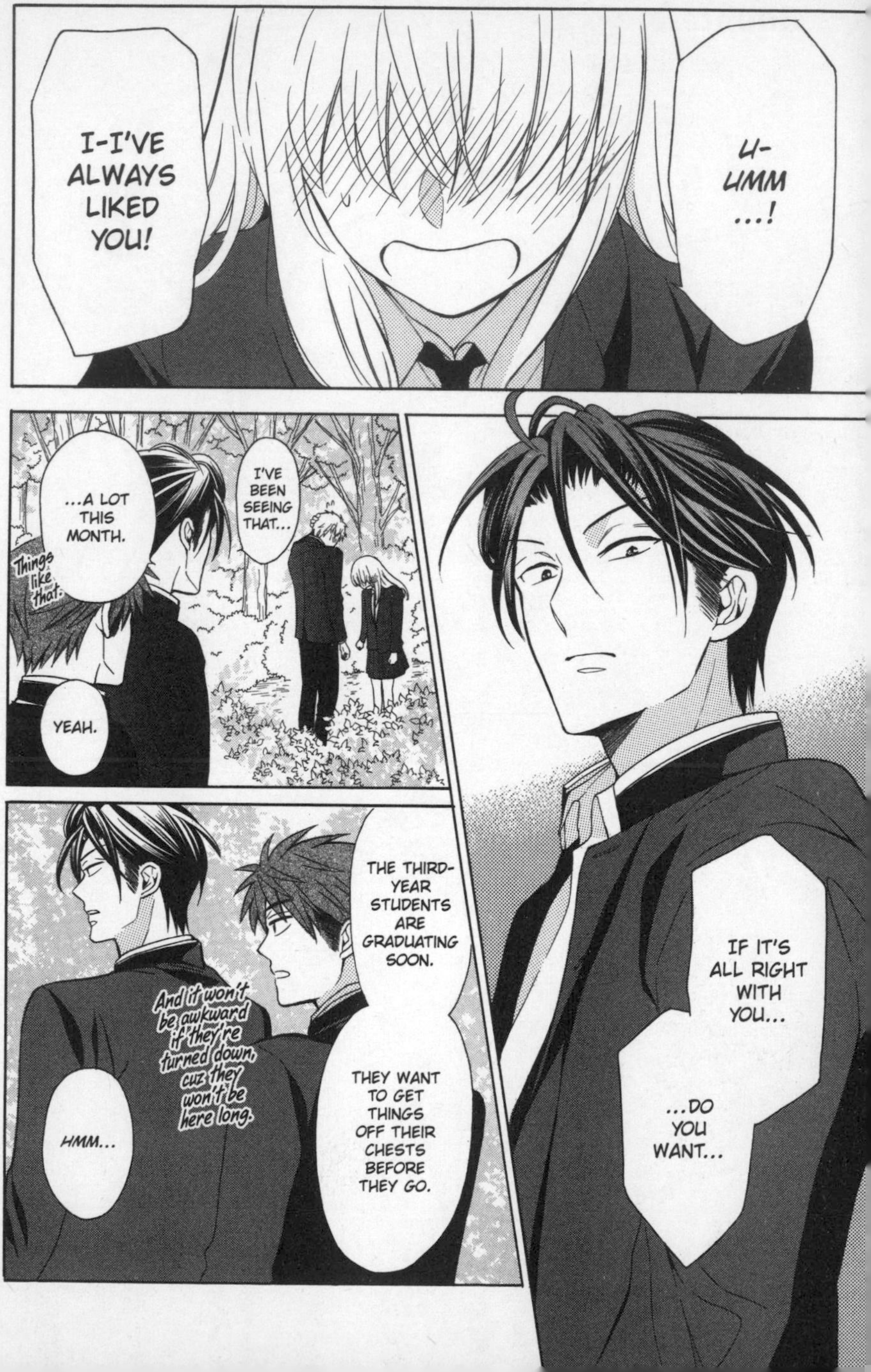
U-UMM...!
I-I'VE ALWAYS LIKED YOU!
IF IT'S ALL RIGHT WITH YOU...
...DO YOU WANT...
I'VE BEEN SEEING THAT...
...A LOT THIS MONTH.
Things like that.
YEAH.
THE THIRD-YEAR STUDENTS ARE GRADUATING SOON.
THEY WANT TO GET THINGS OFF THEIR CHESTS BEFORE THEY GO.
And it won't be awkward if they're turned down, cuz they won't be here long.
HMM...

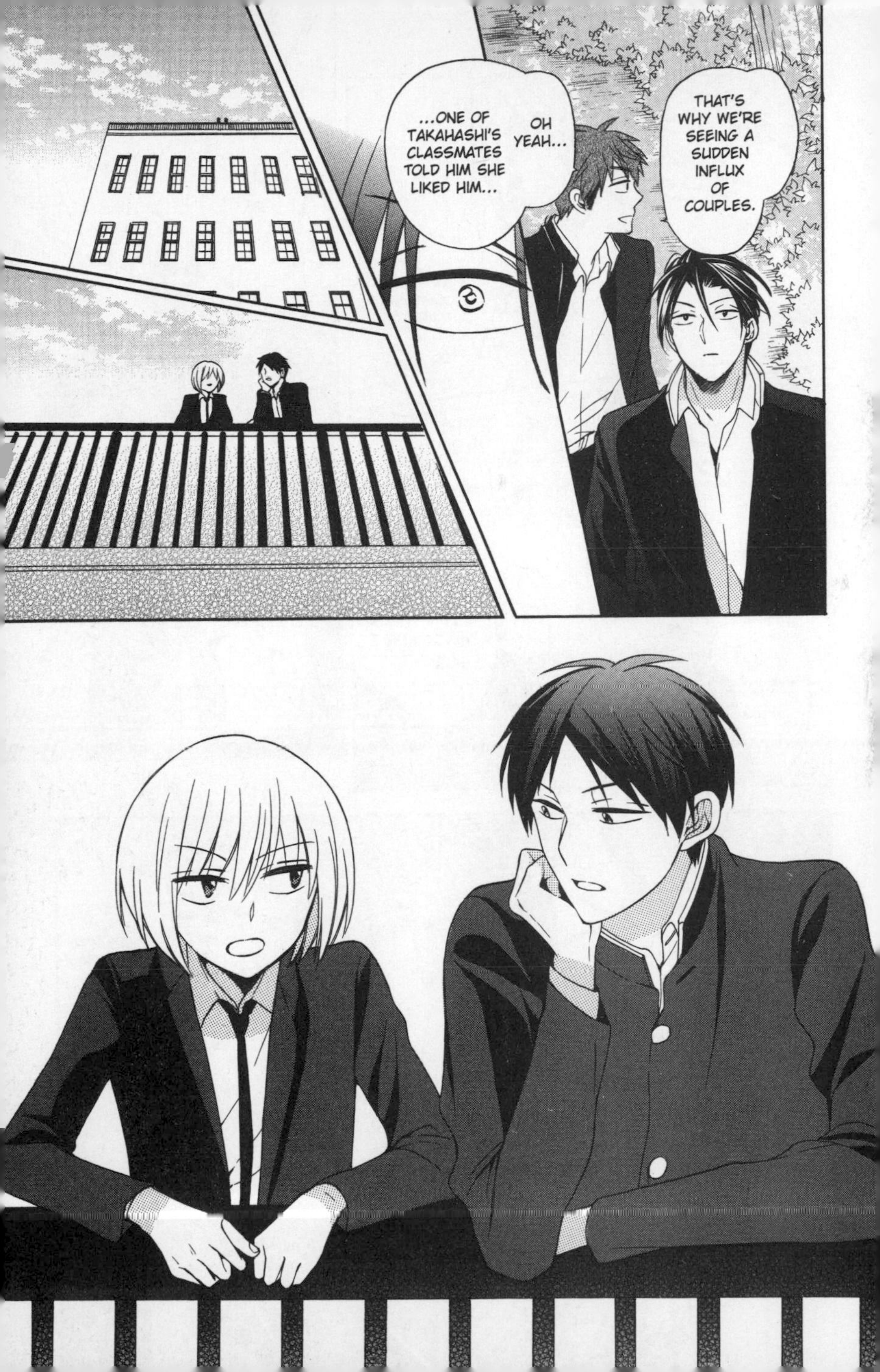
THAT'S WHY WE'RE SEEING A SUDDEN INFLUX OF COUPLES.
OH YEAH...
...ONE OF TAKAHASHI'S CLASSMATES TOLD HIM SHE LIKED HIM...

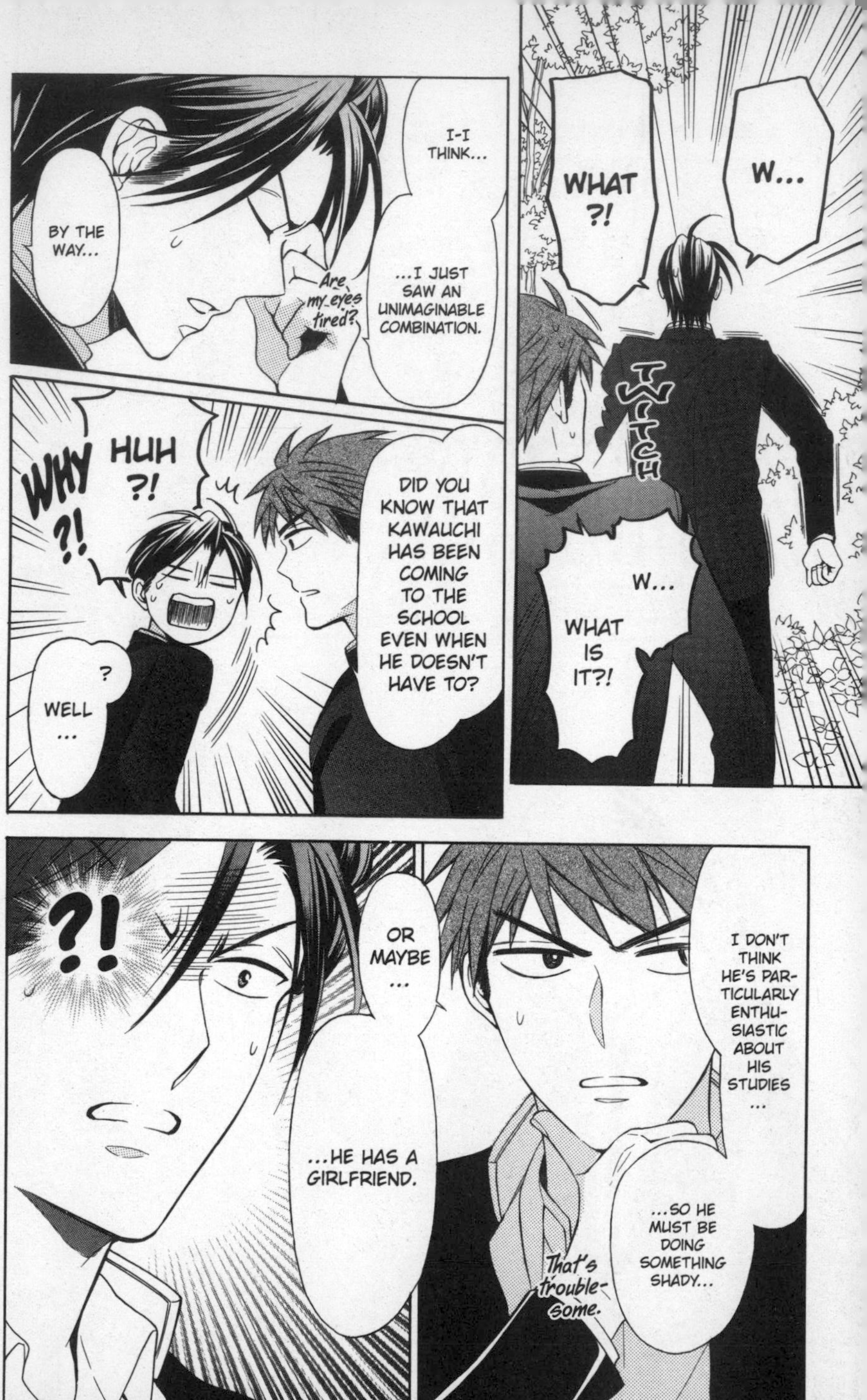
W...
WHAT ?!
WITCH
W... WHAT IS IT?!
I-I THINK...
...I JUST SAW AN UNIMAGINABLE COMBINATION.
Are my eyes tired?
BY THE WAY...
DID YOU KNOW THAT KAWAUCHI HAS BEEN COMING TO THE SCHOOL EVEN WHEN HE DOESN'T HAVE TO?
HUH ?!
WHY ?!
? WELL ...
I DON'T THINK HE'S PARTICULARLY ENTHUSIASTIC ABOUT HIS STUDIES ...
...SO HE MUST BE DOING SOMETHING SHADY...
That's troublesome.
OR MAYBE ...
...HE HAS A GIRLFRIEND.
?!

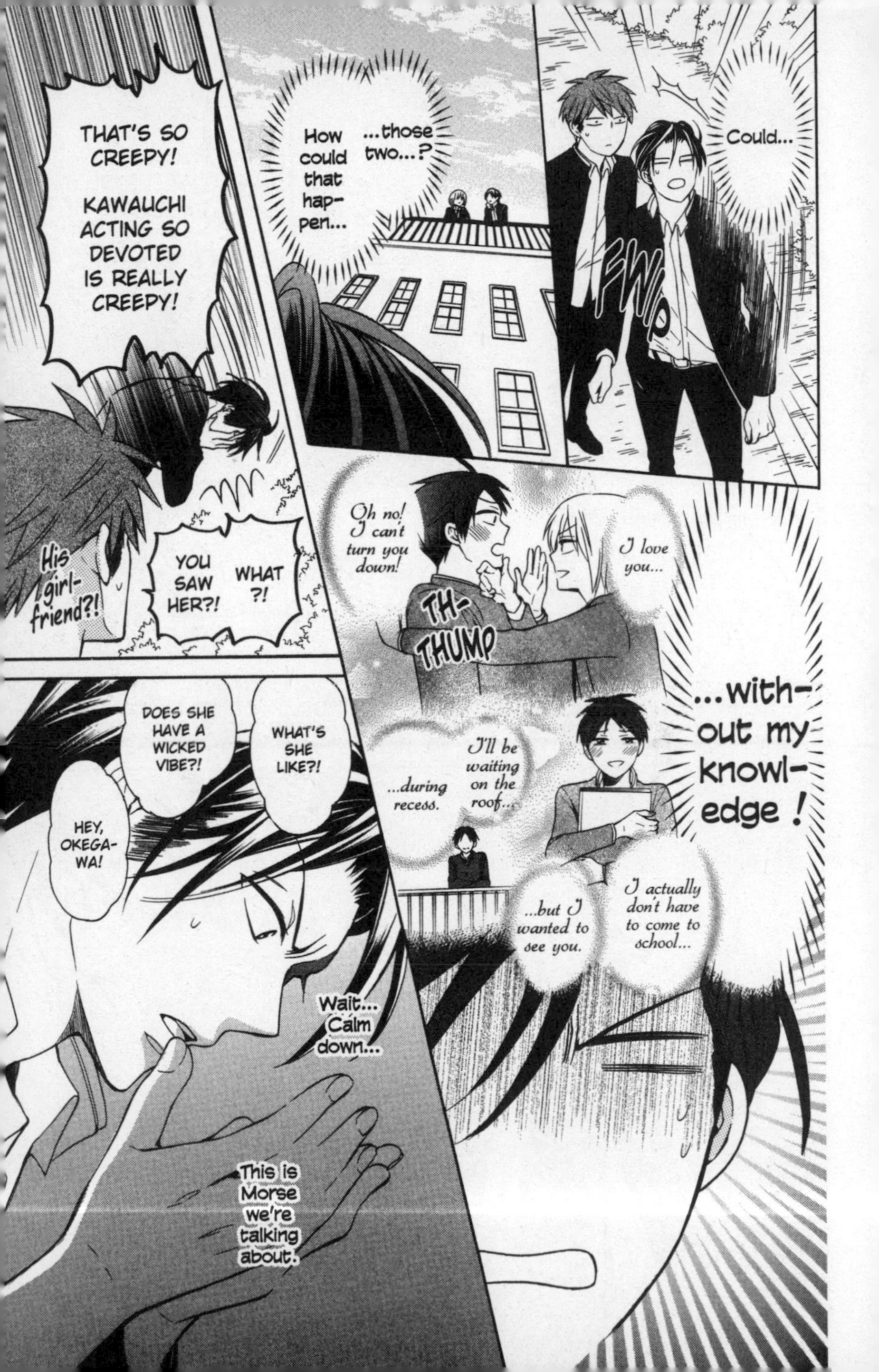

Could...
FWIP
...those two...?
How could that happen...
I love you...
Oh no! I can't turn you down!
TH-THUMP
I actually don't have to come to school...
...but I wanted to see you.
I'll be waiting on the roof...
...during recess.
...without my knowledge!
THAT'S SO CREEPY!
KAWAUCHI ACTING SO DEVOTED IS REALLY CREEPY!
WHAT?!
YOU SAW HER?!
His girlfriend?!
WHAT'S SHE LIKE?!
DOES SHE HAVE A WICKED VIBE?!
HEY, OKEGAWA!
Wait... Calm down...
This is Morse we're talking about.

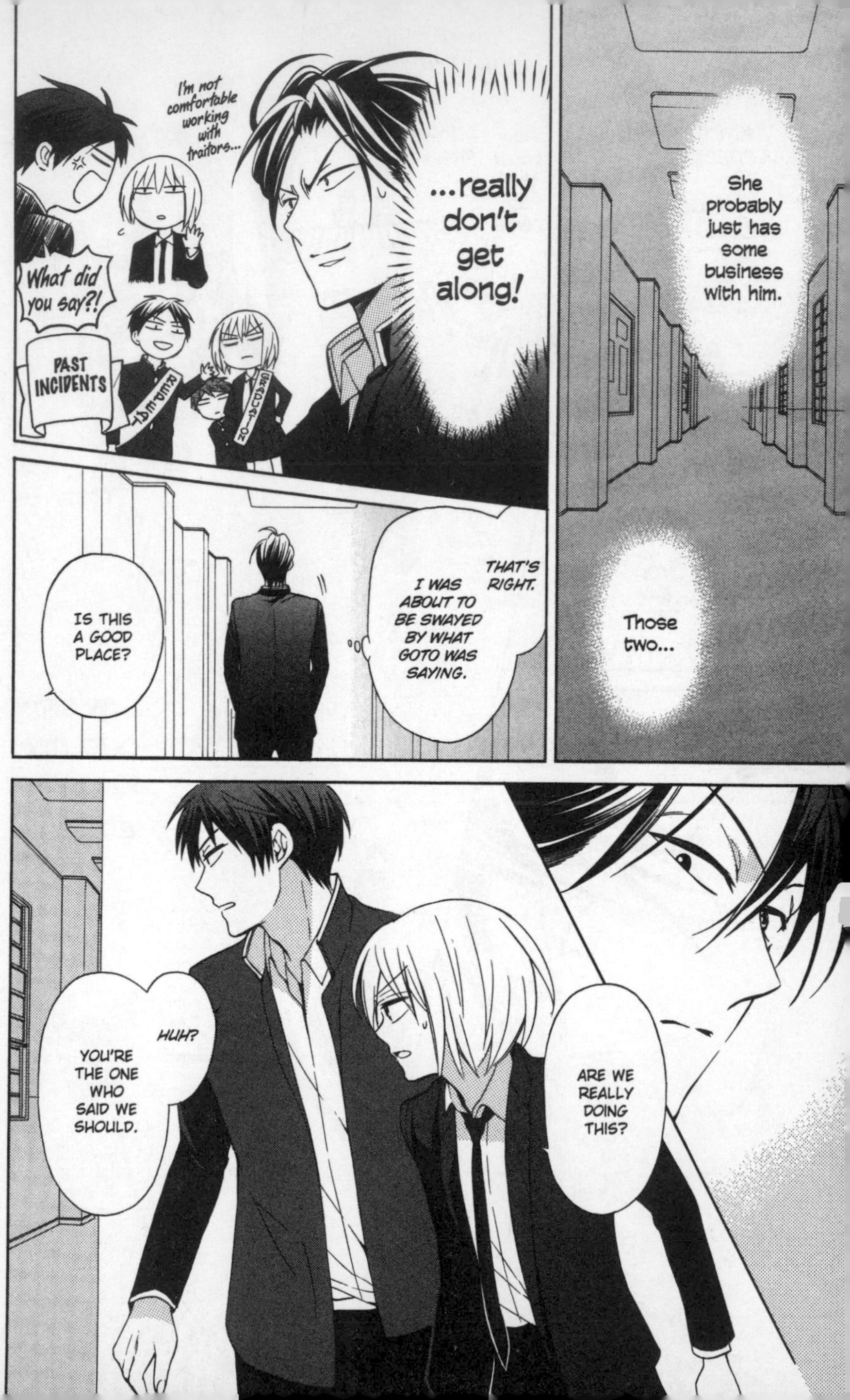

She probably just has some business with him.
Those two...
...really don't get along!
I'm not comfortable working with traitors...
What did you say?!
PAST INCIDENTS
GRADUATION
THAT'S RIGHT.
I WAS ABOUT TO BE SWAYED BY WHAT GOTO WAS SAYING.
IS THIS A GOOD PLACE?
ARE WE REALLY DOING THIS?
HUH?
YOU'RE THE ONE WHO SAID WE SHOULD.

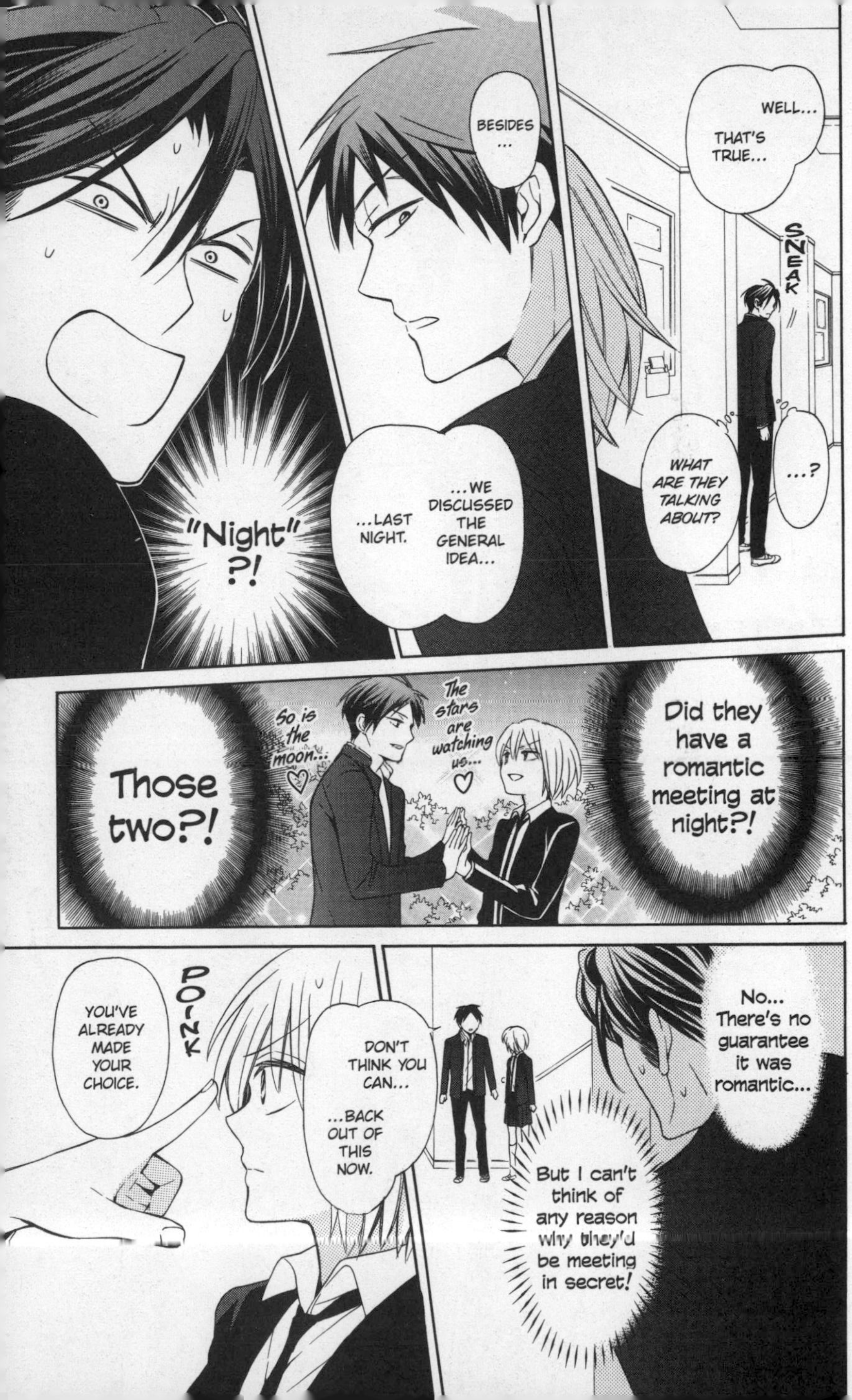
WELL... THAT'S TRUE...
SNEAK
...?
WHAT ARE THEY TALKING ABOUT?
BESIDES...
...WE DISCUSSED THE GENERAL IDEA...
...LAST NIGHT.
"Night" ?!
Did they have a romantic meeting at night?!
The stars are watching us...
So is the moon...
Those two?!
No... There's no guarantee it was romantic...
But I can't think of any reason why they'd be meeting in secret!
DON'T THINK YOU CAN...
...BACK OUT OF THIS NOW.
POINK
YOU'VE ALREADY MADE YOUR CHOICE.

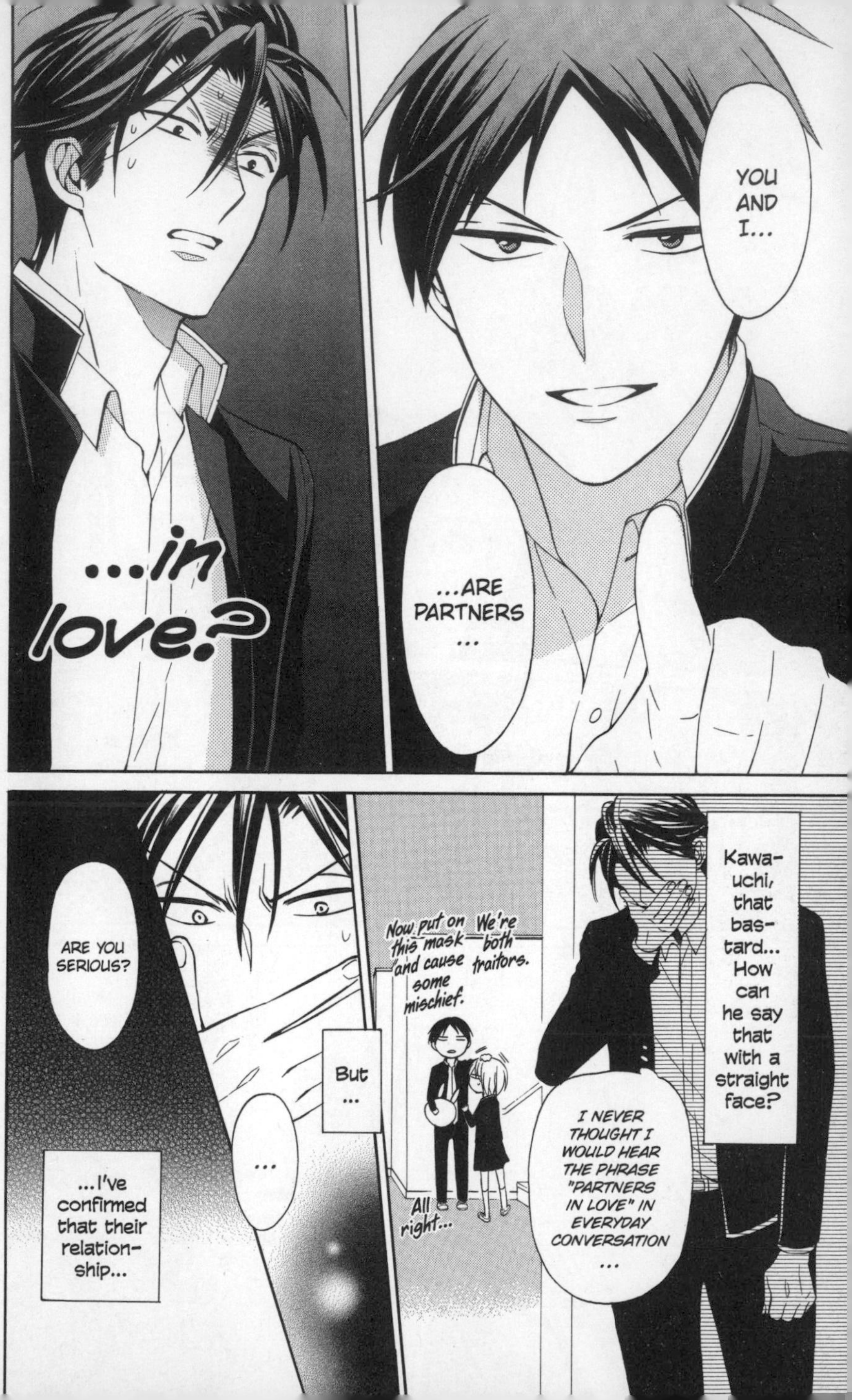
YOU AND I...
...ARE PARTNERS ...
...in love?
Kawa-uchi, that bas-tard... How can he say that with a straight face?
I NEVER THOUGHT I WOULD HEAR THE PHRASE "PARTNERS IN LOVE" IN EVERYDAY CONVERSATION ...
We're both traitors.
Now put on this mask and cause some mischief.
All right...
ARE YOU SERIOUS?
But ...
...
...I've confirmed that their relationship...

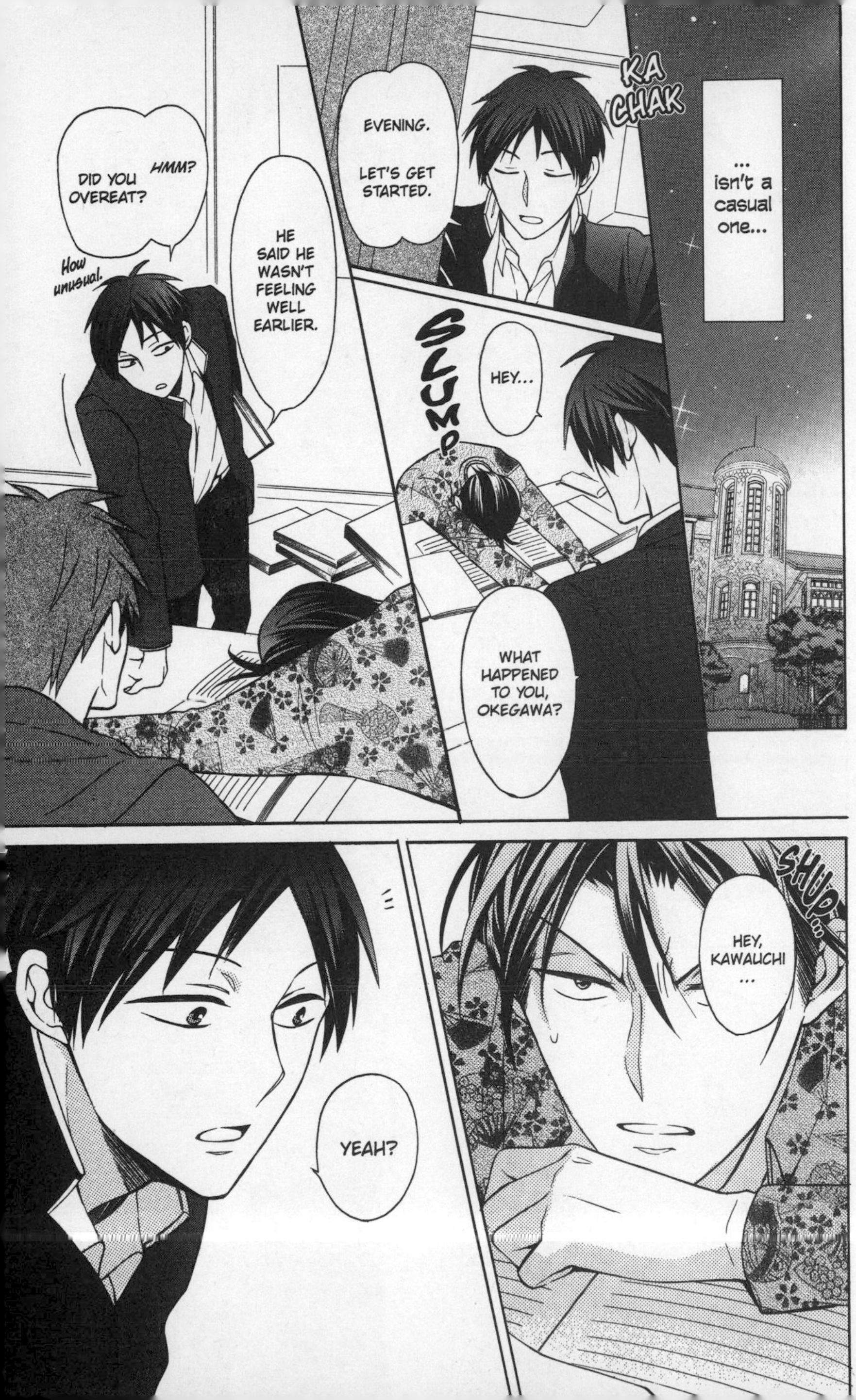

... isn't a casual one...
KA CHAK
EVENING. LET'S GET STARTED.
SLUMP
HEY...
WHAT HAPPENED TO YOU, OKEGAWA?
HE SAID HE WASN'T FEELING WELL EARLIER.
HMM? DID YOU OVEREAT?
How unusual.
SHUP...
HEY, KAWAUCHI ...
YEAH?

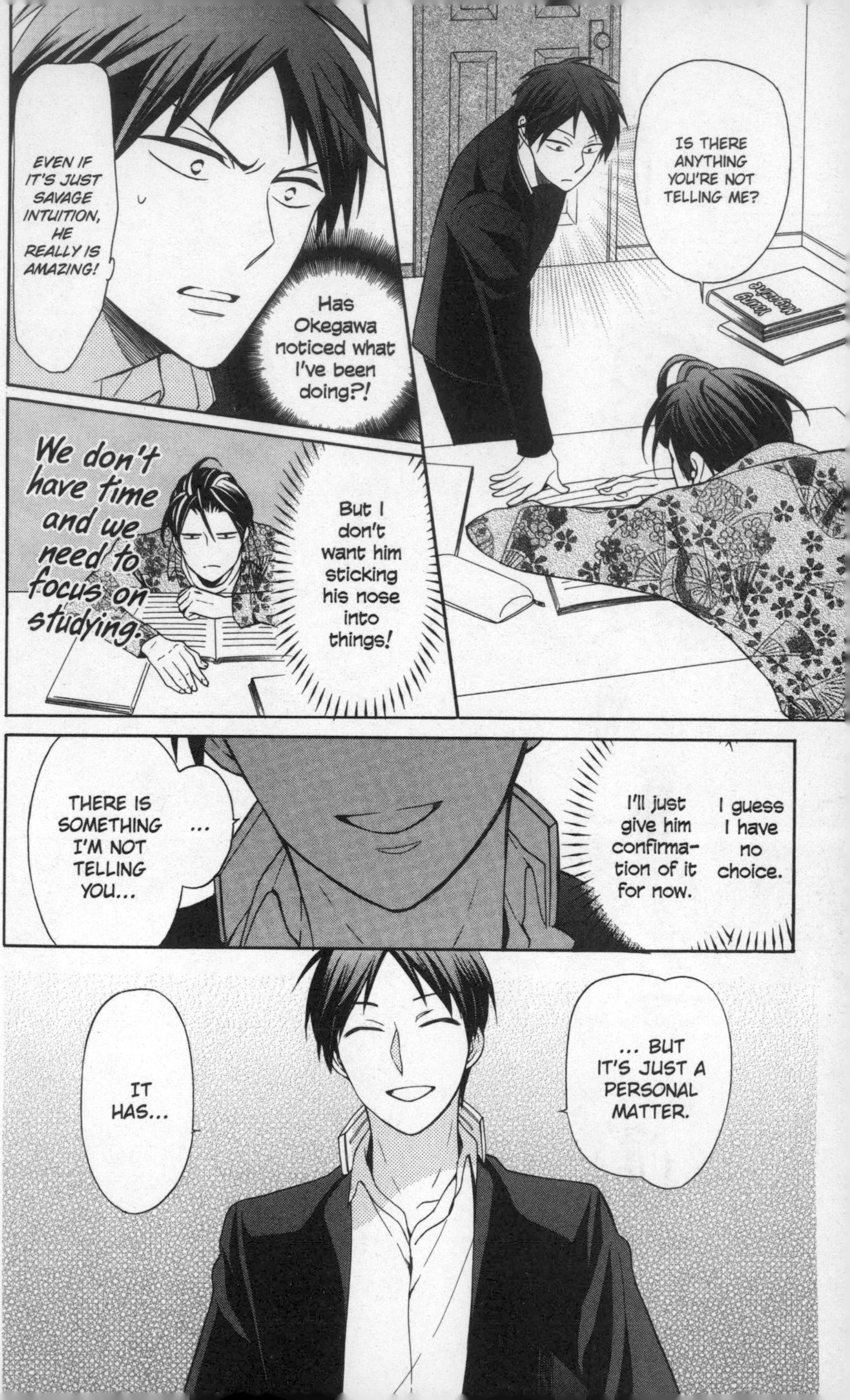
IS THERE ANYTHING YOU'RE NOT TELLING ME?
Has Okegawa noticed what I've been doing?!
EVEN IF IT'S JUST SAVAGE INTUITION, HE REALLY IS AMAZING!
But I don't want him sticking his nose into things!
We don't have time and we need to focus on studying.
I guess I have no choice.
I'll just give him confirmation of it for now.
...
THERE IS SOMETHING I'M NOT TELLING YOU...
... BUT IT'S JUST A PERSONAL MATTER.
IT HAS...

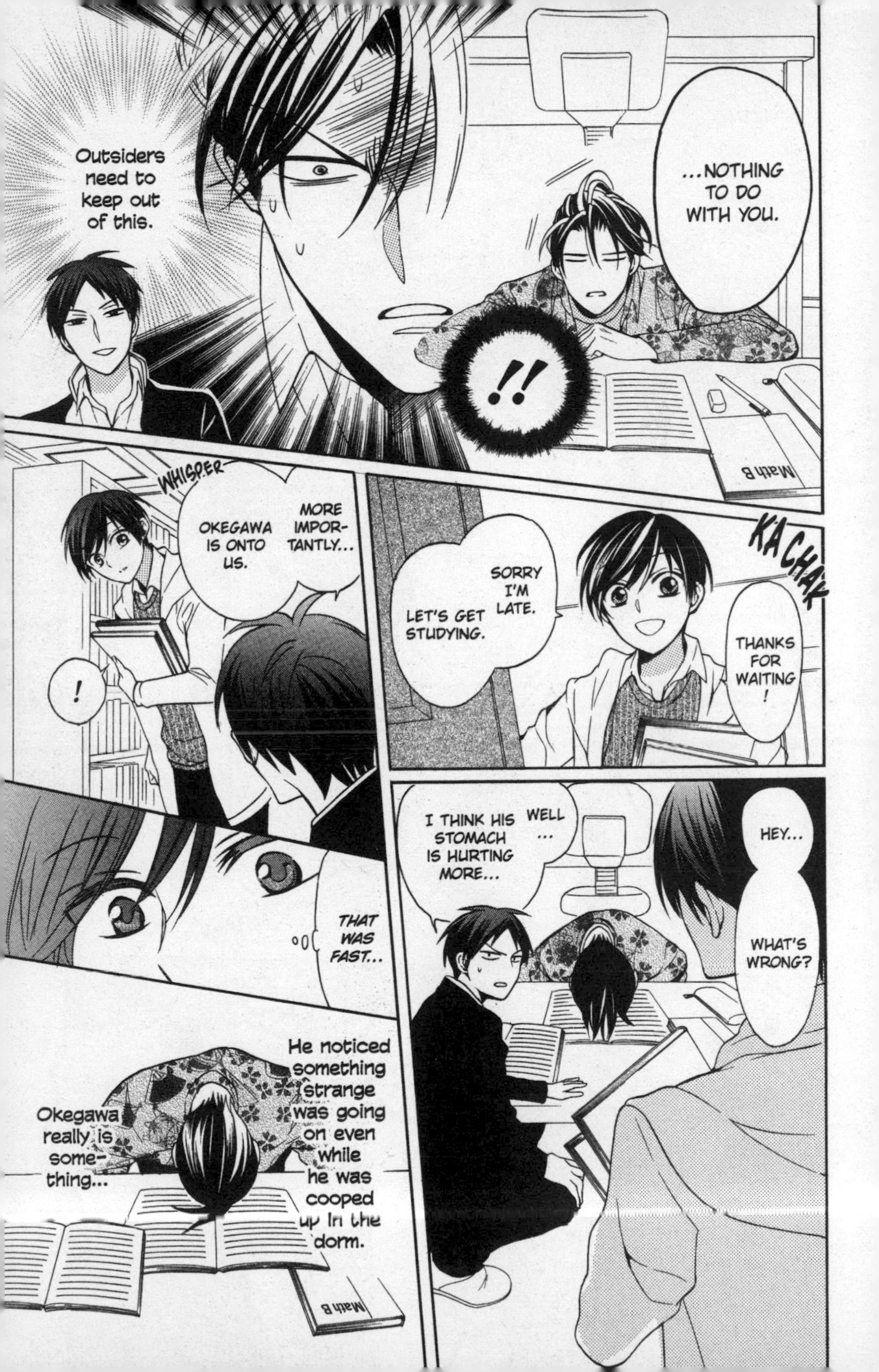
...NOTHING TO DO WITH YOU.
!!
Outsiders need to keep out of this.
KA CHAK
THANKS FOR WAITING!
SORRY I'M LATE.
LET'S GET STUDYING.
WHISPER
MORE IMPORTANTLY...
OKEGAWA IS ONTO US.
!
HEY...
WHAT'S WRONG?
WELL...
I THINK HIS STOMACH IS HURTING MORE...
THAT WAS FAST...
He noticed something strange was going on even while he was cooped up in the dorm.
Okegawa really is something...

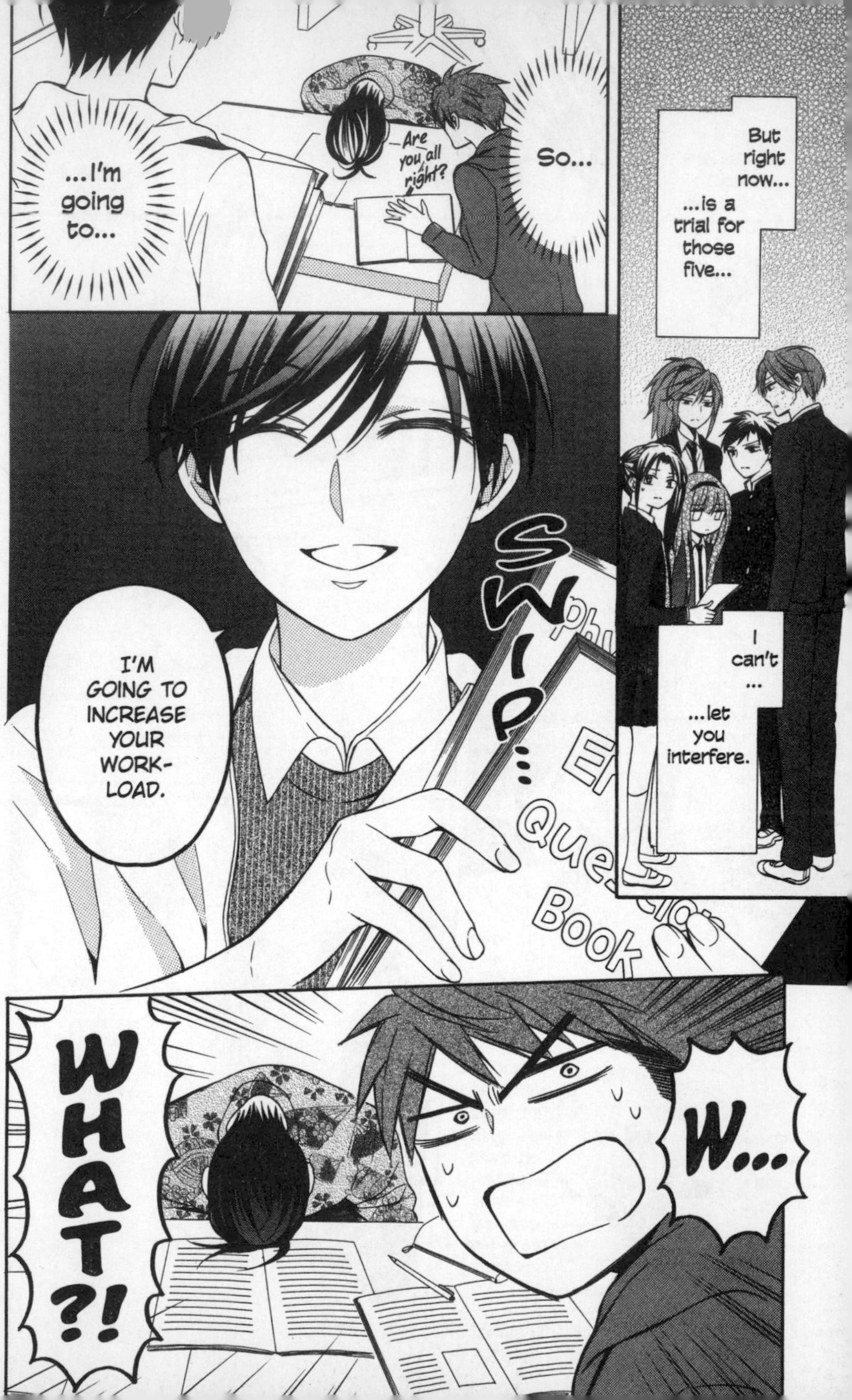
But right now...
...is a trial for those five...
I can't ...
...let you interfere.
So...
Are you all right?
...I'm going to...
I'M GOING TO INCREASE YOUR WORK-LOAD.
SWIP...
Book
W...
WHAT?!

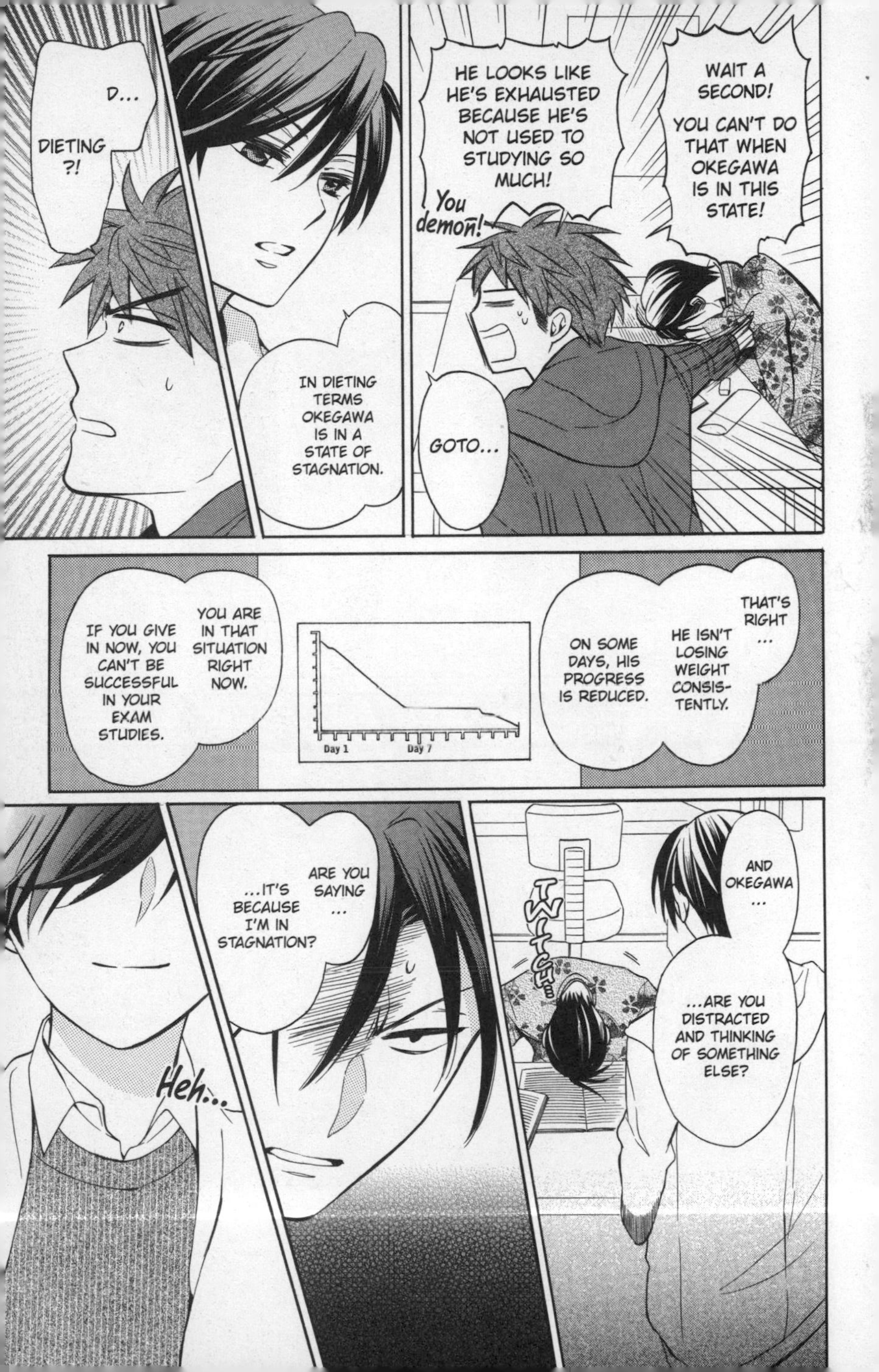
WAIT A SECOND! YOU CAN'T DO THAT WHEN OKEGAWA IS IN THIS STATE!
HE LOOKS LIKE HE'S EXHAUSTED BECAUSE HE'S NOT USED TO STUDYING SO MUCH!
You demon!
GOTO...
IN DIETING TERMS OKEGAWA IS IN A STATE OF STAGNATION.
D... DIETING?!
THAT'S RIGHT...
HE ISN'T LOSING WEIGHT CONSISTENTLY.
ON SOME DAYS, HIS PROGRESS IS REDUCED.
Day 1
Day 7
YOU ARE IN THAT SITUATION RIGHT NOW.
IF YOU GIVE IN NOW, YOU CAN'T BE SUCCESSFUL IN YOUR EXAM STUDIES.
AND OKEGAWA...
TWITCH
...ARE YOU DISTRACTED AND THINKING OF SOMETHING ELSE?
ARE YOU SAYING...
...IT'S BECAUSE I'M IN STAGNATION?
Heh...

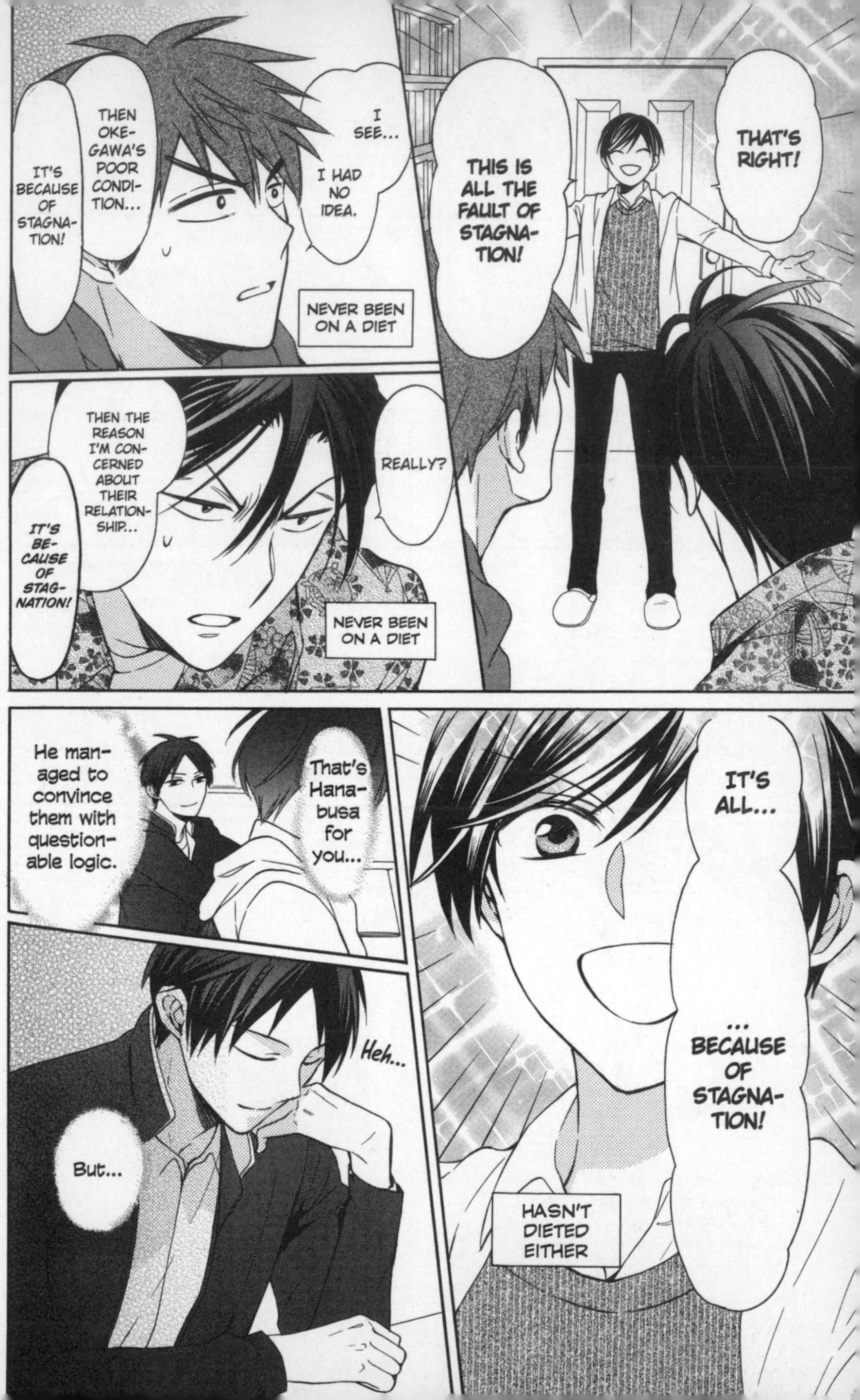
THAT'S RIGHT!
THIS IS ALL THE FAULT OF STAGNATION!
I SEE...
I HAD NO IDEA.
THEN OKEGAWA'S POOR CONDITION...
IT'S BECAUSE OF STAGNATION!
NEVER BEEN ON A DIET
REALLY?
THEN THE REASON I'M CONCERNED ABOUT THEIR RELATIONSHIP...
IT'S BECAUSE OF STAGNATION!
NEVER BEEN ON A DIET
IT'S ALL...
...BECAUSE OF STAGNATION!
HASN'T DIETED EITHER
That's Hanabusa for you...
He managed to convince them with questionable logic.
Heh...
But...

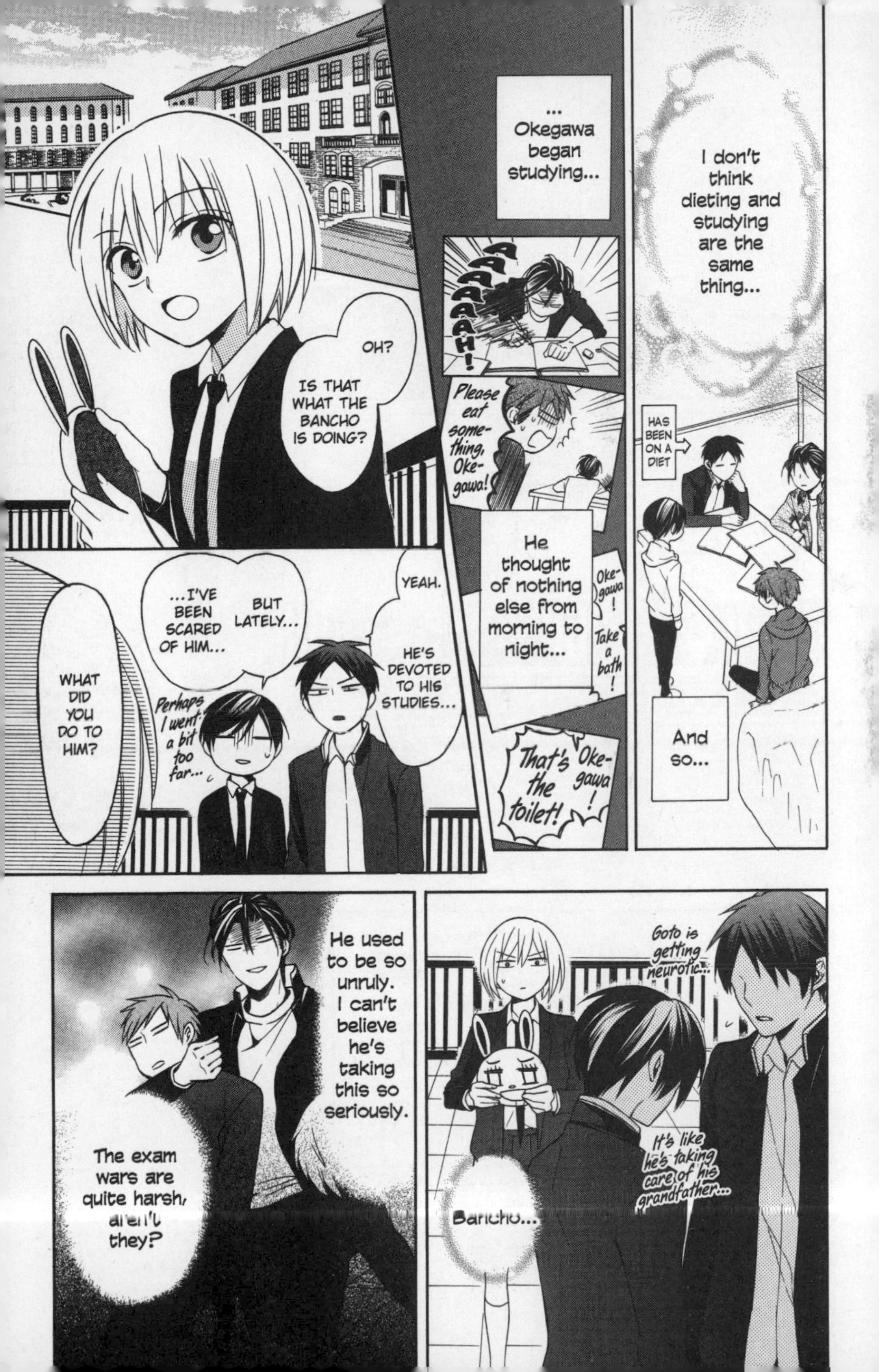
I don't think dieting and studying are the same thing...
HAS BEEN ON A DIET
And so...
... Okegawa began studying...
AAAAAAAH!
Please eat something, Okegawa!
He thought of nothing else from morning to night...
Okegawa!
Take a bath!
Okegawa!
That's the toilet!
OH?
IS THAT WHAT THE BANCHO IS DOING?
YEAH.
HE'S DEVOTED TO HIS STUDIES...
BUT LATELY...
...I'VE BEEN SCARED OF HIM...
Perhaps I went a bit too far...
WHAT DID YOU DO TO HIM?
Goto is getting neurotic...
It's like he's taking care of his grandfather...
Bancho...
He used to be so unruly. I can't believe he's taking this so seriously.
The exam wars are quite harsh, aren't they?

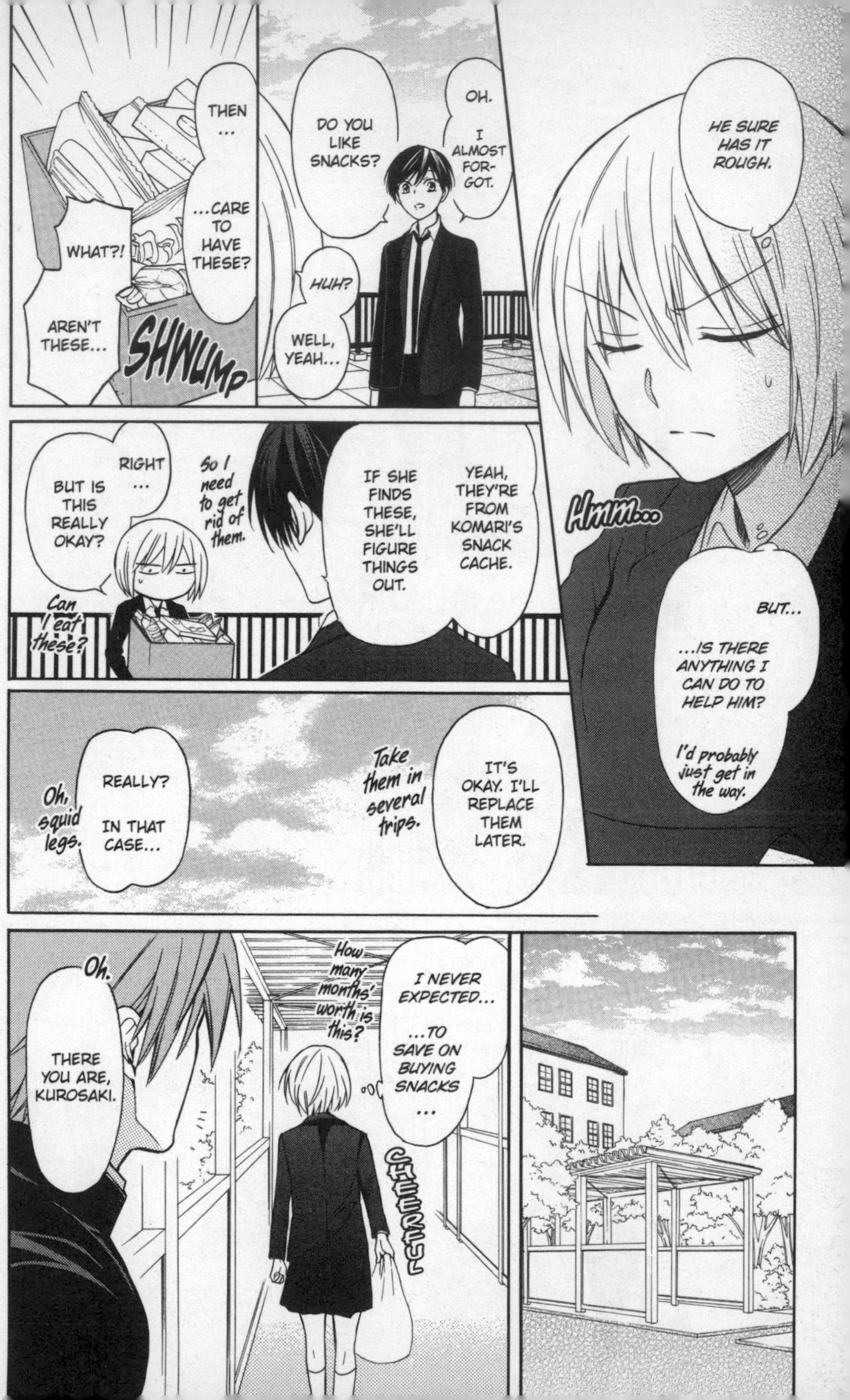
HE SURE HAS IT ROUGH.
Hmm...
BUT...
...IS THERE ANYTHING I CAN DO TO HELP HIM?
I'd probably just get in the way.
OH.
I ALMOST FOR-GOT.
DO YOU LIKE SNACKS?
HUH?
WELL, YEAH...
THEN...
...CARE TO HAVE THESE?
SHWUMP
WHAT?!
AREN'T THESE...
YEAH, THEY'RE FROM KOMARI'S SNACK CACHE.
IF SHE FINDS THESE, SHE'LL FIGURE THINGS OUT.
So I need to get rid of them.
RIGHT...
BUT IS THIS REALLY OKAY?
Can I eat these?
IT'S OKAY. I'LL REPLACE THEM LATER.
Take them in several trips.
REALLY?
IN THAT CASE...
Oh, squid legs.
I NEVER EXPECTED...
...TO SAVE ON BUYING SNACKS...
How many months' worth is this?
CHEERFUL
Oh.
THERE YOU ARE, KUROSAKI.

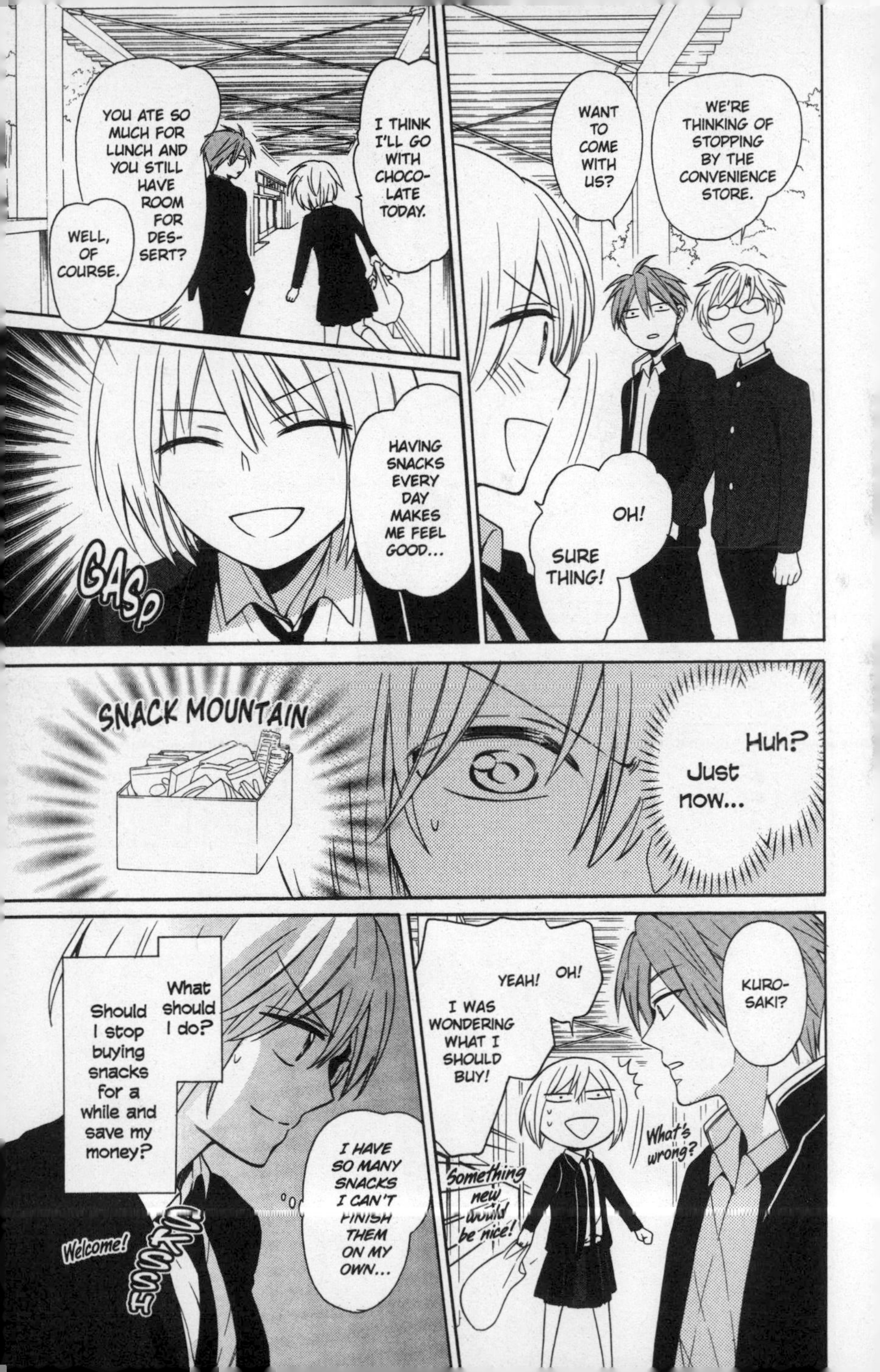
WE'RE THINKING OF STOPPING BY THE CONVENIENCE STORE.
WANT TO COME WITH US?
OH!
SURE THING!
I THINK I'LL GO WITH CHOCOLATE TODAY.
YOU ATE SO MUCH FOR LUNCH AND YOU STILL HAVE ROOM FOR DESSERT?
WELL, OF COURSE.
HAVING SNACKS EVERY DAY MAKES ME FEEL GOOD...
GASP
Huh? Just now...
SNACK MOUNTAIN
KURO-SAKI?
What's wrong?
OH!
YEAH!
I WAS WONDERING WHAT I SHOULD BUY!
Something new would be nice!
What should I do?
Should I stop buying snacks for a while and save my money?
I HAVE SO MANY SNACKS I CAN'T FINISH THEM ON MY OWN...
Welcome!

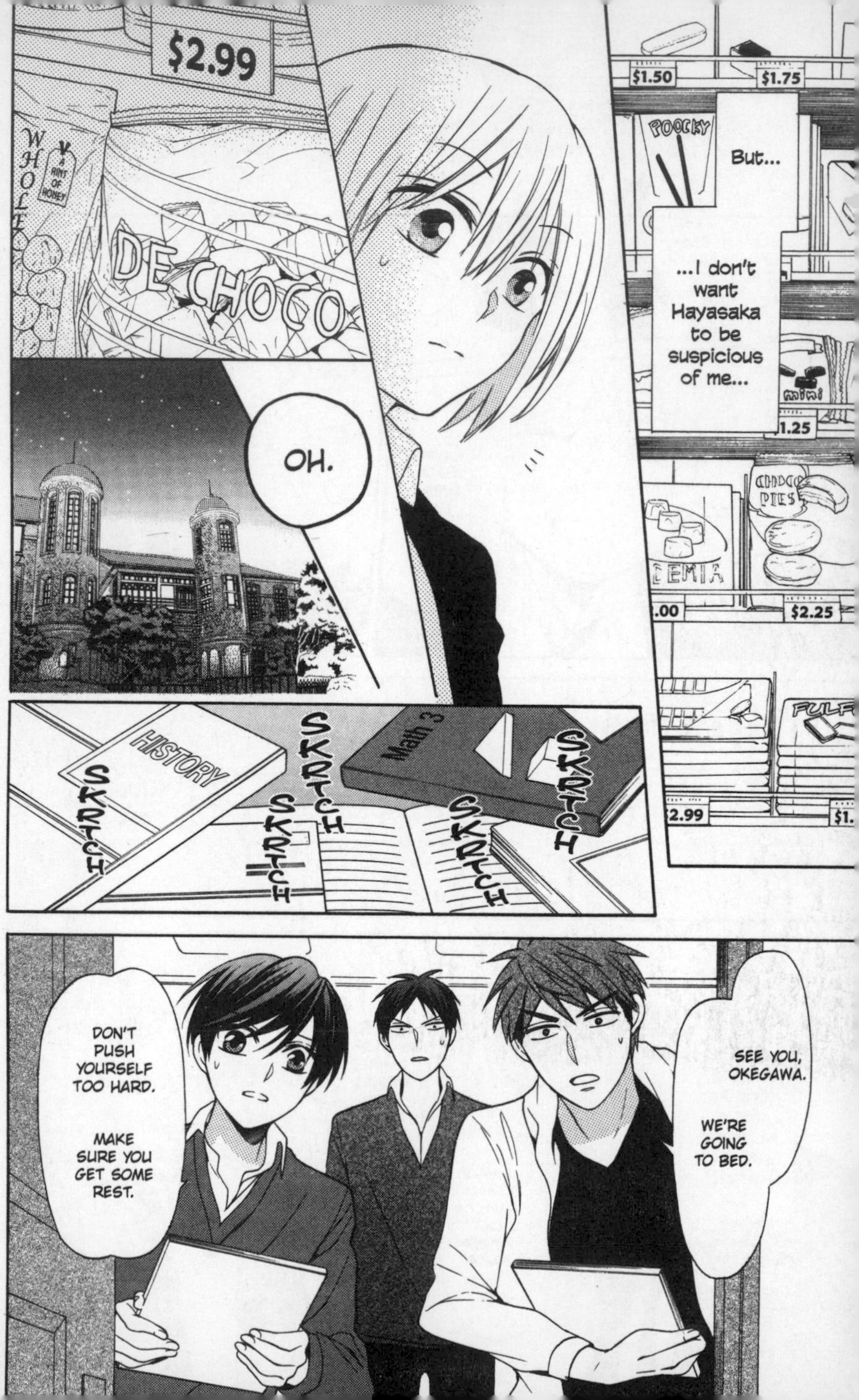
$1.50
$1.75
POOCKY
But...
...I don't want Hayasaka to be suspicious of me...
mimi
$1.25
CHOCO PIES
$2.25
$2.99
$2.99
A HINT OF HONEY
DE CHOCO
OH.
Math 3
SKRTCH
SKRTCH
HISTORY
SKRTCH
SKRTCH
SKRTCH
SKRTCH
SEE YOU, OKEGAWA.
WE'RE GOING TO BED.
DON'T PUSH YOURSELF TOO HARD.
MAKE SURE YOU GET SOME REST.

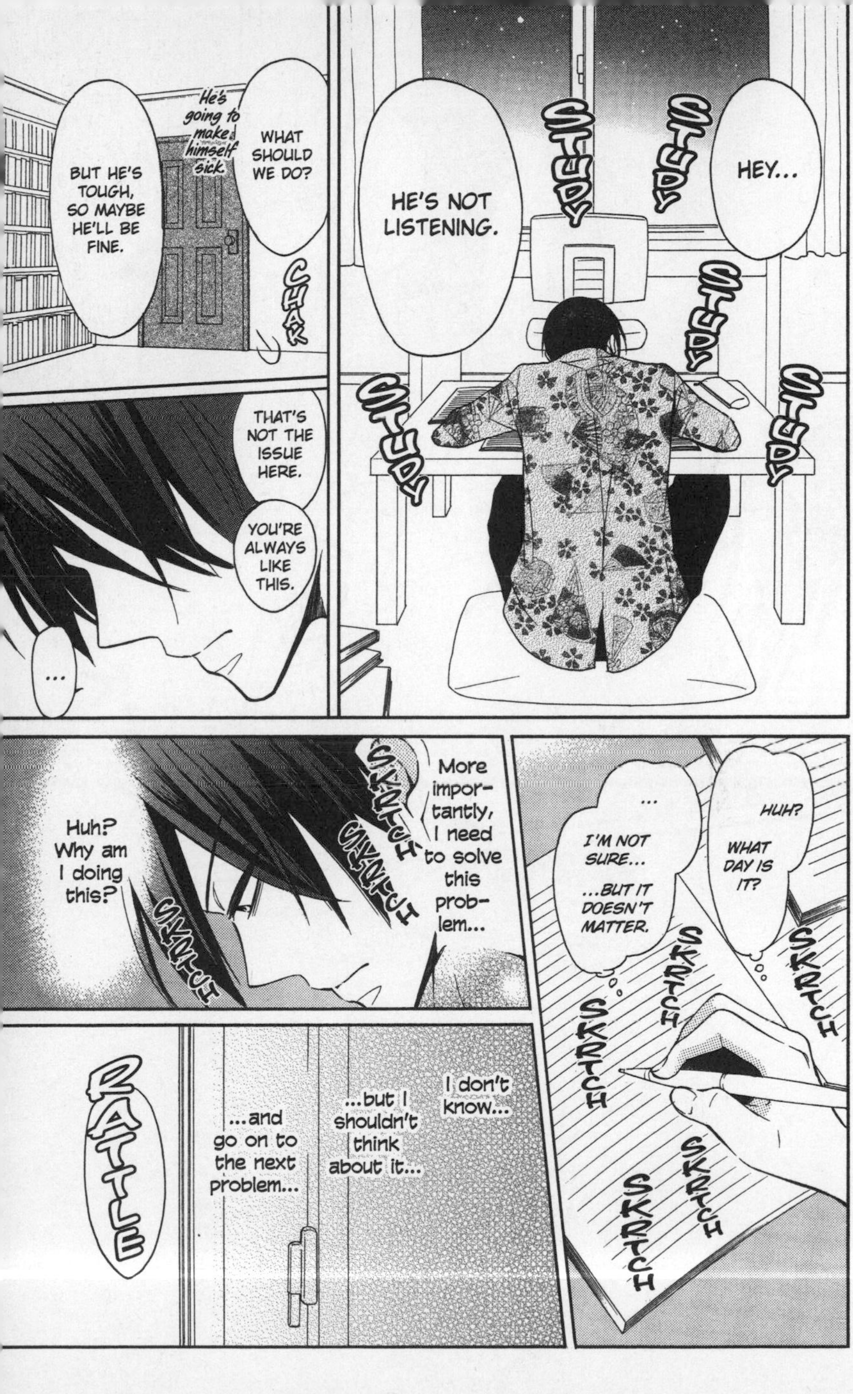
HEY...
STUDY
STUDY
STUDY
STUDY
HE'S NOT LISTENING.
WHAT SHOULD WE DO?
He's going to make himself sick.
BUT HE'S TOUGH, SO MAYBE HE'LL BE FINE.
CHAK
THAT'S NOT THE ISSUE HERE.
YOU'RE ALWAYS LIKE THIS.
...
HUH? WHAT DAY IS IT?
...
I'M NOT SURE...
...BUT IT DOESN'T MATTER.
SKRTCH
SKRTCH
SKRTCH
SKRTCH
SKRTCH
SKRTCH
More importantly, I need to solve this problem...
SKRTCH
SKRTCH
Huh? Why am I doing this?
SKRTCH
I don't know...
...but I shouldn't think about it...
...and go on to the next problem...
RATTLE

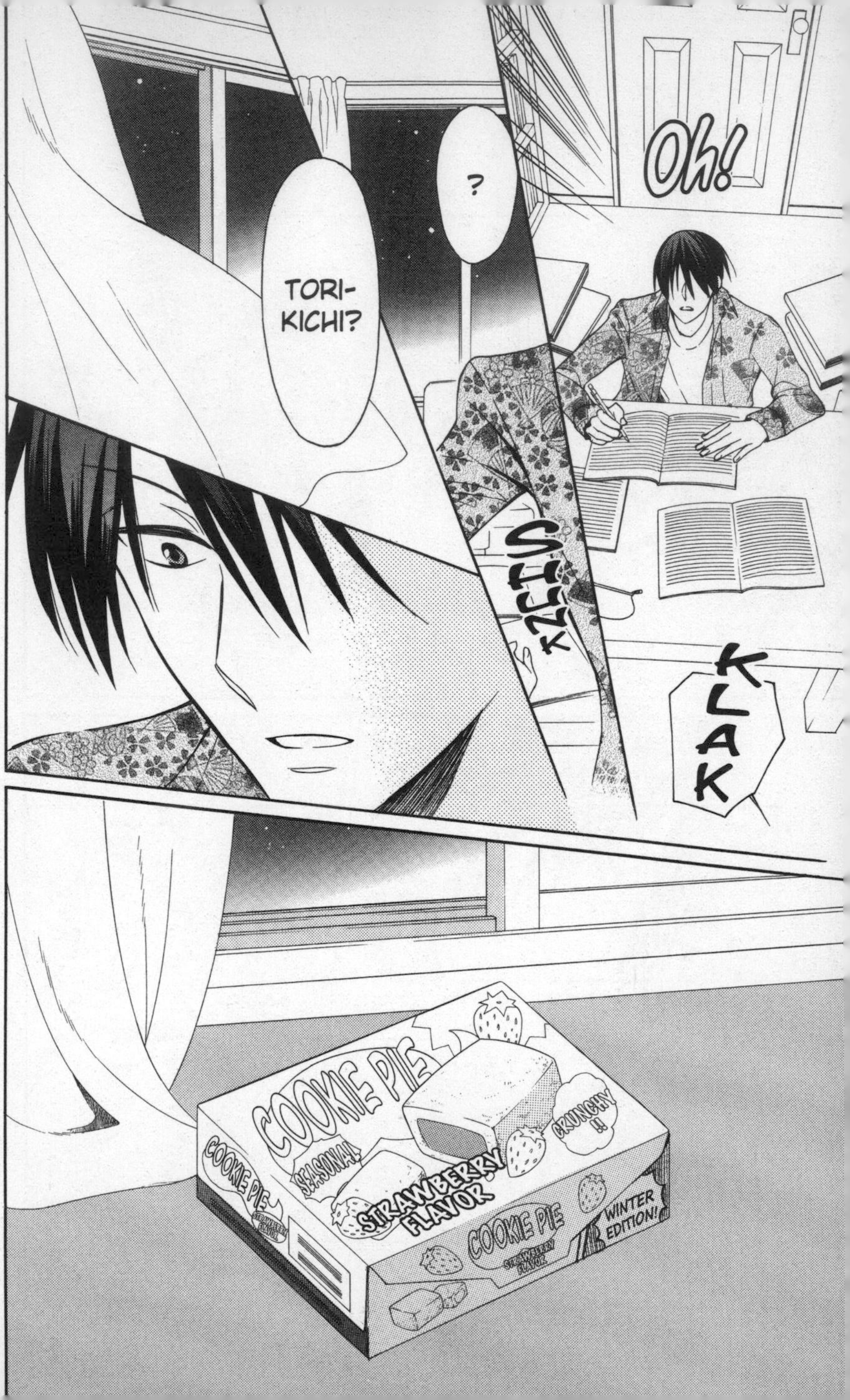
Oh!
KLAK
SHUNK
?
TORI-KICHI?
COOKIE PIE
SEASONAL
STRAWBERRY FLAVOR
CRUNCHY!!
COOKIE PIE
WINTER EDITION!

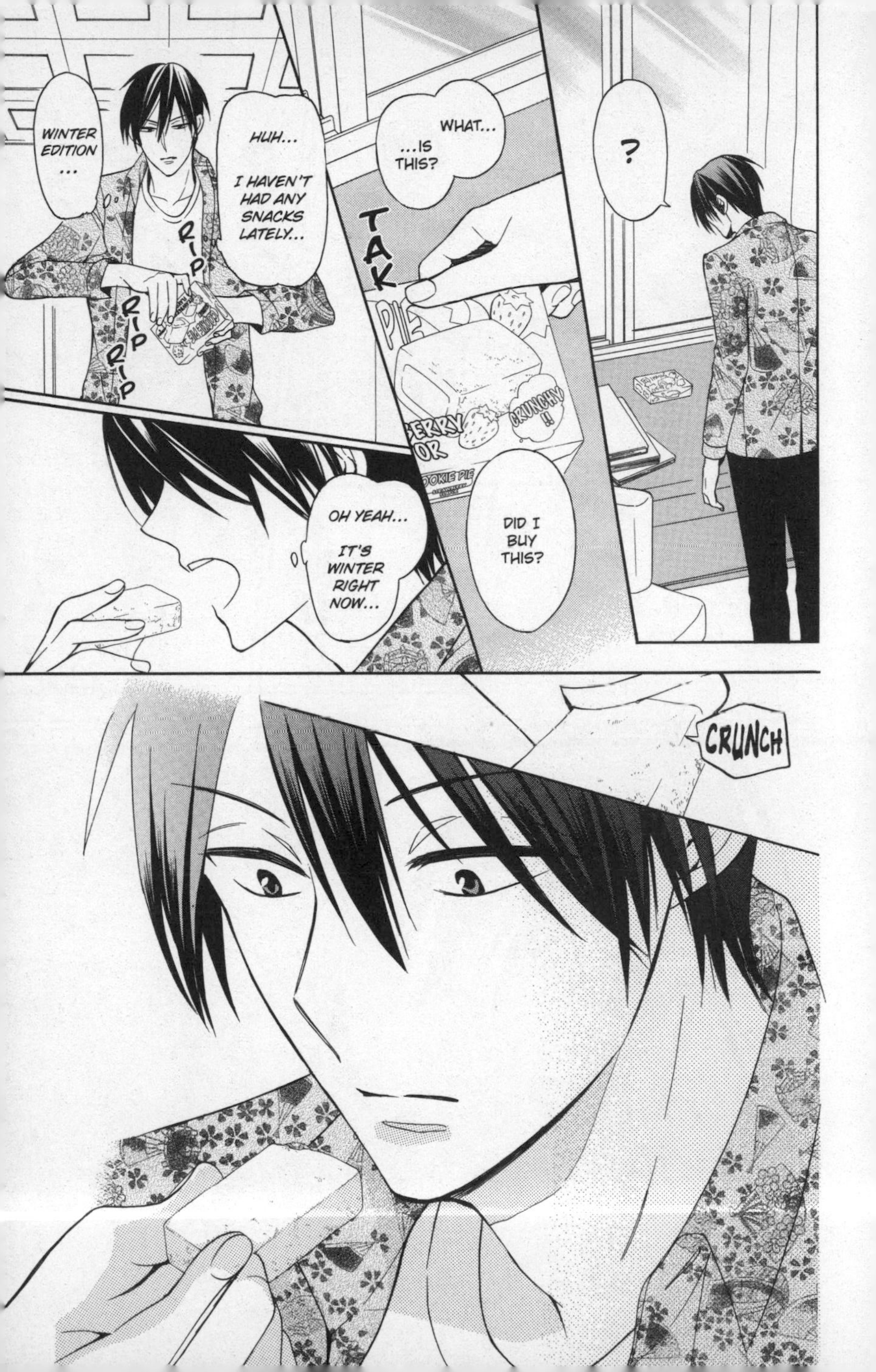
?
WHAT... ...IS THIS?
TAK
CRUNCHY!!
DID I BUY THIS?
HUH... I HAVEN'T HAD ANY SNACKS LATELY...
WINTER EDITION...
RIP RIP RIP
OH YEAH... IT'S WINTER RIGHT NOW...
CRUNCH

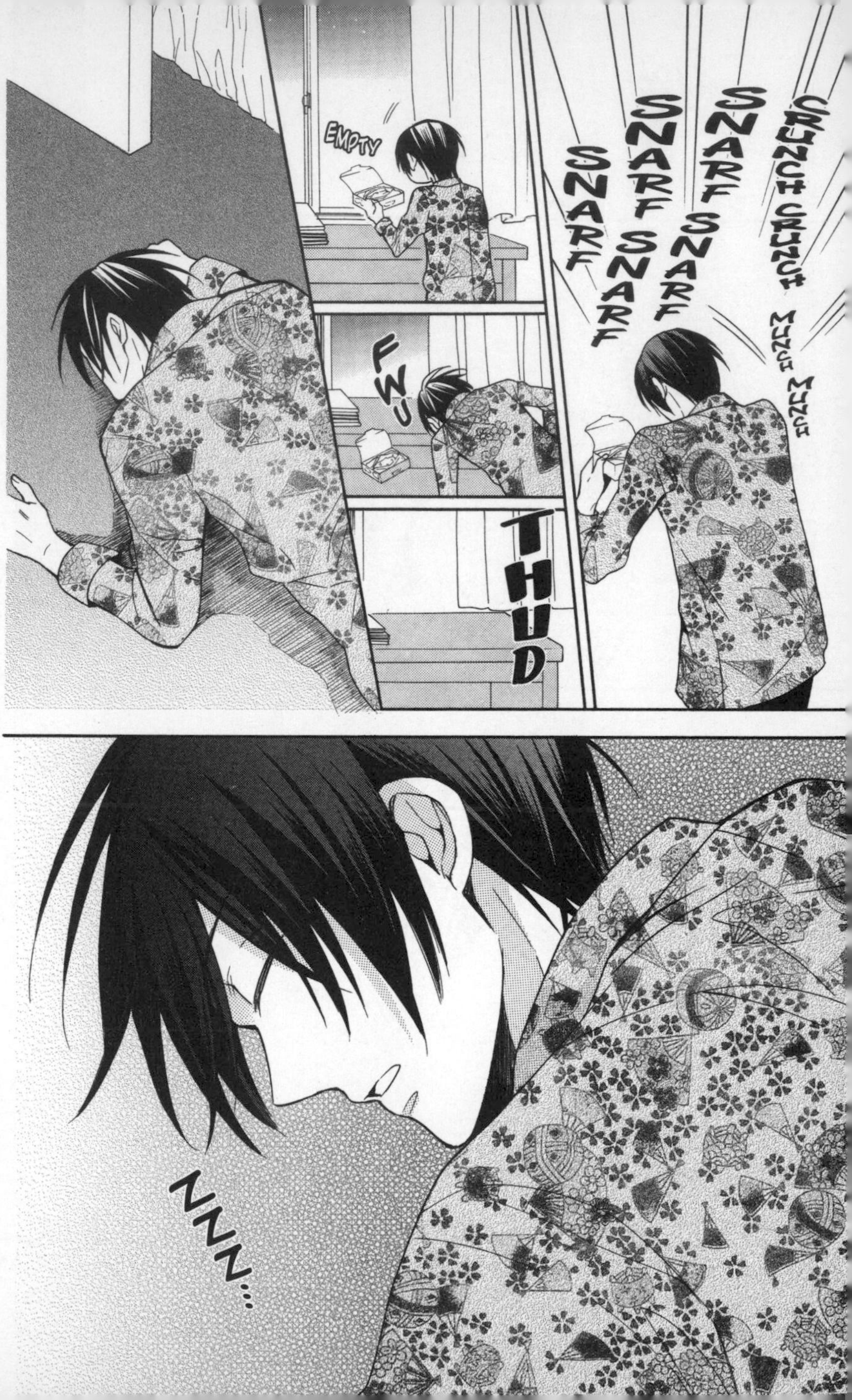
CRUNCH CRUNCH
MUNCH MUNCH
SNARF SNARF
SNARF SNARF
SNARF
EMPTY
FWU
THUD
NNN...

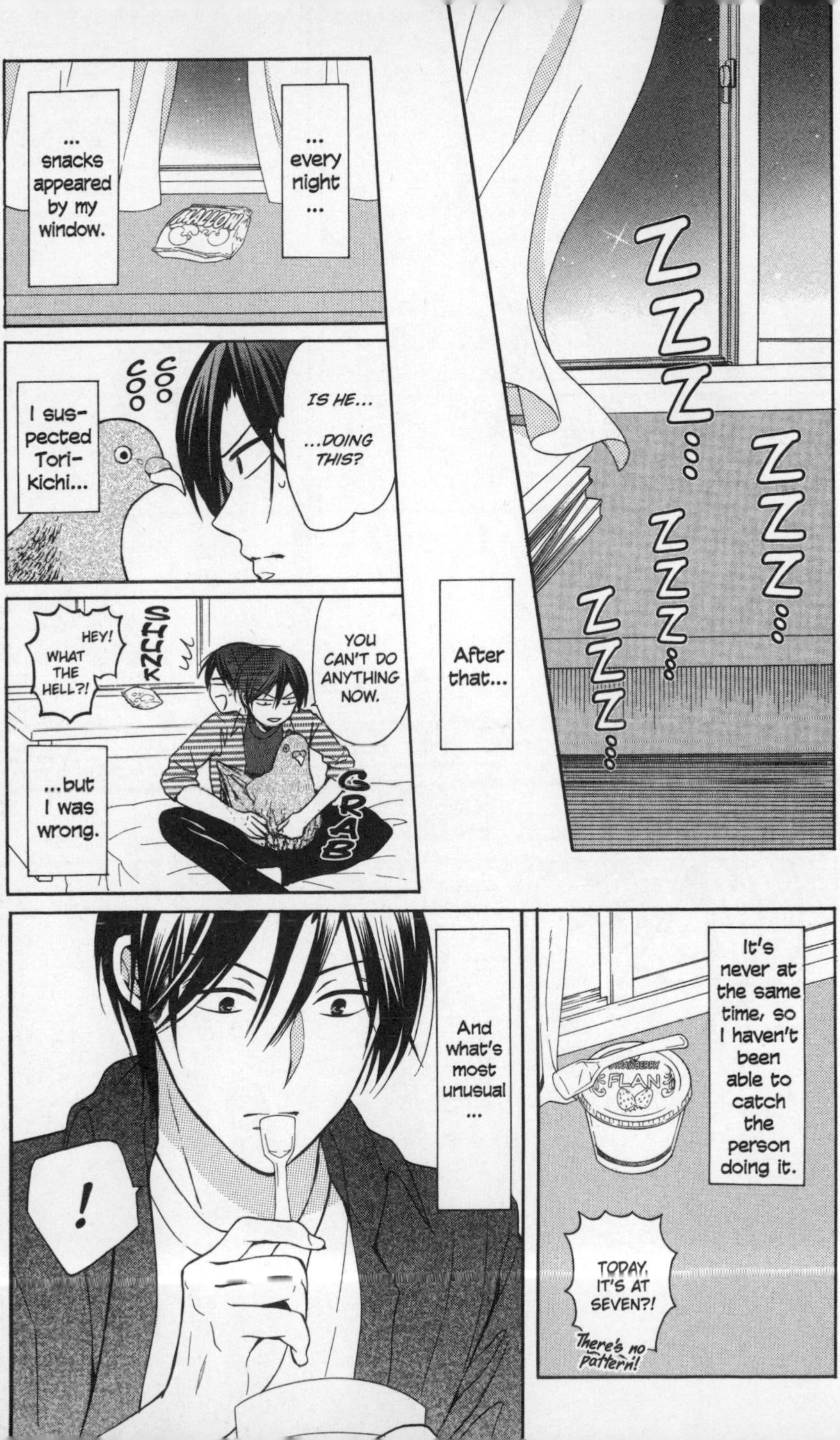
ZZZ...
ZZZ...
ZZZ...
ZZZ...
After that...
... every night ...
... snacks appeared by my window.
MALLOW
COO COO
I suspected Tori-kichi...
IS HE...
...DOING THIS?
YOU CAN'T DO ANYTHING NOW.
SHUNK
HEY! WHAT THE HELL?!
GRAB
...but I was wrong.
It's never at the same time, so I haven't been able to catch the person doing it.
STRAWBERRY
FLAN
TODAY, IT'S AT SEVEN?!
There's no pattern!
And what's most unusual ...
!

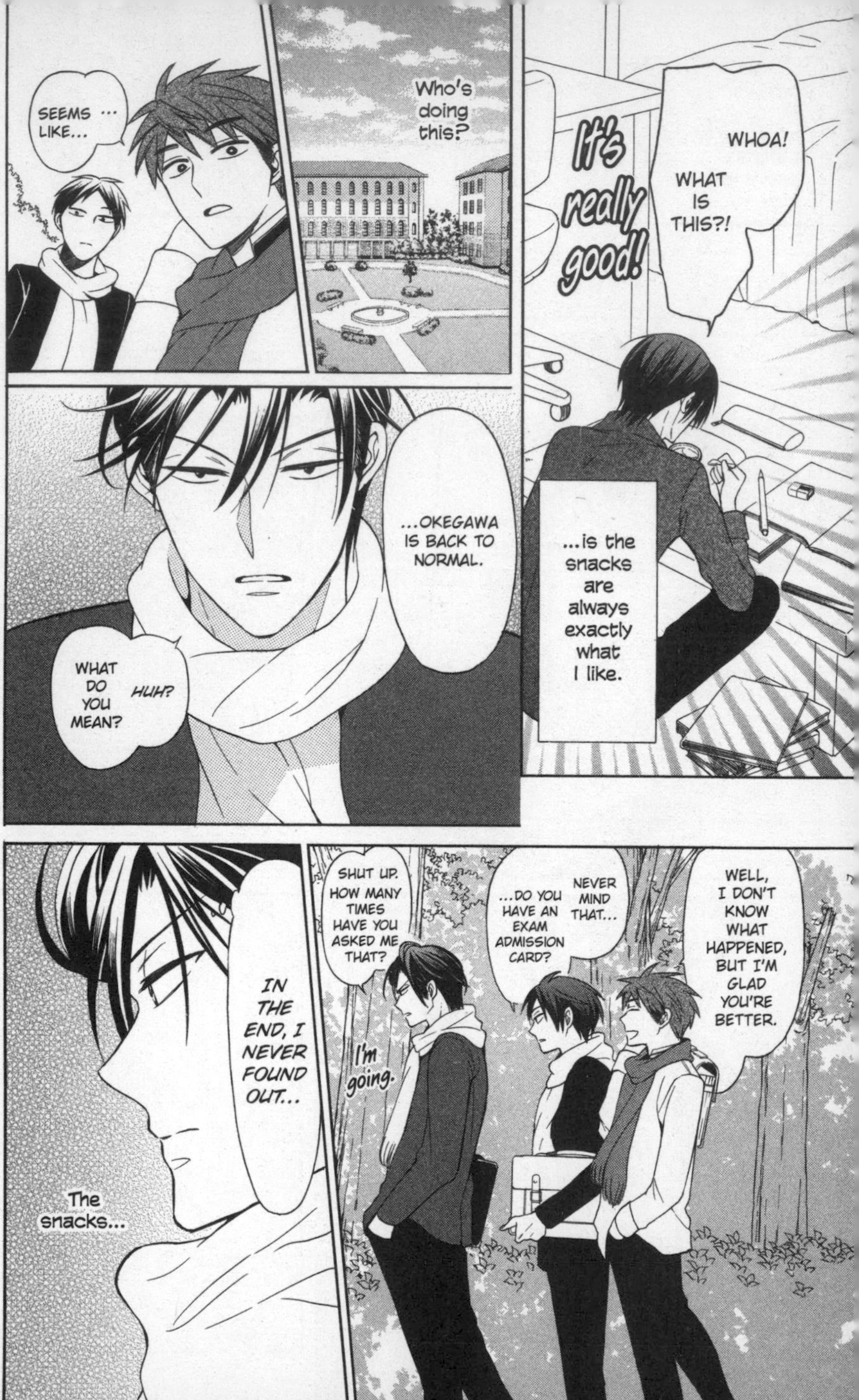
WHOA!
WHAT IS THIS?!
It's really good!
...is the snacks are always exactly what I like.
Who's doing this?
SEEMS ... LIKE...
...OKEGAWA IS BACK TO NORMAL.
HUH?
WHAT DO YOU MEAN?
WELL, I DON'T KNOW WHAT HAPPENED, BUT I'M GLAD YOU'RE BETTER.
NEVER MIND THAT...
...DO YOU HAVE AN EXAM ADMISSION CARD?
SHUT UP. HOW MANY TIMES HAVE YOU ASKED ME THAT?
I'm going.
IN THE END, I NEVER FOUND OUT...
The snacks...

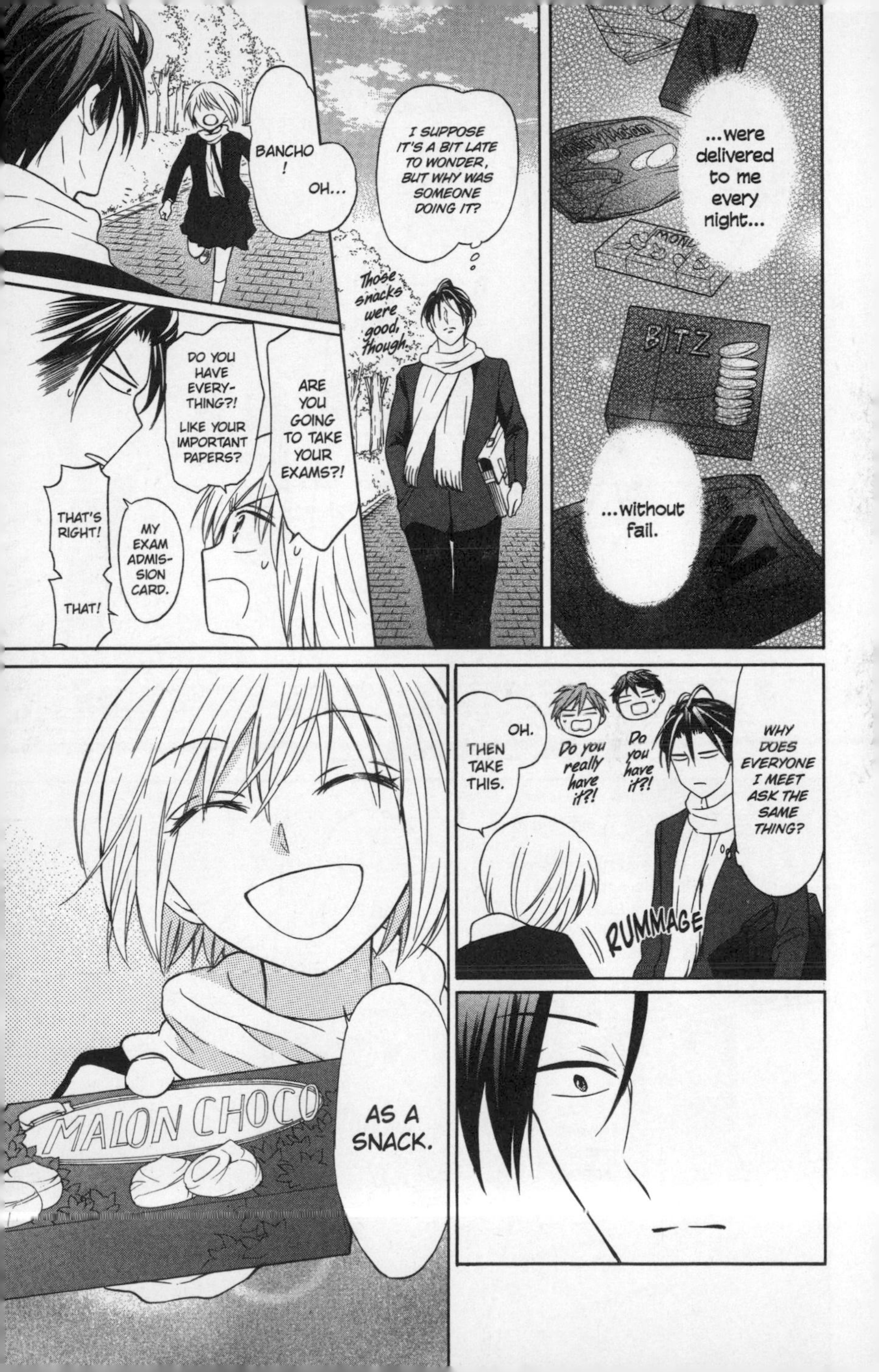

...were delivered to me every night...
...without fail.
BITZ
I SUPPOSE IT'S A BIT LATE TO WONDER, BUT WHY WAS SOMEONE DOING IT?
Those snacks were good, though.
BANCHO!
OH...
ARE YOU GOING TO TAKE YOUR EXAMS?!
DO YOU HAVE EVERYTHING?!
LIKE YOUR IMPORTANT PAPERS?
MY EXAM ADMISSION CARD.
THAT'S RIGHT!
THAT!
WHY DOES EVERYONE I MEET ASK THE SAME THING?
Do you have it?!
Do you really have it?!
OH.
THEN TAKE THIS.
RUMMAGE
AS A SNACK.
MALON CHOCO

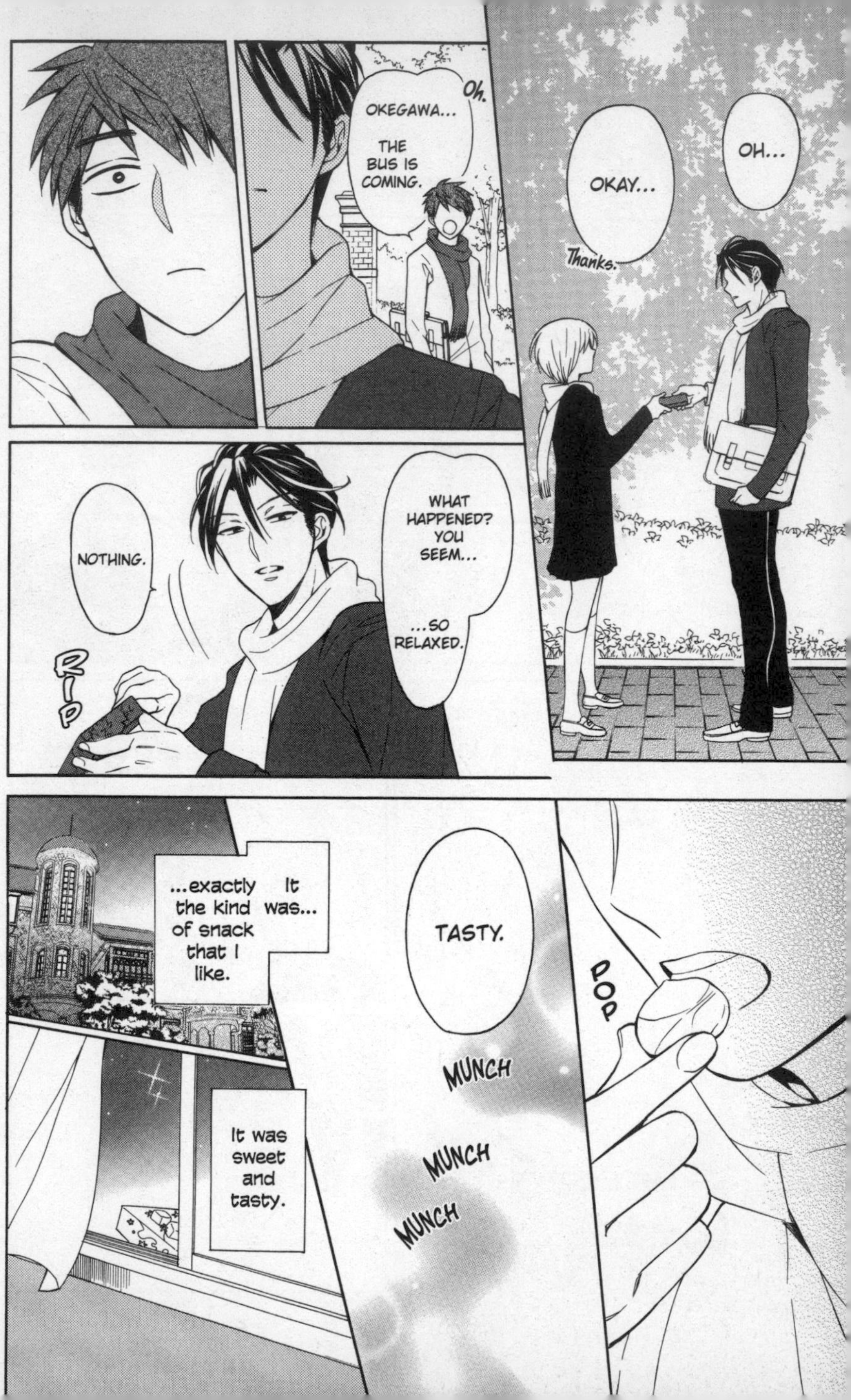
OH...
OKAY...
Thanks.
Oh.
OKEGAWA...
THE BUS IS COMING.
WHAT HAPPENED? YOU SEEM...
...SO RELAXED.
NOTHING.
RIP
POP
TASTY.
MUNCH
MUNCH
MUNCH
It was...
...exactly the kind of snack that I like.
It was sweet and tasty.

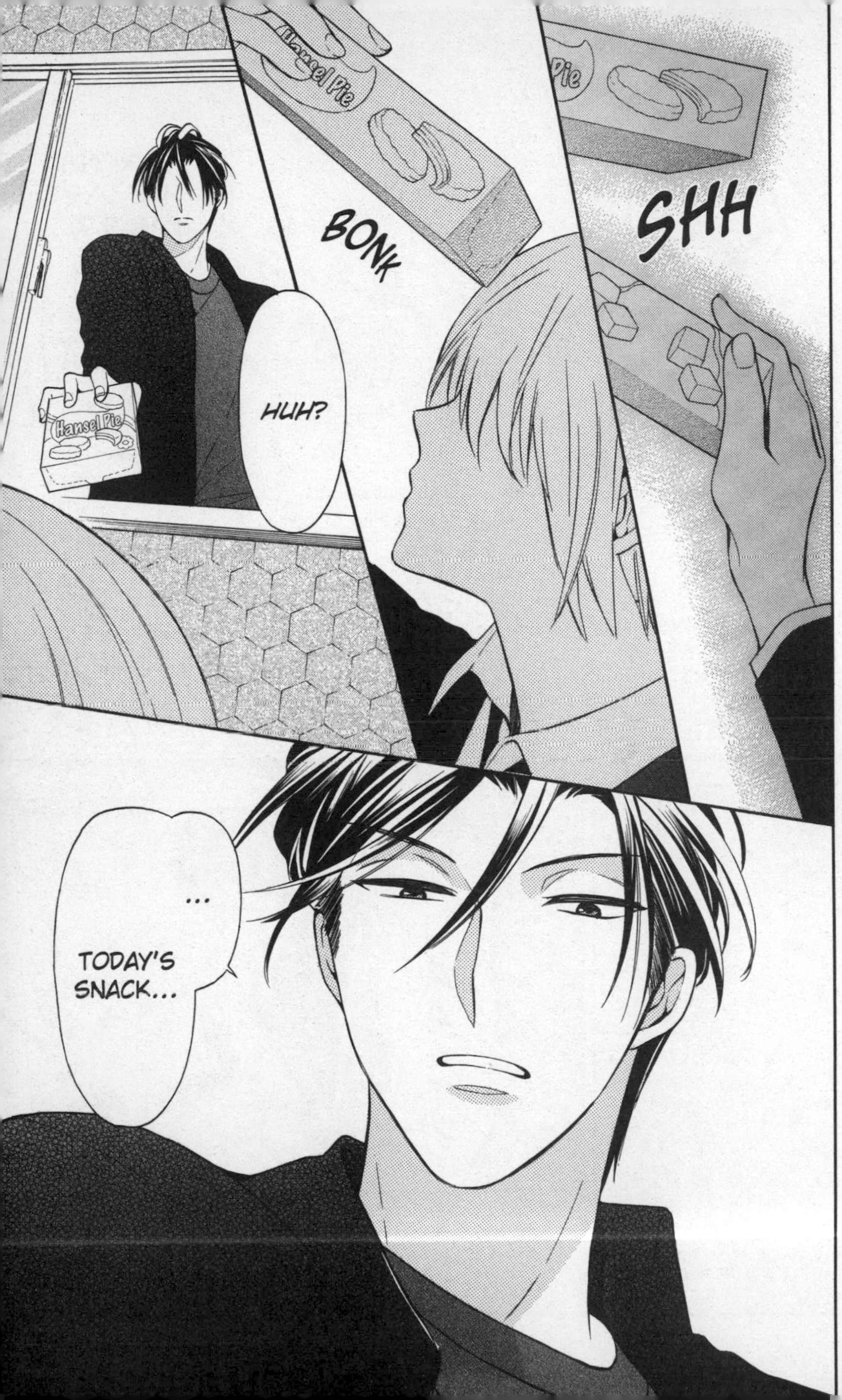
SHH
Hansel Pie
BONK
Hansel Pie
HUH?
...
TODAY'S SNACK...

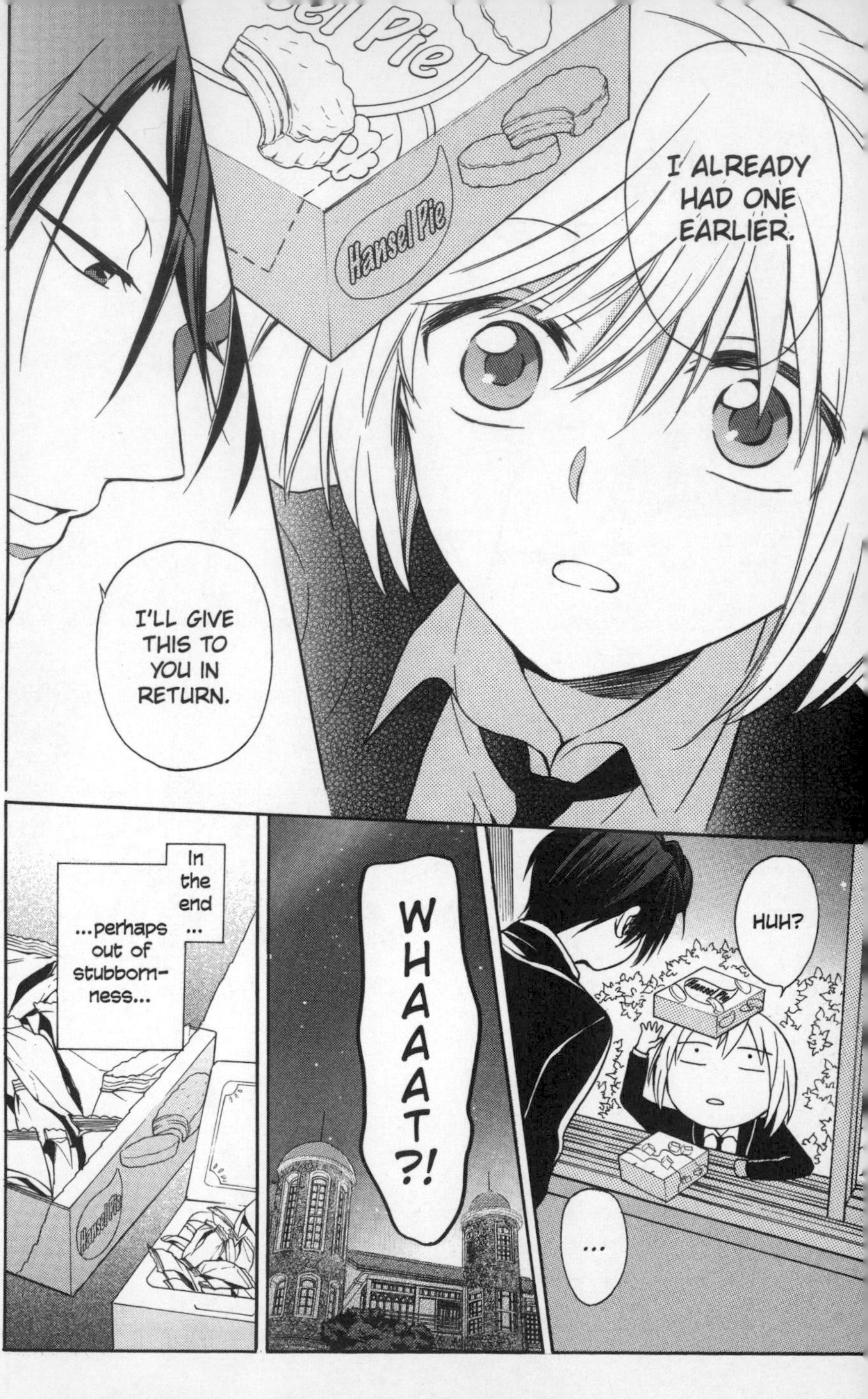
Hansel Pie
I ALREADY HAD ONE EARLIER.
I'LL GIVE THIS TO YOU IN RETURN.
HUH?
...
WHAAAAT?!
In the end...
...perhaps out of stubborn-ness...

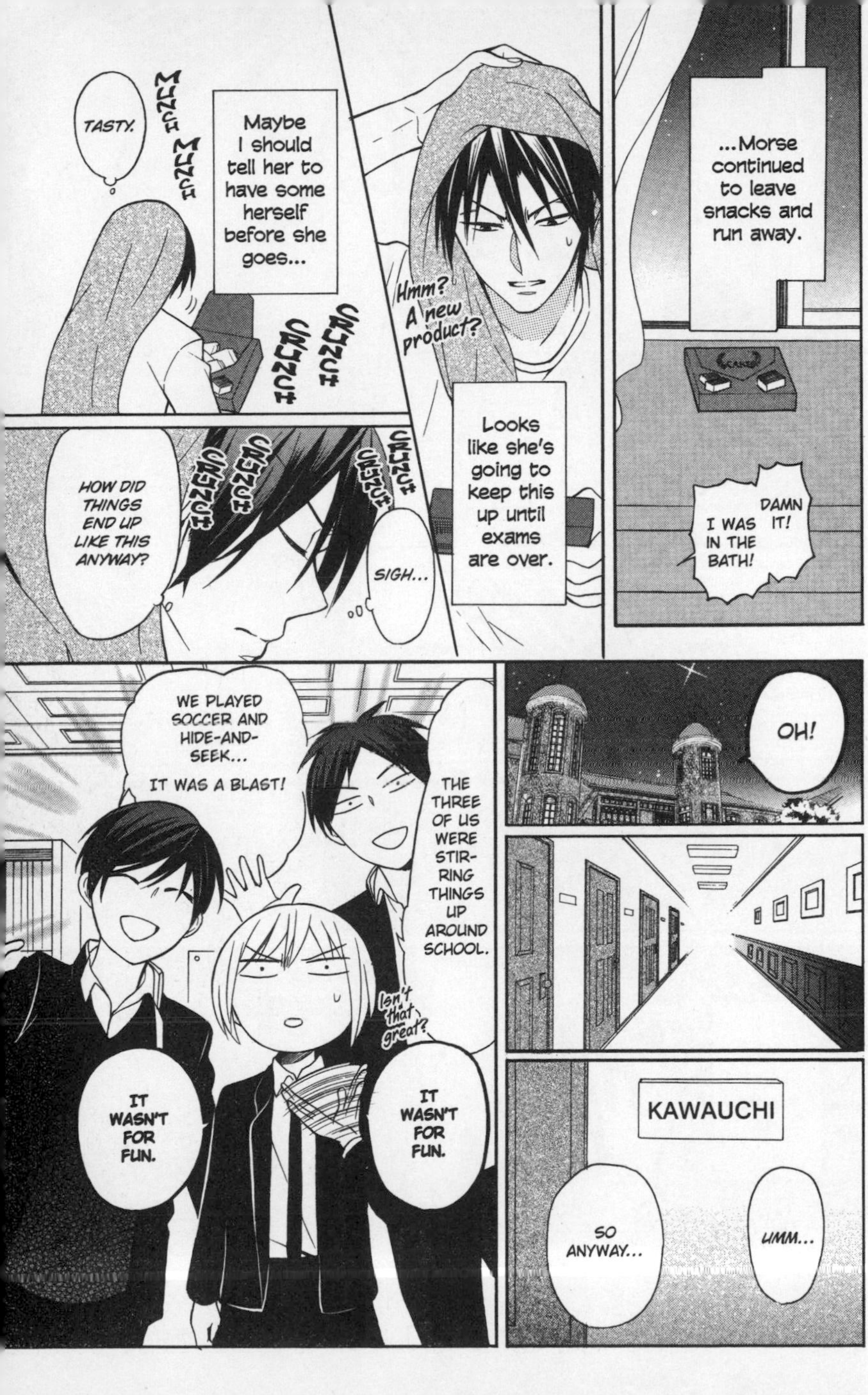
...Morse continued to leave snacks and run away.
I WAS IN THE BATH! DAMN IT!
Hmm? A new product?
Maybe I should tell her to have some herself before she goes...
TASTY.
MUNCH MUNCH
CRUNCH CRUNCH
Looks like she's going to keep this up until exams are over.
SIGH...
CRUNCH CRUNCH
CRUNCH CRUNCH
HOW DID THINGS END UP LIKE THIS ANYWAY?
OH!
KAWAUCHI
UMM...
SO ANYWAY...
THE THREE OF US WERE STIR-RING THINGS UP AROUND SCHOOL.
WE PLAYED SOCCER AND HIDE-AND-SEEK...
IT WAS A BLAST!
Isn't that great?
IT WASN'T FOR FUN.
IT WASN'T FOR FUN.

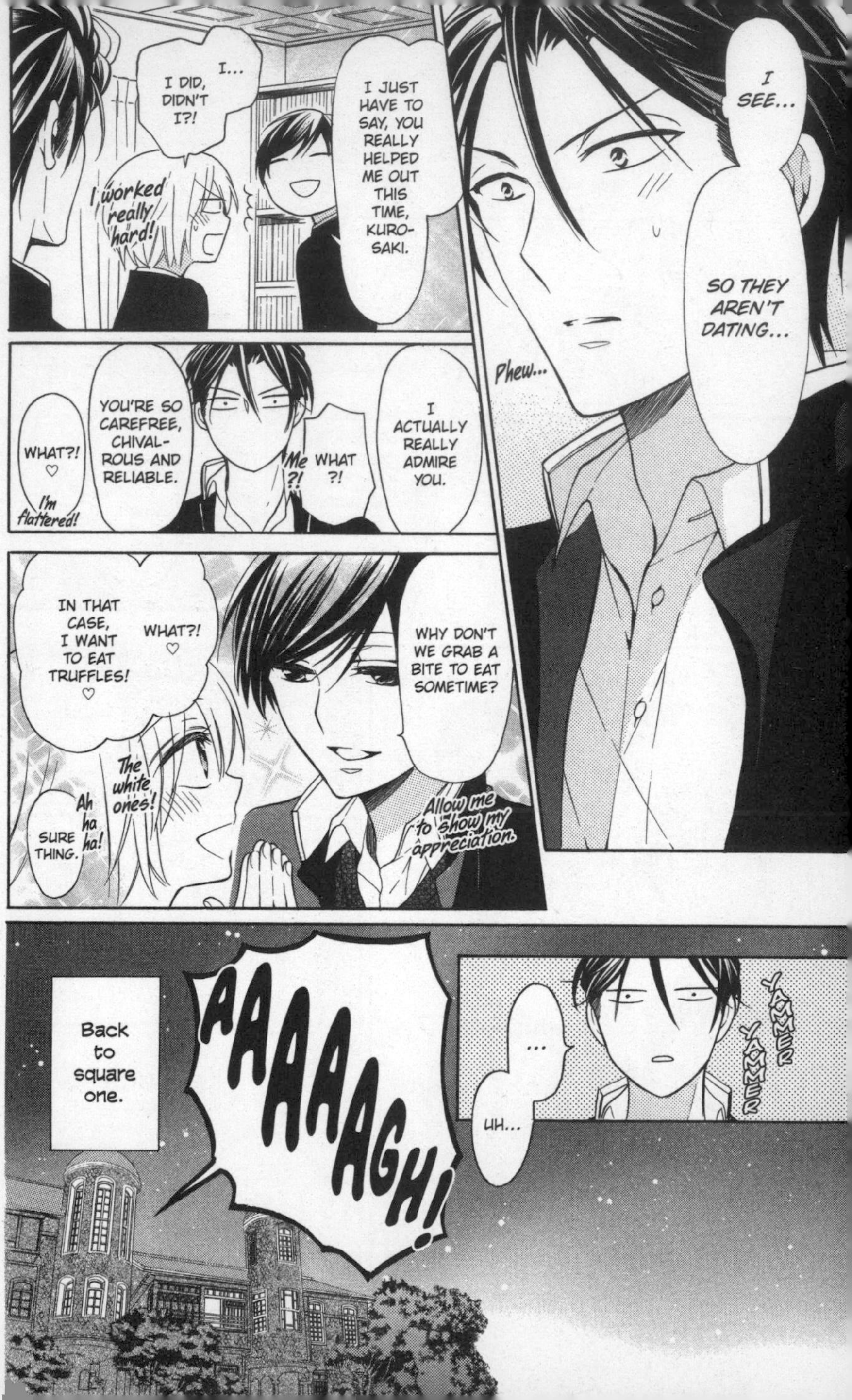
I SEE...
SO THEY AREN'T DATING...
Phew...
I JUST HAVE TO SAY, YOU REALLY HELPED ME OUT THIS TIME, KUROSAKI.
I... I DID, DIDN'T I?!
I worked really hard!
I ACTUALLY REALLY ADMIRE YOU.
WHAT ?!
Me ?!
YOU'RE SO CAREFREE, CHIVALROUS AND RELIABLE.
WHAT?! ♡
I'm flattered!
WHY DON'T WE GRAB A BITE TO EAT SOMETIME?
Allow me to show my appreciation.
WHAT?! ♡
IN THAT CASE, I WANT TO EAT TRUFFLES! ♡
The white ones!
Ah ha ha!
SURE THING.
YAMMER YAMMER
...
UH...
AAAAAGH!
Back to square one.

Chapter 128

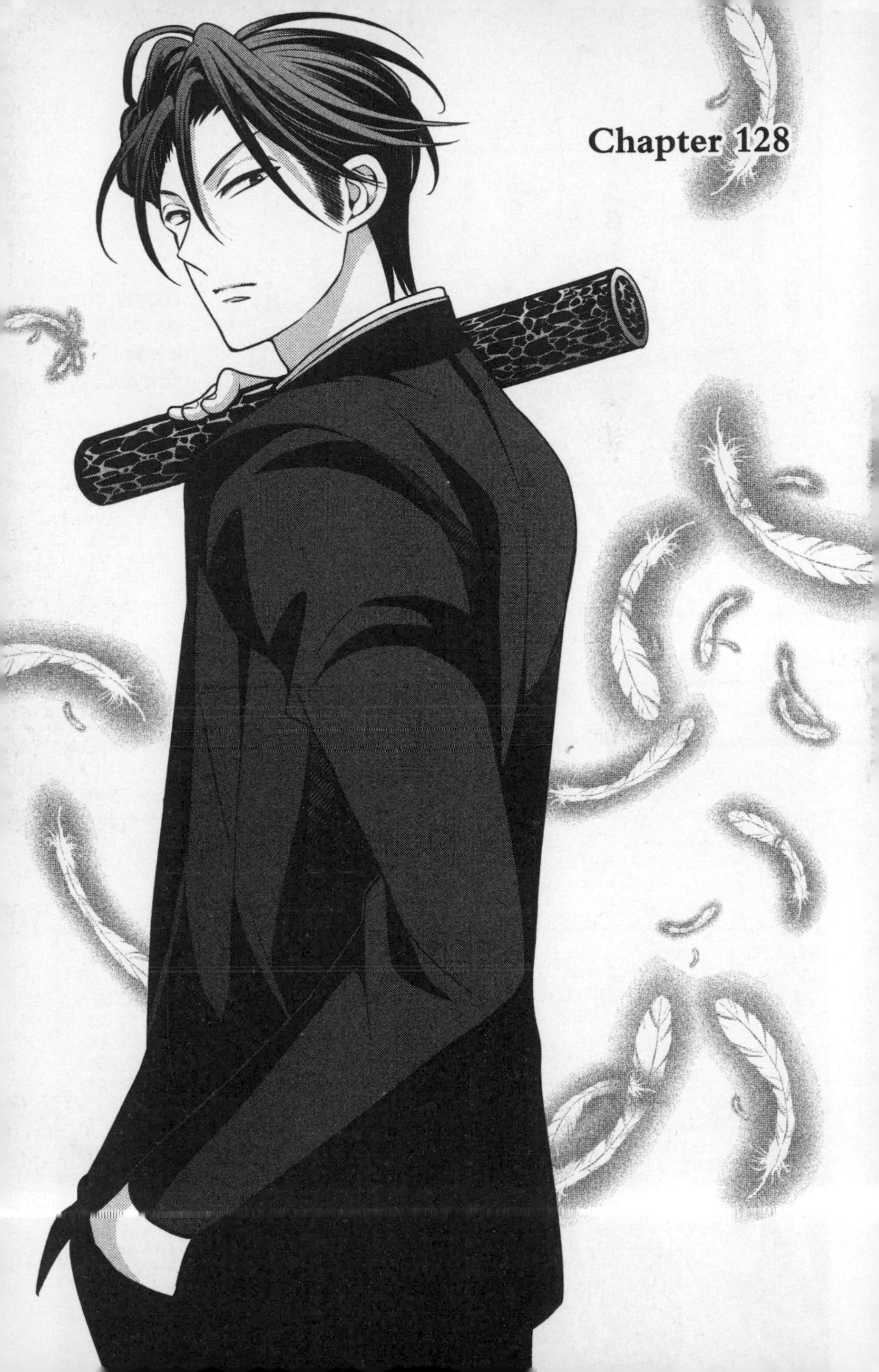

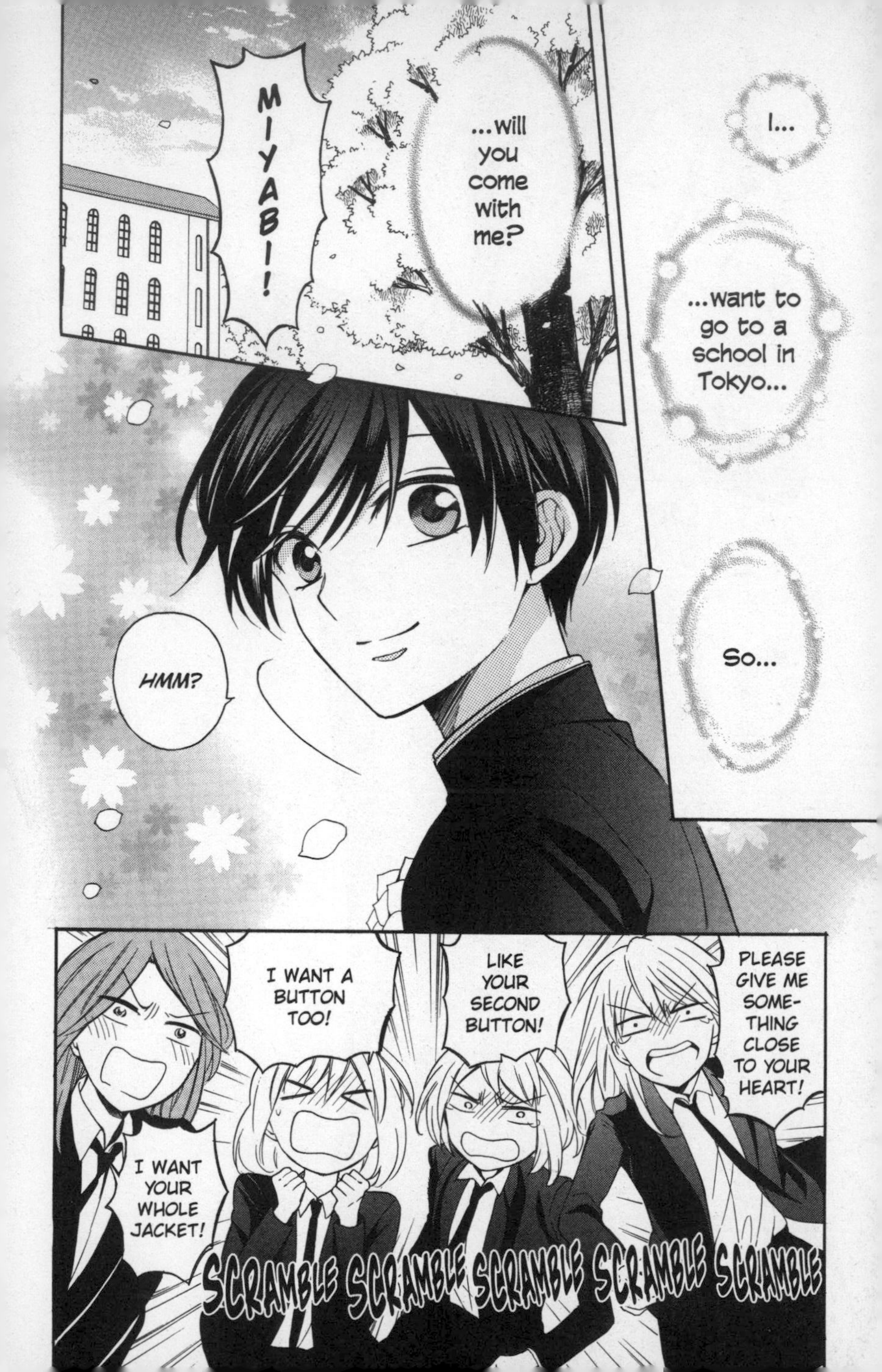
I...
...want to go to a school in Tokyo...
So...
...will you come with me?
MIYABI!
HMM?
PLEASE GIVE ME SOME-THING CLOSE TO YOUR HEART!
LIKE YOUR SECOND BUTTON!
I WANT A BUTTON TOO!
I WANT YOUR WHOLE JACKET!
SCRAMBLE SCRAMBLE SCRAMBLE SCRAMBLE SCRAMBLE

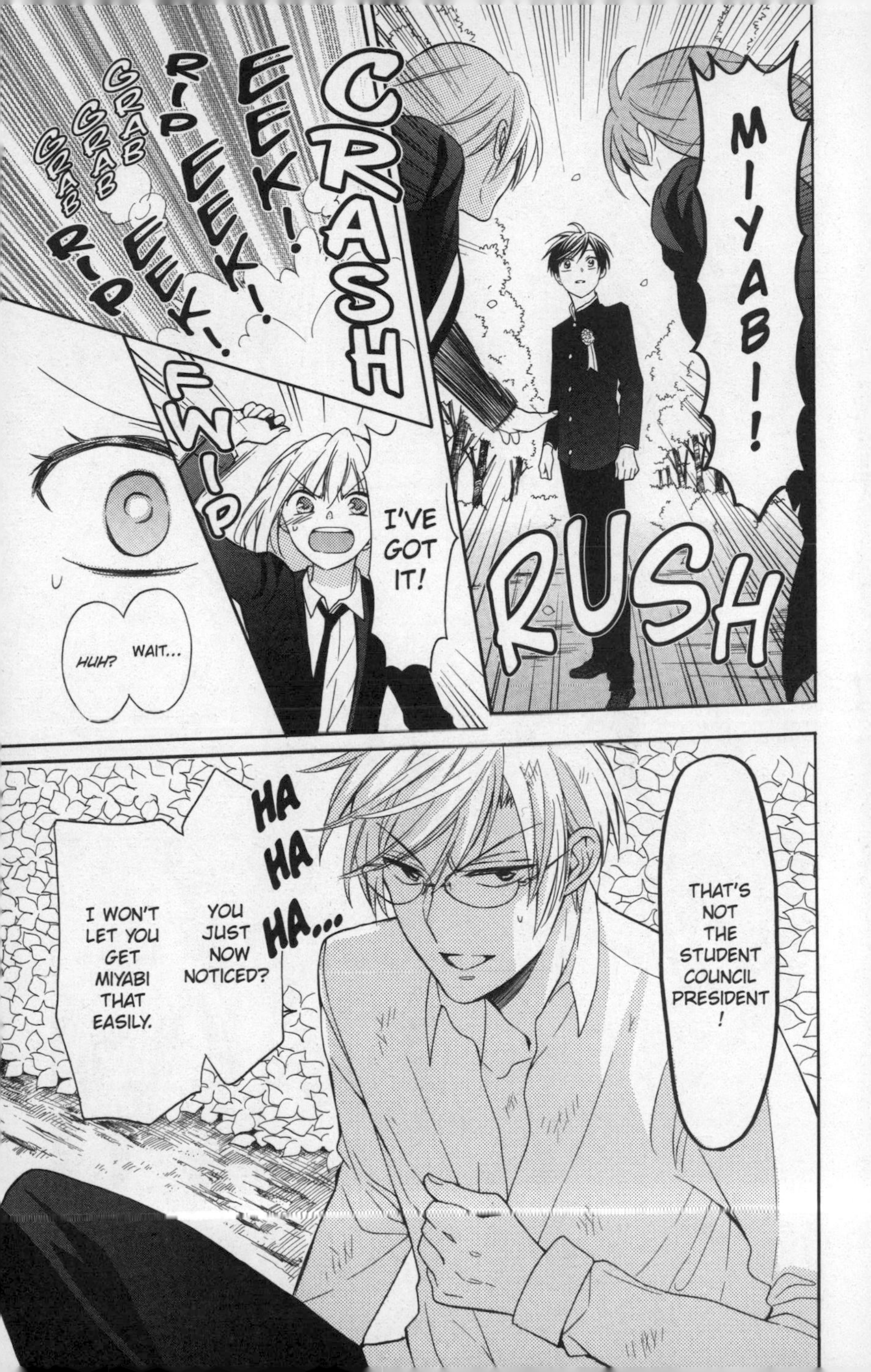
MIYABI!!
RUSH
CRASH
EEK!
EEEK!!
EEEK!!
RIP
GRAB
GRAB
GRAB
RIP
FWIP
I'VE GOT IT!
HUH?
WAIT...
THAT'S NOT THE STUDENT COUNCIL PRESIDENT!
HA HA HA...
YOU JUST NOW NOTICED?
I WON'T LET YOU GET MIYABI THAT EASILY.

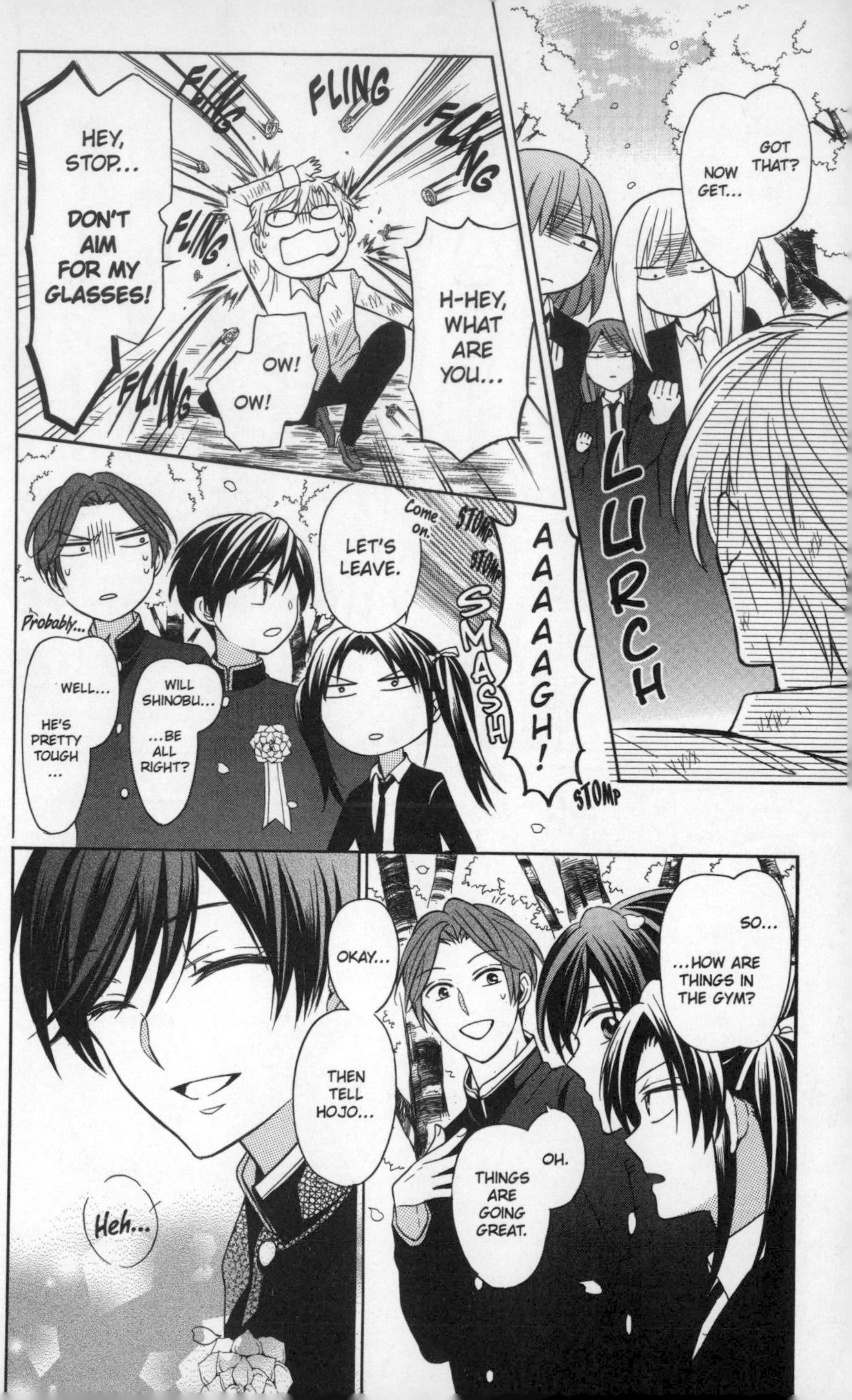
NOW GET... GOT THAT?
LURCH
AAAAAAGH!
SMASH
STOMP
H-HEY, WHAT ARE YOU...
FLING
FLING
FLING
FLING
FLING
OW!
OW!
HEY, STOP...
DON'T AIM FOR MY GLASSES!
LET'S LEAVE.
Come on.
STOMP
STOMP
WILL SHINOBU...
...BE ALL RIGHT?
Probably...
WELL...
HE'S PRETTY TOUGH...
SO...
...HOW ARE THINGS IN THE GYM?
OH.
THINGS ARE GOING GREAT.
OKAY...
THEN TELL HOJO...
Heh...

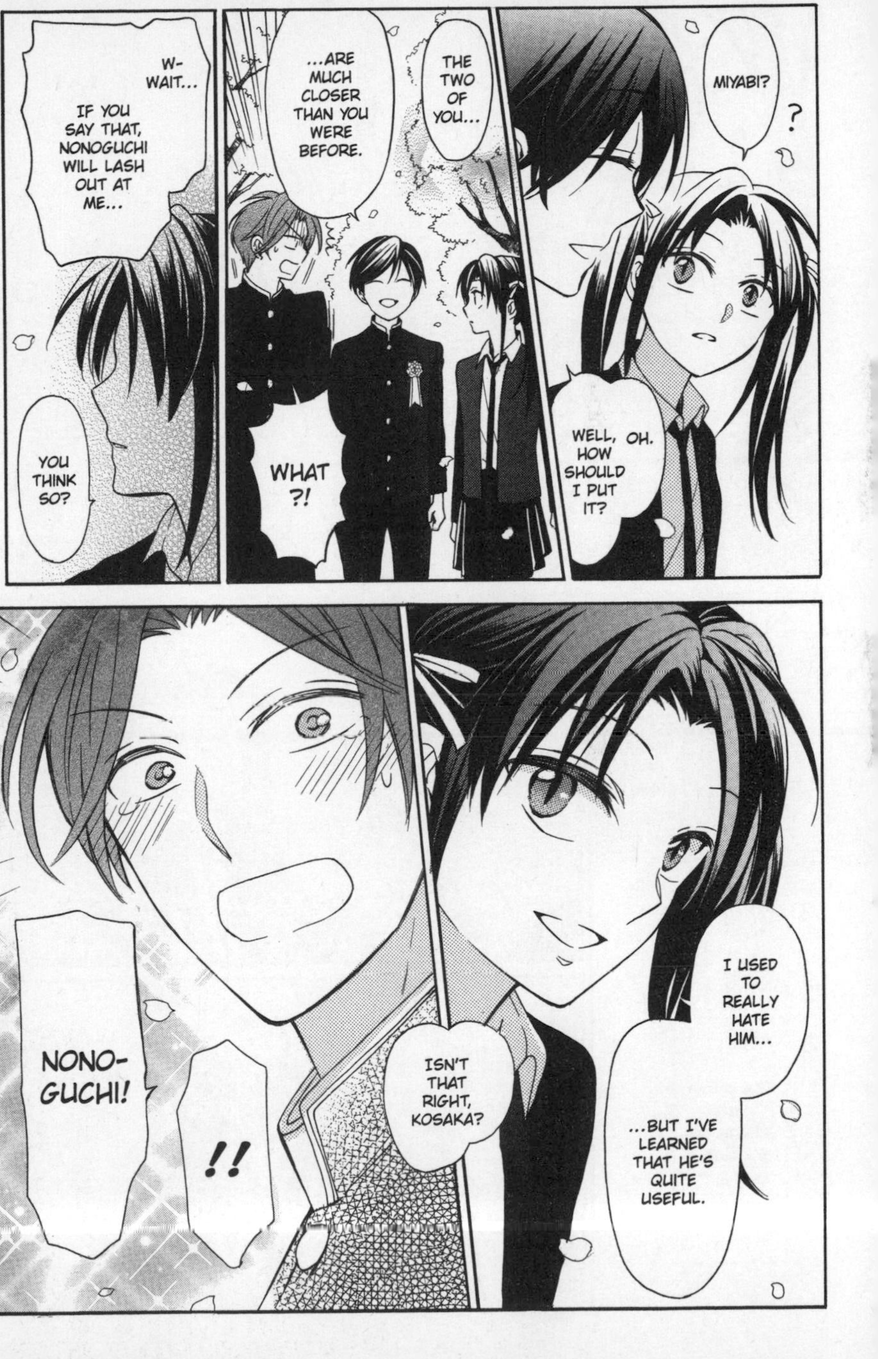
MIYABI?
?
WELL, OH. HOW SHOULD I PUT IT?
THE TWO OF YOU...
...ARE MUCH CLOSER THAN YOU WERE BEFORE.
WHAT?!
W-WAIT...
IF YOU SAY THAT, NONOGUCHI WILL LASH OUT AT ME...
YOU THINK SO?
I USED TO REALLY HATE HIM...
...BUT I'VE LEARNED THAT HE'S QUITE USEFUL.
ISN'T THAT RIGHT, KOSAKA?
!!
NONOGUCHI!

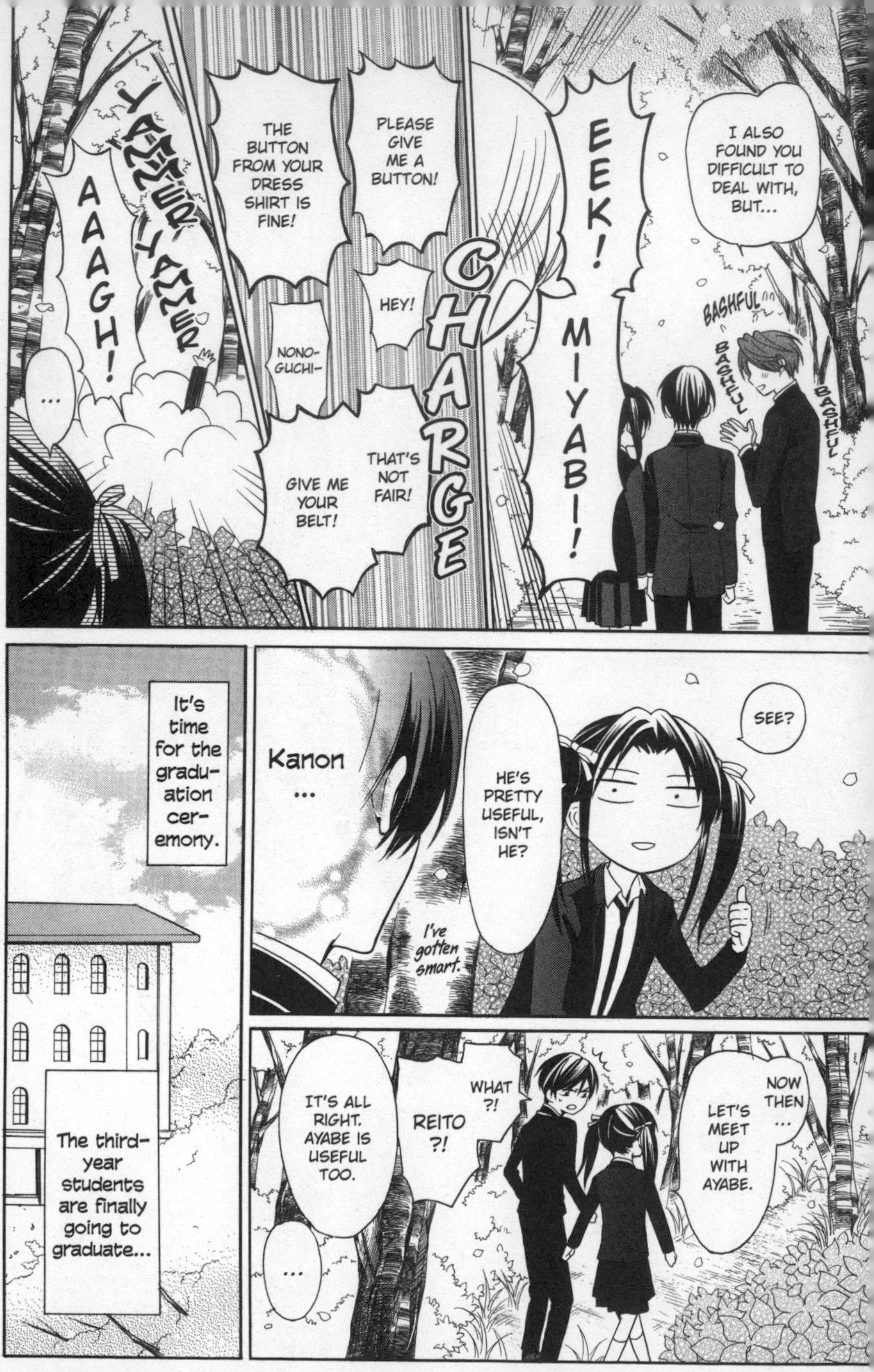
I ALSO FOUND YOU DIFFICULT TO DEAL WITH, BUT...
BASHFUL BASHFUL BASHFUL
EEK! MIYABI!!
CHARGE
PLEASE GIVE ME A BUTTON!
THE BUTTON FROM YOUR DRESS SHIRT IS FINE!
HEY!
NONO-GUCHI-
THAT'S NOT FAIR!
GIVE ME YOUR BELT!
YAMMER YAMMER
AAAGH!
...
SEE?
HE'S PRETTY USEFUL, ISN'T HE?
Kanon ...
I've gotten smart.
NOW THEN ...
LET'S MEET UP WITH AYABE.
WHAT?!
REITO?!
IT'S ALL RIGHT. AYABE IS USEFUL TOO.
...
It's time for the graduation ceremony.
The third-year students are finally going to graduate...

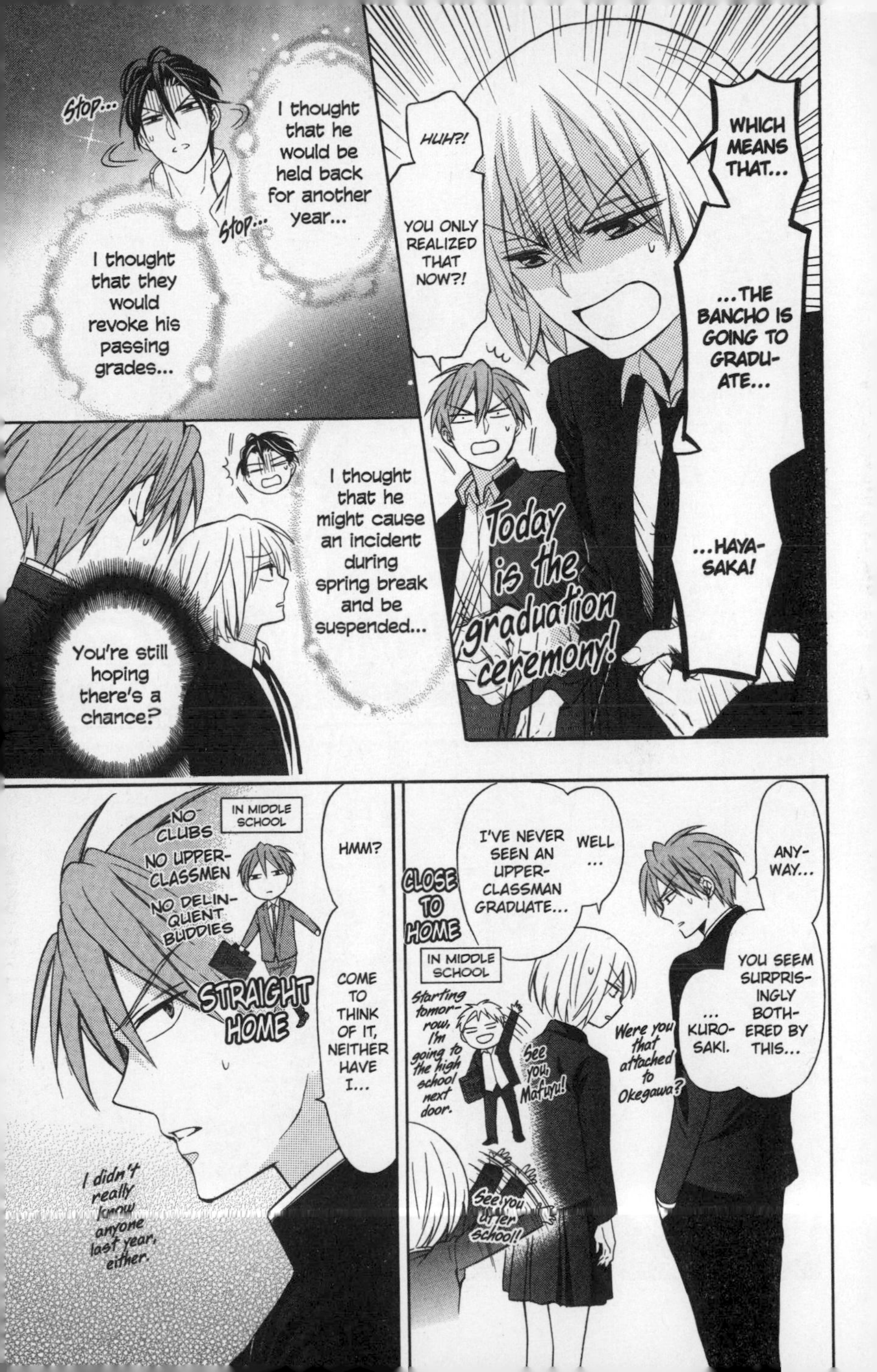
WHICH MEANS THAT...
...THE BANCHO IS GOING TO GRADUATE...
...HAYASAKA!
HUH?!
YOU ONLY REALIZED THAT NOW?!
Today is the graduation ceremony!
I thought that he would be held back for another year...
Stop...
Stop...
I thought that they would revoke his passing grades...
I thought that he might cause an incident during spring break and be suspended...
You're still hoping there's a chance?
ANYWAY...
YOU SEEM SURPRISINGLY BOTHERED BY THIS...
...KUROSAKI.
Were you that attached to Okegawa?
WELL...
I'VE NEVER SEEN AN UPPERCLASSMAN GRADUATE...
CLOSE TO HOME
IN MIDDLE SCHOOL
Starting tomorrow, I'm going to the high school next door.
See you, Mafuyu!
See you after school!!
HMM?
COME TO THINK OF IT, NEITHER HAVE I...
IN MIDDLE SCHOOL
NO CLUBS
NO UPPERCLASSMEN
NO DELINQUENT BUDDIES
STRAIGHT HOME
I didn't really know anyone last year, either.

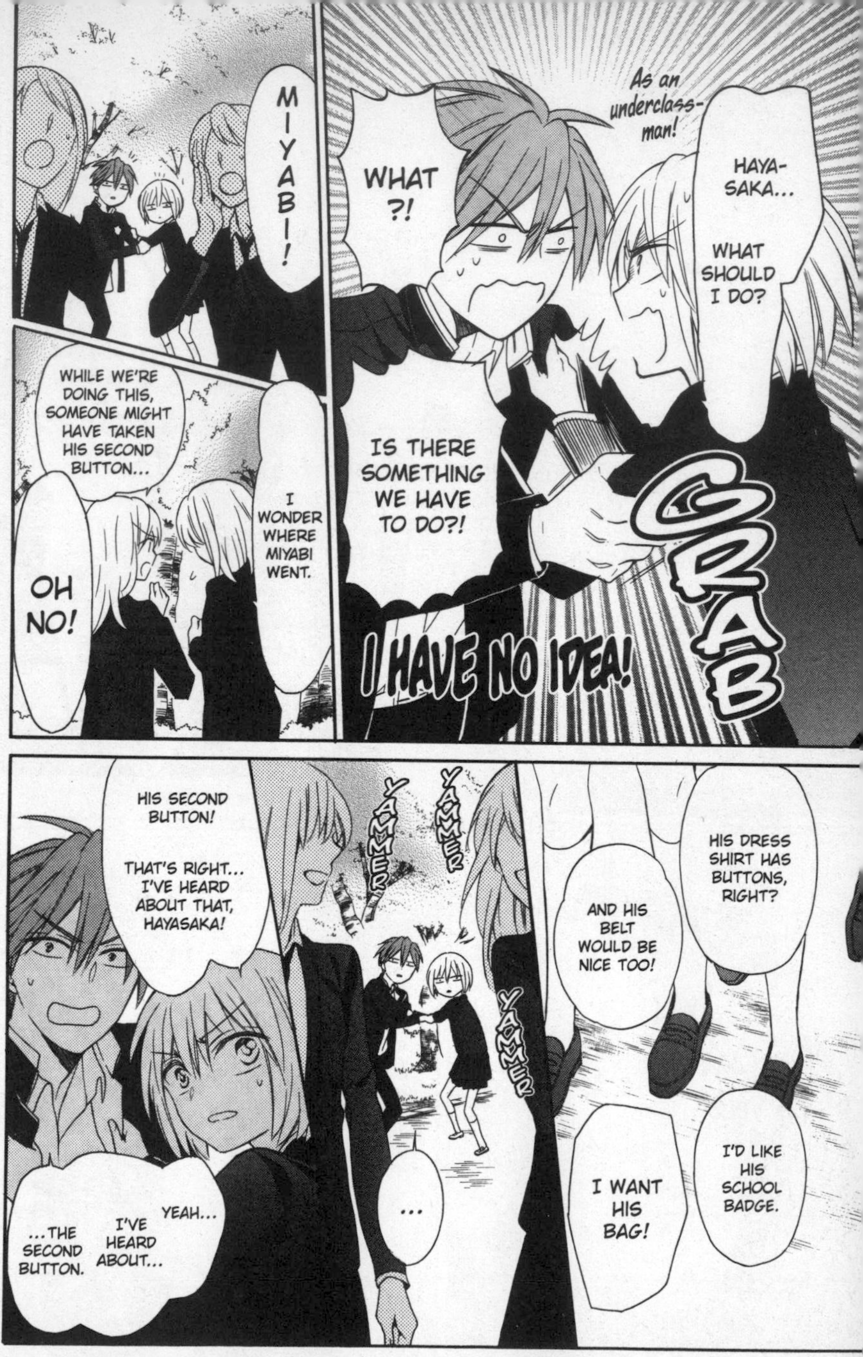
As an underclass-man!
HAYA-SAKA...
WHAT SHOULD I DO?
WHAT?!
IS THERE SOMETHING WE HAVE TO DO?!
GRAB
I HAVE NO IDEA!
MIYABI!
I WONDER WHERE MIYABI WENT.
WHILE WE'RE DOING THIS, SOMEONE MIGHT HAVE TAKEN HIS SECOND BUTTON...
OH NO!
HIS DRESS SHIRT HAS BUTTONS, RIGHT?
AND HIS BELT WOULD BE NICE TOO!
I'D LIKE HIS SCHOOL BADGE.
I WANT HIS BAG!
YAMMER
YAMMER
YAMMER
HIS SECOND BUTTON!
THAT'S RIGHT... I'VE HEARD ABOUT THAT, HAYASAKA!
...
YEAH...
I'VE HEARD ABOUT...
...THE SECOND BUTTON.

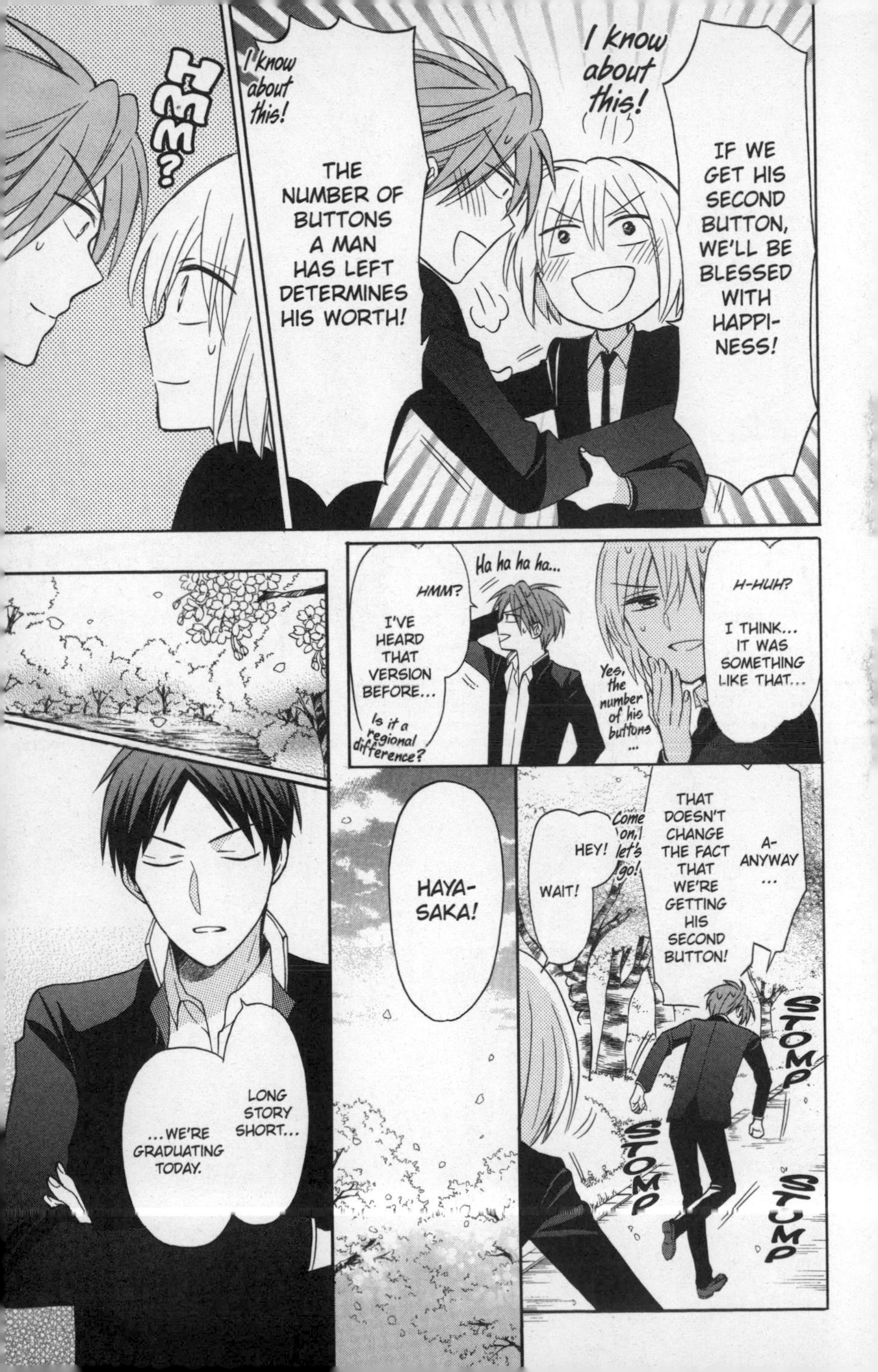
I know about this!
IF WE GET HIS SECOND BUTTON, WE'LL BE BLESSED WITH HAPPINESS!
I know about this!
THE NUMBER OF BUTTONS A MAN HAS LEFT DETERMINES HIS WORTH!
HMM?
H-HUH?
I THINK... IT WAS SOMETHING LIKE THAT...
Yes, the number of his buttons...
Ha ha ha ha...
HMM?
I'VE HEARD THAT VERSION BEFORE...
Is it a regional difference?
A-ANYWAY...
THAT DOESN'T CHANGE THE FACT THAT WE'RE GETTING HIS SECOND BUTTON!
Come on, let's go!
HEY!
WAIT!
STOMP
STOMP
STOMP
STOMP
HAYA-SAKA!
LONG STORY SHORT...
...WE'RE GRADUATING TODAY.

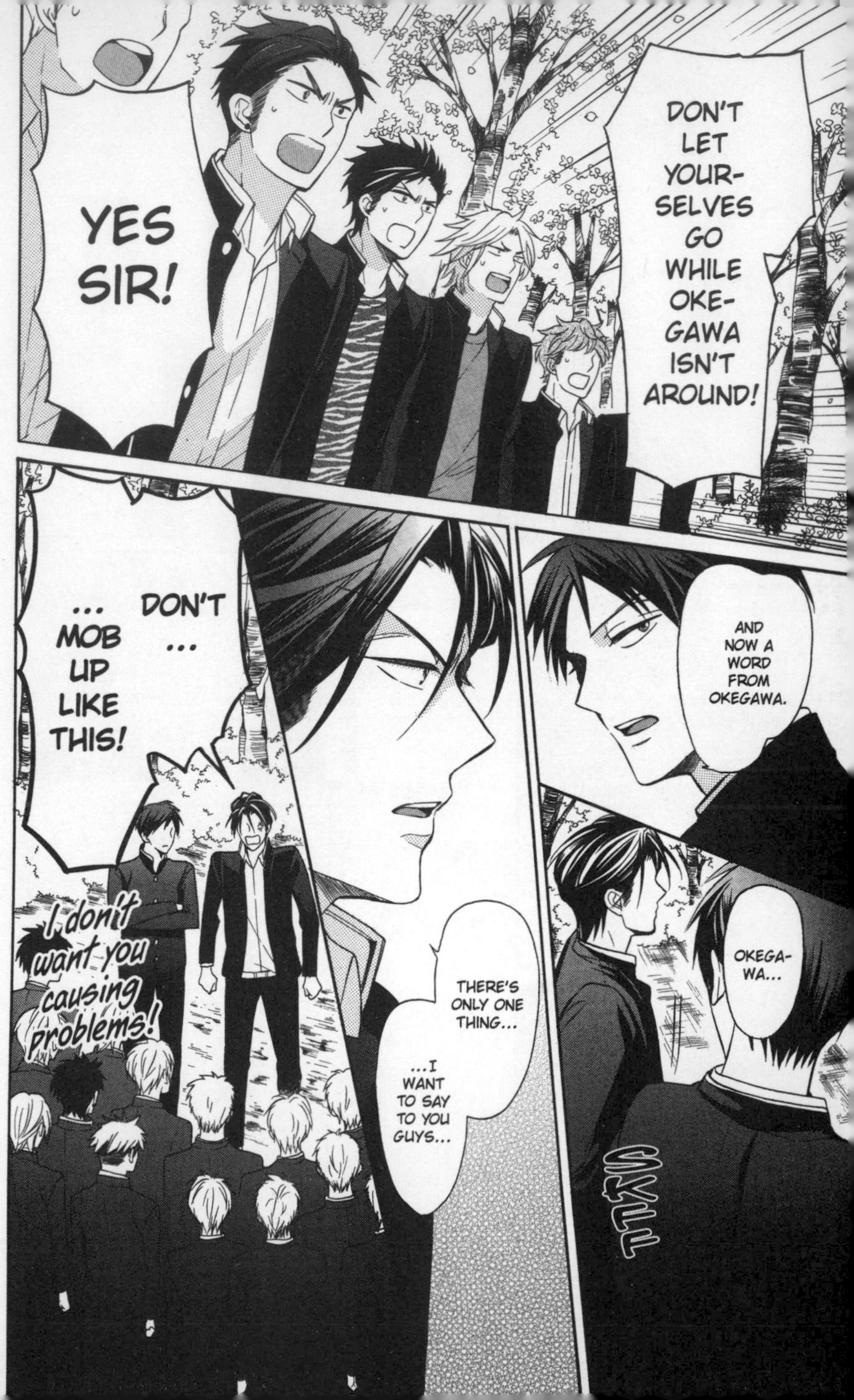
DON'T LET YOUR-SELVES GO WHILE OKE-GAWA ISN'T AROUND!
YES SIR!
AND NOW A WORD FROM OKEGAWA.
OKEGA-WA...
SKFF
THERE'S ONLY ONE THING...
...I WANT TO SAY TO YOU GUYS...
DON'T ...
... MOB UP LIKE THIS!
I don't want you causing problems!

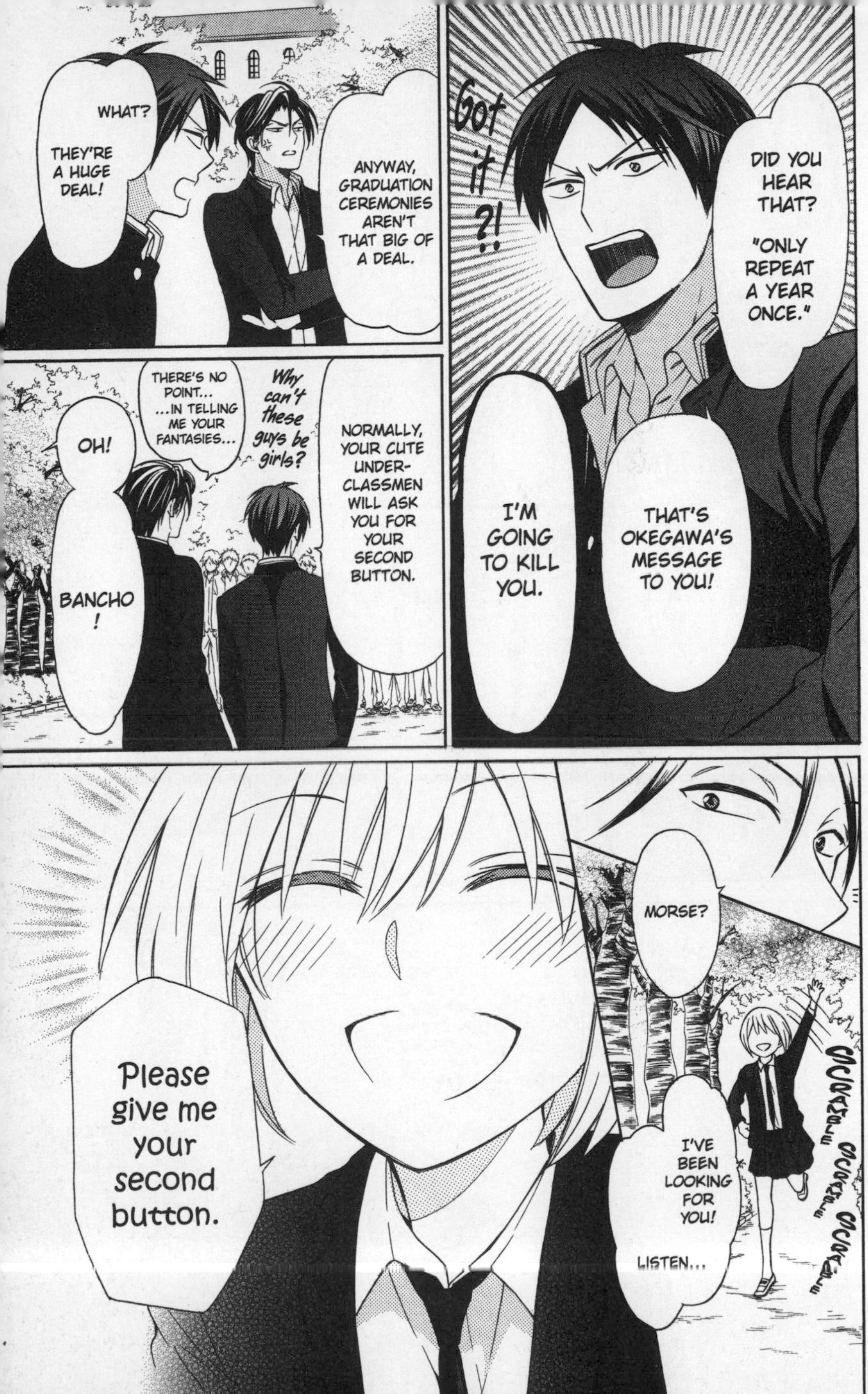
DID YOU HEAR THAT? "ONLY REPEAT A YEAR ONCE."
Got it?!
THAT'S OKEGAWA'S MESSAGE TO YOU!
I'M GOING TO KILL YOU.
ANYWAY, GRADUATION CEREMONIES AREN'T THAT BIG OF A DEAL.
WHAT? THEY'RE A HUGE DEAL!
NORMALLY, YOUR CUTE UNDERCLASSMEN WILL ASK YOU FOR YOUR SECOND BUTTON.
Why can't these guys be girls?
THERE'S NO POINT... ...IN TELLING ME YOUR FANTASIES...
OH! BANCHO!
MORSE?
I'VE BEEN LOOKING FOR YOU! LISTEN...
SCRAMBLE SCRAMBLE SCRAMBLE
Please give me your second button.

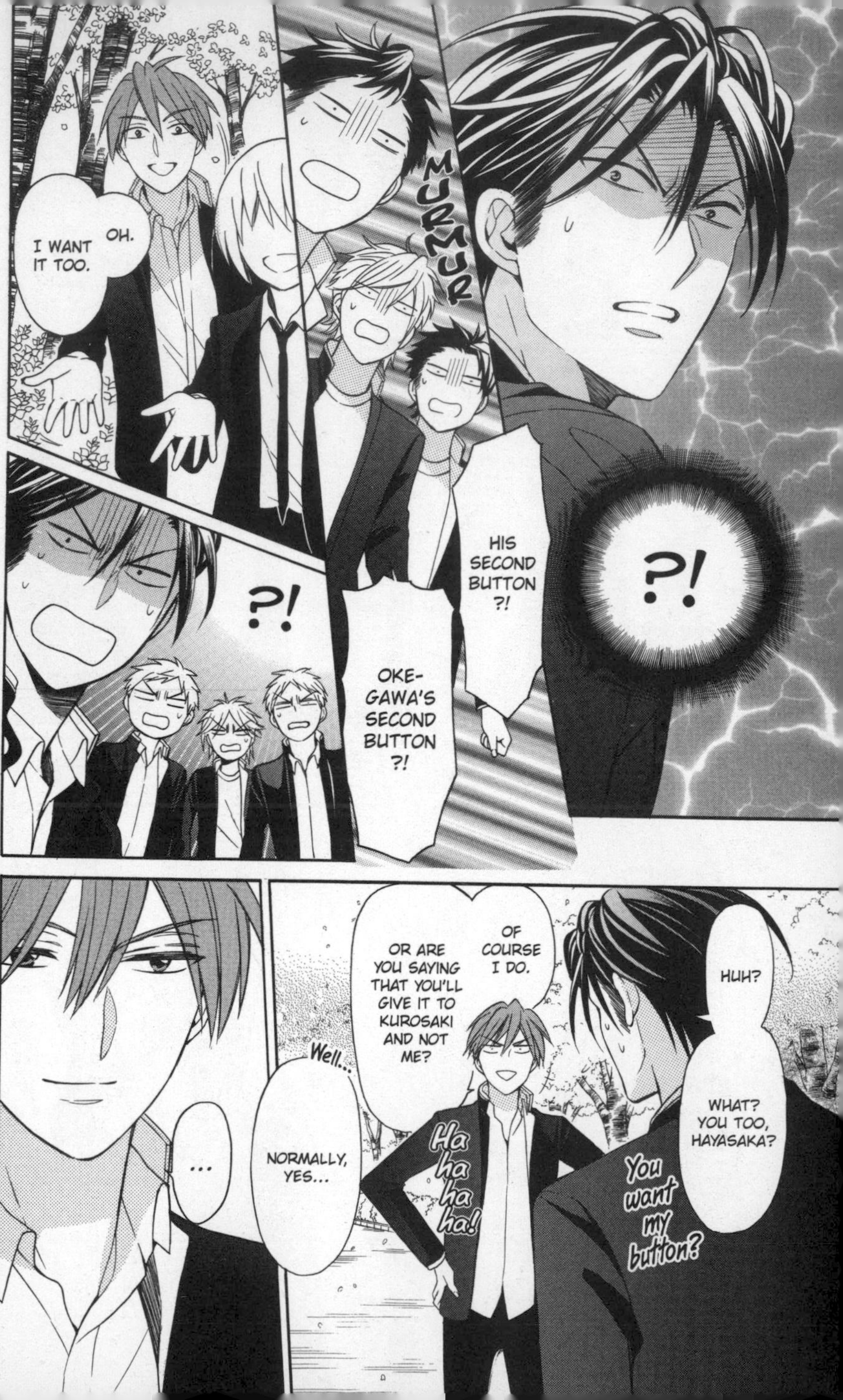
?!
MURMUR
OH.
I WANT IT TOO.
HIS SECOND BUTTON ?!
OKE-GAWA'S SECOND BUTTON ?!
?!
HUH?
WHAT? YOU TOO, HAYASAKA?
You want my button?
OF COURSE I DO.
OR ARE YOU SAYING THAT YOU'LL GIVE IT TO KUROSAKI AND NOT ME?
Ha ha ha ha ha!
Well...
NORMALLY, YES...
...

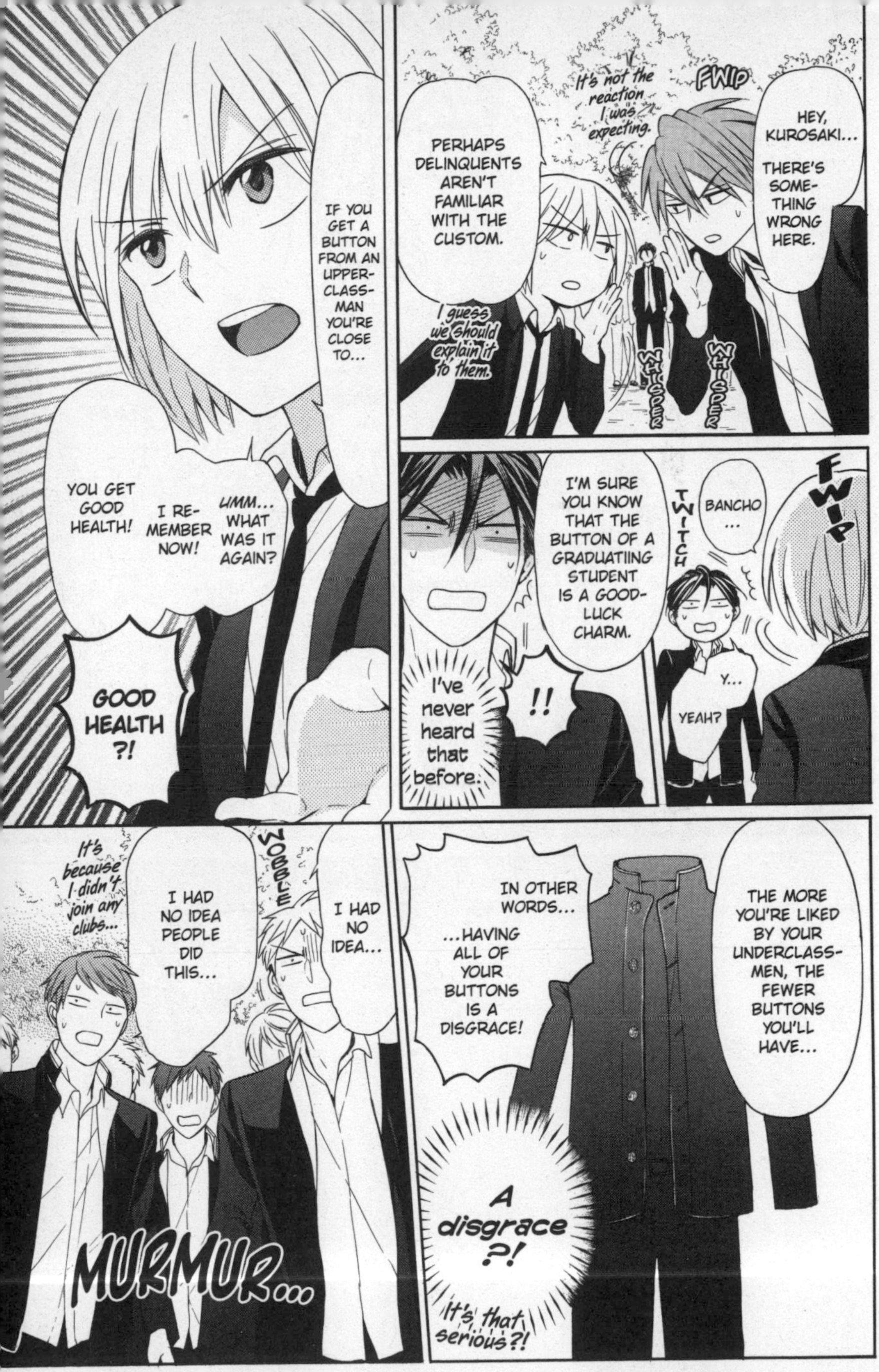
HEY, KUROSAKI... THERE'S SOME-THING WRONG HERE.
FWIP
WHISPER
It's not the reaction I was expecting.
PERHAPS DELINQUENTS AREN'T FAMILIAR WITH THE CUSTOM.
WHISPER
I guess we should explain it to them.
FWIP
BANCHO...
TWITCH
Y... YEAH?
I'M SURE YOU KNOW THAT THE BUTTON OF A GRADUATIING STUDENT IS A GOOD-LUCK CHARM.
!!
I've never heard that before.
IF YOU GET A BUTTON FROM AN UPPER-CLASS-MAN YOU'RE CLOSE TO...
UMM... WHAT WAS IT AGAIN?
I RE-MEMBER NOW!
YOU GET GOOD HEALTH!
GOOD HEALTH?!
THE MORE YOU'RE LIKED BY YOUR UNDERCLASS-MEN, THE FEWER BUTTONS YOU'LL HAVE...
IN OTHER WORDS... ...HAVING ALL OF YOUR BUTTONS IS A DISGRACE!
A disgrace?!
It's that serious?!
I HAD NO IDEA...
WOBBLE
I HAD NO IDEA PEOPLE DID THIS...
It's because I didn't join any clubs...
MURMUR...

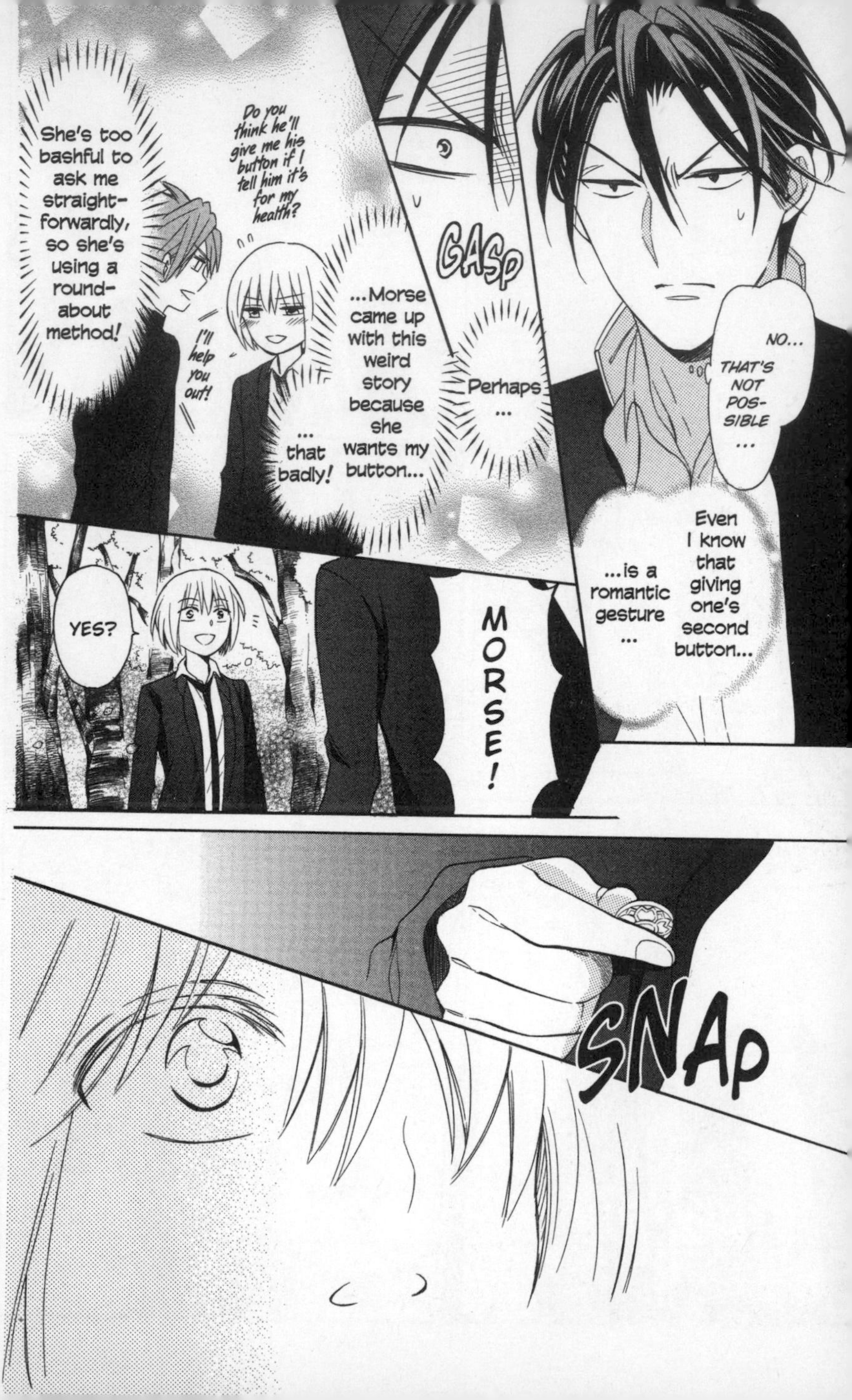
NO... THAT'S NOT POSSIBLE...
Even I know that giving one's second button...
...is a romantic gesture...
GASp
Perhaps...
...Morse came up with this weird story because she wants my button...
...that badly!
Do you think he'll give me his button if I tell him it's for my health?
I'll help you out!
She's too bashful to ask me straightforwardly, so she's using a roundabout method!
MORSE!
YES?
SNAp

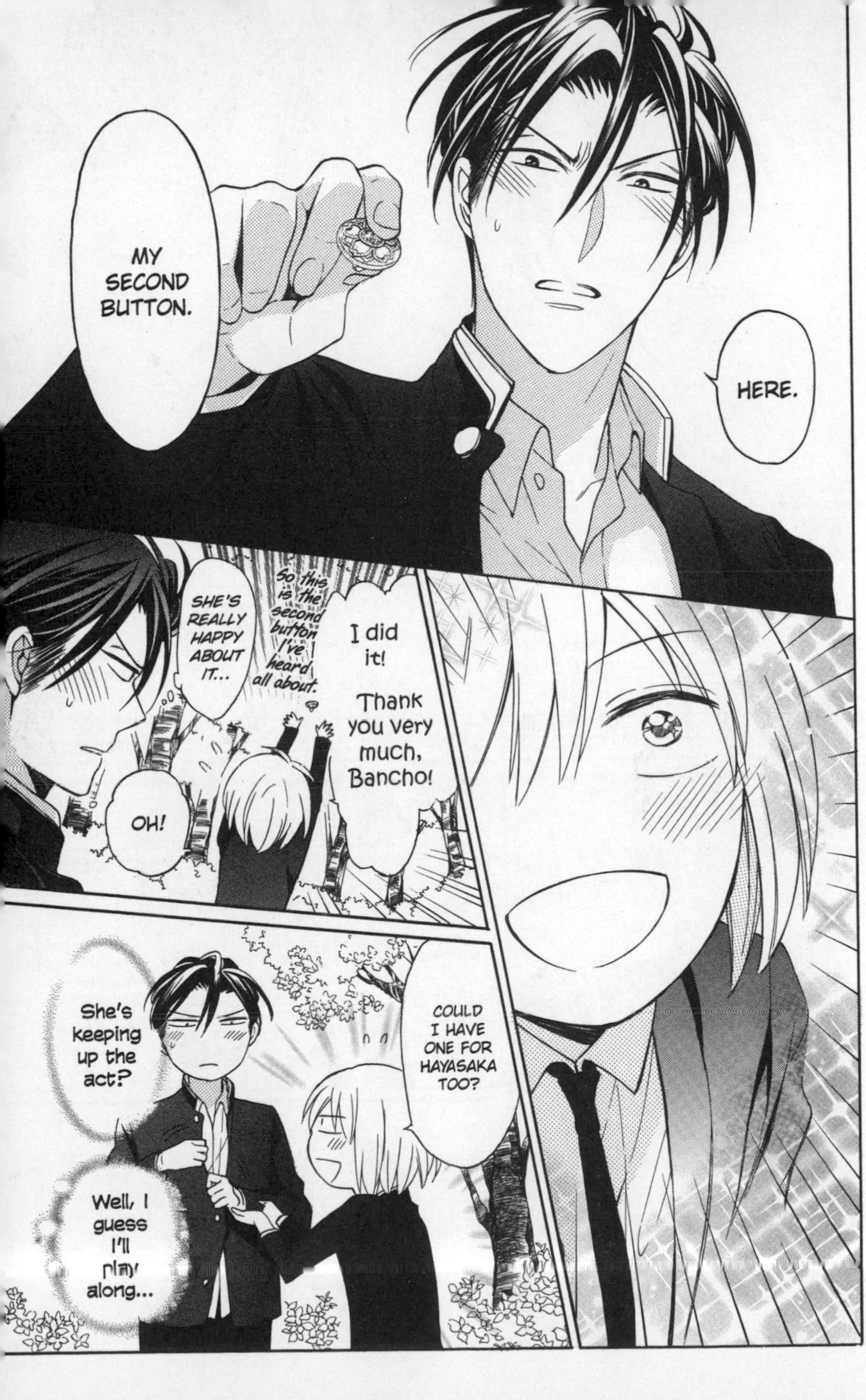
HERE.
MY SECOND BUTTON.
I did it! Thank you very much, Bancho!
So this is the second button I've heard all about.
SHE'S REALLY HAPPY ABOUT IT...
OH!
COULD I HAVE ONE FOR HAYASAKA TOO?
She's keeping up the act?
Well, I guess I'll play along...

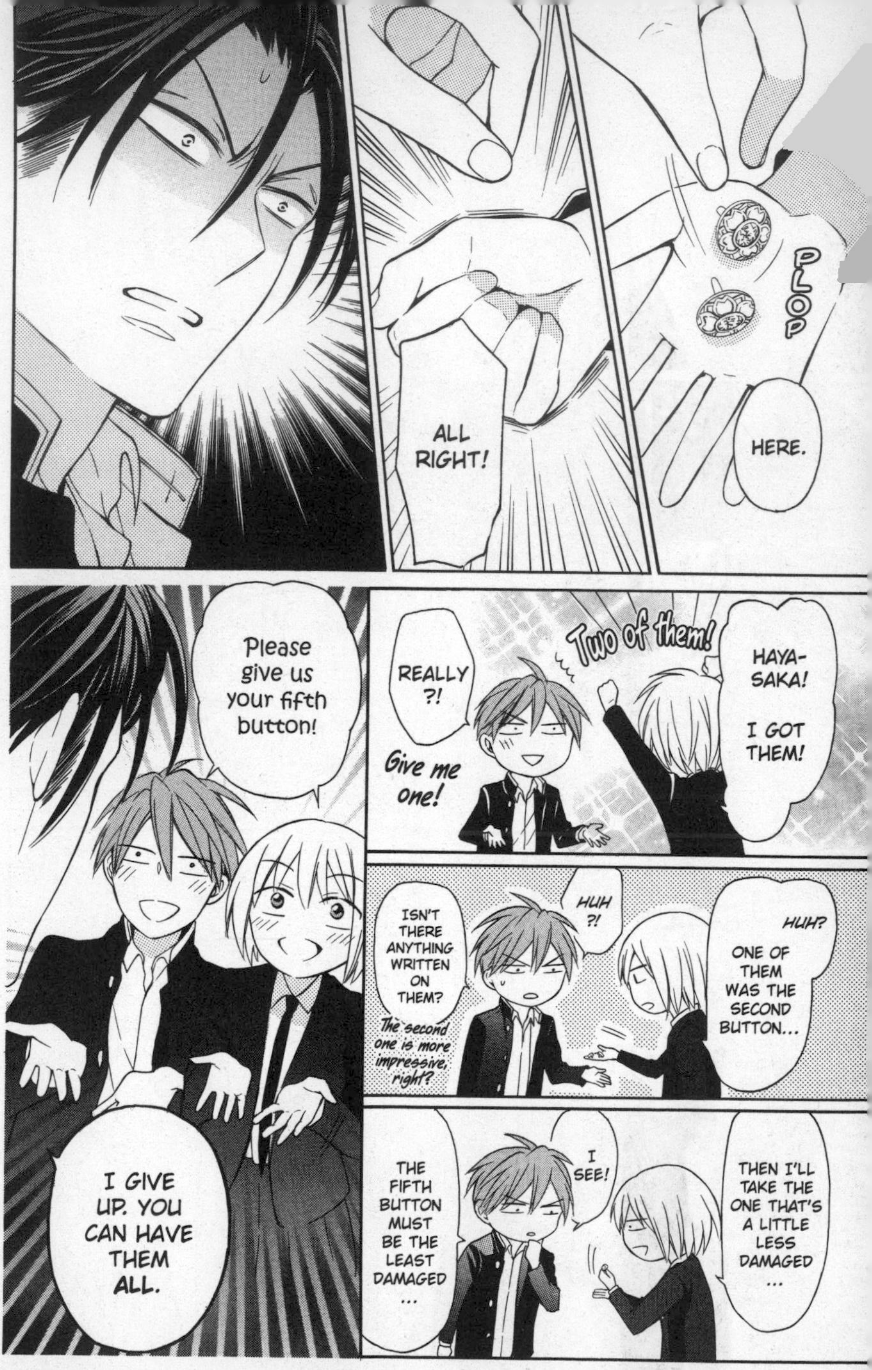
PLOP
HERE.
ALL RIGHT!
HAYA-SAKA! I GOT THEM!
Two of them!
REALLY ?!
Give me one!
HUH? ONE OF THEM WAS THE SECOND BUTTON...
HUH ?!
ISN'T THERE ANYTHING WRITTEN ON THEM?
The second one is more impressive, right?
THEN I'LL TAKE THE ONE THAT'S A LITTLE LESS DAMAGED ...
I SEE!
THE FIFTH BUTTON MUST BE THE LEAST DAMAGED ...
Please give us your fifth button!
I GIVE UP. YOU CAN HAVE THEM ALL.

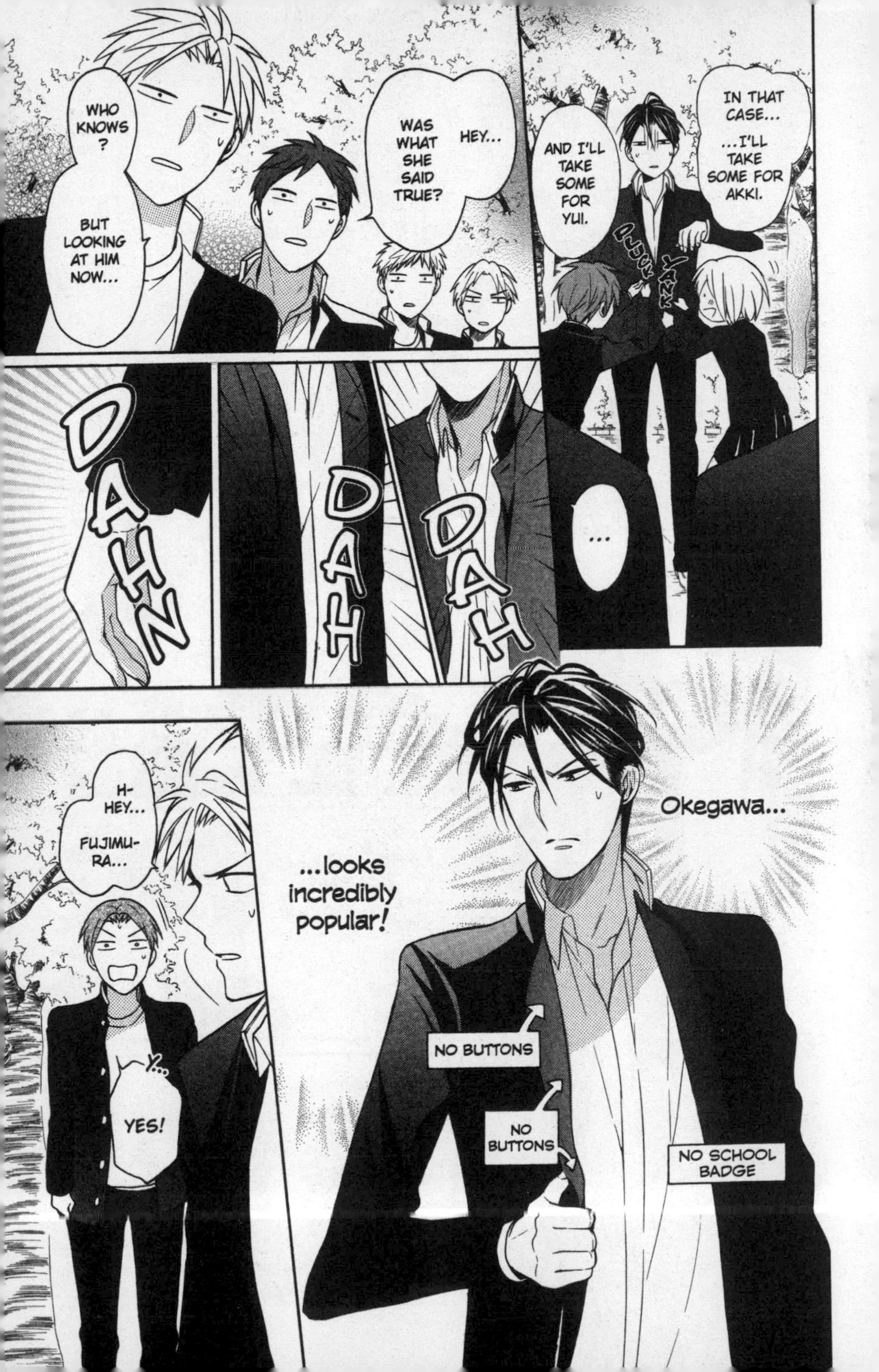
IN THAT CASE...
...I'LL TAKE SOME FOR AKKI.
AND I'LL TAKE SOME FOR YUI.
YANK
PLUCK
...
HEY...
WAS WHAT SHE SAID TRUE?
WHO KNOWS?
BUT LOOKING AT HIM NOW...
DAH
DAH
DAHN
Okegawa...
...looks incredibly popular!
NO SCHOOL BADGE
NO BUTTONS
NO BUTTONS
H-HEY... FUJIMURA...
Y... YES!

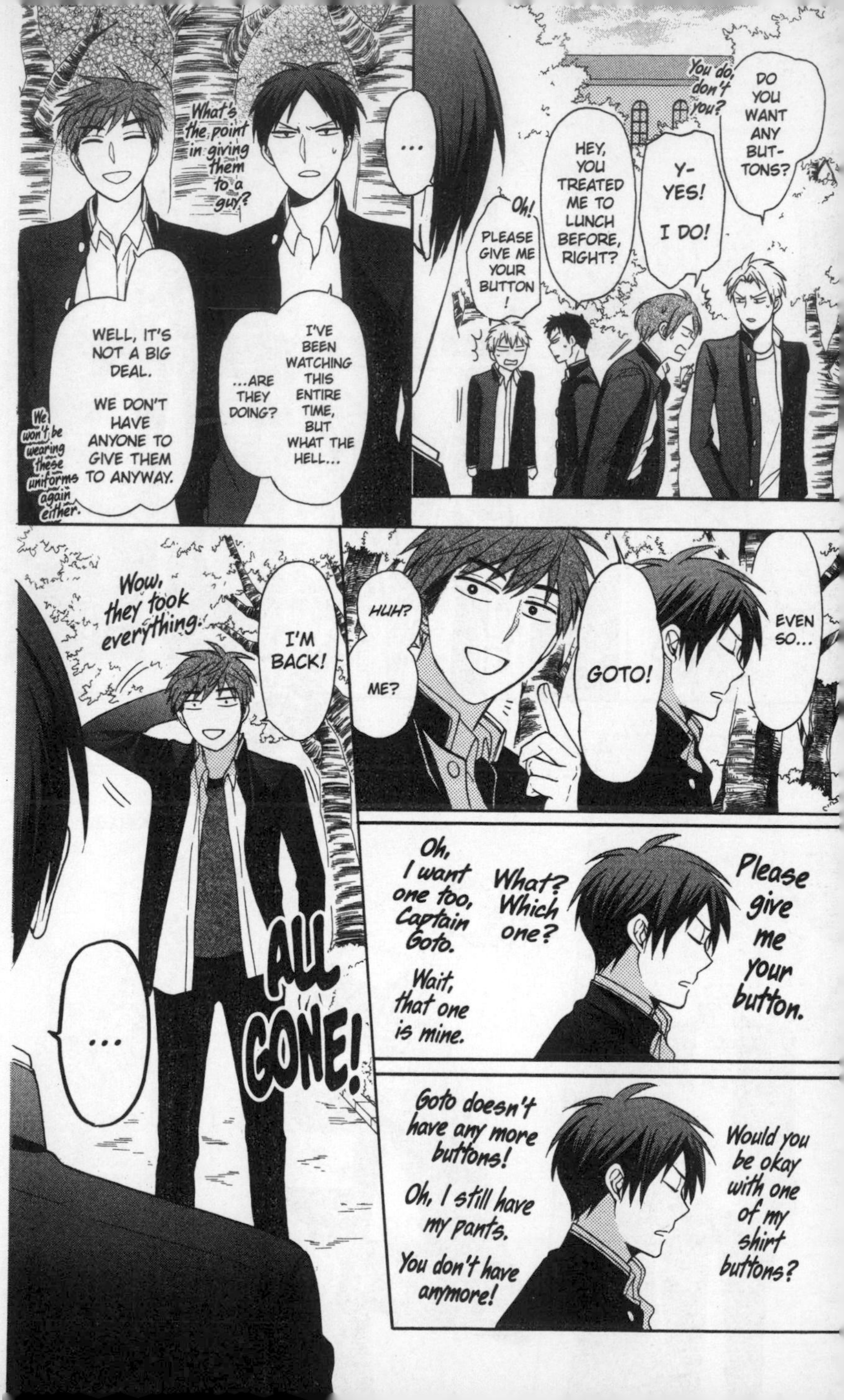
DO YOU WANT ANY BUT-TONS?
You do, don't you?
Y-YES! I DO!
HEY, YOU TREATED ME TO LUNCH BEFORE, RIGHT?
Oh! PLEASE GIVE ME YOUR BUTTON!
...
What's the point in giving them to a guy?
I'VE BEEN WATCHING THIS ENTIRE TIME, BUT WHAT THE HELL...
...ARE THEY DOING?
WELL, IT'S NOT A BIG DEAL. WE DON'T HAVE ANYONE TO GIVE THEM TO ANYWAY.
We won't be wearing these uniforms again either.
EVEN SO...
GOTO!
HUH? ME?
Please give me your button.
What? Which one?
Oh, I want one too, Captain Goto.
Wait, that one is mine.
Would you be okay with one of my shirt buttons?
Goto doesn't have any more buttons!
Oh, I still have my pants.
You don't have anymore!
I'M BACK!
Wow, they took everything.
ALL GONE!
...

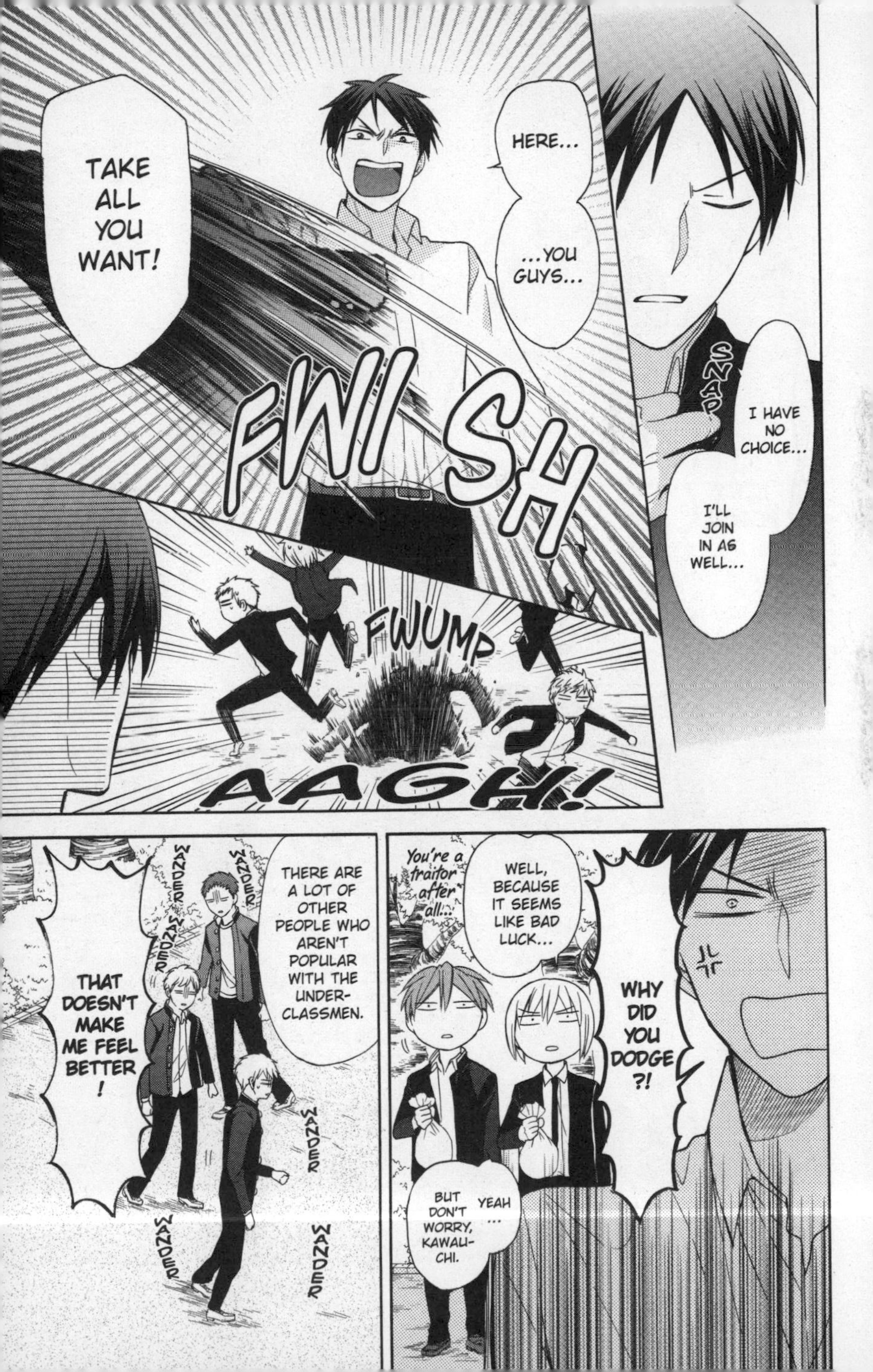

SNAP
I HAVE NO CHOICE...
I'LL JOIN IN AS WELL...
HERE...
...YOU GUYS...
TAKE ALL YOU WANT!
FWISH
FWUMP
AAGH!
WHY DID YOU DODGE?!
WELL, BECAUSE IT SEEMS LIKE BAD LUCK...
You're a traitor after all...
YEAH...
BUT DON'T WORRY, KAWAUCHI.
THERE ARE A LOT OF OTHER PEOPLE WHO AREN'T POPULAR WITH THE UNDER-CLASSMEN.
WANDER
WANDER WANDER
WANDER
WANDER
WANDER
THAT DOESN'T MAKE ME FEEL BETTER!

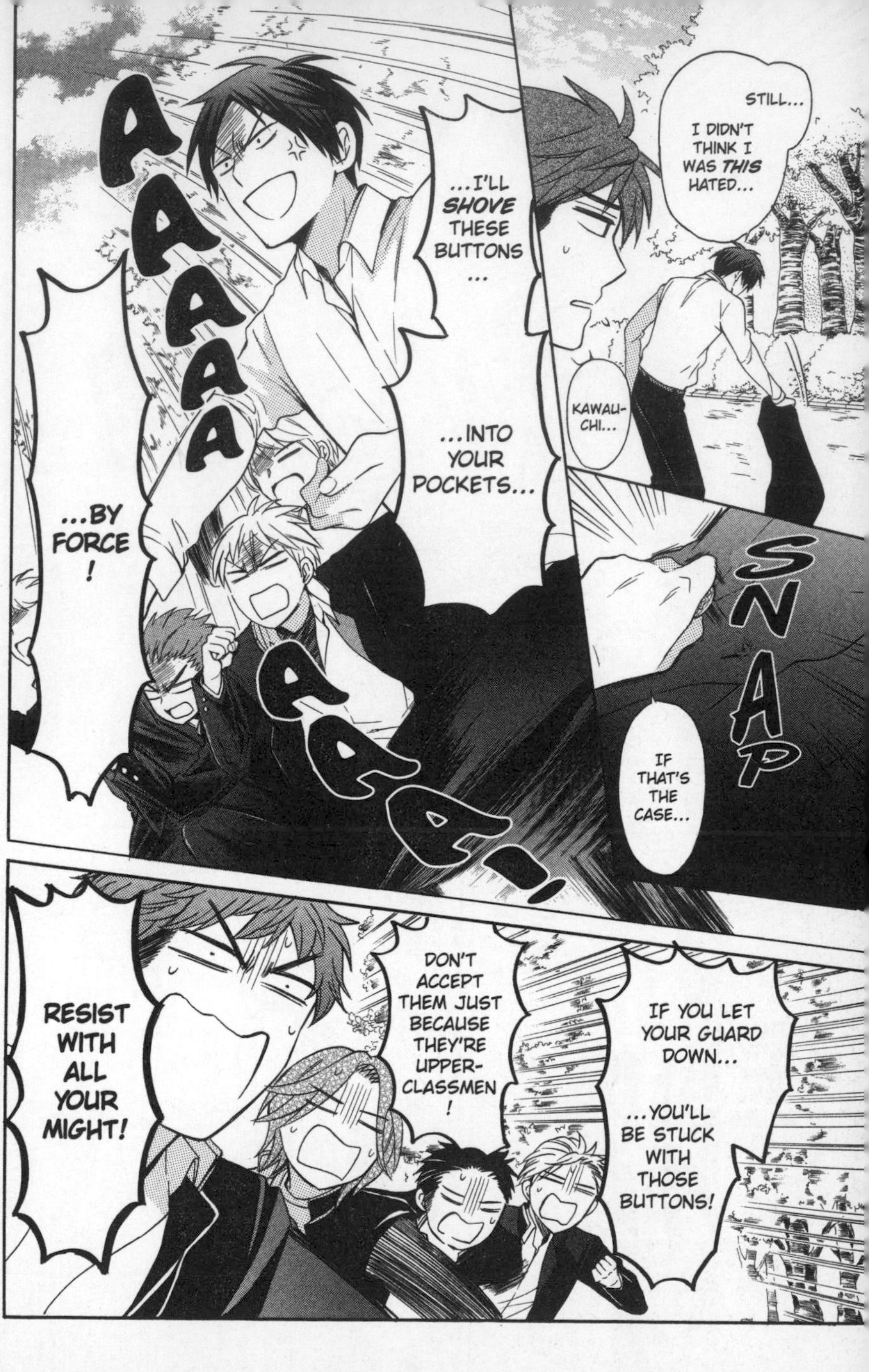
STILL...
I DIDN'T THINK I WAS THIS HATED...
KAWAUCHI...
SNAP
IF THAT'S THE CASE...
...I'LL SHOVE THESE BUTTONS...
...INTO YOUR POCKETS...
...BY FORCE!
AAAAAAA
AAAA--!!
IF YOU LET YOUR GUARD DOWN...
...YOU'LL BE STUCK WITH THOSE BUTTONS!
DON'T ACCEPT THEM JUST BECAUSE THEY'RE UPPERCLASSMEN!
RESIST WITH ALL YOUR MIGHT!

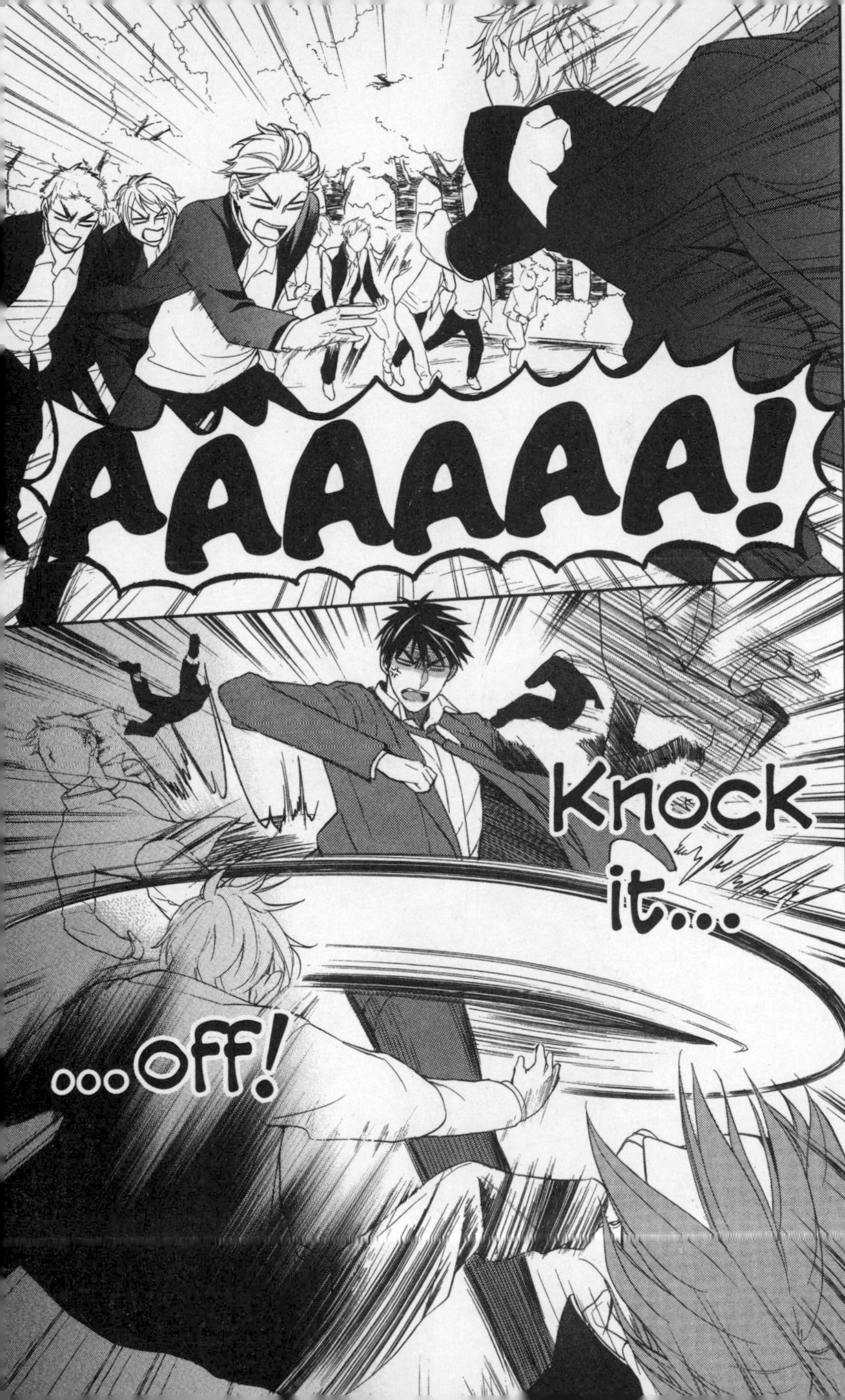
AAAAAA!
Knock it...
...off!

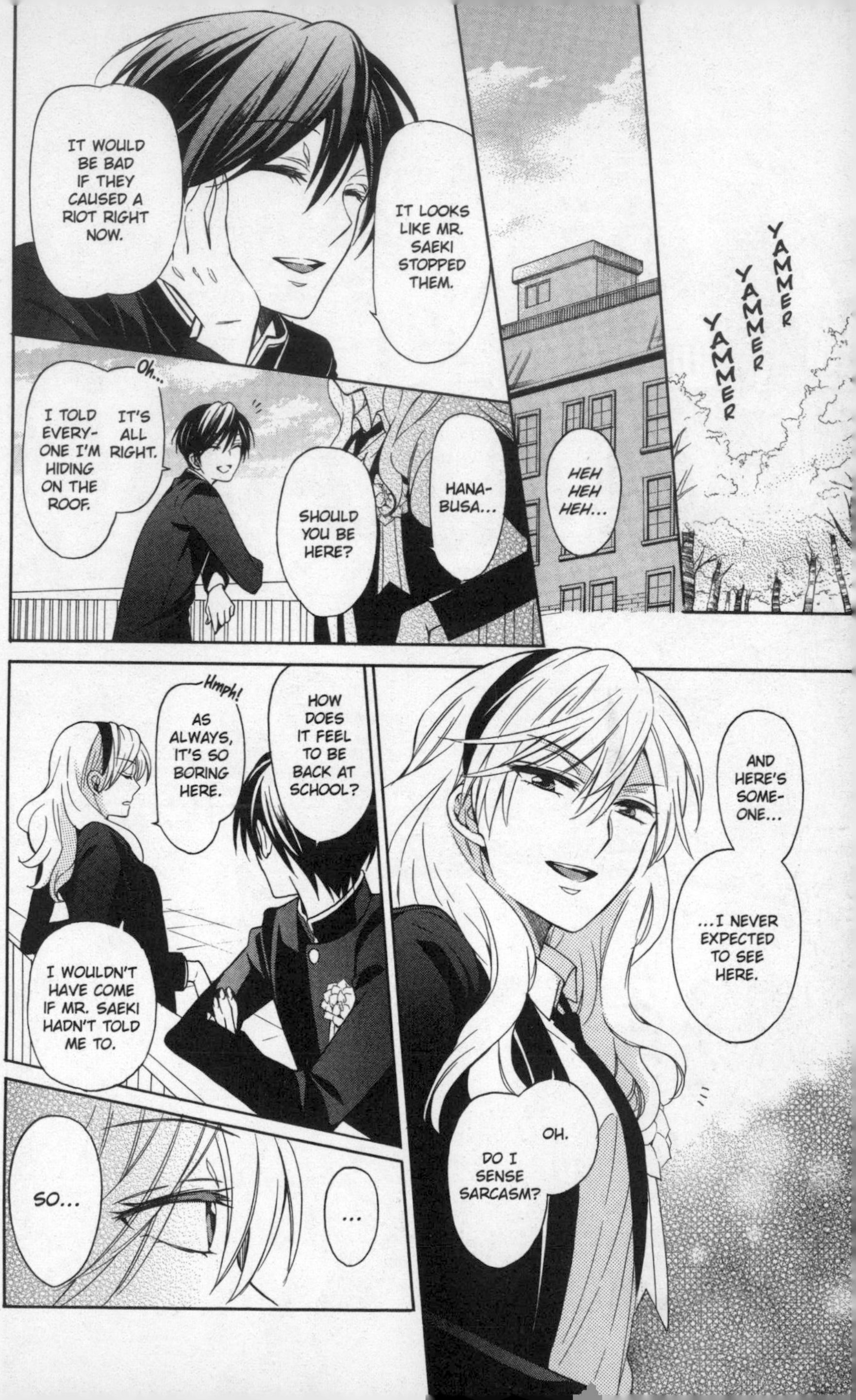
YAMMER
YAMMER
YAMMER
HEH HEH HEH...
IT LOOKS LIKE MR. SAEKI STOPPED THEM.
IT WOULD BE BAD IF THEY CAUSED A RIOT RIGHT NOW.
HANA-BUSA...
SHOULD YOU BE HERE?
Oh...
IT'S ALL RIGHT.
I TOLD EVERY-ONE I'M HIDING ON THE ROOF.
AND HERE'S SOME-ONE...
...I NEVER EXPECTED TO SEE HERE.
OH.
DO I SENSE SARCASM?
HOW DOES IT FEEL TO BE BACK AT SCHOOL?
Hmph!
AS ALWAYS, IT'S SO BORING HERE.
I WOULDN'T HAVE COME IF MR. SAEKI HADN'T TOLD ME TO.
...
SO...

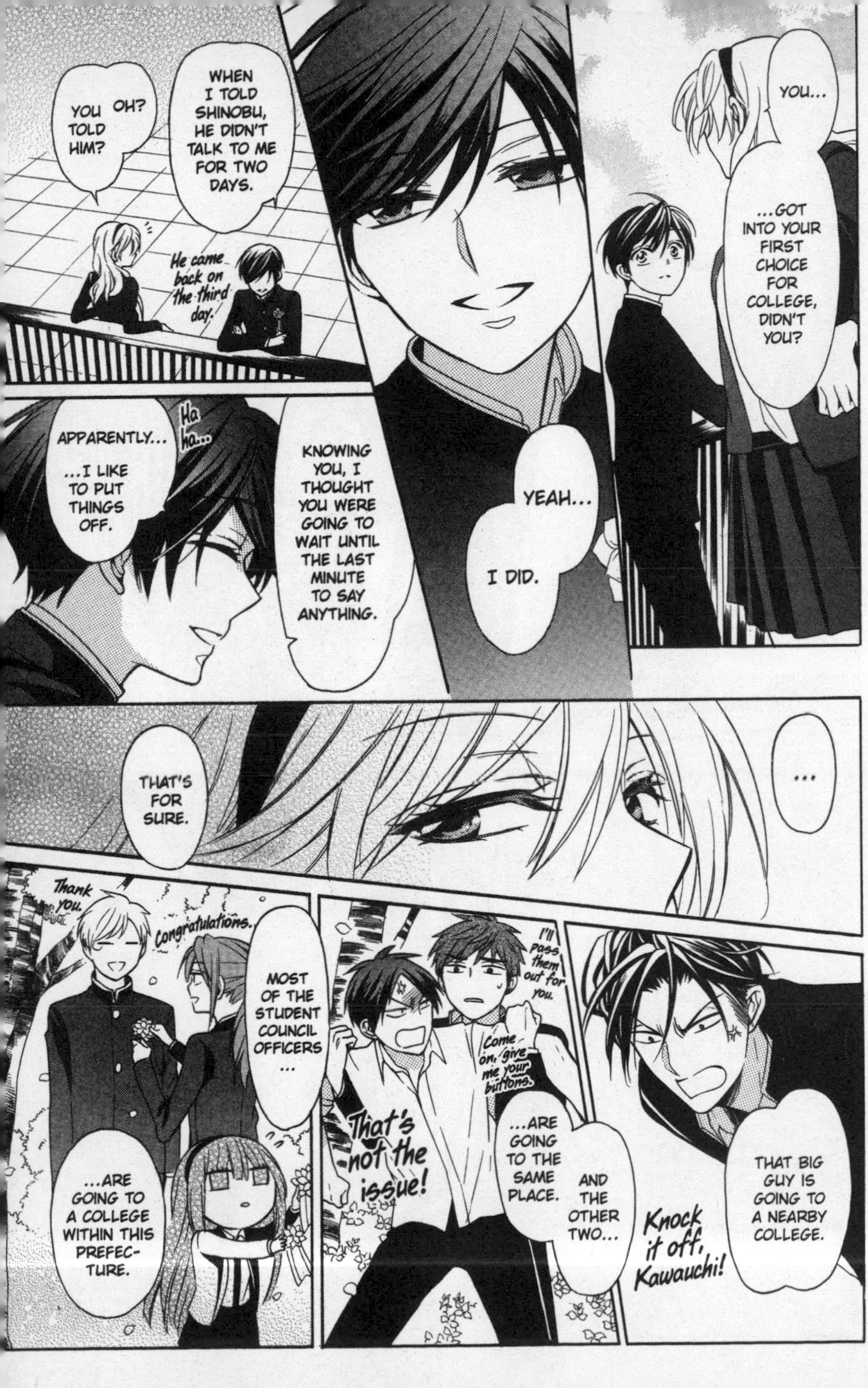
YOU...
...GOT INTO YOUR FIRST CHOICE FOR COLLEGE, DIDN'T YOU?
YEAH...
I DID.
WHEN I TOLD SHINOBU, HE DIDN'T TALK TO ME FOR TWO DAYS.
OH?
YOU TOLD HIM?
He came back on the third day.
KNOWING YOU, I THOUGHT YOU WERE GOING TO WAIT UNTIL THE LAST MINUTE TO SAY ANYTHING.
Ha ha...
APPARENTLY...
...I LIKE TO PUT THINGS OFF.
...
THAT'S FOR SURE.
THAT BIG GUY IS GOING TO A NEARBY COLLEGE.
Knock it off, Kawauchi!
AND THE OTHER TWO...
...ARE GOING TO THE SAME PLACE.
I'll pass them out for you.
Come on, give me your buttons.
That's not the issue!
MOST OF THE STUDENT COUNCIL OFFICERS...
Congratulations...
Thank you.
...ARE GOING TO A COLLEGE WITHIN THIS PREFECTURE.

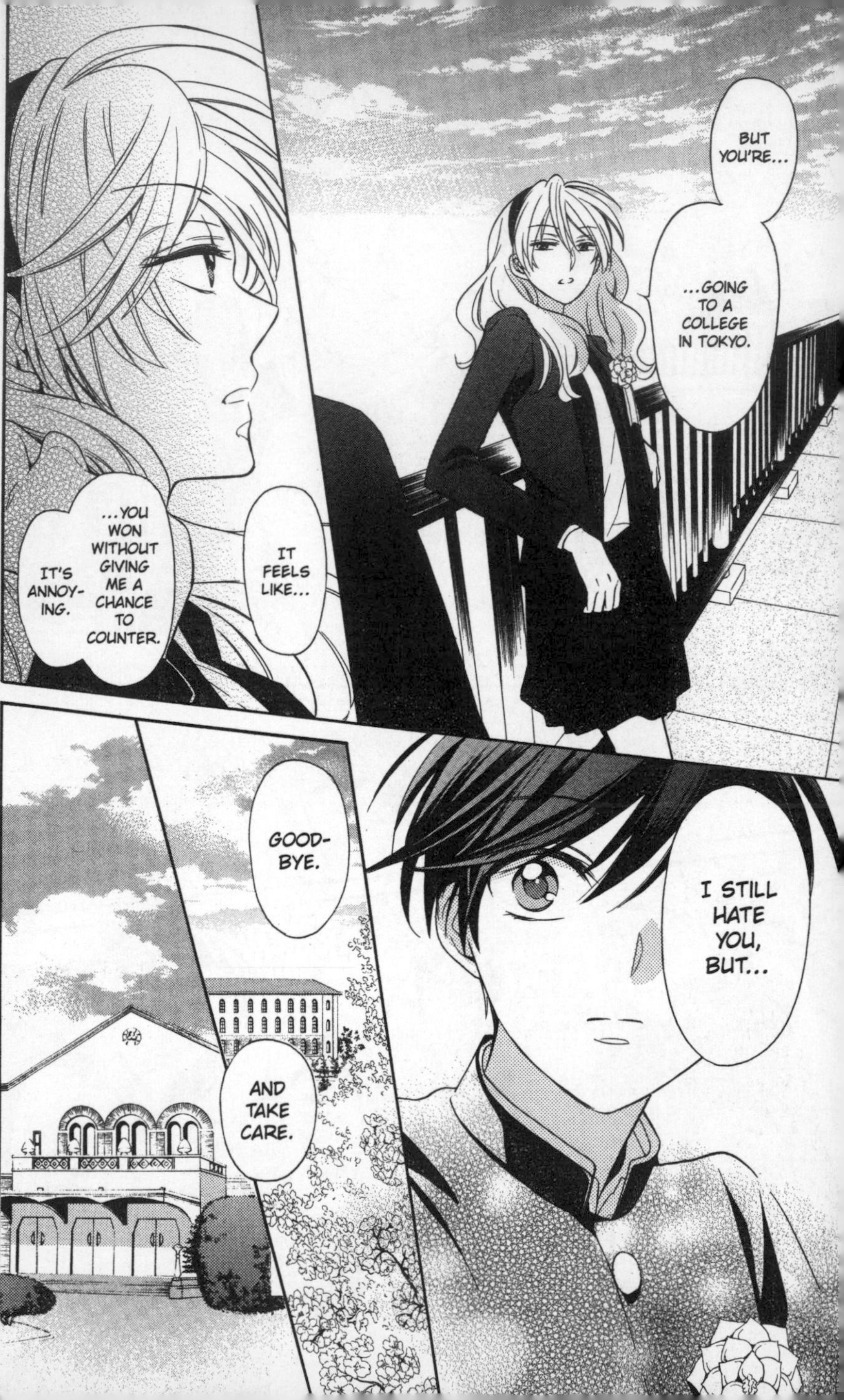
BUT YOU'RE...
...GOING TO A COLLEGE IN TOKYO.
IT FEELS LIKE...
...YOU WON WITHOUT GIVING ME A CHANCE TO COUNTER.
IT'S ANNOY-ING.
I STILL HATE YOU, BUT...
GOOD-BYE.
AND TAKE CARE.

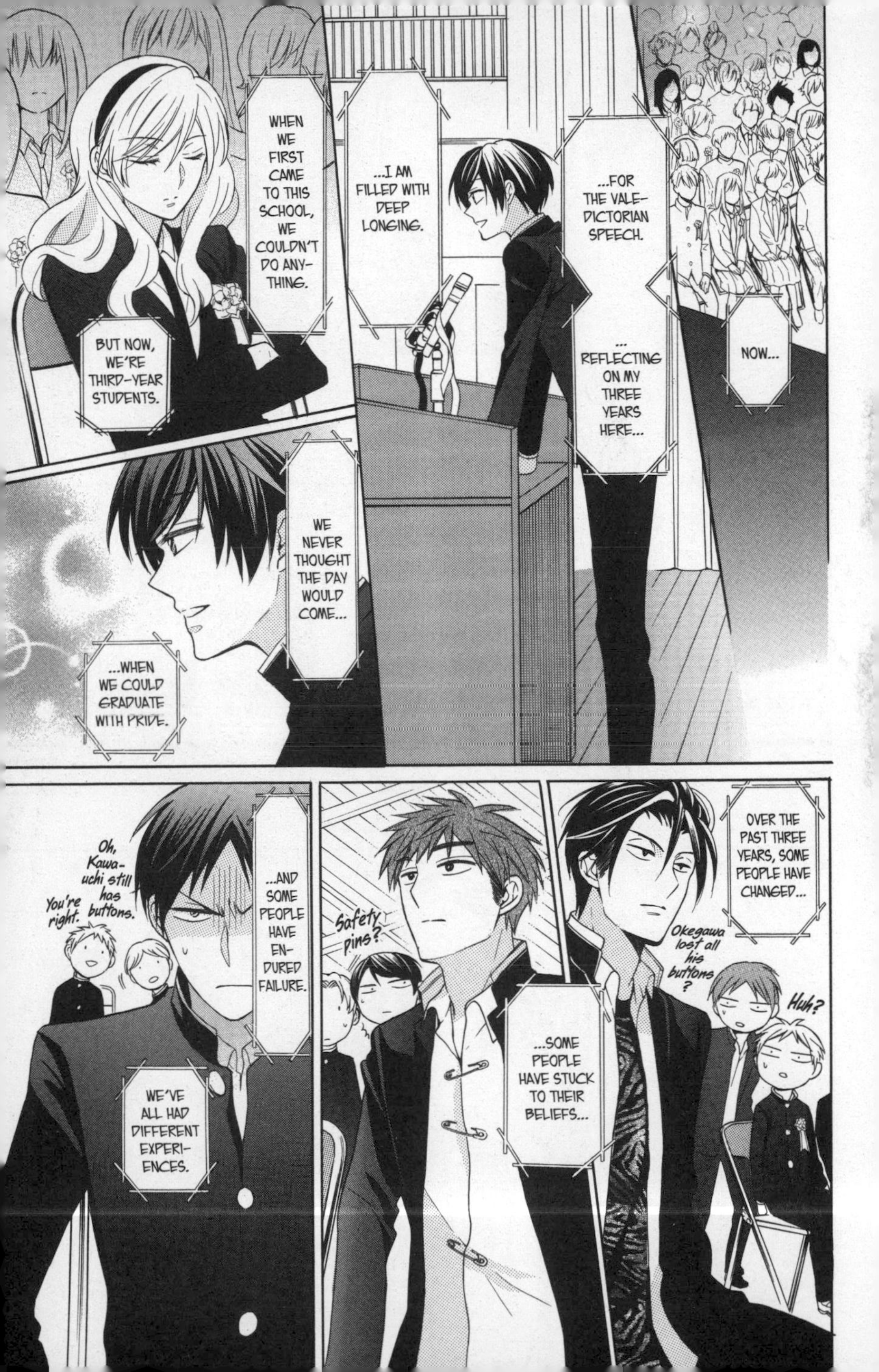
NOW...
...FOR THE VALEDICTORIAN SPEECH.
...REFLECTING ON MY THREE YEARS HERE...
...I AM FILLED WITH DEEP LONGING.
WHEN WE FIRST CAME TO THIS SCHOOL, WE COULDN'T DO ANYTHING.
BUT NOW, WE'RE THIRD-YEAR STUDENTS.
WE NEVER THOUGHT THE DAY WOULD COME...
...WHEN WE COULD GRADUATE WITH PRIDE.
OVER THE PAST THREE YEARS, SOME PEOPLE HAVE CHANGED...
Okegawa lost all his buttons?
Huh?
...SOME PEOPLE HAVE STUCK TO THEIR BELIEFS...
Safety pins?
...AND SOME PEOPLE HAVE ENDURED FAILURE.
Oh, Kawauchi still has buttons.
You're right.
WE'VE ALL HAD DIFFERENT EXPERIENCES.

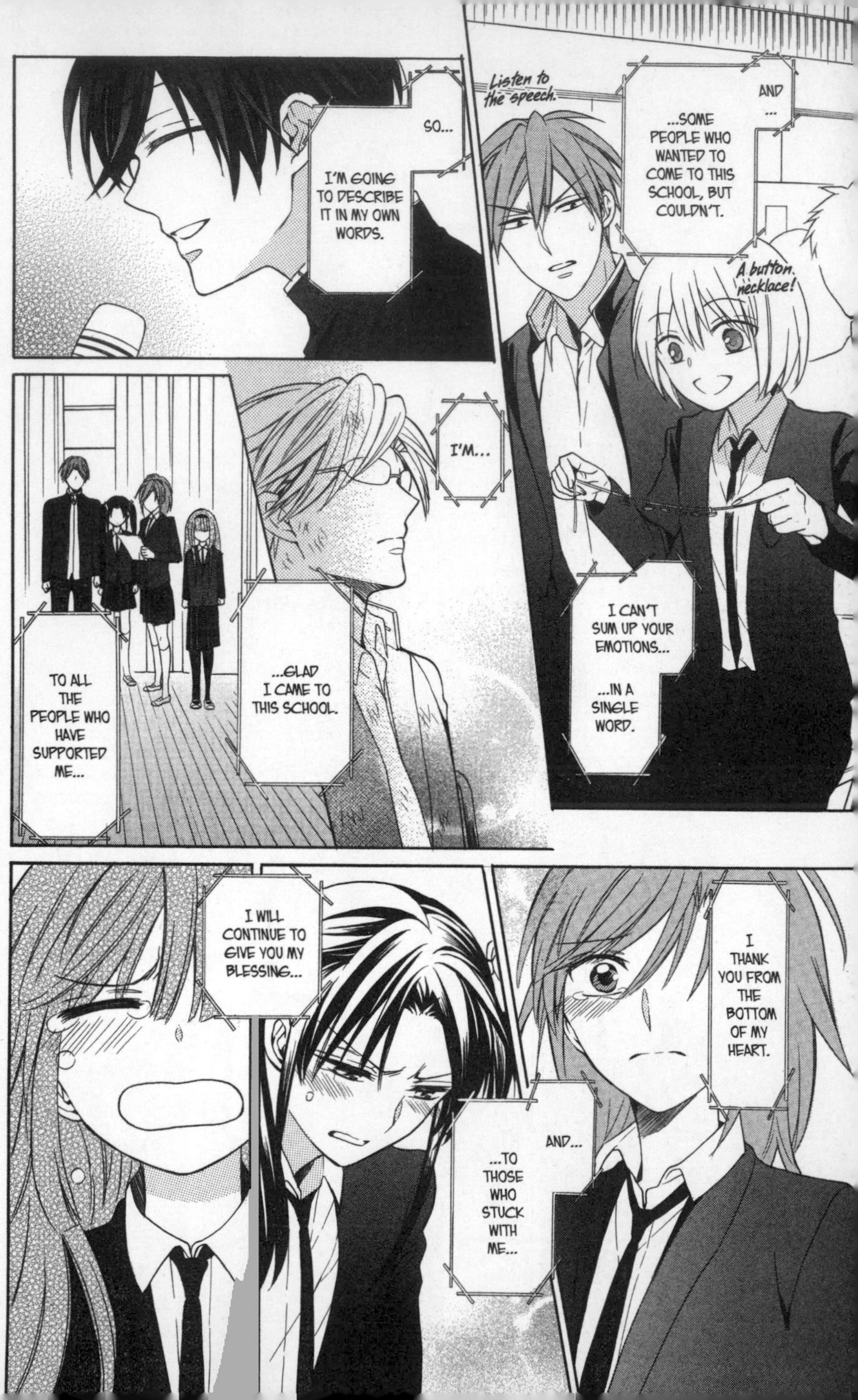
Listen to the speech.
AND...
...SOME PEOPLE WHO WANTED TO COME TO THIS SCHOOL, BUT COULDN'T.
A button necklace!
I CAN'T SUM UP YOUR EMOTIONS...
...IN A SINGLE WORD.
SO...
I'M GOING TO DESCRIBE IT IN MY OWN WORDS.
I'M...
...GLAD I CAME TO THIS SCHOOL.
TO ALL THE PEOPLE WHO HAVE SUPPORTED ME...
I THANK YOU FROM THE BOTTOM OF MY HEART.
AND...
...TO THOSE WHO STUCK WITH ME...
I WILL CONTINUE TO GIVE YOU MY BLESSING...

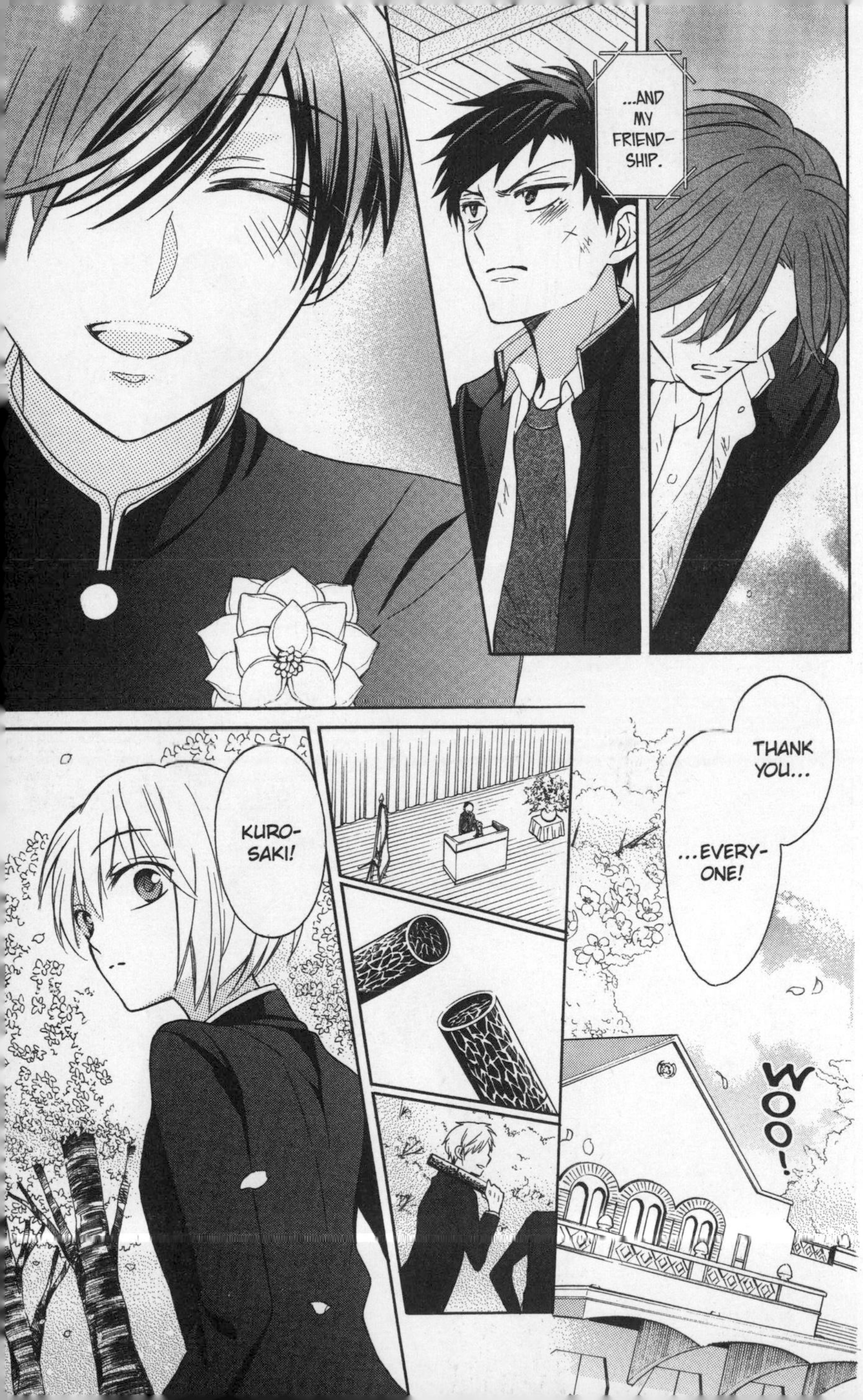
...AND MY FRIEND-SHIP.
THANK YOU...
...EVERY-ONE!
WOO!
KURO-SAKI!

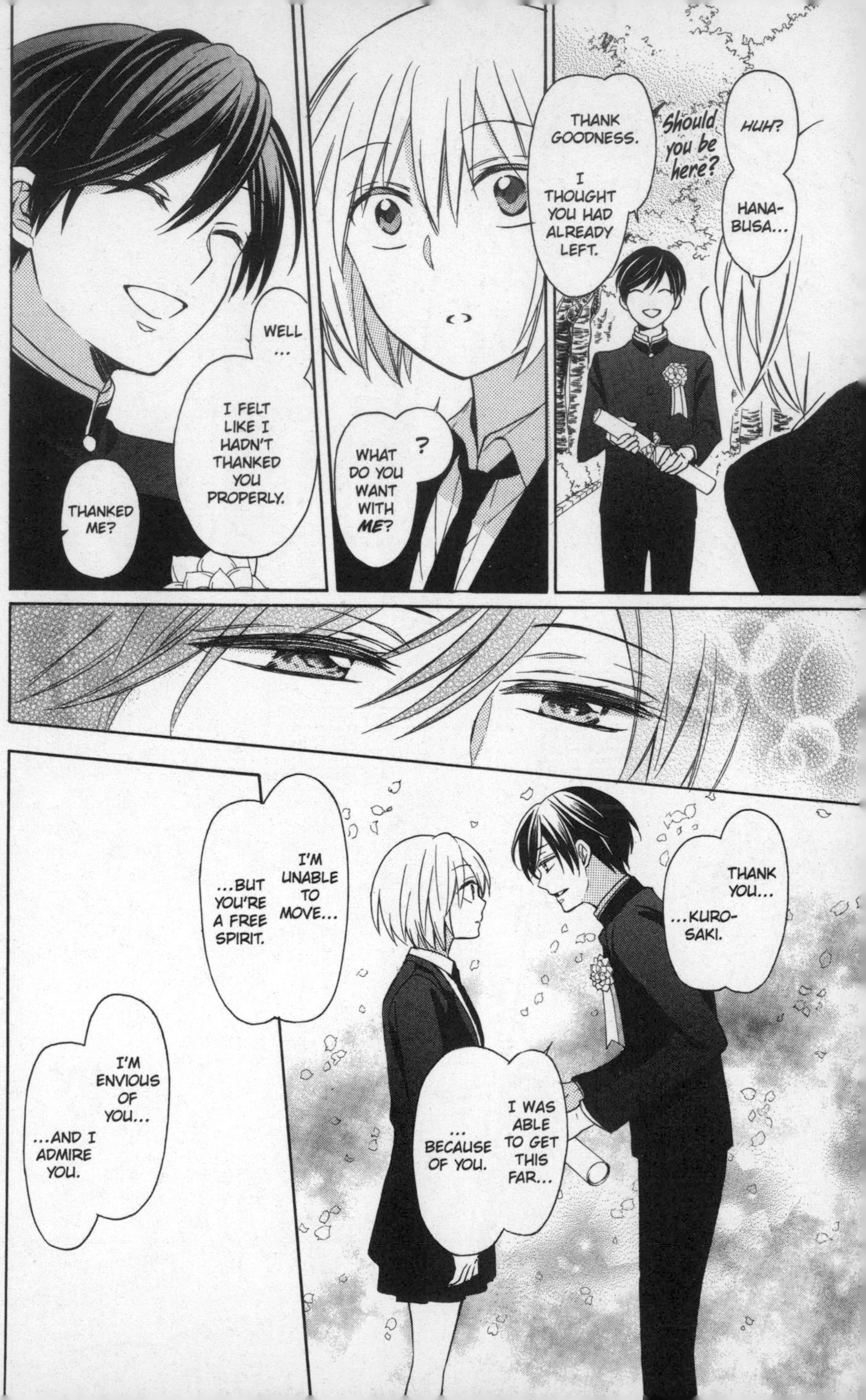
HUH?
HANA-BUSA...
Should you be here?
THANK GOODNESS.
I THOUGHT YOU HAD ALREADY LEFT.
?
WHAT DO YOU WANT WITH *ME*?
WELL...
I FELT LIKE I HADN'T THANKED YOU PROPERLY.
THANKED ME?
THANK YOU...
...KURO-SAKI.
I'M UNABLE TO MOVE...
...BUT YOU'RE A FREE SPIRIT.
I WAS ABLE TO GET THIS FAR...
...BECAUSE OF YOU.
I'M ENVIOUS OF YOU...
...AND I ADMIRE YOU.

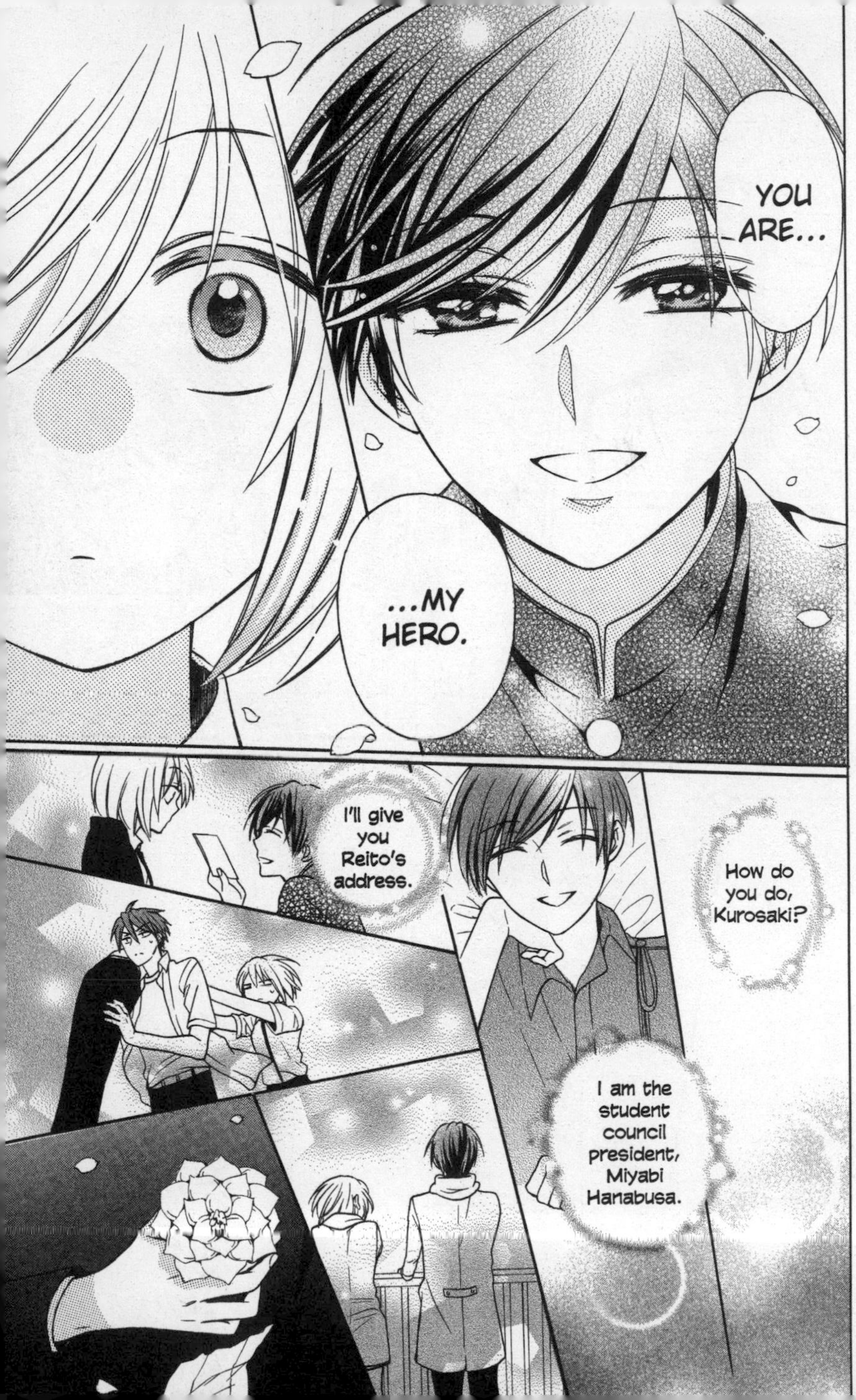
YOU ARE...
...MY HERO.
How do you do, Kurosaki?
I am the student council president, Miyabi Hanabusa.
I'll give you Reito's address.

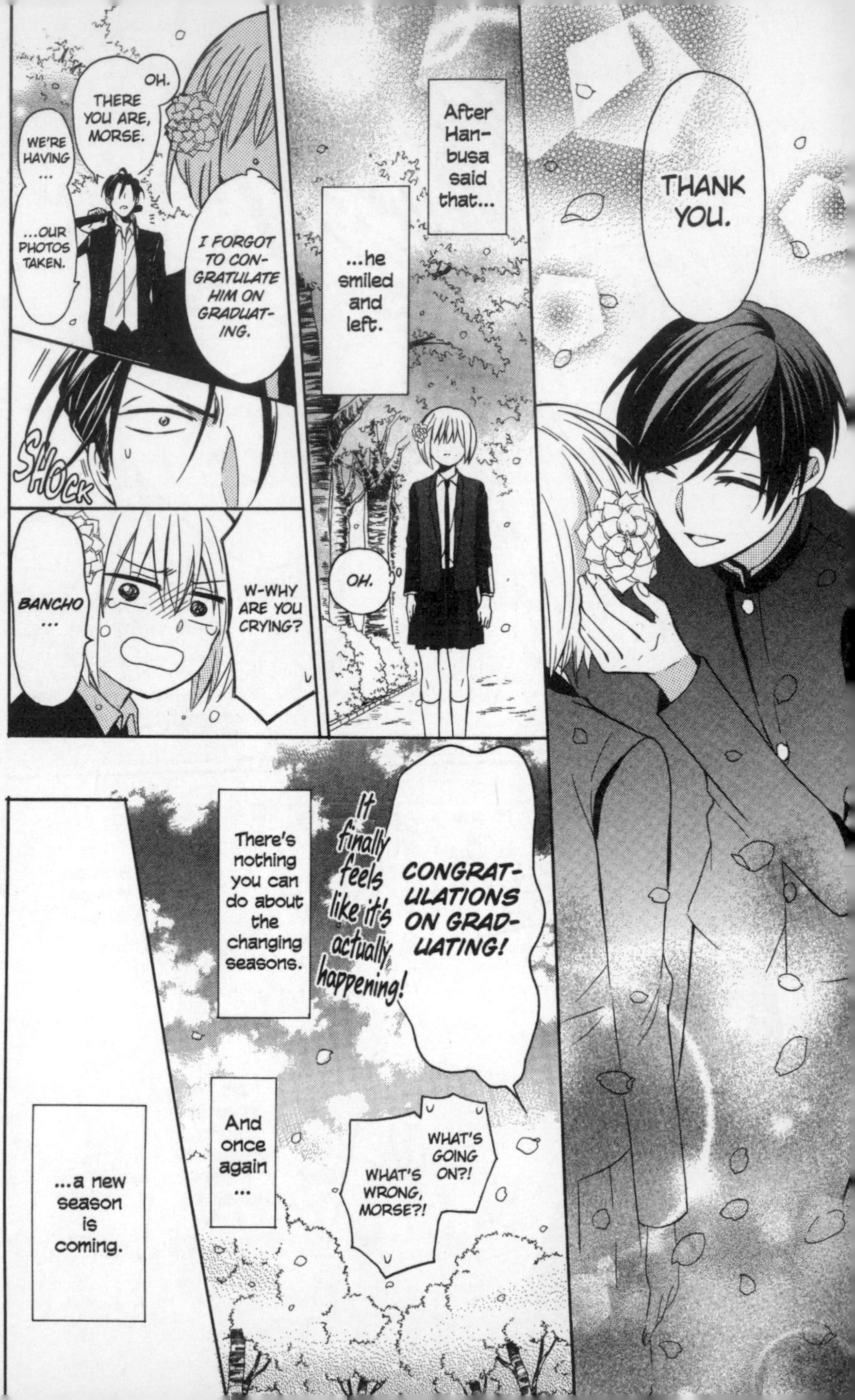

THANK YOU.
After Han-busa said that...
...he smiled and left.
OH.
OH. THERE YOU ARE, MORSE.
WE'RE HAVING...
...OUR PHOTOS TAKEN.
I FORGOT TO CON-GRATULATE HIM ON GRADUAT-ING.
SHOCK
W-WHY ARE YOU CRYING?
BANCHO...
CONGRAT-ULATIONS ON GRAD-UATING!
It finally feels like it's actually happening!
There's nothing you can do about the changing seasons.
WHAT'S GOING ON?!
WHAT'S WRONG, MORSE?!
And once again...
...a new season is coming.

TROUBLESOME UNDERCLASSMEN

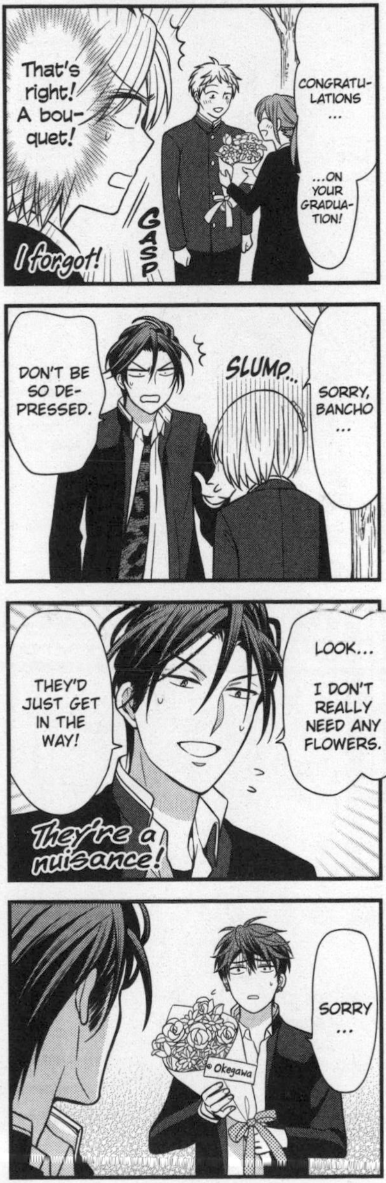
CONGRATULATIONS...
...ON YOUR GRADUATION!
That's right! A bouquet!
GASP
I forgot!
SORRY, BANCHO...
SLUMP...
DON'T BE SO DEPRESSED.
LOOK... I DON'T REALLY NEED ANY FLOWERS.
THEY'D JUST GET IN THE WAY!
They're a nuisance!
SORRY...
Okegawa

DECORATED HEAD

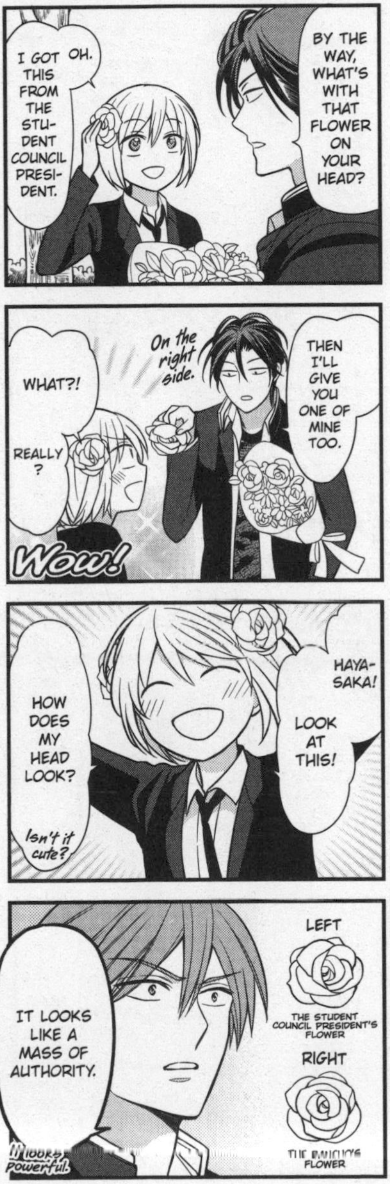
BY THE WAY, WHAT'S WITH THAT FLOWER ON YOUR HEAD?
OH.
I GOT THIS FROM THE STUDENT COUNCIL PRESIDENT.
THEN I'LL GIVE YOU ONE OF MINE TOO.
On the right side.
WHAT?!
REALLY?
Wow!
HAYASAKA!
LOOK AT THIS!
HOW DOES MY HEAD LOOK?
Isn't it cute?
LEFT
THE STUDENT COUNCIL PRESIDENT'S FLOWER
RIGHT
FLOWER
IT LOOKS LIKE A MASS OF AUTHORITY.
powerful.

PLANS FOR LATER

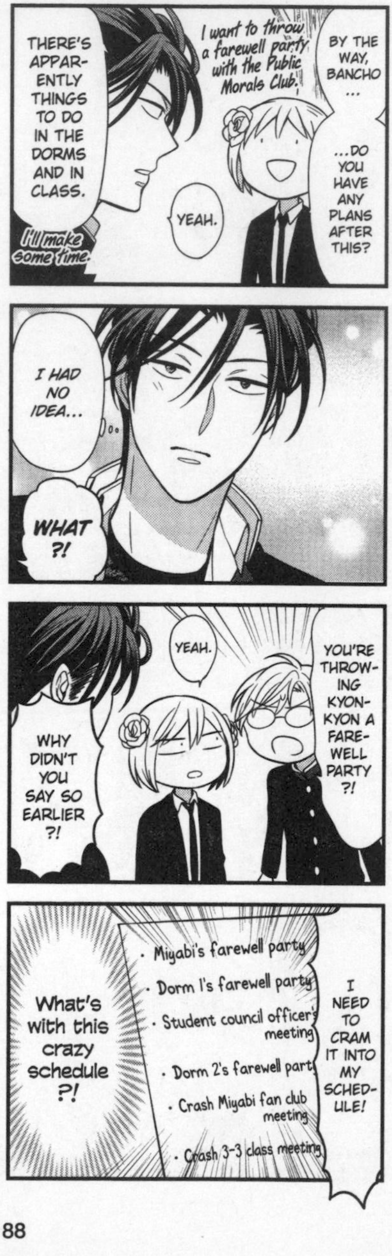
BY THE WAY, BANCHO ...
...DO YOU HAVE ANY PLANS AFTER THIS?
I want to throw a farewell party with the Public Morals Club.
THERE'S APPARENTLY THINGS TO DO IN THE DORMS AND IN CLASS.
YEAH.
I'll make some time.
I HAD NO IDEA...
WHAT ?!
YOU'RE THROWING KYON-KYON A FAREWELL PARTY ?!
YEAH.
WHY DIDN'T YOU SAY SO EARLIER ?!
I NEED TO CRAM IT INTO MY SCHEDULE!
· Miyabi's farewell party
· Dorm 1's farewell party
· Student council officer's meeting
· Dorm 2's farewell part
· Crash Miyabi fan club meeting
· Crash 3-3 class meeting
What's with this crazy schedule ?!

GRADUATION PHOTO SWAP ♡

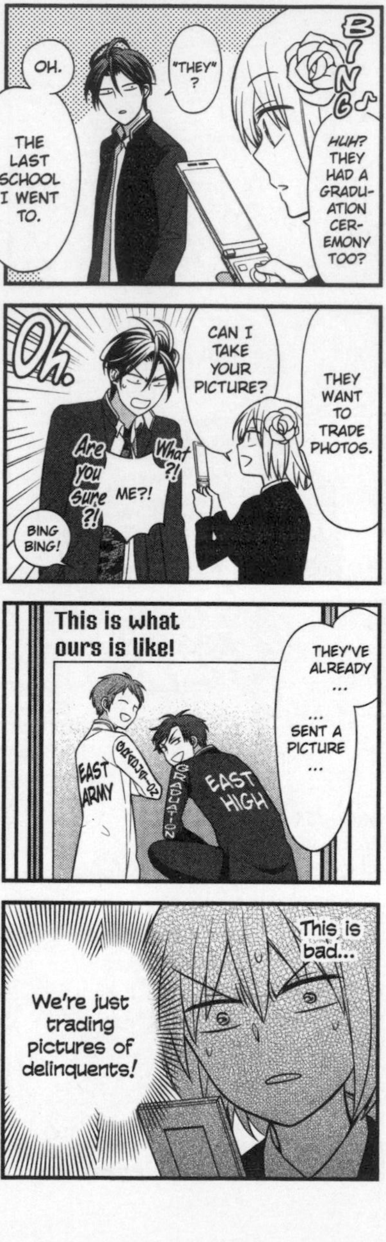
BING ♪
HUH? THEY HAD A GRADUATION CEREMONY TOO?
"THEY" ?
OH.
THE LAST SCHOOL I WENT TO.
THEY WANT TO TRADE PHOTOS.
CAN I TAKE YOUR PICTURE?
What ?!
ME?!
Are you sure ?!
Oh.
BING BING!
THEY'VE ALREADY ...
... SENT A PICTURE ...
This is what ours is like!
EAST HIGH
GRADUATION
EAST ARMY
This is bad...
We're just trading pictures of delinquents!

UNEXPECTED

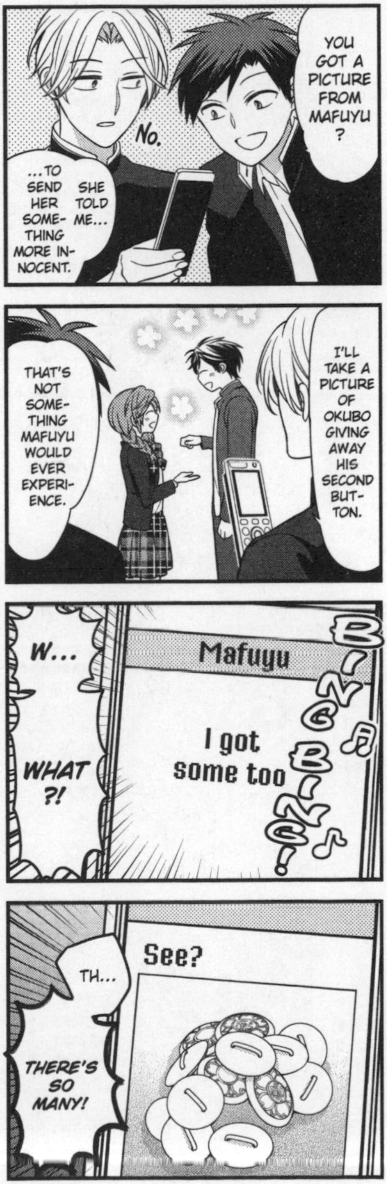
YOU GOT A PICTURE FROM MAFUYU?
No.
SHE TOLD ME...
...TO SEND HER SOMETHING MORE INNOCENT.
I'LL TAKE A PICTURE OF OKUBO GIVING AWAY HIS SECOND BUTTON.
THAT'S NOT SOMETHING MAFUYU WOULD EVER EXPERIENCE.
BING BING!
Mafuyu
I got some too
W...
WHAT?!
See?
TH...
THERE'S SO MANY!

THAT'S TRUE, BUT...

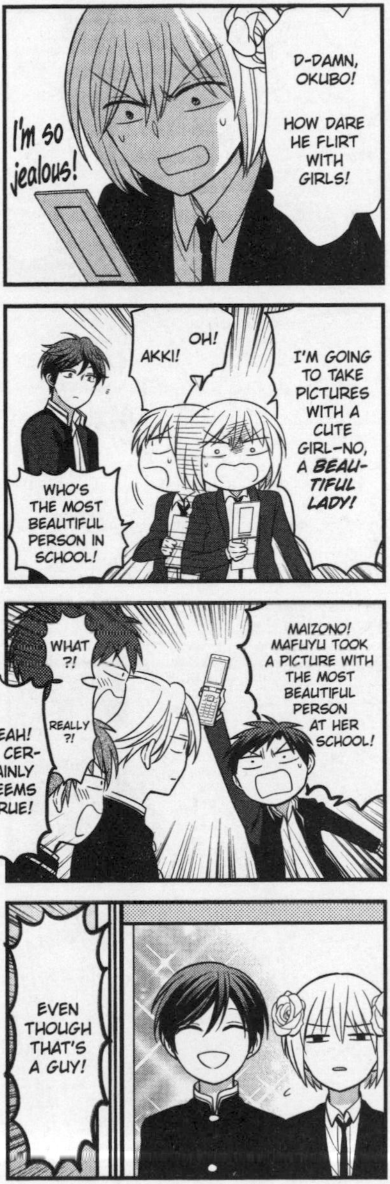
D-DAMN, OKUBO!
HOW DARE HE FLIRT WITH GIRLS!
I'm so jealous!
I'M GOING TO TAKE PICTURES WITH A CUTE GIRL—NO, A BEAUTIFUL LADY!
OH!
AKKI!
WHO'S THE MOST BEAUTIFUL PERSON IN SCHOOL!
MAIZONO! MAFUYU TOOK A PICTURE WITH THE MOST BEAUTIFUL PERSON AT HER SCHOOL!
WHAT?!
REALLY?!
YEAH! IT CERTAINLY SEEMS TRUE!
EVEN THOUGH THAT'S A GUY!

A WORLD I KNOW NOTHING ABOUT

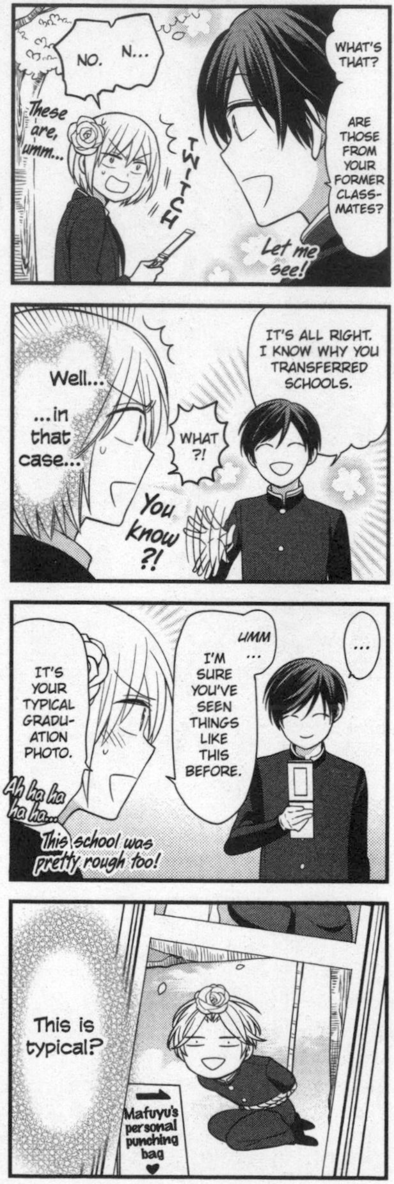
WHAT'S THAT?
ARE THOSE FROM YOUR FORMER CLASS-MATES?
Let me see!
N...
NO.
TWITCH
These are, umm...
IT'S ALL RIGHT. I KNOW WHY YOU TRANSFERRED SCHOOLS.
WHAT?!
You know?!
Well...
...in that case...
...
UMM...
I'M SURE YOU'VE SEEN THINGS LIKE THIS BEFORE.
IT'S YOUR TYPICAL GRADU-ATION PHOTO.
Ah ha ha ha ha...
This school was pretty rough too!
This is typical?
Mafuyu's personal punching bag ♥

WE'LL NEVER CHANGE ☆

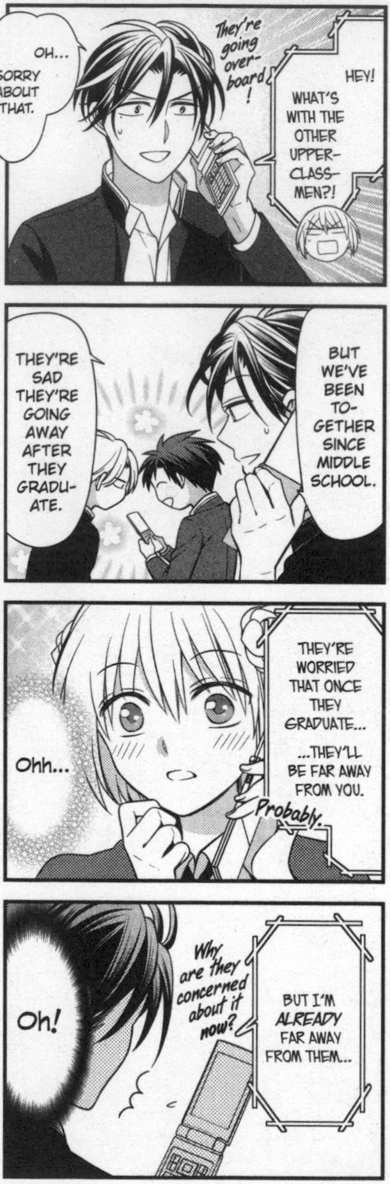
HEY! WHAT'S WITH THE OTHER UPPER-CLASS-MEN?!
They're going over-board!
OH... SORRY ABOUT THAT.
BUT WE'VE BEEN TO-GETHER SINCE MIDDLE SCHOOL.
THEY'RE SAD THEY'RE GOING AWAY AFTER THEY GRADU-ATE.
THEY'RE WORRIED THAT ONCE THEY GRADUATE...
...THEY'LL BE FAR AWAY FROM YOU.
Probably.
Ohh...
BUT I'M ALREADY FAR AWAY FROM THEM...
Why are they concerned about it now?
Oh!